CAMBRIDGE LIBRARY COLLECTION

Books of enduring scholarly value

Religion

For centuries, scripture and theology were the focus of prodigious amounts of scholarship and publishing, dominated in the English-speaking world by the work of Protestant Christians. Enlightenment philosophy and science, anthropology, ethnology and the colonial experience all brought new perspectives, lively debates and heated controversies to the study of religion and its role in the world, many of which continue to this day. This series explores the editing and interpretation of religious texts, the history of religious ideas and institutions, and not least the encounter between religion and science.

The Wisdom of Solomon

Although much about this apocryphal book of the Septuagint (Greek Old Testament) is unknown, it remains an influential and much-studied work. J. A. F. Gregg (1873–1961), who was educated at Christ's College, Cambridge, and later became Church of Ireland archbishop of Dublin and then of Armagh, gives an extensive introduction to his edition of the English version, published in the 'Cambridge Bible for Schools and Colleges' series in 1909. He examines the complicated problem of dating the text, as well as the question of its original language and possible author, concluding this was most likely a Jewish person from Alexandria, at some time after the second century BCE, and not King Solomon himself. The text itself examines many aspects of wisdom, from its inherent nature to its role in the protection of Israelites. Gregg provides notes throughout, making this volume a detailed guide to an important piece of sacred writing.

Cambridge University Press has long been a pioneer in the reissuing of out-of-print titles from its own backlist, producing digital reprints of books that are still sought after by scholars and students but could not be reprinted economically using traditional technology. The Cambridge Library Collection extends this activity to a wider range of books which are still of importance to researchers and professionals, either for the source material they contain, or as landmarks in the history of their academic discipline.

Drawing from the world-renowned collections in the Cambridge University Library, and guided by the advice of experts in each subject area, Cambridge University Press is using state-of-the-art scanning machines in its own Printing House to capture the content of each book selected for inclusion. The files are processed to give a consistently clear, crisp image, and the books finished to the high quality standard for which the Press is recognised around the world. The latest print-on-demand technology ensures that the books will remain available indefinitely, and that orders for single or multiple copies can quickly be supplied.

The Cambridge Library Collection brings back to life books of enduring scholarly value (including out-of-copyright works originally issued by other publishers) across a wide range of disciplines in the humanities and social sciences and in science and technology.

The Wisdom of Solomon

*In the Revised Version
with Introduction and Notes*

EDITED BY J.A.F. GREGG

CAMBRIDGE
UNIVERSITY PRESS

CAMBRIDGE UNIVERSITY PRESS

Cambridge, New York, Melbourne, Madrid, Cape Town,
Singapore, São Paolo, Delhi, Tokyo, Mexico City

Published in the United States of America by Cambridge University Press, New York

www.cambridge.org
Information on this title: www.cambridge.org/9781108039758

© in this compilation Cambridge University Press 2012

This edition first published 1909
This digitally printed version 2012

ISBN 978-1-108-03975-8 Paperback

*THE CAMBRIDGE BIBLE
FOR SCHOOLS AND COLLEGES*

General Editor for the Old Testament
and Apocrypha:—

A. F. KIRKPATRICK, D.D.
DEAN OF ELY

THE
WISDOM OF SOLOMON

CAMBRIDGE UNIVERSITY PRESS WAREHOUSE,
C. F. CLAY, Manager.
London: FETTER LANE, E.C.
Edinburgh: 100, PRINCES STREET.

Berlin: A. ASHER AND CO.
Leipzig: F. A. BROCKHAUS
New York: G. P. PUTNAM'S SONS.
Bombay and Calcutta: MACMILLAN AND CO., Ltd.

THE
WISDOM OF SOLOMON

In the Revised Version

With Introduction and Notes

by

THE REV. J. A. F. GREGG, M.A.

LATE SCHOLAR OF CHRIST'S COLLEGE, CAMBRIDGE

CAMBRIDGE:

at the University Press

1909

Cambridge:
PRINTED BY JOHN CLAY, M.A.
AT THE UNIVERSITY PRESS.

PREFACE

BY THE

GENERAL EDITOR FOR THE OLD TESTAMENT.

THE present General Editor for the Old Testament in the Cambridge Bible for Schools and Colleges desires to say that, in accordance with the policy of his predecessor the Bishop of Worcester, he does not hold himself responsible for the particular interpretations adopted or for the opinions expressed by the editors of the several Books, nor has he endeavoured to bring them into agreement with one another. It is inevitable that there should be differences of opinion in regard to many questions of criticism and interpretation, and it seems best that these differences should find free expression in different volumes. He has endeavoured to secure, as far as possible, that the general scope and character of the series should be observed, and that views which have a reasonable claim to consideration should not be ignored, but he has felt it best that the final responsibility should, in general, rest with the individual contributors.

A. F. KIRKPATRICK.

FROM YOUTH TO OLD AGE TAKE WISDOM
FOR THY SUSTENANCE: OF ALL POSSESSIONS
IT ALONE ABIDETH.

BIAS.

CONTENTS.

Wisdom is a breath of the power of God, and a clear effluence of the glory of the Almighty; therefore can nothing defiled find entrance into her. For she is an effulgence from everlasting light, and an unspotted mirror of the working of God, and an image of his goodness. And she, being one, hath power to do all things; and remaining in herself, reneweth all things: and from generation to generation passing into holy souls she maketh *men* friends of God and prophets.

Wisdom vii. 25—27.

INTRODUCTION.

§ 1. *Title.*

The book is known as the *Wisdom of Solomon* in the three oldest extant Gk. MSS., אAB, and in each case occupies the same position relatively to the other Wisdom-books, i.e. it follows Proverbs, Ecclesiastes (and Song of Solomon), and precedes Ecclesiasticus, the position of Job being variable[1].

In the Syriac Version, it is known as the "Book of the Great Wisdom of Solomon, son of David," and in the Arabic, as the "Book of the Wisdom of Solomon, son of King David, who ruled over the children of Israel."

Cyprian (d. 258) quotes Wisdom frequently, and habitually refers to it as *Solomon*, or the *Wisdom of Solomon* : Tertullian (*praescr. haer.* vii.) had cited it under the latter title. Jerome (*praef. in libr. Salom.*) unhesitatingly describes it as pseudepigraphic, and, doubtless under his influence, the title given to it in the Vulgate was simply *Liber Sapientiae* : while St Augustine (*Civ. Dei* xvii. 20), though aware of the tradition of the Solomonic authorship, acknowledged that the best writers denied its truth, although an early ecclesiastical custom in the West had lent authority to it (see also Aug. *de doct. Chr.* ii. 13).

The reference in the Western "Muratorian Canon" (about 220 A.D.?) to "Wisdom, written by the friends of Solomon in his honour," is very obscure ; but cp. Intr. p. xx, n. 1.

Among the Greek fathers, Clement of Alexandria (*Strom.* iv.

---

[1] The title varies thus:—Σοφία Σαλωμῶνος B. Σ. Σαλομῶντος א. Σ. Σολομῶντος A and Cod. Ven. For the names given to *Wisdom* in Patristic and Synodical lists of the Eastern and Western Church, see Dr Swete's *Introd. to O.T. in Greek*, pp. 203—214.

16) and Origen (*Ep. ad Rom.* vii. 14) both call it the *Divine
Wisdom*, although the former also knows it as the *Wisdom of
Solomon* (*Str.* vi.), and the latter refers to it as the "Wisdom
named that of Solomon" (*adv. Cels.* v. 29). The *Wisdom*
mentioned by Melito (Eus. *H. E.* iv. 26) is almost certainly the
Book of Proverbs, the canon to which he refers being Palestinian
(cp. that of Origen, Eus. *H. E.* vi. 25). Epiphanius (*de mens. et
pond.* § 4) and John of Damascus (*de fid. orth.* iv. 17) call it
ἡ πανάρετος, "The Wisdom which comprises all virtues[1]." This
title was probably given in connection with the series of attributes ascribed to Wisdom in ch. vii. 22 f, and is also accorded to
Proverbs by Clement of Rome (*Ep. ad Cor.* § 57), and by Hegesippus and Irenaeus (Eus. *H. E.* iv. 22), and to *Ecclesiasticus*
by Jerome (*praef. in libr. Salom.*).

§ 2. *Date.*

As will be seen below, the Solomonic date for the Book of
Wisdom is impossible. Some writers have placed it as early as
the end of the 3rd cent. B.C., others as late as the middle of the
1st cent. A.D.

Wisdom could not have been written before the beginning of
the 2nd cent. B.C. This is proved by its relation to the Greek
version of the prophets and hagiographa. Undoubted use is
made of the Greek version of Isaiah (ii. 12, cp. Is. iii. 10; xv. 10,
cp. Is. xliv. 20), the author quoting from the Greek where it
differs from the Hebrew; and of Job (xii. 12, cp. Job ix. 12, 19):
accordingly Wisdom was written after these books were translated. But, inasmuch as the LXX. version of the Pentateuch
was not made until the reign of Ptolemy Philadelphus (284—
246 B.C.), it is unlikely that the canon of the prophetic and historical books which was not fixed until about 300—250 B.C. (see
Hastings, *D. B.* iii. 612), and still less the canon of the hagiographa, would call for translation into Greek, either in whole
or in part, until some considerable time later. Therefore, the

---

[1] Πανάρετος is the alternative title given to *Wisdom* in the list of
books prefixed to Cod. A. Epiphanius calls it "The Wisdom of
Solomon called ἡ πανάρετος"; John of Damascus "ἡ πανάρετος, that
is, the Wisdom of Solomon."

earliest approximate date for a book which made use of these translations is the beginning of the 2nd century B.C.

On the other hand, Wisdom might have been written before 132 B.C. By that date, a Greek version of the prophets and possibly of the hagiographa was known to the translator of the Wisdom of the Son of Sirach (Swete, *Introd. to O.T.* pp. 23, 24), and was apparently not quite new.

If any definite indebtedness to the Greek version of Ecclesiasticus could be established, Wisdom could be dated with certainty *after* 132 B.C. But although there is some similarity of tone between such Wisdom-passages in Ecclus. as iv. 11—15; vi. 18—28 ; xv. 1—8, and Wisd. vi., viii. (cp. also Wisd. iv. 3 and Ecclus. xxiii. 25 ; Wisd. vi. 18 and Ecclus. i. 26 ; Wisd. xv. 7, 8 and Ecclus. xxxiii. 10—13), the relation is too general to warrant any conclusion upon which an argument might with safety be based.

Two considerations however lend strong support to a date within the last quarter of the 2nd century B.C.

(A) *The references to the relations between Egypt and the chosen people.*

Under the early Ptolemies, the Jews had received great consideration. Whatever may have been the feelings of their native subjects, these kings had treated the Jews with marked favour, and it was not till the reign of Ptolemy VII. (Euergetes II., surnamed Physcon, 145—117 B.C.), that any official action was taken against them. Josephus (*contr. Ap.* ii. 5) records the vengeance of Physcon upon the Alexandrian Jews for their loyalty to Cleopatra, in words which preserve an older version of the tradition adapted by the writer of 3 Macc. (see W. Fairweather, in Hastings' *D. B.* vol. iii. p. 193 b).

Wisdom xi. and xvi.—xix. display a strong national antipathy to the Egyptians, while iii. 1 ; v. 1 ; vi. 5—9 were evidently written by way of consolation to sufferers. But such passages could not have been written, had there been no other collision between the Egyptians and the Jews than that at the time of the Exodus : besides, they would have been impolitic as well as gratuitous under the gracious rule of the earlier Ptolemies.

They point to almost contemporary circumstances the memory of which yet rankled in the Jewish mind.

On the other hand, the literary treatment of the subject-matter is too passionless and academic to belong to a period of actual persecution : the writing is dictated by calm and reasoned prejudice rather than by the vehement indignation that is provoked by personal suffering. These conditions point to a time (about 120—100 B.C.) when the persecution under Physcon was a thing of the past, while its memory had not yet faded from the minds of the older generation of Jews.

(B) *The author is evidently unacquainted with the Philonic doctrine of the Logos.*

In spite of the remarkable similarity (in some cases amounting almost to identity) of the language of Philo and that of Wisdom, there is one vital difference which points to a considerably earlier date for the latter.

The Logos-idea is the leading feature of Philo's system, and there is in Wisdom no trace of the Philonian Logos, nor is the Divine Wisdom ever even identified with the Logos. In Philo's time the Logos-doctrine must have belonged to current Alexandrian thought : had Philo been its originator, he would have asserted it in a more polemical manner.

Accordingly, time must be allowed for the development of a doctrine which Philo found ready to his hand, and that length of time must have separated the composition of Wisdom from the writings of Philo. The inference (see Grimm, *Intr.* p. 34) is that Wisdom was composed a considerable time, perhaps a century, before Philo, who was born about 20 B.C., began to write.

If this argument is valid, it is unnecessary to discuss whether the persecutions of the Jews hinted at in Wisdom could have been those under Nero, or Caligula, or Cleopatra. Grätz and Noack saw in ch. xiv. 16—20 a reference to the command of Caligula that his statue should be placed in the Temple at Jerusalem, and to the erection of his effigy in the Synagogues of Alexandria. Grimm however points out that the reference in ch. xiv. would be very mild in view of such an outrage upon the Jewish conscience, while divine honours had long previously been paid to the Seleucidae and to Ptolemy Lagi and his wife. For the same reason, those writers who, like Plumptre (*Expositor*, vol. i. "The Writings of Apollos"), place its composition after Christ on the ground of its similarity with, and indebtedness to, the writings of Philo, fail to sustain their case. Without doubt, a superficial comparison of Wisdom and Philo brings to light remarkable resemblances of language and expression. The numerous cases of similarity in the interpretation or amplification of O.T. passages between Philo and the latter half of Wisdom might be urged as indicating the dependence of the latter (note especially the interpretation of the garments of the high priest in Wisd. xviii. 24).

But the writer is Jewish in spirit throughout, and although we find in Wisdom Philonic turns of expression and even philosophical terms, he is not an advanced Alexandrian like Philo, but an orthodox Jew.

The explanation of this similarity of interpretation and amplification must be sought not in the dependence of one writer upon another, but in their common dependence on a third source, viz. Palestinian *Midrashîm*, or Commentaries. Many of these must have been known to the Jews resident in Alexandria, and their exegesis largely influenced Alexandrian writers.

Finally, although our knowledge of the formation of the Canon of the Greek O.T. is exceedingly small, it is hard to understand how a work composed about A.D. 45 should have found a place in the Greek O.T., even taking precedence of Ecclesiasticus. Origen quotes from it as the "Divine Word" (*adv. Cels*. iii. 72), or as "the prophet" (*in Levit. Hom*. v. 2), while Eusebius (*praep. Evang*. i. 11) describes a quotation from it in almost identical terms.

The conclusion is that no date satisfies the general requirements of the book so well as about 125—100 B.C.

§ 3. *Language of the original.*

It was seen in the preceding section that in two cases at least[1] the author used the Greek version of Isaiah. The strong pre-

---

[1] ii. 12; xv. 10.

sumption hereby raised that the original language of Wisdom was Greek, is confirmed by a closer examination of the phraseology of the book.

Although the writer is not a philosopher, he draws very largely upon the vocabulary of Greek philosophy[1], and uses terms for which it would be hopeless to find equivalents in Hebrew. An ingenious attempt was made by D. S. Margoliouth (*Journ. of the Royal Asiatic Soc.* 1890) to prove a Hebrew original, but was refuted by Freudenthal (*Jewish Quarterly Review*, 1891). A very cursory survey will show the difference between Wisdom and Ecclesiasticus : the retranslation of the former into a Semitic language would be a *tour de force.* Such passages as Wisd. vii. 22—viii. 1, and xiii. 1—9 are altogether Greek, while the references in vii. 17, 18, and xi. 17 are equally decisive. Although the writer was at heart a Jew and Hebraistic expressions abound[2], his philosophical interests made Hebrew or Aramaic an impossible medium.

Further, the Greek of Wisdom is spontaneous and altogether free from the constraint which is inevitable in a translation. The many reminiscences of O.T. language as rendered by the LXX.[3], have not been carefully fitted into the text by a translator,

---

[1] viii. 7 the four cardinal virtues; ix. 15 b a Platonic touch ; xi. 17 ὕλη ἄμορφος; xiv. 3, xvii. 2 πρόνοια; xvi. 21 ὑπόστασις; xvi. 24 ἐπίτασις, ἄνεσις; xix. 18 στοιχεῖα, and metabolism, cp. xvi. 21.

[2] e.g. i. 1 singleness of heart. ii. 9 portion, lot. ii. 15 paths (in moral sense). ii. 16 accounted as. iv. 13 fulfil time. iv. 15 God's holy ones. vii. 29 ; viii. 11 to find (in sense of *recognise*). ix. 3 uprightness of soul. ix. 9 what is pleasing in the eyes of God. xi. 1 in the hand of. viii. 21 with a whole heart. ix. 6 sons of men. (From Grimm).

[3] i. 1 ; 1 Chr. xxix. 17. i. 2 ; Is. lxv. 1. i. 13 b, 14 a ; Is. liv. 16. i. 16 ; Is. xxviii. 15. ii. 7 ; Is. xxv. 6, 7. iii. 8 b ; Ps. x. 16. iii. 9 c; Ps. lxxxiv. 11. iii. 11; Prov. i. 7. iv. 10; Gen. v. 24. iv. 18 b ; Ps. ii. 4. v. 2 ; Is. xiii. 8. v. 14 a ; Job viii. 13; Is. xxix. 5. v. 14 d ; Is. xxxviii. 12. v. 22 c; Song viii. 7. vi. 1 ; Ps. ii. 10. vi. 7 ; Deut. i. 17. viii. 12; Job xxix. 9, 21. ix. 1; Dan. ii. 23. ix. 5; Ps. cxvi. 16. xi. 4 b; Deut. viii. 15. xi. 23; Job xlii. 2. xii. 12; Job ix. 12, 19. xiii. 18; Is. viii. 19. xvi. 13; 1 Sam. ii. 6. xix. 17; Gen. xix. 11.

but fall involuntarily from the pen of a writer whose memory is
stored with expressions drawn from the Book of his daily
meditation.

But the writer was more than a student of philosophy: his
flexible style, "redolent of Greek eloquence" (Jerome, *praef. in
libr. Salom.*), betrays the student of classical Greek literature[1].
If his clauses are more often loosely bound together by the
conjunctions *and, but, therefore, wherefore,* he is nevertheless
able to construct sentences in true periodic style (xii. 27; xiii.
11—15).
If again some of his utterances recall the studied parallelism
of Hebrew poetry (cp. ch. i. *passim*), he employs on the other
hand the Greek rhetorical figures of *Chiasmus* (cp. ch. i. 1, 4, 8;
iii. 15) and *Sorites* (ch. vi. 17—20).
There are not a few indications that his taste had been formed
by hearing or reading the Greek poets. His fondness for
accumulated epithets (ch. vii. 22, 23) and for compound words[2]
(in the construction of which[3] he shows no small skill) is almost
Aeschylean.   His manner has at times the freshness[4] or the
lightness of touch[5] of Greek lyric poetry, and occasionally his
words fall into an iambic or hexameter rhythm[6].
Finally, it would be hard to account for the various examples

[1] It is true that his writing contains two apparent solecisms,
iv. 12 μεταλλεύειν, cp. xvi. 25.   xi. 26 φιλόψυχος.
[2] i. 4 κακότεχνος (Homeric).   vii. 23 παντεπίσκοπος.   x. 3 ἀδελφοκτό-
νος.   xii. 5 σπλαγχνοφάγος.   xiii. 5 γενεσιουργός.   Cp. Swete, *Intr. to
O.T.* pp. 269, 311, 312.
[3] vii. 1 πρωτόπλαστος.   xi. 7 νηπιοκτόνος.   xiii. 3 γενεσιάρχης.   xiv. 23
τεκνοφόνος.   xv. 8 κακόμοχθυς.
[4] xvii. 17—19.
[5] ii. 6—8.
[6] (a) x. 9 ἐκ πόνων ἐρρύσατο.   xiv. 26 ψυχῶν μιασμός, γενέσεως ἐναλ-
λαγή.   xv. 4 εἶδος σπιλωθὲν χρώμασιν.   5 ποθεῖ τε νεκρᾶς εἰκόνος...
ὧν ὄψις ἄφροσιν εἰς ὄνειδος ἔρχεται.   6 κακῶν ἐρασταί.
(b) x. 3 συναπώλετο θυμοῖς.   xviii. 4 αἰῶνι δίδοσθαι.
In this connection, the rhythmical tendency so frequently observable
through the book is of considerable importance.   See an article by
H. St J. Thackeray in *Journ. of Theol. Studies,* vol. vi. pp. 232—237.

WISDOM   b

of alliteration[1], assonance[2], and paronomasia[3] in a work which was only a translation. The occurrence of a few instances might be put down to accident, but the occurrence of several suggests the author's deliberate intention.

We need have little hesitation in concluding that Wisdom has reached us in the language in which it was composed[4]: Jerome (*praef. in libr. Salom.*) actually writes that though he had found Ecclus. in Hebrew, "Wisdom is nowhere among the Hebrews."

§ 4. *Place of writing.*

It is a very reasonable inference from the evidence supplied by the book, that Wisdom was written by one who was resident in Egypt.

We have seen the close connection between the language of Wisdom and of the Alexandrian (LXX.) Version of O.T., and a similar connection may be traced between Wisdom and 3 and 4 Maccabees, both of which books show marks of Alexandrian origin.

Although obviously a Jew (xii. 22), the writer could not have been a Palestinian. He was a Hellenist, and among the Jews of Palestine Hellenism was tantamount to unpatriotism. Josephus (*Ant.* xx. 11, 2) writes with reference to Greek learning, "Our nation does not encourage those that learn the languages of many nations." This prejudice was very natural, considering the Hellenizing efforts of Jason the high priest under Antiochus

---

[1] ii. 10 πρεσβύτου...πολιὰς πολυχρονίους. ii. 14 βαρὺς...καὶ βλεπόμενος. iii. 8 κρινοῦσιν...κρατήσουσιν. iii. 16 τέκνα...ἀτέλεστα. iv. 5 περικλασθήσονται κλῶνες. v. 12 βέλους βληθέντος. v. 18 κόρυθα κρίσιν ἀνυπόκριτον. Cp. ii. 23; vi. 10; xii. 15.

[2] i. 10 οὖς...θροῦς. iv. 2 ποθοῦσιν ἀπελθοῦσαν. v. 14 ἀσεβοῦς...χνοῦς. vii. 13 ἀδόλως...ἀφθόνως. xiii. 11 εὐμαθῶς...εὐπρεπῶς.

[3] v. 3 στενοχωρίαν...στενάξονται. v. 10 ἀτραπὸν τρόπιος. v. 22 ποταμοί...ἀποτόμως. xvii. 12, 13 προδοσία, προσδοκία.

[4] Cp. Dr Westcott's remarks on *Style and Language* in Smith, *B. D.* iii. 1780, "No existing work represents perhaps more completely the style of composition which would be produced by the (Alexandrian) sophistic school of rhetoric."

Epiphanes (2 Macc. iv. 7—15), the effect of which was to lead men "to make of no account the honours of their fathers, but to think the glories of the Greeks best of all [1]."

On the other hand, the author of Wisdom writes about the old-time dwellers in Egypt with a warmth that has something personal in it, and hardly tries to conceal his antipathy for the Egyptians of his own day under a historical mask (chs. xi., xvi. —xix.); and again, he writes of the gods of the Egyptians (xii. 23—27; xv. 18, 19) from a first-hand experience. He has looked upon them, and felt the loathing excited by their hideous appearance.

At the same time, he makes no effort to disguise his sympathy with Hellenic thought. He is a Euhemerist in his account of the origin of idol-worship (ch. xiv.): he is a Platonist in his sense of the beauty of the world, and in his argument that its beauty points to a supreme First Cause. He draws on Plato for his doctrine of pre-existing matter (xi. 17), of the pre-existence of the soul (viii. 19), and of the body as an obstacle in the path to spiritual knowledge (ix. 15).

The teaching of the Stoics suggested to him the penetrating-ness of Wisdom (vii. 24), and her quickness of understanding (νοερόν, vii. 22). The doctrine of Providence (xiv. 3), and the conception of the four cardinal virtues (viii. 7), were a loan partly from Plato and partly from the Stoics.

This combination of knowledge of Egypt and sympathy with Greek studies points plainly to Alexandria; and the inference is strengthened by a comparison of Wisdom with the writings of the Alexandrian Philo. For the affinity between them is so close, that the author has been styled a pre-Philonic Philonist. Like Philo (but in a more uncompromising way), he is a Jew loyal to the national religion; and no centre offered the same opportunities as did Alexandria for a Jew, who wished to unite a liberal eclecticism with his traditional faith.

He displays the Alexandrian tendency which was Greek in its origin, and is illustrated in Philo later, to allegorize Scripture

---

[1] Heriot (*Philon le Juif*, p. 23) writes that about 64 B.C. a curse was pronounced against any parents giving their children a Greek education, cp. Baba Kamma, 82 b, 83 a; Menahoth. 64 b: Sota, 49 b.

(x. 7 the pillar of salt; x. 17 the cloud; xvi. 5—7 the brazen serpent; 28 the manna; xvii. 21 the Egyptian darkness).

He holds the Alexandrian belief in the transcendence of God, which he endeavours (like Philo later with the Logos-theory) to balance with the doctrine of a vicarious intermediary, the Wisdom of the many names and functions; and in order to reconcile the religious sentiment with the divine transcendence, he applies the Greek philosophical idea of a world-soul, and thus contrives (while neither dethroning God nor deifying Wisdom) to elaborate a doctrine of immanence.

He shows no hesitation in placing the doctrines of Israel side by side with the philosophy of Greece, thus leading where Philo followed later. It would be possible to produce a very lengthy catena of quotations to show the similarity that exists between the language and thought of Wisdom and Philo, but it would be out of place here.

What has been said makes the conclusion very reasonable that the writer was a Jew of Alexandria[1].

§ 5. *The Author.*

From the conclusions reached in the preceding sections, it will be seen that, although it is unlikely we shall ever know the name of the author of Wisdom, certain points seem to be fairly established. The writer lived about 100 B.C., and was an Alexandrian Jew, possessing considerable acquaintance with the poetry and philosophy of Greece.

He may have been a professional religious teacher: his words in vi. 23 seem like a defence in advance against the charge of cupidity levelled by Philo against his profession, and probably not less unmerited at this period by the "sophists" of Alexandria

---

[1] Grimm (*Intr.* p. 20) names as specifically Judaeo-Alexandrine the doctrine of Love as the moving principle in God's activity as Creator and Sustainer of the world (xi. 24), and the designation of God as "He that is" (xiii. 1).

It should be observed that the writer's doctrine of the life after death is quite distinct from the Palestinian doctrine of the resurrection of the body (see Hastings, *D. B.* v. 305, 306), nor does his eschatological scheme contain any allusion to a personal Messiah.

than by those of Athens in the time of Socrates. Although inclined to eclecticism, as was only natural in a capital where all religions met, he was an unfaltering adherent of the national faith. He speaks of the law of Moses as "the incorruptible light of the law" (xviii. 4); he is unsparing in his condemnation of his renegade fellow-countrymen (chs. i.—v.); with the incapacity for appreciation fostered by the Mosaic legislation, he stands unmoved before the triumphs of art, regarding all visible representations of natural objects as indications of impiety if not insanity (xiv. 18—21; xv. 4—6).

Idolatry was for him the beginning and cause of every moral and social evil (xiv. 27): though he could view with tolerance the nobler forms of nature-worship, his residence among the votaries of less elevated cults had done nothing to blunt his abhorrence for those who "invested stones and stocks with the incommunicable Name" (xiv. 21).

Again, he is a blind particularist in dealing with his own nation. The Israelites are the holy people, the blameless seed (x. 15), the just (xi. 14): their enemies the impious, the lawless (xvi. 16, xvii. 2). Not only does his desire to heighten the contrast lead him into unfairness, but he occasionally colours history in stating the case for the Israelites. They cry to God for water (xi. 4), when Exodus xvii. relates that they murmured against God. The Scriptural account of the incidents that led up to the Brazen Serpent is ignored, and Israel is viewed as the object of Divine deliverance almost to the exclusion of the thought of chastisement (xvi. 5—14). The loathing of the people for the familiar manna is forgotten, in order that the author may credit it with the miraculous property of gratifying every taste (xvi. 21). Again, not a word is said as to the reason why the plague fell upon Israel (xviii. 20—25).

But although we may say thus much about the circumstances and prepossessions of the author, it is easier to say who he was not than who he was. Many conjectures have been hazarded, but he must remain nameless.

He was not *Solomon* (see §§ 2—4). The Solomonic authorship is a purely literary artifice. For the same reason, he could not have been *Zerubbabel* (Faber); or the *Son of Sirach* (a suggestion made by St Augustine but withdrawn later); or *the older Philo*, who according to Josephus was a heathen.

Nor was he *Aristobulus* (Lutterbeck); holding as he did a privileged position in Egypt as friend of Ptolemy Philometor, he could not have written the passages in which kings are reproached for their abuse of authority, while under that king the Jews enjoyed considerable advantages.

The celebrated *Philo*[1] was held to be the author by Luther among others, and there is more to be said for this hypothesis than for any of the preceding.

But it was seen in § 2 that there are no traces in Wisdom of the specifically Philonic Logos-doctrine. While this in itself would seem almost conclusive, Grimm (*Intr.* pp. 24, 25) adds that the author seems, unlike Philo, to have been but a casual student of Greek philosophy, knowing of it little more than what filtered down into the popular mind. Again, there is no trace in Wisdom of the Platonic tripartite psychology, and doctrine of ideas, which played so important a part in Philo's system. The fundamental dualism of Philo, if not unseen in Wisdom, is at any rate only hesitatingly touched. Again, in Wisdom the devil is represented as an active agent (ii 24), whereas the advance of speculation has banished him from the writings of Philo.

Furthermore, the difference in style must not be overlooked. Philo's sentences are periodic, and his thought abstract and unemotional: the first nine chapters of Wisdom on the other hand recall the short sententious style of the gnomic books of the O.T., while in the latter half the author's manner is glowing and picturesque. Philo thinks overmuch, the author of Wisdom has no system and lacks precision of thought: the former is a philosopher, the latter a rhetorician.

Grimm is therefore probably right in concluding that Wisdom presents an earlier stage of development in the type of thought

---

[1] The ingenious conjecture of Dr Tregelles (Canon Murat. p. 53) may be mentioned. The words in which the book is described are "*et Sapientia ab amicis in honorem ipsius scripta*," and he suggested that "*ab amicis*" stands for ὑπὸ Φίλωνος in the Greek original, which was mistaken for ὑπὸ φίλων.

whose ripened fruit appears in Philo. This conclusion militates
against the theory of Noack, warmly supported by Dean
Plumptre (*Expositor*, vol. ii. "The Writings of Apollos"), that
Wisdom was written by the Alexandrian *Apollos* before he
became a Christian, being the precursor of the Epistle to the
Hebrews written by him after his conversion: Apollos would
hardly revert to a pre-Philonic stage of thought.

The further suggestion that Wisdom is by *a Christian hand* is
met by the reply that there is not in the book one characteristically Christian conception.

§ 6. *Purpose of the Book.*

(A) The book opens with an address to rulers (i. 1 ; vi. 1—11),
but except in those passages, and vi. 20—25, there is no other
reference to them. But Wisdom is far from being a treatise
on statesmanship, the first section (which contains the only
mention of rulers) dealing almost entirely with moral and
spiritual considerations, in a personal rather than a social
connection. Accordingly, the address to rulers would seem to
be a purely rhetorical artifice, screening the real purpose of the
book, which is to give warning and encouragement to faithful
Jews.

But even supposing, as we may (cp. the connection between
i. 16 and ii. 1), that the writer has in view "not heathen rulers
but powerful personages in the Jewish environment who...had
apostatized...and attached themselves to the heathen government" (Siegfried, Art. "Bk of Wisdom," Hastings' *D. B.*), he
only addresses them for the benefit of his readers, not expecting
that his words will penetrate to high places, in the same manner
as the O.T. prophets addressed warnings and prophecies to
absent foreign princes and peoples with a direct view to the
consolation of Israel.

At the same time, a criticism of the lives of those powerful
Jews who had fallen from the faith provided him with the
opportunity of exposing the worst consequences of a liberalizing
tendency prevalent among all Alexandrian Jews, which although
by no means harmful in its earlier stages needed careful guiding
if it was not to issue in open hostility.

(B) The readers contemplated are plainly Jews.

(*a*) The book teems with allusions to historical events and characters, and yet not a single proper name (either of person or of place) occurs throughout. The allusive character of the writing makes it plain that the readers are expected to be capable of interpreting the half concealed references for themselves, through familiarity with the O.T. Scriptures.

(*b*) Certain characteristic O.T. conceptions are carefully placed in the light of a more inward philosophy of life.

This world is no longer to be regarded as the sole theatre for rewards and punishments; while again the outward must be interpreted in connection with the inward, so that the short lived man may be seen to have been spiritually long lived, and the childless to have had a portion better than sons or daughters.

(C) Wisdom was written by a Jew who was pained to see that, as a body, his countrymen in Egypt were weakened by unfaithfulness within and harassed by oppression from without. He aimed at consoling and strengthening his people, negatively, by showing them the bankruptcy of materialism and the futility of idolatry, and positively, by commending to them the pursuit of the Almighty Wisdom.

(*a*) Materialism was always a snare to the Jews, in view of their doctrine of a future life.

If the only prospect after death was that of a non moral existence in Sheol, there was to grosser natures no reason why the cup of pleasure should not be drunk inordinately: and further, there was no satisfying solution of the problem of the prosperity of the wicked and the sufferings of the righteous. Few but those who are possessed by an overwhelming sense of the presence of God (like the Psalmists), or of the claims of man (like the Comtists), can regard their life as limited to the present world, without giving way to a fatalistic sensuality.

Very few men are idealists; and with the breakdown of the theocratic system, and on the one hand the Hellenizing of Palestine in the early years of the second century B.C., and on the other the solvent influence of philosophic thought and heathen morals upon the religion of the Jews resident in Egypt, the standard of life in all but the most spiritually minded declined rapidly. When further, those who were Jews by heredity and not by conviction found themselves exposed to the ridicule of foreigners who scorned the rigorisms of the Hebrew system, and were also (like Tiberius Alexander, Philo's nephew, in later days) made aware of the advantages to be derived from a politic change of creed, a serious leakage from Judaism manifested itself. And when in addition the apostates, not content with their infidelity, not only mocked those who remained faithful, but even persecuted them for their loyalty, the outlook was black indeed. (For an account of the apostasy in Palestine under Antiochus Epiphanes, cp. 1 Macc. i. 11—16, 43—64; 2 Macc. iv. 10; and for that in Egypt under Physcon, cp. 3 Macc. ii. 31, and generally, Philo, *Mos.* i. 6, "They despise countrymen and friends, they transgress the laws under which they were born and brought up, they change their national customs against which no fault can be alleged, and they live under an alien rule and for the sake of present advantages forget all their old associations"; see also id. *Conf. l.* § 2.) It is against apostates of this type apparently that chs. i.—v. were directed, although the author had in view in this section the further object of spiritualising the ideas of the still faithful Jews, who found as much bewilderment as the apostates found security in the difficulties arising out of their traditional doctrines of the Sheol-existence and earthly retribution. He revised some of their inherited conceptions, teaching that death opened a gate of blessedness for the righteous, that posterity and length of days were not the criterion of a successful life, and that persecution was only one side of a picture, the other (and strangely unexpected) side of which would be revealed after death.

(*b*) But if Judaism was torn with inner dissensions, it suffered no less from pressure from without. Nothing else will account for the intensity of the writer's hatred of Egypt, which he gratifies as he lingers over the bondage of the Israelites, and labours the contrast between the fortunes of oppressors and oppressed (x. 16 ff. ; xi. 1 ff. ; xvi.—xix.).

History repeats itself, and he regards the study of history as the best remedy for national depression. If it was in respect of its divinities that Egypt was smitten in the time of Moses, and if idolatry is not only folly but the cause of all social and civic decadence (xiii.—xv.), the suppressed conclusion is that the Egypt which still harries the resident Jews and has not yet repented of its beast-worship, will once again bend before Israel. It should be noted that the section on false cults starts from Egypt (xii. 24, cp. xi. 15) and leads back to Egypt (xv. 18).

(*c*) In face of internal weakness and external pressure, the author propounds his positive teaching. His most orthodox readers had been coming unconsciously to be affected by Hellenic speculation, and in the Wisdom of the Book of Proverbs he found a means of reconciling traditional Hebrew thought with the cosmic ideas of Stoicism. Alexandrian Jews were looking for a philosophy of experience, and they failed to find such in any truly speculative sense, except in the later Sapiential books.

Accordingly, he propounds his doctrine of Wisdom as a fundamental unifying principle, which coordinates Greek thought with Hebrew revelation, and correlates (as functions of the same being) the various operations of creative activity, guidance of history, advancement of science and philosophy, moral elevation of mankind, and mediation between God and man.

In this way he hopes, while never passing the bounds of orthodoxy, to show that Judaism is not merely an insulated national creed, but one standing in relation with truth wherever found. Further, nothing but the Wisdom revealed to the Hebrews can avert the doom threatening those rulers who have wrongly administered God's kingdom on earth.

(D) It has been maintained that Wisdom was written with a "definite polemical aim in opposition" to Ecclesiastes (Siegfried, "Bk of Wisdom" in Hastings' *D. B.*, and Plumptre, *Ecclesiastes*, p. 70), but such a view is based on very insecure evidence.

Ecclesiastes was apparently composed about B.C. 200, and was Palestinian in origin. We do not know when it reached Egypt, or when it was translated ; but it can have been only in its Greek form that it was studied at Alexandria. It was probably one of the latest O.T. books to be translated, as its canonicity was long in dispute, and continued so to be for many years after Wisdom was composed (if 100 B.C. is accepted as the date of Wisdom). It may therefore have not been yet translated, when Wisdom was written[1].

Further, it is hard to see why a book with so little authority should require so strenuous a refutation. For it probably began its career in Egypt with little, if any, precedence over Ecclesiasticus, with which it is about contemporary in composition and from which it is equally impossible to prove that Wisdom made any borrowings[2].

If the aim of Wisdom is to denounce renegade Jews, it is hardly a reasonable suggestion that such men had found a champion for their principles of life in Solomon, and that therefore a counter-standard of a pious and orthodox Solomon needed to be erected. Apostates would not look for a justification of their life to the Scriptures of a religion they derided and renounced and persecuted.

But besides this, the resemblances between Wisdom and the Gk. version of Eccl. are very few and doubtful. There is not in Wisdom a single expression which can be decisively shown to be drawn from Eccl. There is no part of the Greek Bible that bears more clearly or crudely the marks of a translation from Hebrew than Eccl., but any of the few Hebraisms common to both books (such as μερὶς, ii. 9; Eccl. iii. 22) can be traced elsewhere in LXX.

Again, of isolated thoughts there are only a few for which even distant and general parallels (such as may be found anywhere) are seen in Eccl. (cp. ii. 3, 9; Wisd. vii. 11 a. iv. 14; Wisd. vi. 20. vii. 12; Wisd. viii. 17. vii. 19; Wisd. xvi. 17, 24. viii. 8; Wisd. ii. 5. x. 8; Wisd. xi. 16, but cp. Ecclus. xxvii. 27. xii. 7; Wisd. xv. 8, 16). Further, in the Stoic and Epicurean philosophy of life (in which the main resemblance is held to lie),

---

[1] Barton (Ecclesiastes, p. 9, in *Int. Crit. Comm.*) concludes that the earliest Gk. version of Ecclesiastes was that of Aquila at the end of the first century A.D.

[2] Plumptre even suggests that the "copy, affording no small instruction" referred to in the Prologue to Ecclus. was Ecclesiastes.

Eccl. finds a parallel only in Wisd. i. 16—ii. 10. And even here, there is no further relation between Eccl. and Wisdom than might be expected between the reflective writings of any two Jews acquainted with Job and Proverbs. Epicureanism is a fault of the heart as much as of the head, and can be accounted for without the hypothesis of a literary dependence. Finally, the standpoint of the hedonist in Eccl. is altogether different from that of the voluptuaries of Wisd. ii. Koheleth never rejects his religion: he summarizes the whole matter with "Fear God and keep His commandments." They, on the other hand, praise unbridled licence as the supreme goal of life, and above all become persecutors of their faithful fellow countrymen. In short, what Wisdom refutes is something not contemplated by Eccl.

For these reasons, the theory that Wisdom was prompted by opposition to Eccl. may be confidently rejected.

(E) The name of Solomon was probably chosen for two reasons, (i) because Wisdom-literature was traditionally associated with his name, as psalmody with that of David, and (ii) because of the address to rulers. Although it is hard to imagine that Wisdom would be read by any heathen rulers, and by more than a few (if any) ex-Jewish rulers, yet dramatically it would be fitting that the Hebrew king famed above all others for his administrative wisdom should be the writer's mouthpiece.

It should be noted that the writer brings Solomon upon the stage in his youth, ignoring the moral declension of his later life.

§ 7. *Unity of the book.*

The principal attacks upon the unity of Wisdom were made by Houbigant, Eichhorn, and Bretschneider.

Houbigant, struck by the difference between the earlier and later parts of the book, divided it into two sections, suggesting that Solomon himself wrote chs. i.—ix. in Hebrew, while chs. x.—xix. were added in Greek, possibly by the translator of chs. i.—ix.

Eichhorn divided the book differently, and conjectured that

chs. i.—xi. 1 were the work of a different author from chs. xi. 2—
xix., or of the same author at a different period of his life.

Bretschneider divided the book into three parts, i.—vi. 8;
vi. 9—x.; xii.—xix. According to him, the first part was a
fragment of a larger Hebrew work written in the time of Antiochus Epiphanes by a cultivated Palestinian Hellenist. The
second part was the work of an Alexandrian Jew, a contemporary
of our Lord. The third part was composed by a Jew of crude
conceptions, writing about the same time. Ch. xi. served as a
ligature between parts ii. and iii.

Into the arguments on either side there is no need to enter.
Attacks upon the unity of the book have failed, and no serious
effort to dispute it has recently been made.

It cannot be denied that, from the point of view of style,
Wisdom divides itself into certain distinct sections, only loosely
bound together, and not marked by any pronounced uniformity
of treatment. But the author was a rhetorician, to whom "no
class of writings and no mode of combination appear to be
unfamiliar." Uniformity of style is not to be looked for, when
a man of wide reading and great imitative versatility handles a
variety of topics. As he passes from one class of subject to
another, the *motif* of the moment imposes upon him the style in
which he is accustomed to find it treated.

Too much importance may easily be assigned to superficial
differences[1], while the underlying homogeneity of the book (as
to general tone and manner of thought) is ignored. The careful
study of Wisdom as a whole will reveal sufficient evidence of
unity of idea and relation between its parts to justify the belief
in its composition by a single author. Grimm, who combats in
detail (*Intr.* pp. 9—15) the arguments adduced in favour of the
disintegrating hypotheses, concludes by saying that "the unity
of the book is securely established by the consistent character
of the language, as well as by the unity of the literary situation

---

[1] E.g., the eschatological interest is confined to the first part, and
the haggadistic interpretation to the second. Part i. is concerned with
the life of the individual, part ii. with a philosophy of national history.
Wisdom is the central figure in chs. i.—ix.: she is almost ignored in
chs. xi.—xix.

and tendency." The two objects of attack, apostasy and idolatry, represent the two great enemies of later Judaism. (See also Dr Westcott, in Smith's *D. B.* iii. p. 1780.)

It may be added that a love of extended antitheses is a feature of the book throughout. Chs. i.—v. contain three lengthy comparisons of the fortunes of the godly and the ungodly, while chs. xvi.—xix. are devoted to five laboured contrasts between the experiences of the Israelites and the Egyptians (cp. also chs. xi. and xii.).

§ 8. *Wisdom-literature.*

Wisdom-literature represents a definite direction of the Hebrew mind, parallel to that which it took in prophecy. Three classes of men are spoken of in Jer. xviii. 18, *prophets, priests,* and *wise men*; and from this passage amongst others it seems clear that the wise (*ḥakāmîm*) formed, if not a school, at any rate a class among the Jews, whose activities took their place as a recognised department of Jewish national life.

The wise men probably rendered a quiet but solid assistance to the prophets, whose message was delivered in more general terms and with uncompromising vehemence: being the casuists and moral advisers of the day the *ḥakāmîm* were in a position to individualize the prophetic message and to present it in a more conciliatory manner.

The earliest form which Wisdom took was the elaboration of riddles (Jdg. xiv. 14), fables (Jdg. ix. 8—15), parables (2 Sam. xii. 1—6), and proverbs (Ez. xviii. 2), the proverb (*māshāl*) being a terse generalisation based upon human experience, or upon the observation of nature.

The reflective tendency produced famous wise men from the days of Solomon downwards (1 Kings iv. 30), but Wisdom was not confined to the Israelites: the men of Edom were famed for their sagacity (cp. Jer. xlix. 7; Obad. 8).

Wisdom-literature began with the formation of collections of the sayings of the wise, the most famous being, of course, that known as the Book of Proverbs.

But it was after the Exile, that Wisdom-literature attained its highest development. "Wisdom" served as a corrective of legalism, when, after the religious reorganisation under Ezra,

the intellectual life of the people was gradually "confined by
the priests within the limits of rigid law." The wise men were
no longer represented in literature by collections of detached
aphorisms, but they appeared as writers on popular morals,
handling ethical subjects at length in narrative style. The
canonical examples of their work are seen in Job and Eccl.,
and perhaps Ps. lxxiii.

But the unofficial work of the wise men was an unspoken
criticism of that of prophets and priests, who accordingly regarded them with some jealousy and suspicion. They were the
"humanists" of Israel, and made their influence felt against a
too rigid institutionalism.

Their teaching was, it is true, directed to the establishment of
morality, but its practical aim made them indifferent to that
insistence upon national topics which marked the prophet, and
that attention to ceremonial considerations which marked the
priest. The wise men were not concerned with the central
prophetic ideas of the Kingdom of God, the Chosen People, or
the Messiah, or with the priestly ritual connected with sacrifice
and Temple-service. Occupied as they were with the analysis
of human conduct, and the observation of the sequences of cause
and effect in connection with it, they studied experience chiefly
in a subjective light. They were the first among the Israelites
to begin to allow for the action of general laws. They were so
occupied with the contemplation of nature and man, that they
assigned increasing importance to laws of action and reaction
which worked themselves out automatically without calling for
any direct intervention on the part of God.

Thus the operation of spiritual laws plays a larger part in the
Wisdom-books than in the prophetic writings: "Thus saith the
Lord" tends to disappear, and psychological analysis becomes
more prominent.

But God is not banished from the writings of the wise: it is
only that greater room is allowed for that power divinely planted
in men and things, of obeying the laws written in their constitution. Experience is stated in terms of man. Far from being
atheists, the wise men represent a tendency altogether opposite
to that of the Greek speculators. In fact, it might even be

said that the Jewish Wisdom (*Ḥokmah*) was no philosophy at all. The wise men of Israel never approached their enquiries without theological presuppositions. They had no desire to investigate final causes; they started from a fundamental axiom "In the beginning God...." This postulate indicates the character of their studies, which were not so much speculative as practical: their desire was not so much to understand the works of God, as to acquaint themselves with their harmonies, beauties, and adaptations, and all this with the final object of knowing and doing the will of God.

But while the basis of Hebrew enquiry was thus provided by Revelation, and the only atheists were the immoral who said in their heart "There is no God," there were no bounds to its range. The entire field of practical life came within its purview: kings, husbandmen and traders alike were governed by the moral principles which formed the study of the wise.

To the class of Wisdom-literature belong the Palestinian *Ecclesiasticus*, and the Alexandrian *Wisdom* (and 4 *Macc.*). The former, owing to its relation to the law and the prophets, shows traces of having not altogether thrown off the legalistic tendency, while Wisdom, as we saw earlier, lays Greek philosophical terms under contribution, although hardly deviating (cp. xi. 17) from the strictest Jewish orthodoxy. It should be noted that, in the latter half of Wisdom, the writer deserts one of the most characteristic canons of Wisdom-literature, and exhibits a violent national prejudice (cp. also Ecclus. xxiv. 8). It may be, however, that in passing from the more strictly gnomic to the descriptive part of the book, a change in the tone of his thought effected itself spontaneously upon a change in the mode of literary treatment.

Perhaps the main contribution of the Book of Wisdom to Sapiential literature is the clearness of its witness to life beyond the grave. Prof. A. B. Davidson (*Expositor*, xi. pp. 335 ff.) has noted three phases of Wisdom-literature: (i) That of Prov. x. ff. in which occurrences never violate the O.T. principles of earthly reward and retribution. This world supplies a broad enough platform upon which to complete the entire drama of human life: the righteous live long, the wicked are not delivered.

(ii) That in which exceptions occur, cp. Ps. lxxiii. and Job, and the godly are perplexed by the prosperity of the wicked and the sufferings of the righteous. (iii) That in which difficulties no longer perplex, e.g. Eccl., but are acquiesced in as a permanent and useful element of experience.

Wisdom puts forward unhesitatingly as a solution of the difficulty that eschatological hope which was tentatively held by the thinkers of the second phase. The life beyond the grave (in the form of the Greek doctrine of the immortality of the soul) was perhaps the greatest spiritual consolation that could have been offered in days when the promises to the chosen people seemed to be irretrievably falsified by a bitter experience of oppression without and faithlessness within.

§ 9. *The Divine Wisdom.*

Wisdom-literature is so called because it contains the practical wisdom of the *ḥakāmîm*, and not because it reveals the Divine Wisdom.

But in Prov. and Job, as well as in Ecclus. and Wisdom, a personified, almost hypostatised, Wisdom is introduced, a conception the development of which must be traced, if we are to grasp the leading idea of the Book of Wisdom.

It may be said at once that Wisdom, as it appears in the Book of Job, will hardly concern us, except as an arrested phase of a development exhibited in greater completeness in Prov., Ecclus. and Wisdom. In Job Wisdom is "the idea or principle lying under the order of the universe," the world-plan. It is the moral constitution of the world, comprising not only physical phenomena, but also the life and destinies of men. This "world-order with all its occurrences is nothing but God fulfilling Himself in many ways, but these ways may be reduced to one conception, and this is Wisdom, which is thus conceived as a thing having objective existence of its own." This Wisdom is a possession of God alone. When therefore to the question, "Where shall Wisdom be found?" the answer is returned "The fear of the Lord that is Wisdom," there is no identification of Wisdom with the fear of the Lord, nor even explanation of it in those terms. The meaning is that a man cannot attain to the

WISDOM   *c* intellectual apprehension of the underlying principle of the universe, but that God has given him a *substitute*, viz. the fear of the Lord (see A. B. Davidson, *Job*, pp. 198—201, and W. R. Inge, *Faith and Knowledge*, p. 29).

In Proverbs (chs. i.—ix.) the system of the universe, moral and physical, is regarded as a unity pervaded by an immanent God. Then the Divine principles which manifest themselves in the life of the world are abstracted from God their source, and these principles are viewed "as an articulated, organised whole, outside of God Himself, the expression of His mind, but having an existence of its own alongside of God." To this system of principles consciousness is attributed; it is personified as Wisdom, in whom are summed up the principal attributes of God: Wisdom even becomes the child of God, "playing" (Prov. viii. 30) before Him in the days of creation.

But though personified, the function of Wisdom is mainly humanitarian: her delights are with the sons of men (Prov. viii. 31, 32). Her work is that of a public teacher: the picture of her in Prov. viii. "could only have been drawn by combining many materials together, such as the public teaching of the prophets, the more private conversational instruction of the wise, the judicial procedure of the public law at the gates, and the many lessons of social order and well-being which the thronging thoroughfares presented....She is the personification of everything that had a voice to speak to men, and impress upon them the principles of Divine order in the world" (A. B. Davidson, *Expositor*, xii. p. 456).

The conception of Wisdom in Ecclus. is clearly borrowed from Proverbs, and (although slightly expanding the earlier teaching) makes no real advance upon it. Wisdom was created before the world (xxiv. 9); she came forth from the mouth of the Most High (*v.* 3). She has a possession in every people and nation (*v.* 6), but her special portion is with Israel (*v.* 8), and upon Mount Sion (*v.* 10). The picture is free from all traces of Hellenism, and shows Wisdom as a purely moral agent (as in Prov.), and not employed as intermediary in creation. Wisdom is still a personification, and not a person.

But it is when we come to the Book of Wisdom, that we find

the most complete development of the conception. But even there the last thing we must look for is a definite, clear-cut presentment of Wisdom. The writer breathes an atmosphere charged with vague and indeterminate conceptions, some Greek and others Hebrew, which seem to approach one another, but never quite to meet. Possessed of little precision of thought, he fails to produce a logically perfect synthesis: but he makes a remarkable advance upon his predecessors in effecting the fusion of Greek and Hebrew ideas.

If we desire to arrive at the author's conception, we must consider first (i) the synonyms, (ii) the attributes, (iii) the functions, of Wisdom.

(i) *Synonyms for Wisdom.* The writer was acquainted with the Stoical theory of an all-penetrating Logos, which took shape in the universe as rational order, and in man as reason. Round this Divine principle gathered, and with it were identified, such varied ideas as providence, destiny, justice, truth, cause, nature, necessity.

The author could not introduce the Logos into his philosophy, but he could take the authorised Hebrew conception of the Wisdom, and handle it in a manner altogether analogous to that of the Stoic Logos. To the potentialities of such a cosmic figure as the Wisdom of Prov. and Ecclus., practically no limits could be set. Accordingly, he identifies Wisdom with

(a) *The spirit of the Lord* (ix. 17). If the spirit of the Lord fills all things, and is in all the world (i. 7 ; xii. 1), so is Wisdom (vii. 24 ; viii. 1). Not only does a holy spirit of discipline behave in the same manner in face of sin as does Wisdom (i. 4, 5), but we learn that Wisdom is herself a spirit (i. 6 ; perh. vii. 22).

Further, the same functions are ascribed to Wisdom in chs. vii.—ix., as in O.T. to the spirit of God, which leads man in the right way (Job xxxii. 8; Ps. li. 12; cxliii. 10), and gives wisdom to kings (Is. xi. 2), inspiration to artists (Ex. xxxi. 3), and vision to prophets (1 Sam. x. 6).

(b) The *Logos*, or *Word*, in O.T. sense. What the Word of the Lord does, that Wisdom does. They are instruments of creation (ix. 1, cp. viii. 6; ix. 2, 9). They are remedies against

c 2

evil (xvi. 12, cp. ix. 18 and x.). They are used to chastise Egypt (xviii. 15, cp. x. 19). They are both all-powerful (xviii. 15, cp. vii. 23); both sit on God's throne (xviii. 15, cp. ix. 4). It should be observed, however, that although the functions of the Word are all conceded to Wisdom, the converse is not true in this book.

(c) *Power*, i. 3, cp. x. 8.

(d) *Providence*, xiv. 3, cp. x. 4.

(e) *Hand of God*, xiv. 6, cp. x. 4.

(f) *Justice*, i. 8; xiv. 31, cp. x. 14, 16.

(g) *Angel of the Lord*. The destroying angel of O.T. is represented by the Logos in xviii. 15; but in Wisd. x. 17 Wisdom controls the pillar of cloud, being thus identified with the "angel of God" in Ex. xiv. 19.

Thus Wisdom unites in herself a number of floating conceptions: though alone in kind, she is manifold (vii. 22), see H. Bois, *Origines*, pp. 233—241.

(ii) *Attributes*. From ch. vii. 22—24 we learn the nature of Wisdom. She possesses intelligence, holiness, beneficence, omnipotence, omniscience (ix. 11). She is mobile, enjoying such rarity of being that she can penetrate into every place and discern every pure spirit. These qualities belong to her because of her ineffably close relation to God, whence come her stainless beauty and indefeasible security (vi. 12; vii. 25, 29, 30).

(iii) *Functions*. Wisdom, being a cosmic figure, is concerned with the two great departments of creation, nature and man, but as in Proverbs, her chief interest is man.

(a) *Nature*. She fills the world (i. 7); holds all things together (i. 7); renews all things (vii. 27); orders all things (viii. 1); works all things (viii. 5). She was an instrument in God's creating work (ix. 2); was therefore present at creation (ix. 9); knows God's works (ix. 9), and chooses them out (viii. 4).

(b) *Man*. She convicts him of unrighteous words (i. 8); she forestalls those who seek her (vi. 13—16); she promotes to a kingdom (vi. 20); brings good things with her, of which she is the mother (vii. 11, 12); helps to the Divine friendship (vii. 14,

27); makes men prophets (vii. 27); teaches the sciences (vii. 16—22), the four virtues (viii. 7), experience and foresight and intuition (viii. 8); gives man counsel and encouragement (viii. 9), glory and honour (viii. 10), immortality (viii. 13), power to govern (viii. 14), knowledge of the Divine counsel (ix. 17). She alone makes man to be held in account (ix. 6); corrects the ways of earth-dwellers (ix. 18); is a saviour (ix. 18); and was the director and deliverer of the heroes of antiquity (chs. x., xi).

We come now to the discussion of the nature of Wisdom. Her functions and attributes mark her out as being very near to God Himself, and the writer accumulates such expressions as breath, effluence, effulgence, mirror, image (vii. 25, 26), in order to assert her divineness without attributing to her deity. She is pictured as a "solar energy, emanating from the focus of power, and though exerting characteristic influences on every variety of object, yet never breaking loose into separate existence, or violating the indissoluble unity of her source." With this central source she is one : yet, though possessing all that God has to give, she does so only by derivation.

This aspect of her being is carefully emphasised. She sits by God on His throne (ix. 4); she is initiated into His knowledge, and actually chooses out His works (viii. 3, 4); she is with God, and was present with Him when he was making the world (ix. 9) : and yet, she is God's servant, completely at His disposal. He is her guide (vii. 15); He gives her (ix. 4), and sends her from on high (ix. 17); He bids her go from the throne of His glory to dwell with men (*id.*).

Nevertheless, Wisdom is not hypostatised. Drummond writes (*Phil. Jud.* i. p. 226) that she is personal, but not a person. If the distinction is valid, it expresses well the nature of a Being which is allowed to possess all the moral qualities of God without His self-determination. She is holy, and possesses intelligence; God loves her: and yet she does not exist out of Him. She is rather the result of God's being and the reflection of His volitional movements, than a Being standing over against Him. She is a channel of His will, rather than a voluntary agent on its behalf. She personifies the train of causal sequences that connect the act of will in the mind of God with the object upon which He wills to act. And yet the writer regards her as far more than a merely literary personification: in view of viii. 16—18 it must be granted that he conceded to her a refined, supersensuous personality. But psychological analysis had not reached its present development, and the *differentia* of personality would be stated now in very different terms from those which he would have employed. No modern psychologist would allow personality to Wisdom, on the data advanced in the book.

In conclusion, it is plain that Wisdom is a creation of thought (not of necessity consciously so to the writer), representing the answer to the question, how to bring a transcendent God into relation with phenomena. Wisdom is not an attribute, nor the sum of the attributes, of God: such an explanation would not take account of all the properties postulated of Wisdom, nor would it allow for the completeness of the Divine transcendence. Wisdom again is not God in manifestation: she is too distinct from Him to be merely a theoretical aspect of Himself. Lastly, she is not a Being, personal and distinct from God: she emanates from Him, but emanation has not terminated. No birth-severance has taken place, giving her independent life.

No better summary could be offered than the words of Drummond (*Phil. Jud.* i. p. 225) "Wisdom is a self-adaptation of the inviolable spirituality of God to material conditions, an assumption of the necessary community of nature, in order to bring the infinite and eternal into those relations of space and time which are implied in the creation and government of the world of sense."

§ 10. *The Logos.*

The Philonic doctrine of the Logos, or Word, is not found in this book: the author advances nowhere beyond the Jewish use of the word. But Philo's doctrine of the Wisdom is almost identical with that of Pseudo-Solomon, and any anticipations in this book of Philo's doctrine of the Logos are to be found in connection with it rather than with the term Logos.

The Philonic Logos, owing to its Greek philosophical implications, has the meaning of "reason," or the rational thought and ideal of God: but of the six passages in which the word is used in Wisdom, in one only can the Logos have the sense of "reason," and then not in a cosmic sense, but with reference to human nature (ii. 2, "reason is a spark").

In ch. ix. 1, 2 we read "who madest all things by Thy Logos, and by Thy Wisdom Thou formedst man." Here Logos is rightly rendered "Word." The passage is Hebrew in tone, recalling Ps. xxxiii. 5, 6, and no contrast is intended between the two clauses. They are parallel, and "wisdom" is used in the second as a poetic variant for "word" in the first. Wisdom here is not the Divine semi-hypostatised Being, but the Divine attribute of Wise-ness, as in Ps. civ. 24 "in Wisdom hast Thou made them all." There is no contrast suggested between the functions of Wisdom and of the Logos, as if the former were the agent in the making of man, and the latter in the making of things: for Wisdom is the "artificer of all things" (vii. 22, cp. viii. 6).

Again, as far as the Book of Wisdom is concerned, a distinction between the Wisdom as representing the immanence of God, and the Word as representing His activity, cannot be maintained. Wisdom is consistently presented as an agent throughout ch. x.

Ch. xii. 9 and xviii. 22 present no difficulty, as Logos in these passages plainly has the meaning of "word," while xvi. 12 is based upon Ps. cvii. 20, "He sent His word and healed them."

But the celebrated passage in xviii. 15 has been claimed as an example of the Philonic use of the Logos. This, however, is not the case. The use of Logos in this passage must be determined both by its use elsewhere in Wisdom and by the character of the chapter.

(i) We have seen that the Divine Logos has no Greek philosophical associations in any other passage in this book. See ix. 1; xii. 9; xvi. 12, cp. Ps. cxlvii. 15, 18. In each of these passages, it is the expression of the will of God in action, cp. the parallel use in xviii. 22.

(ii) This ch. is Hebraic in thought, and not Greek. *v.* 24 is undoubtedly borrowed from Hebrew commentaries, to which

Philo and Josephus later had access.   It is probable that *vv.* 9,
15 are drawn from a similar source.

The Logos is treated in this verse in a highly rhetorical way:
there is a great advance upon such a passage as Is. xi. 4 LXX.
"He shall smite the earth with the Logos of His mouth," or
Hos. vi. 5 LXX. "I slew them by the word (ῥήματι) of My
mouth," or even upon Ps. cxlvii. 15 LXX. "His Logos shall
run." Not only is independent action attributed to it, "It
leaped," but it is personified as "a stern warrior."

Now Wisd. xviii. 15 seems to be based upon 1 Chr. xxi. 15,
where the agent is the angel of the Lord.   But the ministry of
angels has no place in Wisdom; accordingly, the change to
Logos is accounted for: and the presence of the angel in the
source-passage tells at first sight in favour of the independent
personality of the Logos here.

But the writer may have drawn upon the passage in 1 Chr.
xxi. without necessarily identifying the Logos in Egypt with the
angel of the plague.   Moreover, the Logos in Wisd. xviii. 15
corresponds exactly with the "punisher" of xviii. 22, and the
"destroyer" of xviii. 25; and it is curious to note that the latter
expression is not taken from the account in Numbers from which
the rest of the narrative (*vv.* 20—25) is drawn, but is introduced
from Ex. xii. 23, which relates to the death of the firstborn.

Now, although in Wisd. xviii. 15 the Logos is the agent in the
destruction of the firstborn, and although in the *Jerusalem
Targum* (Etheridge, p. 477) it is the "Word of the Lord" that
slew all the firstborn in the land of Egypt, yet in the source-
passages, Ex. xi. 4 and xii. 29 (LXX.), God Himself is spoken of
as the agent.   Hence it seems plain that the writer had no
intention of hypostatising the Logos, but had in mind only the
customary Jewish periphrasis for the Lord, i.e. the "Memra of
Jehovah." This expression means "the Divine Being in self-
manifestation" (see Etheridge, *Targums*, Introd. pp. 14—20).

The inference that the personification of the Logos is purely
poetical is supported by those Biblical narratives, in which the
agent is now spoken of as God, and again as the angel of the
Lord (cp. Gen. xxxi. 11 and 13; xxxii. 24 and 30; Ex. xiv. 19
and xiii. 21).   The same tendency may be observed in later

versions of an earlier account (cp. Acts vii. 30 and 32[1]; also Acts vii. 38, 53; Gal. iii. 19; Heb. ii. 2, as compared with Ex. xix. 19; xx. 1). In these passages we see how strongly the Jews felt that what in God is capable of manifestation must be distinguishable from His transcendent existence, and yet that they only ventured to provide themselves with a formula to express God in self-manifestation: they were very far from postulating a second "eternal." And similarly, in Wisd. xviii. 15, no valid reason exists for regarding the Logos as more than a rhetorico-poetical personification of the Divine will and energy.

It has been argued that the Logos in xviii. 15 is to be identified with the Wisdom, cp. Ecclus. xxiv. 3, and perhaps Wisd. ix. 1, 2. The same epithet "all powerful" is applied to both (vii. 23); Wisdom sits beside God on His throne (ix. 4); Wisdom possesses unlimited mobility, and her power reaches from one end of the world to the other (vii. 24; viii. 1). That Wisdom like the Logos is not associated with creative acts only may be seen from her destructive actions in x. 19.

But the preceding argument shows that the Logos is not conceived of in this book as a personal intermediary in the same rank with Wisdom, and either coequal or identical with her, but as merely a rhetorical personification. The writer would not identify a substance with a shadow.

§ 11. *Doctrine of God.*

The Book of Wisdom does not ask, "Does God exist?" His existence is taken for granted. But there is another question "What is His nature?" and to it no definite answer is given, although many hints are furnished as to the writer's view.

God is supreme, and His supremacy is seen in His work as Creator (xi. 17) and Upholder (xii. 15). But what are His relations to His world? Is He immanent or transcendent? Is He rightly described as its Creator, or only as its Organiser?

Wisdom emphasises, as might be expected in an Alexandrine work, the distance of God from His world. Even omnipresence

---

[1] Cp. the Alexandrian Jewish poet, Ezekiel, in Eus. (*Praep. Ev.* 441 a) "The Divine *Logos* shineth upon thee out of the bush."

is only indirectly attributed to God: it is the spirit of God, or Wisdom, that fills the World. And if God searches hearts and reins, and hears the secret words of men, it is because His deputy lays them open to His mind (i. 6—10).

It is as a transcendent God that the book presents Him. He is indeed Creator, Artificer, Author of the world's beauty (i. 14; ix. 9; xiii. 1; *id.* 3), but not directly; His creative action was mediated through Wisdom: and similarly, though He might be said to order the course of the world (xii. 15), yet Wisdom is His appointed agent (viii. 1). All things were made through Wisdom, and without her was not anything made.

God is more rightly named Organiser than Creator. His hand did not make the world out of nothing, but out of formless matter (xi. 17). No explanation is offered as to the source of this pre-existing material, and the hypothesis of a double creation (i.e. first, the production of matter, and later, its arrangement) may be discarded, because, as Grimm well says, the production of the elemental substance is a far greater marvel than the reduction of it to order, and when the writer could have spoken of the more marvellous, he would hardly have confined himself to the less. Accordingly the verb κτίζω (create) used in xi. 17 (cp. κατασκευάζω, ix. 2; xiii. 4) indicates that "to create" as used in i. 14, ii. 23 emphasises not so much the manner of creation as the personal action of the Creator.

Besides this dualism of God and matter, the author incidentally mentions another. God made the world for life (i. 14), but His creation has been intruded upon by death (i. 16). Now death is not God's handiwork (i. 13), but what the source is from which death springs, the writer does not discuss: through the envy of the devil it entered into the world, but the devil is not viewed as its author, only as its channel (ii. 24). But even if death does not hold the rank of a rival eternal principle, it is nevertheless a terrible fact thwarting God's purposes for men.

The giving of the name of Wisdom to His supreme intermediary, indicates the aspect under which the author found his chief pleasure in contemplating the transcendent God.

We have seen what are the attributes of Wisdom: what the servant is, that, and more, must the Master be (vii. 16—26).

Next to His wisdom, the omnipotence of God as qualified by
His goodness, appeals to him. God has to answer to no
overlord for His conduct (xii. 12—14); He is the self-existent
(ὁ ὤν, xiii. 1); the eternal light (vii. 26); He has all power
(xi. 21, 23; xii. 18); and yet He does not employ His might
capriciously or irresponsibly (xi. 23; xii. 16, 18). Nothing but
love can explain His self-restraint (xi. 24, 26). Nothing could
have come into being and continued in being without His will
(xi. 25), and He could never have called into existence a thing
that He hated (xi. 24). Love therefore must be viewed as His
motive in creation: and this principle is demonstrated in His
patient forbearance towards sinners (xi. 26; xii. 1). The world
is so minute in His sight (xi. 22), that in very pity He seeks to
make it possible for sinners to repent (xi. 23; xii. 10, 20).

And yet, if God exercises a beneficent providence caring for
all alike (vi. 7), He has His moral prepossessions. He detests
idolaters (xiv. 9); He detested the Canaanites for their abominations (xii. 3); He will laugh at the wicked (iv. 18). But the
souls of the righteous are in His hand (iii. 1); He loves those
who dwell with Wisdom (vii. 14, 28), and He will visit His saints
(iv. 15).

Again, to the Jews He was a Father, disciplining them with
an educative purpose, but to the Egyptians a stern King,
chastening them in displeasure and in token of condemnation
(xi. 9, 10).

May God be known? Does the fact that He manifests
Himself through Wisdom prove that He must do so, because
otherwise He is hidden, incomprehensible, unknowable? Carefully as His transcendence is emphasised, still greater care is
taken to prove His revelation of Himself. The external world
cannot indeed give an adequate knowledge of God, but it can
prove His existence (xiii. 1). And it can do more: by its power
and beauty, it can symbolise (as Plato and the Stoics had seen)
the moral force and loveliness of its author (xiii. 3—5). But
there can be a direct self-manifestation of God to the soul that
prepares itself for Him (i. 1, 2; xv. 1—3); men may be His
friends (vii. 27); incorruption brings them near to Him (vi. 19);
He inspires them with right words and thoughts (vii. 15, 16).

And yet, even here the mediation of Wisdom is asserted (vii. 28; ix. 17).

The truth is that no statement of the theology of Wisdom can be made without qualifications. The writer felt the influence of two types of thought, without giving a complete adhesion to either. He acknowledged the direct action of God upon the world, and yet his Alexandrine sympathies forced upon him the doctrine of an intermediary. At first sight, the anthropomorphisms of the book might seem to bear witness to the direct action of God; because, if the writer had been completely possessed by the Judaeo-Alexandrine doctrine of God's aloofness, he would have written of the Divine powers rather than as in iii. 1; v. 16; vii. 16, of God's hand and arm. On the other hand, the later Judaeo-Alexandrine writers had ceased to be afraid of anthropomorphisms. The LXX. translators tried to eliminate them (cp. Josh. iv. 24, where "hand of God" becomes "power"), but the growth of the allegorical method was seen to rob them of all dangerousness. The work of Aristobulus represented a deliberate effort to explain them away by treating them as formulae standing for some divine attribute, and to show that the hands, arm, face, and feet of God were to be interpreted as divine powers (see Eus. *Praep. Ev.* viii. 9, 10).

Accordingly, it is easy and very possibly correct to view some of the anthropomorphisms in this book as merely synonyms of Wisdom (see x. 20; xi. 17, 21; xvi. 15; xix. 8). Again such a passage as v. 16 is so clearly poetical that it does nothing to prove that the author thought anthropomorphically, or did not hold exaggerated views of divine transcendence.

§ 12. *Doctrine of Man.*

Man is composed of body and soul (i. 4 ; viii. 19, 20). This is the only analysis accepted by the writer, although xv. 11 seems at first to distinguish between soul and spirit. But the distinction is only superficial : the contrast really suggested is between the two epithets applied to the one principle.

The seat of personality is not clearly defined. In the earlier part of the book the writer identifies the blessed dead with their souls which are in the hand of God (iii. 1—9), but he is not

consistent. In viii. 19 Solomon says that he received a good
soul, thus seeming to imply that personality is to a certain
extent independent of the soul: but immediately afterwards he
corrects himself, and personality is identified with the soul
"I came into a body undefiled" (viii. 20). In ch. xv. however
it is not clear whether that which receives the soul or spirit
(*v.* 11) is the man, or merely his body: nor again in *v.* 8 whether
that which surrenders the soul-loan is the man himself,
or merely his mortal body (cp. *v.* 16, and St Luke xii. 20. *Is*
the soul the man and does he go with his soul? Or does he
continue to exist apart from his soul?) This spiritual endowment comes from God (xv. 11), and joins the body at birth.
Hence a certain pre-existence is taught, which is due doubtless
to Greek influence, but not pre-existence of the developed Platonic type (*Phaedr.* 245 C, D; *Meno* 86 A). The writer leans, if
anything, to the Greek position, but he has no consistent view:
in viii. 19 he takes the Greek view, while xv. 11 plainly recalls
Gen. ii. 7. However, the doctrine of the immortality of the soul
which he adopts unreservedly, follows upon the doctrine of pre-
existence more logically than upon the O. T. doctrine. See
Hastings' *D. B.* iv. 63, 164; v. 291.

Pre-existence involves a measure of predestination (cp. Ecclus.
xxxiii. 10—13), which theoretically is only towards goodness,
although practically experience produces many exceptions.
But the writer makes no attempt to effect a reconciliation. On
the one hand he writes that God created man for incorruption,
making him in His own image (ii. 23); Solomon, who was
ex hypothesi like any other man, received a good soul and an
undefiled body. On the other hand, the children of ungodly
parents are destined to an evil end (iii. 12, 16—19; iv. 3—6).

Whatever may constitute the bias towards evil, men possess
free will and are responsible agents. Thus they brought King
Hades into God's world and made terms with him (i. 16);
Adam's transgression was his own; Cain revolted from Wisdom
and so fell into sin (x. 1, 3, cp. *v.* 8). But equally, men may
seek God in such a spirit as to find Him (i. 1, 2); kings must
honour Wisdom if they would reign securely (vi. 21); men may
obtain Wisdom by asking for her (viii. 21).

The writer does not place the principle of sin in the body, although the tendency to depreciate the body has begun (ix. 15). The mere fact that Solomon came into an undefiled body proves that the writer was aware of no law that the body is inherently sinful : similarly, when he says that Wisdom will not dwell in a sin-enslaved body (i. 4), the inference is that inasmuch as Wisdom does dwell with some men, *all* bodies are not held in pledge by sin. It would seem that theoretically the body shares the ethical quality of the soul, and that " the soul's tenement is in itself morally neutral, reflecting the hues of virtue or guilt which belong to the animating spirit" (Drummond, *Ph. Jud.* i. 202). This may be seen from viii. 19, 20, and from i. 4 which is its counterpart, the reference in the two clauses of the latter *v.* being not to two individuals so much as to the one evildoer in his twofold aspect of body and soul. Ch. ix. 15 illustrates the Platonic dualism, to which Philo yielded a complete assent, but which is only an incipient tendency in Wisdom. The body is not an active agent of evil, it is rather a passive check upon the soul : if the soul is not always on God's side, neither is the body invariably His enemy in man.

It is a mistake to urge, as has been done, that the writer gives evidence of a dualistic tendency by an advocacy of asceticism and celibacy (see iii. 13, 14). He views childlessness not as a merit, but as a misfortune, for which spiritual compensations are promised to the sinless.

But however perfect the natural man may be, he will be held in no account apart from Wisdom (ix. 6); but in kinship unto her lies immortality (viii. 17). For the wise man is the righteous man (compare iv. 17 with ii. 12), and righteousness is immortal (i. 15). Righteousness is shown to be closely related to spiritual intuition (cp. x. 10 *b*). The righteous man's boast is his knowledge of God (ii. 13): inadequate knowledge is the misfortune of men which Wisdom alone remedies, while right knowledge is the path to the pleasing of God (ix. 13—19). Again, the supreme righteousness is the knowledge of God, and in the knowledge of His might lies the root of immortality (xv. 3), but ignorance of God is sin entailing condign punishment (xii. 27, cp. x. 8, xiii. 6—9, xv. 11).

But although righteousness is thus seen to depend on knowledge, the content of piety is not thereby exhausted. The duty
of prayer and thanksgiving is prescribed (xvi. 28, cp. viii. 21),
while trust in God, which issues in temporal benefits (xvi. 24,
26), leads to the understanding of truth and to lasting fellowship
with Him (iii. 9).

§ 13. *Death and Immortality.*

By nature, man is immortal, in a spiritual though not in a
physical sense. Physical death is viewed in an altogether non-
moral light, and the author displays no acquaintance with the
penal doctrine of Ecclus. xxv. 24 " Because of her [Eve] we all
die." This is clear from i. 15 "Righteousness is immortal":
the righteous are subject to physical death, and yet their death
has not even remotely a moral significance (cp. iii. 1 ff.). Death
is a universal and purely physical contingency, and the word
"death" is used in this sense in various passages, ii. 20, 24;
xvi. 13; xviii. 12, 16, 20; xix. 5.

But there are some passages where "death" cannot denote
merely physical death. In i. 13 we read "God made not death";
but the writer accepts physical death as part of the normal
economy of nature (cp. xvi. 13). We find ourselves therefore in
presence of a moral death which stands related to moral action
(cp. i. 11 "A lying mouth destroyeth a soul"). This death men
"court in the error of their life" (i. 12): God did not make it,
but they draw it upon themselves by their voluntary action (i. 12,
13). Men cannot blame their circumstances for it, for there is
no moral evil in nature (i. 14). In fact, as long as he remains
true to righteousness, man is free from spiritual death: it is
only those who deliberately bring into their moral world an
intruding rival to God, King Hades, who are subject to it (i. 16.
Bois identifies Pluto, the king of the lower world, with the devil,
Origines, p. 295).

The path to moral death is specified in ch. ii. as sensuality,
apostasy, and oppression of the faithful. The view of life
present and to come, held by those who tread it, is seen in ii.
1—5. Being materialists in practice and philosophy, they view
physical death as extinction : they have discarded even the old

Sheol-conception, and regard death as the end. Led astray by the blindness of their view and by their spiteful jealousy, they think to punish the righteous man by killing him (ii. 20, 21). But they forget the reward of holy souls : the immortality for which God destined all, but the enjoyment of which has now been restricted to the faithful (ii. 22), will cheat them of their desired vengeance. The righteous man cannot be killed except in body: his spirit retains God's image with the incorruption of life that he has preserved. But envy will have its way. Envy introduced murder into the world, when Cain killed his brother, and envy will repeat that first crime to the end (ii. 23, 24, see notes *ad loc.*). The devil's party habitually resort to murder as the final means of clinching their argument with the righteous (ii. 24).

But physical death is the revelation of the meaning of immortality and spiritual death. No doubt these have been in process of development during the earthly life, and death (far from causing any interruption in them) is only a signal for a more rapidly advancing maturity. Immortality lies in obedience to, and fellowship with, Wisdom (vi. 18; viii. 17), and its root is the knowledge of God's power (xv. 3; cp. i. 1, 2 and St John xvii. 3), while on the other hand spiritual death is the state of those whose thoughts are crooked, whose souls devise evil, and whose bodies are pawned to sin (i. 3—5). But death confirms and consummates the righteous : perhaps they have even been snatched away in the best interest of their soul (iv. 11—13). Their souls are in the hand of God (iii. 1): they themselves are in peace (iii. 3) and rest (iv. 7). They died full of hope, and their hope was strong because they carried immortality within them (iii. 4). In the eternal world they receive a crown (iv. 2), and God Himself is their defence and reward (v. 15).

In contrast with this immortality consisting in union with God (the scene of which is not specified), the real meaning of spiritual death comes to light. The souls of the wicked persist, but *metaphorically* they are (and were) dead. They have forfeited the holy immortality of the righteous, and their own condition deserves no other name than death. In fulfilment of their earthly choice, they pay an appropriate penalty (iii. 10).

They have no hope or consolation (iii. 11, 18; v. 14): they lie in the darkness of their own hearts (xvii. 21). They suffer spiritual pain (iv. 19), being tortured with foreboding fears (v. 2) and the tardy but desperate discovery of the falseness of the principles of their earthly life (v. 1—14).

The "day of judgment" is conceived of somewhat vaguely. Wisdom is not a Palestinian book, and therefore the thought of the dead returning to earth (whether without bodies or re-incarnate) to take their part in it, does not necessarily belong to the writer's conception.

This day (of searching out, i. 9; of visitation of souls, iii. 13; of decision, iii. 18; of reckoning up of sins, iv. 20) is spoken of in terms borrowed from current Jewish eschatological belief, but nothing is said as to the scene of the judgment. This judgment declares itself immediately after death, and, without waiting for a resurrection, the souls pass by a kind of selective affinity to reward or retribution[1].

Wisdom contains no doctrine of the annihilation of the wicked. They shall be "a perpetual desolation" in that they have lost their truest life, but no period is stated as being put to their suffering (iv. 19). The continued existence of all is assumed.

It will be seen that all conceptions are spiritualised. Immortality is of a purely ethical kind. The resurrection of the body is not suggested. The writer's doctrine is influenced by Plato and the Stoics.

The persistence of the soul as a separate entity was not a Hebrew conception (Sheol being not a place of departed *spirits*, but of shadow-like personalities), but its individual survival is a salient doctrine of Wisdom. The Stoics who viewed the soul as a fiery current diffused through the body and awaiting ultimate re-absorption into the primal fire, were (like the Jews) vague as to details : they were unable to say, e.g. whether the

---

[1] That the condemnation of the wicked by the righteous (iv. 16) is ideal and inward, may be inferred from the tone of reflection and self-reproach prevailing in v. 1—14. Grimm, however, holds that iii. 13, iv. 6, 20 point to an external and local final judgment (*Weisheit*, p. 110).

soul was re-absorbed immediately after death, or whether it preserved its distinctness until the great conflagration. But there
can be no doubt that in Greek thought upon this subject the
author tended to find matter more to his mind than in Jewish
speculation.

§ 14. *Eschatology.*

Strictly speaking, there is no Messianic hope in Wisdom,
although there are two passages with an outlook over a glorious
future, which in a wider sense might be so described. These
are iii. 7—9 and v. 16—23, which are both capable of interpretation in three ways.

They may be viewed :

(*a*) as vivid and pictorial descriptions of an ethical and
spiritual future, the concrete being the only way of presenting
the inward reality.

(*b*) as definite and literal promises concerning a concrete
earthly future, when the Jews shall be restored to their theocratic
preeminence.

(*c*) as representations of the popular Jewish eschatology,
which looked forward to a universal Messianic world-sovereignty
for Israel, in which the dead would partake, having been restored
to earth by a bodily resurrection.

The view adopted in this commentary is (*a*), which is most
consonant with the Alexandrine tone of Wisdom, and allows
for many discrepancies in detail which cannot be harmonized.
Drummond writes "His thoughts evidently stray to the ultimate
victory of righteousness in the world ; but the language is so
highly figurative that it would be hazardous to fix upon him
any defined eschatology. His deliberate convictions we may
sum up in a single pregnant phrase, 'Incorruption causes to be
near to God'" (*Philo Judaeus*, i. p. 212).

It is only right however to mention that Grimm deliberately
adopts (*b*). In his interpretation of iii. 7—9, he views "they
shall shine forth" as referring to a restitution of power, dignity,
and happiness to God's people in this world, after their long
night of misery and subjection. Further, he regards the

destruction of the stubble by the sparks as a picture of a future extermination of the wicked by the righteous which can have place nowhere except in this world. He anticipates the objection that there is too sudden a leap from the eternal world to the present in iii. 7 by claiming that in a passage where all belongs to the realm of belief the transition is natural and not violent.

The victory of *v.* 7 is followed by the Messianic rule of *v.* 8, which, although exercised upon earth, will be wise and righteous, being carried on by the wise who through association with Wisdom are trained for kingship (vi. 9, 20). He claims that it gives too attenuated a meaning to *v.* 8 to interpret it in the purely spiritual sense of the attainment of freedom and blessedness in the life to come. He clinches his argument by pointing to the latter half of v. 23, which has obvious reference to the accompaniments of an earthly misrule.

§ 15. *Analysis of Contents.*

Part I. Chs. i.—ix.

A. The praise of Wisdom, as the source of true happiness and immortality. Contrast between the estimates, ideals, hopes, and destinies of the godly and the ungodly (chs. i.—v.).

Ch. i. 1—5 Wisdom will dwell only with the upright in thought,

6—11 and in word.

12—15 Life, through righteousness, is the destiny for which God created men.

Three comparisons between materialists and spiritualists, i.e. those who despise and those who follow Wisdom.

I (*a*) Ch. i. 16—ii. 24 Sensuality, and the consequent false estimates of life and death.

(*b*) Ch. iii. 1—9 The meaning of death for the righteous man.

II (*a*) Ch. iii. 10—iv. 6 Earthly immortality is discounted, when the sins of parents are visited on their children.

(*d*) Chs. xvi.—xix. 21 A series of five contrasts between the
    fortunes of Israel and Egypt, in respect of

  (i) *animals*, ch. xvi. 1—14 :
      (*a*) quails *vv.* 1—4,
      (*b*) fiery serpents *vv.* 5—14.

  (ii) *fire and water, heat and cold*, ch. xvi. 15—29.

  (iii) *light and darkness*, ch. xvii. 1—xviii. 4.

  (iv) *death*, ch. xviii. 5—25.

  (v) *passage of the Red Sea*, ch. xix. 1—21.

Nature generally was made subservient to the purposes of
God for His people, and against their enemies.

(*e*) Ch. xix. 22 Conclusion.

§ 16. *MSS. and Text.*

The chief uncial Greek MSS. which contain Wisdom are Cod.
Sinaiticus (א), Vaticanus (B), Alexandrinus (A), Cod. Ephremi
Syri (C, palimpsest) containing viii. 5—xii. 10, xiv. 19—xvii. 18,
xviii. 24—end, and Venetus (V). For a description, see Swete,
Intr. to O.T. in Greek, pp. 125—132.

There are numerous cursives, the best being 68 (Holmes and
Parsons).

˙The Authorised Version of 1611 was based chiefly on the text
of the famous Complutensian Polyglott Bible, 1514 (see Swete,
Introd. pp. 171, 2). The Revised Version, which is used in this
volume, mainly follows the text of B, which is taken as the
standard in Dr Swete's *Old Testament in Greek*, the variant
readings of א, A, and C being given in an *apparatus criticus* at
the foot of each page. The work of revising the English translation of Wisdom and 2 Maccabees was entrusted to the Cambridge Committee, consisting finally of Dr Hort, Dr Westcott,
and Dr Moulton, who began their work in 1881, and completed
it in 1892. "The singular difficulty and importance of the Book
of Wisdom led the revisers to review the version a third time"
(Pref. to Apocr. R.V., cp. also *Life and Letters of F. J. A. Hort*,
vol. ii., pp. 233, 386, 450).

The Greek text is, on the whole, in a good condition : there
are, as might be expected, a number of minor variations, but

there are very few passages (such as xii. 5, 6) in which it seems
hopeless, with the materials extant, to arrive at a true reading.
B gives the best text, but it can not infrequently be corrected
by ℵA, while C (with one brilliant exception, xvi. 3) seems less
trustworthy than A.

The version found in the Latin Bible is the old Latin Version.
Jerome expressly states that he did not revise the translation of
Wisdom (*praef. in Libr. Sal.*). It is possible that in chs. i. 15,
ii. 8 it preserves lines which have dropped out of Greek MSS.,
but for the most part the translation agrees closely with the
existing text.

A collation of the Florentine *Codex Amiatinus* may be found
in Lagarde, *Mittheil.* i. pp. 241—282. See Hastings, *D. B.* iv.
886.

§ 17. *Wisdom and the New Testament.*

There is no direct quotation from the Book of Wisdom in
the N.T., but there is little doubt that its influence was felt by
some of the N.T. writers.

(a) In St Luke xi. 49 our Lord says "Therefore said the
wisdom of God," but the words which follow are not from the
Book of Wisdom (see Plummer *ad loc.*). In a few cases the
language of St Luke may possibly be a reminiscence of expressions in the book. Lk. ii. 7 recalls Wisd. vii. 4, where the
homely detail of the royal child being wrapped in swaddling
clothes is recorded. Lk. xii. 20 τὴν ψυχήν σου αἰτοῦσιν resembles Wisd. xv. 8 τὸ τῆς ψυχῆς ἀπαιτηθεὶς χρέος. Lk. ix. 31
has the unusual word for decease (ἔξοδος) found in Wisd. iii. 2,
while Lk. xix. 44 has the same phrase "time of visitation" as
Wisd. iii. 7. But these similarities may be purely accidental, or
may be due to the influence of St Paul on the mind of the
Evangelist.

(β) In the Fourth Gospel, a more definite connection may
be traced. Not only does the Logos-doctrine of the Prologue
exhibit close affinities with the Wisdom-doctrine of our book,
but many thoughts in the discourses are closely parallel to
thoughts in Wisdom.

(a) St John's Logos-doctrine differs from Wisdom-doctrine

in only one point, but that is the vital one, which marks the distinction between two dispensations, viz. "The Word was God." The similarity of the two doctrines may be seen when we consider that it is possible to substitute the name of Christ for that of Wisdom in the doctrinal parts of Wisdom, and to find a fairly complete anticipation (except in the one particular) of Johannine Logos-doctrine. One reason why in N.T. "Word" not "Wisdom" is employed, is probably that the feminine associations of the latter conception as developed in the Book of Wisdom would make the name (though not the doctrine for which it stood) unsuitable for application to the God-Man.

John i. 1. In the beginning   Wisd. ix. 9. Cp. Prov. viii. 23
The Word was with God   viii. 3; ix. 4
i. 3. All things...made by him (διὰ)   vii. 12 b, 22 a; viii. 6
i. 5. The light shineth   vi. 12
Darkness overcame it not   vii. 29, 30
i. 9. The true light   vii. 10
i. 12. As many as received him   vii. 27 b
i. 14. Glory as of the only be-   vii. 25, 26 (cp. v. 22
gotten   μονογενές)
i. 16. Of his fulness   vii. 11, 12
Grace for grace   iii. 14
i. 18. He hath declared him   ix. 17

Pauline Logos-doctrine is naturally anticipated, cp. Col. i. 13 *the son of his love* (Wisd. viii. 3), while the redemptive work of Christ is foreshadowed by that of Wisdom (i) at the Exodus, x. 15, (ii) in the moral sphere, ix. 18; x. 8, 9. If Christ is the εἰκών (image), Col. i. 15, so is Wisdom (Wisd. vii. 26, cp. ἀπαύγασμα in same v. with Hebr. i. 3). Col. i. 16 *In him were all things created* recalls Wisd. ix. 1, 2; Col. i. 17 *In him all things consist* recalls Wisd. i. 7; and 1 Cor. i. 24 *The power of God* recalls Wisd. i. 3.

Bp Westcott has shown (*Gospel of St John*, Intr. p. xviii) that Johannine Logos-doctrine is "not intelligible as an application or continuation of the teaching of Philo": is it unreasonable to argue that, since in the Book of Wisdom was to be found the most highly developed pre-Christian orthodox speculation on the subject of an intermediary between God and the world, either St Paul, or the writer of the Fourth Gospel, or the un-named pioneer in Christian Logos-doctrine, availed himself of what he found there? When so great a resemblance between earlier and later writers is observable, it is more natural to explain it by the influence of one upon the other, than to regard it as purely fortuitous. The writings of the Christian Church do not represent an unrelated new beginning: they are grounded in those of the Jewish Church.

(*b*) A few parallelisms of thought and expression are selected from a much larger list.

John iii. 5, xv. 5, 6		Wisd. ix. 6
iii. 13.	That came down from heaven	ix. 10
iii. 36.	The wrath...abideth	xvi. 5; xviii. 20
v. 20.	Loveth the Son, and sheweth	viii. 3; ix. 9
v. 23.	Honour the Son	vi. 21
v. 26.	To have life in himself	vii. 27
vi. 57.	He shall live by me ($\zeta\acute{\eta}\sigma\epsilon\iota$ $\delta\iota'$ $\grave{\epsilon}\mu\acute{\epsilon}$), cp. xiv. 19	viii. 13 $\acute{\epsilon}\xi\omega$ $\delta\iota'$ $\alpha\mathring{\upsilon}\tau\grave{\eta}\nu$ $\grave{\alpha}\theta\alpha\nu\alpha\sigma\acute{\iota}\alpha\nu$ (cp. *v.* 17)
vi. 63.	The words	xvi. 12
vi. 65.	Except it were given	viii. 21; ix. 4
vii. 7.	Me it hateth, because I testify of it	ii. 12
viii. 31, 32.	If ye continue..., ye shall know (cp. vii. 17)	iii. 9
viii. 44.	A murderer, cp. 1 John iii. 8, 12	ii. 24 (see note)
viii. 46.		vii. 25, nothing defiled can find entrance into her
viii. 51.	If a man keep..., he shall never see death	vi. 18 b
ix. 2.		iv. 6

John xii. 35.	Darkness come upon you	Wisd. xvii. 21
xiii. 15.	An example	xii. 19
xiv. 15.	If ye love me, keep	vi. 18 a
xiv. 21.	Will manifest myself	vi. 16
xiv. 26.	The Holy Ghost, whom the Father will send	ix. 17 b
xiv. 27.	Peace, not as the world giveth	xiv. 22
xvi. 27.	Loveth you, because ye have loved me (cp. xiv. 6 b)	vii. 28
xvii. 3.	Life eternal, that they may know thee	xv. 3
xvii. 15.	Not that thou shouldest take them out of the world	iv. 10, 11
xix. 11.	No power at all, except...from above	vi. 3

(γ) The question has been frequently debated whether St Paul owed any of his thought to the author of Wisdom. Grimm (*Intr.* p. 36) holds that any apparent likeness must be traced to the common circle of ideas in which both writers moved. But E. Grafe (*Theol. Abhandl.* Freiburg i. B. 1892), who examines the question in minute detail, is firmly convinced of the debt of St Paul to Wisdom, while Sanday and Headlam (*Romans*, pp. 51, 52, 267—9) print certain passages in Rom. i. and ix. in parallel columns with the related passages in Wisdom.

An illustration of the similarity of thought may be seen in St Paul's doctrine of predestination.

Rom. ix. 19, 20. Thou wilt say then unto me, Why doth he still find fault? For who withstandeth his will?

Shall the thing formed say to him that formed it, Why didst thou make me thus?

Wisd. xi. 21. The might of thine arm who shall withstand?

Wisd. xii. 12. For who shall say, What hast thou done? Or who shall withstand thy judgement? And who shall accuse thee for the perishing of nations

which thou didst make? Or
who shall come and stand
before thee as an avenger for
unrighteous men?

Rom. ix. 21. Or hath not
the potter a right *over the clay,
from the same* lump to make
one part *a vessel* unto honour,
and another unto dishonour?

Wisd. xv. 7. *A potter,...,*
mouldeth each several vessel
for our service: nay, *out of the
same clay* doth he fashion both
the *vessels* that minister to
clean uses, and those of a contrary sort, all in like manner;
but what shall be the use of
each..., the craftsman himself
is the judge.

Rom. ix. 22, 23. What if
God, willing to shew his wrath,
and to make his power known,
endured with much longsuffering vessels of wrath *fitted unto
destruction*: and that he might
make known the riches of his
glory upon vessels of mercy...?

Wisd. xii. 10. But judging
them by little and little thou
gavest them a place of repentance.

xii. 20. For if on them that
were enemies of thy servants
and *due to death* thou didst
take vengeance with so great
heedfulness and indulgence,
giving them times and place
whereby they might escape
from their wickedness; with
how great carefulness didst
thou judge thy sons,...!

Grafe notes three common thoughts (i) the irresistible power
of God, (ii) His longsuffering towards His enemies, although
He knows it will be of no avail, (iii) the contrast between the
fortunes of the enemies and the sons of God.

Further, the use in similar passages of the same image of the
potter points towards the dependence of St Paul upon Wisdom,
and even Grimm admits that he knows no literary parallel for
the idea of the potter making of the same clay vessels for
different purposes. There is again a remarkable similarity of
expression between Rom. ix. 22 vessels, *fitted unto destruction*

and Wisd. xii. 20 *due to death*. At the same time the words of S. and H. (p. 269) should be borne in mind " If St Paul learnt from the Book of Wisdom some expressions illustrating the Divine power, and a general aspect of the question, he obtained nothing further. His broad views and deep insight are his own. And it is interesting to contrast a Jew who has learnt many maxims which conflict with his nationalism but yet retains all his narrow sympathies, with the Christian Apostle, full of broad sympathy and deep insight."

Grafe also observes (pp. 271 ff.) a similarity between St Paul's treatment of idolatry (Rom. i. 20—29) and that of Wisdom (chs. xii.—xiv.). In Wisdom a distinction is recognised between the cruder (xii. 24; xiii. 10) and the more refined forms of idolatry (xiii. 1—5): while a twofold verdict is given, making allowance for the ignorance of men (xiii. 1), and yet condemning them for not drawing the inference from the glory of the creation that it was meant to suggest (xiii. 1, 9).

The same distinction appears in St Paul's writings. He deals mildly with the nature-worship of the Galatians (Gal. iv. 8—10), but is unsparing (Rom. i. 20 *without excuse*) in his condemnation of image-worship. The Galatians were allowed to have erred because they "knew not God": image-worshippers "knew God," but denied Him (Rom. i. 19, 21).

But the leading point of resemblance between St Paul and Wisdom is that both give a long catalogue of the social evils resulting from false worship (Rom. i. 24—32; Wisd. xiv. 23—27). The details are not the same, but the important thing is that both writers, after a disquisition on the nature and wickedness of idolatry, emphasise its consequences, laying special stress on the unchastity and unnatural vices which it engenders.

Among other Pauline passages which possibly contain points of contact are:

Rom. v. 12	Wisd. ii. 24
Rom. viii. 28	xvi. 17
1 Cor. ii. 16	ix. 13
1 Cor. vi. 2	iii. 8
2 Cor. v. 1—5	ix. 15
Phil. i. 23	iii. 1—3

A passage that calls for special notice is Eph. vi. 13—17.
There is an undoubted connection between these *vv.* and Wisd.
v. 17—19; but the question of dependence is complicated by
the fact that the source-passage for Wisd. v. 17 is Is. lix. 17
(cp. in the same way 1 Cor. ii. 16 above, with Is. xl. 13). Grafe
is satisfied that St Paul borrows from Wisdom, on the ground
that *panoply* occurs in both, but not in Isaiah, and also that
shield and *sword* are found in Wisd. and Eph., but are missing
from Isaiah.

On the other hand, it may be urged that St Paul borrows the
phrase *helmet of salvation* from Isaiah, and uses Greek words for
helmet, shield, and sword different in each case from those in
Wisdom. It is plain also that when the same image is used in
1 Thess. v. 8, St Paul is borrowing direct from Isaiah. Isaiah
however had not the picture of the classical panoply before his
eyes, but the writer of Wisdom developed Isaiah's idea by
introducing the familiar word, and with it two important parts of
the full equipment, viz. *sword* and *shield*, all of which St Paul
employs. Accordingly, in spite of the fact that St Paul applies
the picture to the Christian while Wisdom (like Isaiah) applies
it to God, and uses different Greek words to denote the various
pieces of armour, it is hard not to conclude from the presence of
panoply and *shield* and *sword*, that the Apostle was conscious
of the influence of Wisdom when elaborating his picture.

(δ) A few other passages which seem to show traces of the
influence of the Book of Wisdom are appended:

James	Wisd.
i. 5	viii. 21
i. 10, 11	ii. 7, 8
i. 13, 14	i. 12—14
i. 17	i. 14
i. 19	i. 11
ii. 6	ii. 10
ii. 13	vi. 6
iii. 17, 18	vii. 22, 23
iv. 8	vi. 19
v. 5	ii. 6—9
v. 6	ii. 12, 20

Heb.	i. 3	Wisd. vii. 26
	iv. 12	xviii. 15, 16
	xii. 17	xii. 10
		See also Plumptre in *Expositor*,
		vol. ii. "The Writings of Apollos."
Rev.	ii. 16	v. 20
	ii. 21	xii. 10, 20
	iii. 12	iii. 14
	xvi. 6	xvi. 9
	xix. 13	xviii. 15

It will thus be seen that the Book of Wisdom exercised no small influence upon N.T. Though not directly quoted, it belonged to the mental furniture of the N.T. writers. The extent to which such influence operated must remain indeterminate, but we should not be dealing fairly with the evidence, if we refused to allow that, out of the many coincidences between N.T. and Wisdom, some are due to a reminiscence, whether conscious or unconscious, of the earlier book.

§ 18.   *Literature.*

The most important commentaries are those of

GRIMM, C. L. W., Das Buch der Weisheit (Kurzgefasstes exegetisches Handbuch zu den Apokryphen des A.T.), Leipzig, 1860.

DEANE, W. J., The Book of Wisdom, The Greek Text, The Latin Vulgate, and the Authorised English Version with Intr., Crit. App., and a Commentary, Oxford, 1881.

FARRAR, F. W., in the Speaker's Commentary.

For lists of other commentaries, see Grimm, pp. 45, 46, Deane, pp. 42, 43 and Schürer, *Jewish People in the time of Jesus Christ*, § 33 (E.T., div. II. vol. iii. pp. 236, 237 : 3rd German ed. 1898, vol. iii. pp. 382, 383).

Among other books which may be consulted with advantage are

SWETE, H. B., The O. T. in Greek, 3 vols., Cambridge, 1891.

COHN AND WENDLAND, Philonis Alexandrini opera quae supersunt, 4 vols., Berlin, 1896–1902.

ETHERIDGE, J. W., The Targums on the Pentateuch, 2 vols., London, 1862.

DRUMMOND, J., Philo Judaeus, or the Jewish-Alexandrian Philosophy in its development and completion, London, 1888.

HERIOT, Philon le Juif.

BOIS, HENRI, Essai sur les origines de la philosophie Judéo-Alexandrine, Toulouse, 1890.

MENZEL, PAUL, Der Griechische Einfluss auf Prediger und Weisheit Salomos, Hallé a S., 1889.

ANDRÉ, L. E. T., Les Apocryphes de l'ancien testament, Florence, 1903.

WESTCOTT, B. F., Art. "Wisdom of Solomon" in Smith's D.B., vol. iii.

SIEGFRIED, C., Art. "Wisdom," and "Book of Wisdom" in Hastings' D.B., vol. iv.

TOY, C. H., Art. "Wisdom (Book)" in Enc. Bibl., vol. iv. (edd. Cheyne and Black).

KAUTZSCH, Die Apokryphen und Pseudepigraphen des Alten Testaments, vol. i. (C. Siegfried).

N.B. The references to Philo follow (except where otherwise stated) the sectional divisions as marked in Cohn and Wendland's smaller edition.

THE
WISDOM OF SOLOMON.

Love righteousness, ye that be judges of the earth,   **1**
Think ye of the Lord ¹with a good mind,

¹ Gr. *in goodness.*

PART I. A.

CH. I.—CH. V.

The character of Wisdom : how she is found, and how forfeited.
Contrast between the worldly fortunes of the righteous and the wicked,
and between their experiences after death.

CH. I. THE PURE IN HEART FIND WISDOM: DEATH IS THE
REWARD OF IMMORALITY.

CH. I. 1—5. GOD CANNOT DWELL WITH EVIL: WISDOM CAN
ASSOCIATE ONLY WITH THOSE WHO RESEMBLE HER.

1. The book opens without a preface : neither its author nor its
destination are known. The *judges of the earth* (cp. ch. vi. 1) who are
addressed in this *v.* are rulers in general, an address in keeping with the
ex hypothesi Solomonic authorship : to none would a king appeal more
fitly than to kings. It is hardly conceivable that if (as has been supposed
by some commentators) the book was a protest to the Roman authorities
against injustices perpetrated upon the Jews at Alexandria, it should be
so devoid of feeling and savour so consistently of the study.

Love righteousness] Cp. Ps. xlv. 7. Righteousness in its widest
sense, not merely for purposes of right government, but as conformity of
thought and deed to the will of God.

judges of the earth] from Ps. ii. 10, and again in ch. vi. 1. *Judges*
means rulers, one principal function of rulers being to dispense justice,
cp. Ps. lxvii. 4, 1 K. iii. 9. Vulg. *Diligite iustitiam qui iudicatis
terram.* Dante (*Par.* xviii. 91) sees a band of spirits group themselves
into the form of the 35 letters, representing them successively.

Think ye of the Lord with a good mind] lit. *in goodness.* Men's
conceptions of God vary with their characters. " Pectus facit theo-
logum." Marg. makes the writer's meaning more clear. Knowledge

And in singleness of heart seek ye him;
2 Because he is found of them that tempt him not,
And is manifested to them that do not distrust him.
3 For crooked thoughts separate from God;
And the *supreme* Power, when it is brought to the proof,
¹putteth to confusion the foolish:

¹ Gr. *convicteth.*

of God is moral rather than intellectual, cp. Heb. xii. 14; for the
sense, cp. Dt. xxviii. 47 LXX.
singleness of heart] from 1 Chr. xxix. 17, where also God is said to
"love righteousness." For the Greek word, see Sanday and Headlam,
on *Rom.* xii. 8. Cp. Col. iii. 22. The "single-minded" man has no
private ends to serve: there is no reservation or *arrière-pensée* in his
allegiance. See Charles, *Test. xii Patr.*, note on Iss. iii. 1.
seek ye him] i.e. covet fellowship with God, cp. Dt. iv. 29. Grimm
quotes Philo (*de Mon.* § 5) "There is nothing better than to seek the
true God, even though it be beyond the power of man to find Him."
    2. *he is found*] The doctrine of spiritual affinity pervades the book.
Cp. ch. vi. 12, 16. See Prov. viii. 17; St John vi. 37, xviii. 37.
tempt him not] Men tempt God by immoral lives. These words
correspond to "with a good mind" in *v.* 1.
is manifested] Cp. Is. lxv. 1; St John xiv. 21.
do not distrust him] i.e. God's will to bless. This clause answers to
"in singleness of heart" in *v.* 1. The single-minded throw themselves
upon God, and (like Browning's grammarian) "unperplexed, seeking
shall find Him." Cp. James i. 6—8.
    3. *For*] *vv.* 3—5 stand in contrast with *v.* 2. God is as inaccessible
to the perverse, as He is approachable for the upright.
crooked thoughts separate] Cp. Is. lix. 2, 7—9. For *crooked*, cp.
Prov. xxi. 8; Dt. xxxii. 5.
thoughts] The Gk. word (λογισμοί) has generally a bad sense, cp.
ch. xi. 15, and James ii. 4 (διαλογ.), but cp. 4 Macc. xviii. 2. For the
sense, cp. Philo, *Mut. Nom.* § 46 "God standeth afar off from sinners,
but He walketh within the souls of the upright."
the supreme *Power*] R.V. plainly points to God as the power in
question. This is no doubt possible, but *the power* is more likely to
be a synonym for Wisdom (cp. *a holy spirit, v.* 5). Wisdom is seen
being "brought to the proof" in *vv.* 4, 5. Thus she is spoken of in
vv. 3, 4, 5, but (for literary reasons) under a different name in each
case. Bois (*Essai sur les origines de la phil. Jud.-Alex.* p. 237) recalls
Philo's use of *power*, and prefers this interpretation.
brought to the proof] applicable either to God or to Wisdom, when
challenged by man's unbelief, cp. Ps. xcv. 9 "Your fathers proved me"
(ἐδοκίμασαν LXX.).
putteth to confusion] by increasing their blindness (Grimm). The

Because wisdom will not enter into a soul that deviseth 4
evil,
Nor dwell in a body that is held in pledge by sin.
For a holy spirit of discipline will flee deceit,   5
And will start away from thoughts that are without under-
standing,
And will be ¹put to confusion when unrighteousness hath
come in.

¹ Gr. *convicted*.

Greek word indicates punishment and final loss rather than the lighter
meaning of "convicting and putting to shame." The writer thinks of
the wicked as ungodly by nature, and incapable of restoration : therefore remedial discipline would be futile.

the foolish] Morally foolish. The word is euphemistically used in
O.T. to express the practical foolishness of immoral living which
ignores God. Cp. Ps. xiv. 1 "The fool hath said."

4. *Because*] *v.* 4 supports the assertions of *v.* 3, the truth of which
rests on the essential nature of Wisdom.

wisdom] See Introduction § 9, and cp. *vv.* 3, 5. The question is
not whether a soul that devises evil things can ever be wise, but
whether it can have affinity with the Wisdom of God.

a soul that deviseth evil] The adj. (κακότεχνος) is poetic, occurring
in Homer, *Il.* xv. 14, and is found again ch. xv. 4. Cp. 4 Macc. vi. 25.
For the friends of Wisdom, see ch. vi. 12—16.

Nor dwell] Cp. Philo, *Somn.* 1. 23 "Strive to be a house of God, a
holy temple, a fair dwelling-place for Him."

held in pledge] i.e. wilfully surrendered to sin. The Greek word
denotes "one mortgaged to sin." Cp. Rom. vii. 14, and St John viii. 34.

In this *v.* the writer views soul as well as body as liable to sin : elsewhere he traces temptation to the body, cp. ch. ix. 15. He is not
however a thorough-going dualist like Philo, who writes (*Migr.* § 2)
of "that loathsome prison-house, the body." On the other hand, like
Philo, he regards the human personality as twofold, *soul* (or *spirit*) and
body, cp. ch. ii. 3 and Philo, *Mos.* iii. 39 "man being twofold, body
and soul." See Introd. § 12.

5. *holy spirit of discipline*] Bois (*op. cit.* p. 234) urges that this
expression is a paraphrase for Wisdom, see Introd. § 9. For Wisdom
as a spirit of discipline, cp. ch. vi. 11. She is a spirit, *v.* 6; there is a
holy spirit in her, ch. vii. 22. This is the first use of πν. ἅγιον in the
Gk. Bible, cp. ch. ix. 17.

will flee deceit] Her hatred of deceit may be inferred from the
description of her origin in ch. vii. 25, 26.

thoughts...without understanding] in a moral sense, see *v.* 3.

put to confusion] like modesty in the presence of the obscene. Or
"will be scared away" (Grimm).

6 For ¹wisdom is a spirit that loveth man,
  And she will not hold a ²blasphemer guiltless for his lips;
  Because God beareth witness of his reins,
  And is a true overseer of his heart,
  And a hearer of his tongue:
7 Because the spirit of the Lord hath filled ³the world,

  ¹ Some authorities read *the spirit of wisdom is loving to man.*
  ² Or, *reviler*   ³ Gr. *the inhabited earth.*

vv. 6—11. GOD NOT ONLY REFUSES WISDOM TO THE IMPURE (*vv.*
3—5), BUT HE ACTIVELY PUNISHES THEM. IF HE CAN SEARCH
HEARTS, SINFUL WORDS CANNOT ESCAPE DETECTION.

6. *wisdom is a spirit*] Text follows אB, and is preferable to the
reading of A and Vulg. See marg.
  that loveth man] lit. *philanthropic*, cp. ch. vii. 23. See Prov. viii.
for this humanitarian aspect of Wisdom (Introd. § 9). She is indeed
humane, but exacts punishment when deserved, so loving is she towards
the souls of men. Cp. Ps. lxii. 12. Wisdom reflects the mind of God
who created all things but loves men best of all, as being the noblest
product of Wisdom's work. Cp. ch. ix. 2, 3; Prov. viii. 31. φιλάνθρωπος
is very frequent in Class. lit., but is not found in O.T. (except Apocr.)
or N.T.; N.T. however has its corresponding adv. and subst. Acts
xxvii. 3; xxviii. 2.
  a blasphemer] Marg. *reviler.* "Blasphemy" is not confined to
words directed against God, but includes all slander and calumny, see
Eph. iv. 31. The writer probably has in view such utterances as those
in ch. ii. 1—20.
  beareth witness] Cp. Ps. xxxiii. 15; cxxxix. 1—5. The *reins* are
viewed as the seat of the feelings, and the *heart* as the source of
thoughts and ideas.
  Grimm sees in the sequence *reins, heart, tongue* an inverted climax:
God knows men's feelings, their unexpressed thoughts, their spoken
words. For *hearts and reins,* cp. Ps. vii. 9; Jer. xi. 20.
  a true overseer of his heart] Cp. Job xx. 29, LXX.; Ecclus. xlii. 20.
The Greek word is generally used in LXX. in an official sense, "task-
master," or "captain," but here in the same sense as in Philo, *Somn.*
i. 15 "God is the overseer of all, to whom all things are open, even all
that is done invisibly in the depths of the heart." Cp. *Clem. Rom.* lix.
3 "Creator and overseer of all spirits." *True,* in that God fulfils the
highest functions of overseer. He cannot be deceived, or biassed; He
cannot forget: there is no human shortcoming in the scrutiny He exercises.
  a hearer of his tongue] Cp. Epict. ii. 8 "If an image of your God
was in the room, you would not behave as you do, and yet when God
is within you and oversees and overhears everything, you are not
ashamed to think and act in this way." Cp. Philo, *Jos.* § 43.
  7. *the spirit of the Lord hath filled*] The proof of the preceding

And that which holdeth all things together hath knowledge
of *every* voice.

Therefore no man that uttereth unrighteous things shall be 8
unseen;
¹Neither shall Justice, when it convicteth, pass him by.

¹ Some authorities read *Nor indeed.*

assertions. Either mediately or in person God fills the universe. It is
not clear whether *the spirit of the Lord* stands for God or the Wisdom
of God. Wisdom in ch. viii. 1 is given the attributes of omnipresence,
while in this book there is no mention of divine omnipresence. The
Alexandrine idea was that God acted upon the world through the Logos,
while the Wisdom mediated His immanence. And so here, it seems
more in keeping with the author's view of the universal activity of
Wisdom, to see in her the medium whereby knowledge of the words
of men is brought to God: Wisdom is the "ear of jealousy" (*v.* 10).

On the other hand for O.T. writers, the spirit of God denotes God in
His activity in the world, and we have in Ps. cxxxix. 7 and Jer. xxiii. 24
the more characteristically Jewish conception of God's immediate
presence, which is to be found also in Philo, *Leg. All.* iii. 2 "God hath
filled all things, and hath passed through all things, and hath left nothing
void or unoccupied by Himself." Cp. *ibid.* i. 14, *Sacr.* 18, *Moses* ii. 31.
Farrar quotes Pope :—

> "All are but parts of one stupendous whole
> Whose body nature is and God the soul;
> That...
> Lives through all life, extends through all extent,
> Spreads undivided, operates unspent."

the world] οἰκουμένη (see marg.) cp. Prov. viii. 31; no limitation of
the sphere of Wisdom is intended, but her activity in this passage is
directed towards human objects.

holdeth all things together] Cp. Ecclus. xliii. 26 "By his word all
things consist"; Col. i. 17; Heb. i. 3; and ch. vii. 17 "the constitution
(lit. *consistence*) of the world." The idea of a world-principle holding
the sum of things together appears in Aristotle (*de Mundo* 6) "the all-
containing cause." The author is employing what is a Stoic and by no
means a Jewish conception, which was adopted by the Alexandrian
Jews, and appears constantly in Philo, cp. *Q. R. D. H.* § 38 "The
Logos is the universal chain, who has filled all things with his being";
id. *plant.* § 2; Clem. Rom. § 27.

Cicero (*de Nat. Deor.* i. 15, 39) writes of the Stoic deity "holding
together nature and all things." The Stoic God was soul, spirit, reason
of the world, providence, destiny, universal law.

8. *Therefore no man*] Cp. Jer. xxiii. 24 of false prophets, "Can any
hide himself in secret places that I shall not see him?" and Job xxxiv.
21—23.

Neither shall] Text follows ℵA (οὐδὲ μὴ).

Justice] Personified, cp. Acts xxviii. 4 R.V. In ch. xiv. 31 occurs

9 For in *the midst of* his counsels the ungodly shall be
    searched out;
    And the sound of his words shall come unto the Lord
    To bring to conviction his lawless deeds :
10 Because *there is* an ear of jealousy *that* listeneth to all
    things,
    And the noise of murmurings is not hid.
11 Beware then of unprofitable murmuring,
    And refrain your tongue from backbiting;

"the Justice of them that sin," which answers to the inner law of moral
compensation which cannot be evaded even by successful sin. Philo,
Post. C. § 4 tells of the Justice that punishes the ungodly waiting for
Cain, cp. id. *de conf. l.* § 24 "an avenging and incorruptible Justice."
    pass him by] Justice is no casual wayfarer : she is the inevitable
reaction upon wrong-doing.
    9. *his counsels*] The Gk. word (διαβούλια), cp. *v.* 3, is used in a
bad sense, implying *craftiness*. Cp. Ps. x. 2; Hos. iv. 9. For the
sense, cp. Epict. ii. 14 "Philosophers say that men should learn before
anything else that God exists and governs the world, and that it is
impossible to hide from Him our deeds or even our thoughts."
    Perhaps the rendering of this line should be "There shall be exami-
nation into the counsels of the ungodly." Cp. forensic use of ἐξέτασις in
3 Macc. vii. 5.
    To bring to conviction his lawless deeds] rather *lawlessnesses*, cp.
Dt. xv. 9, i.e. the counsels and the words referred to in the preceding lines. Philo, *Dec.* § 17 writes "the conviction that is innate
in and inhabits each man, at once his accuser and his judge, wages a
truceless war with the disobedient."
    Although the writer has in mind an exposure of the sinner by
Wisdom, and Philo rather the stings of conscience, psychologically
the inner reality is one and the same.
    10. *an ear of jealousy*] Philo, evidently recalling the teaching of
Zeno (cp. Diog. Laert. *Zeno* § 79) writes *de Somn.* i. § 22 "the highest
and purest spirits do not enter into human bodies, but act as eyes and
ears of the great King, overseeing and hearing everything." For the
genitive of quality, cp. Num. v. 14 LXX. "a spirit of jealousy."
    God's jealousy is shown in O.T. (1) on behalf of the chosen people,
(2) for His own honour. It is in the latter sense that God is spoken of
here as jealous, as He watches the words and thoughts of men.
    noise of murmurings] An intentional resemblance in the Gk.
between *ous* (ear) and *throus* (noise). Even the unspoken murmurings
of the heart are overheard. Cp. Ex. xvi. 7, 8, 9, 12, where God hears
the murmuring of the people.
    11. *unprofitable murmuring*] "unprofitable" is a softened ex-
pression for *soul-destroying*. For *murmurers*, cp. Jude *vv.* 14—16.
    backbiting] Better *blasphemy*. The Gk. word (καταλαλιά) has in

Because no secret utterance shall go on its way void,
And a mouth that belieth destroyeth a soul.
Court not death in the error of your life;   12
Neither draw upon yourselves destruction by the works of
  your hands:
Because God made not death;   13

N.T. the same sense of speaking evil of *men.* But the corresp. vb.
is used in LXX. to denote speaking against God (Numb. xxi. 5;
Ps. lxxviii. 19); and this is the meaning here. There may be a
reference to those apostate or wavering Jews of Alexandria who did not
hesitate to express their despair of the theocracy openly.

go on its way void] For this use of *void* (κενόν), cp. Is. lv. 11, where
Cod. Marchal. has "So shall my word be; it shall not return to me
void." The whispered word may be physically unsubstantial, but it
has concrete moral effects.

a mouth that belieth] lit. *that speaketh falsely against* (*God*). Philo,
fuga § 15 writes "It leaves an incurable stain upon the soul when one
says that God is the author of evil."

destroyeth a soul] This expression is used of physical death in
Ecclus. xxi. 2. Here it refers to the loss of spiritual life (Introd. § 13).
Physical death as the penalty of sin is not in question: the writer is
thinking of that soulless existence of the wicked (present and future)
which, metaphorically speaking, is death.

> *vv.* 12—15. GOD'S WILL FOR MEN IS THAT THEIR SOUL
>   SHOULD LIVE.

12. *Court not death*] The last words of *v.* 11 introduce the subject
of *vv.* 12—15. For *courting death* cp. next *l.*, and *v.* 16. The persistence of the wicked in their evil ways seems explicable on no other
hypothesis than that they desire spiritual death. Cp. Prov. viii. 36,
xxi. 6.

in the error of your life] Generally, for "any ways of life that go
astray." *Your life* supplies a rhetorical antithesis to *court not death.*

neither draw upon yourselves] Both *court* and *drag* are strong
words, the former implying violent desire and the latter violent effort.
LXX. uses the same Gk. word in Is. v. 18, cp. ch. xix. 3.

works of your hands] Philo (*det. pot.* § 32) writes "Moses says it
is not God who is the author of our evils, but our own hands, by which
he intends the voluntary preference of our minds for the worse course."
Cp. Enoch xcviii. 4 "Sin has not been sent upon the earth, but man of
himself has created it."

13. *Because God made not death*] Nothing evil can have its origin in
God, who is altogether good. Such is the doctrine of Philo, reiterated
consistently through his writings, and anticipated here. Philo's
inference is interesting, if not (on account of its somewhat unworthy

Neither delighteth he when the living perish:
14 For he created all things that they might have being:
And ¹the generative powers of the world *are* healthsome,

¹ Or, all *the races* of creatures *in the world*

view of God's motives) convincing. Cp. *de mut.* § 4, and especially *de conf. ling.* § 35, 36. "'Let us make man.' Why is the plural used? In order that men's successes may be attributed to God, but their failures may be laid upon others. For it did not seem right to God to fashion with His own hand the downward inclination in man, wherefore He entrusted this portion of the work to His subordinate agents. God is the author of good things alone, and of nothing at all that is evil, since He is Himself the highest of all things that exist and the most perfect good."

There is no solution here of the problem of evil and death. If Philo refuses to charge God with being Creator of evil, he takes away with one hand what he gives with the other. For his position is essentially dualistic, and he makes evil to be something standing over against God and independent of Him. An evil that is co-eternal with God is a more terrible problem than an evil permitted by God.

Neither delighteth he] Cp. Ezek. xxxiii. 11 "I have no pleasure in the death of the wicked." *The living* may be either *living men* or *things that have life.*

The passage seems to contain a reminiscence of Is. liv. 16 LXX. "But I created thee not for destruction, to cause thee to perish."

14. *created all things...being*] "All things" includes the irrational part of creation, and the various stages of growth and decay through which the brutes and the plants pass. God created all things to partake in some real degree of His own nature, which is fundamentally Being. Cp. Ex. iii. 14 (LXX.) "I am He that is." Epict. iii. 24 writes "God created all men for happiness, for stability." Cp. Philo, *Moses* ii. 8 "For seeing that God alone hath existence of a truth, He is Maker, since he bringeth into existence things that are not."

The gift of positive being to the creation by the Creator here suggested, involves something of the same intimateness of relation as was perhaps expressed in St John i. 3, 4 "That which hath been made was life in him."

and the generative powers] Marg. "all *the races* of creatures *in the world.*" The rendering of text is hardly possible. The alternative rendering in marg. indicates a doubt in the mind of the translators whether the Gk. word can have an active sense. There are four uses of γένεσις in LXX. and Apocrypha: (*a*) birth, (*b*) the process of coming into being, (*c*) a generation, (*d*) a tribe, or species. If the author meant *generative powers*, a subst. with a different termination would be demanded. The "process of coming into being" passes readily into the "things which have come to be," but not into "that which brings things into being." Marg. must accordingly be followed,

And there is no poison of destruction in them:
Nor hath Hades ¹royal dominion upon earth,
For righteousness is immortal:　　　　15

¹ Or, *a royal house*

which has the support of Vulg. *nationes terrae*, i.e. the products of the earth. The meaning is that herbs are not by nature poisonous, nor wild beasts destructive, but human sin has caused a general marring of the divine scheme. Gk. might be rendered *natural processes*, in which case there would be an antithesis between this line and the preceding, the originating decree of the Creator being distinguished from those subsequent processes whereby things seem to make themselves. With γενέσεις cp. the designations of God in ch. xiii. 3, 5, γενεσιάρχης, γενεσιουργός.

healthsome] The Gk. word is frequently found in Philo in an active sense, cp. *ebr.* § 3, *Moses* i. § 17.

poison of destruction] Vulg. *medicamentum exterminii*. The soundness of the physical world in which men are placed is contrasted with the moral evil that works within them. It is not from God's world that men derive the poison that inflames their souls.

Nor hath Hades royal dominion] Marg. *a royal house*. Text gives the better sense, though both renderings are permissible. If the Gk. word βασίλειον be translated as in marg., 'a royal house' stands for the external symbol of the royal dominion, the part for the whole. But text is simpler, and presents a more solid antithesis to *God made not... neither delighteth he...for he created*, etc. Emphasis is laid on the rival sovereignties. For Gk. in the sense of *dominion* see 1 K. xiv. 8; 2 Macc. ii. 17; and of *palace* Prov. xviii. 19. In ch. v. 16 it means *royal crown*. Hades is here personified, and practically corresponds to the Greek Pluto, the God of the lower regions.

15. *righteousness is immortal*] Either righteousness leads its followers to immortality, or (abstr. for concr., in contrast with *ungodly men*, *v.* 16) the righteous are immortal, i.e. possess the life spiritual.

Righteousness is introduced somewhat abruptly. We should expect a link between *vv.* 14 and 15, such as "For [God destined His creation for righteousness, and] righteousness is..." The nature of God as revealed in O.T. points to a fundamental identity between the Good and the Existent. Contrast with Philo's "Folly is an undying evil" (*det. pot.* § 48). Vulg. supplies a new line *iniustitia autem mortis acquisitio est*: no Greek MSS. have this line, which was probably introduced to complete the parallelism. Grimm however is in favour of it. For the life-giving power of Wisdom, cp. Prov. iii. 18. Philo, *plant.* § 27 has "The nature of the Good is incorruptible." Cp. Antisthenes in Diog. Laert. vi. 1, 4 "Those who would be immortal must live piously and righteously."

16 But ungodly men by their hands and their words called
    ¹death unto them :
  Deeming him a friend they ²consumed away,
  And they made a covenant with him,

¹ Or, *Hades* Gr. *him.*   ² Or, *were consumed* with love of him

CH. I. 16—CH. V. 23.

At this point begins a series of three comparisons between the thoughts, character, and destiny of the righteous and the wicked. The distinctions are fairly clearly marked, five out of the six sections beginning with a keyword distinctive of the section, while the sixth begins with what is certainly a false reading and with a word that is readily emended into the necessary distinctive word. It will be noticed that the sections devoted to the wicked are much longer than the others, two of them being occupied with rather tedious monologues. The sections are as follows :—

I. {I. 16—II. 24, ἀσεβεῖς δὲ. (But ungodly men...)
   {III. 1—9, δικαίων δὲ. (But...of the righteous...)

II. {III. 10—IV. 6, οἱ δὲ ἀσεβεῖς. (But the ungodly...)
    {IV. 7—14, δίκαιος δὲ. (But a righteous man...)

III. {IV. 15—V. 14, οἱ δὲ *ἄνομοι*. (But the lawless...)
     {V. 15—23, δίκαιοι δὲ. (But the righteous...)

The sections devoted to the righteous are all of an eschatological character, but those which deal with the ungodly present a distinct time-sequence.

COMPARISON I. (*a*) CH. I. 16—CH. II. 20. THE MATERIALIST—
HIS HOPELESSNESS, HIS SENSUALITY, HIS INTOLERANCE.

16. *But ungodly men*] This *v.* repeats *v.* 12 with emphatic irony.
  by their hands] i.e. by their works, see *v.* 12. The writer pictures the words and deeds of wicked men as constituting an invitation to God's rival.
  death] Marg. *Hades.* Gk. has *him.*
  a friend] Cp. ch. xv. 6 "lovers of evil things," and Prov. viii. 36 "They that hate me love death."
  consumed away] either lit., in consequence of their misplaced friendship, or metaph. as in marg. The latter use is seen in Ps. cxxxix. 21, and is to be preferred. The lit. use appears in Lev. xxvi. 39 LXX. If the vb. (ἐτάκησαν) is taken metaphorically, there is a fine climax in which men's frantic love for self-destruction is vigorously pictured. First, they invite the guest; next, they pine with love for him; and finally they pledge themselves in covenant with him.
  made a covenant] perhaps drawn from Is. xxviii. 15 LXX. "We made a covenant with Hades, and a bond with Death." Cp. Philo, *Quod Deus* § 11 "who made a treaty and agreement with their body," and *Migr.* § 3.

Because they are worthy to be of his portion.

For they said ¹within themselves, reasoning not aright,   **2**
Short and sorrowful is our life;
And there is no healing when a man cometh to his end,

¹ Or, *among*

they are worthy] A leading doctrine in this book is that of a spiritual selective affinity, similar to that traceable in the Fourth Gospel. Cp. in a good and bad sense, Rev. iii. 4 and xvi. 6 "They are worthy." The wicked are "worthy" of Hades because by a kind of fate like always gravitates to like.

of his portion] the words reappear in ch. ii. 24. Gk. means *a possession*, esp. by inheritance. The wicked are made over to their natural king and become his property by their own choice, and yet a choice that was inevitable. They have given themselves to sin, and are prisoners of their own limitations. For *portion*, cp. Col. i. 12, and 4 Macc. xviii. 3.

In connection with this *v.*, Pfleiderer holds that Wisdom was written by one who desired to attack the Pagan mysteries, and that this *v.* was specially directed against the initiated. The Greeks had come to identify the god of death (Hades) with the god of life (Dionysus), and this identification the author accepts. But he denies that this conflate divinity is a god of life. The God of life is the God of the Jews. Their God is not Hades, the true God stands in no relation whatever to death (Bois, *op. cit.* p. 295).

ii. 1. Speculative materialism is not in question, rather a practical materialism like that of Ps. xiv. 1. Cp. "Every one that doeth evil hateth the light." The anti-social effects of a life of sensuality are pointed out; in *v.* 10 the selfish lawlessness which gives pain for the sheer delight of exercising brute force, and in *vv.* 12—20 the spite which wreaks itself on those whose religious profession and conduct are a galling condemnation of the hedonist.

For] The charges in *v.* 16 are made explicit.

they said within themselves] A.V. *For* the ungodly *said, reasoning with themselves*, follows Vulg. which has *cogitantes apud se*, but for reasons of rhythm the division of the words adopted by the text is the better. For *saying within oneself*, cp. St Luke vii. 39, xvi. 3: for *reasoning within oneself*, cp. St Matt. xvi. 7, 8, xxi. 25. Marg. offers the alternative *among themselves*, but that would suggest rather the deliberations of a council (*vv.* 10—20) than the reflections which arise in periods of reaction and depression (*vv.* 1—9). Perhaps however a *double entendre* was intended.

Short and sorrowful] Cp. Eccl. ii. 23, v. 17 LXX. Job x. 20 "Is not the life of my time short?" LXX.; *id.* xiv. 1; Gen. xlvii. 9.

no healing] Vulg. *refrigerium*, possibly under the influence of theological conceptions. But the Gk. is common in LXX., and bears

And none was ever known that ¹gave release from Hades.
2 Because by mere chance were we born,

¹ Or, *returned out of Hades*

its usual meaning here, *no remedy*. Cp. Nah. iii. 19; Jer. xiv. 19; Ps.
xxxviii. 3, 7. The words express either a cheerless fatalism, or else a
positive disbelief in the power or will of God to postpone the evil day.
They take no account of such testimonies as Ps. xxx. 2 "Thou hast
healed me," or Is. xxxviii. 17.

that gave release] This rendering gives only a repetition of the prec.
line:—"there is no remedy, and none to administer one." Further,
instead of the aor. we should have expected the pres. or fut. participle
for the transitive sense. Marg. *that returned* is preferable, as offering
a wider variation of sense:—"there is no remedy, and there is no exception to the fatal law."

But is the Gk. vb. transitive here? It is used trans. in ch. xvi. 14 in a
somewhat similar connection, and it appears in the passive in ch. v. 12,
but in all the six other passages in Apocr. where it is found in the
active, it is intransitive, in the sense of *return*, cp. Eccl. viii. 8. The
negative is much stronger, and the despair more pronounced, when it is
denied that any human soul has ever returned from the grave, than
when the achievements of Elijah and Elisha, and the legends of
Heracles and Orpheus, are merely ignored.

Hades] For the O.T. conception, cp. in this series, Kirkpatrick,
Psalms Vol. I. pp. xciii—xcvii, and Davidson, *Job*, note on
pp. 103, 4.

There is a touch of irony in the involuntary confession on the part of
those who are making terms with Hades, that there are *uestigia nulla
retrorsum*.

The regret here expressed finds no place in the philosophy of Epicurus. Epicureanism proper made light of death. It argued that death
is not terrible when present but only when expected. For while we
live, death is non-existent for us; when we are dead, we are unconscious that we are so. And so, for the living as well as for the dead,
there is no such thing as death. Diog. Laert. x. § 125. Cp. Epict. ii.
5 § 12 "What is born, must be again resolved. I am not an age, only
a man; a part of the whole, even as an hour is part of the day. I
must be present like the hour, and I must become past like the hour.
What does it concern me how I pass?" Cp. Lucr. iii. 830 ff.

2. *Because by mere chance were we born*] Vulg. wrongly *ex nihilo*.
There is a flavour of Epicureanism about the passage, and Epicurus
taught that nothing is made out of nothing (Diog. Laert. x. § 38). He
held that as the atoms fell through the void of space, slight accidental
deviations occurred, and by this means there ensued a continual process
of combination between the atoms. By this process of fortuitous
amalgamation, the world of things as we see it was to be accounted
for. Contrast Cic. *Tusc.* i. 49 "Non temere nec fortuito...creati sumus."

And hereafter we shall be as though we had never been :
Because the breath in our nostrils is smoke,
And ¹while our heart beateth reason is a spark,
Which being extinguished, the body shall be turned into 3
  ashes,
And the spirit shall be dispersed as thin air ;
And our name shall be forgotten in time,   4

¹ Or, *reason is a spark* kindled *by the beating of our heart*

we shall be as though we had never been] Cp. Obadiah 16 LXX. א
has the variant ὑπάρχοντες, probably a reminiscence of Obadiah.
  Because the breath in our nostrils is smoke] Cp. Job xxvii. 3 LXX.
There is a different use of the same simile in Job xli. 20. For smoke,
as a symbol of unsubstantialness, cp. Ps. cii. 3.
  and while our heart beateth reason is a spark] The superficial meaning of these words is that our best life is little better than a spark, so
precarious is our position. But it is hard to avoid the conclusion that
there is a half-concealed cynical allusion to the speculations of Greek
philosophy. Heraclitus held that fire was the origin of all things, and
Zeno developed the idea further. He held that the soul was a fiery
principle with which we are inspired and by which we move (Diog.
Laert. vii. § 157). If this theory is treated sarcastically, by a process of
reductio ad absurdum, its followers are landed in the cheering thought,
that our soul is a spark, and our breath the smoke of its smouldering.
The Logos, or reason, in a man, was supposed to reside in the governing
part of his being which was closely connected with the heart (*ibid.* § 159):
the ancient philosophers had not grasped the secret of the functions of
the brain.   For this reason the marginal reading is to be preferred,
reason is a spark kindled *by the beating of our heart*. The Greek
philosophers "supposed that the beating of the heart produced thought
in the form of gleams or sparks from the fire-substance of the soul.
'Breath' and 'thoughts' to them are merely the results of mechanism"
(Farrar). There is something singularly modern in this early speculation. Modern materialists hold that thought is produced by molecular
change; cp. Cabanis "The brain secretes thought as the liver bile."
For ὁ λόγος (reason) one cursive has ὀλίγος (little), following which A.V.
renders *a little spark*.
  3. *the body...into ashes*] Life is a spark of fire which gradually
consumes the body and leaves only ashes (Deane). Probably, however,
the words are only an adaptation of Job xiii. 12 LXX. "Your boasting
shall become like ashes, and your body clay."
  dispersed] For the Gk., cp. ch. v. 14, where the word is used of
smoke.
  thin air] lit. *gaping*. Air is fugitive and unsubstantial.
  4. *our name shall be forgotten*] The greatest calamity that could
befall a man. In earlier ages, when the idea of personal immortality had

And no man shall remember our works;
And our life shall pass away as the traces of a cloud,
And shall be scattered as is a mist,
When it is chased by the beams of the sun,
And ¹overcome by the heat thereof.
5 For our allotted time is the passing of a shadow,
And ²our end retreateth not;

¹ Gr. *weighed down.*   ² Or, *there is no putting back of our end*

not emerged, future life meant no more than remembrance by future generations. Cp. 2 Sam. xviii. 18; Ps. xlix. 11. In the Egyptian Book of the
Dead, several chapters are devoted to the preservation of the name in
the next world. The Hebrew and Egyptian ideas, though not identical,
agree in this, that unless an object had a name it could not exist, and if
the name were lost, it perished. For the perishing of the name, cp.
Dt. ix. 14; Ps. cix. 13 (note in this series); Job xviii. 17, 19.
   shall remember] Cp. Eccl. i. 11.
   pass away] For the Gk. word, cp. 1 John ii. 17.
   as...a cloud] Cp. Philo, *Quod Deus* § 36 "Like a cloud, her great
good fortune has passed away." Cp. Hos. xiii. 3; Job vii. 9.
   a mist] Cp. Job xxiv. 20 LXX.
   chased] Farrar quotes Ov. *Trist.* ii. 142:—
         "Nube solet *pulsa* candidus ire dies."
   overcome] βαρυνθεῖσα, lit. *weighed down*, Vulg. *aggrauata*. The
word does not seem very appropriate. One cursive has μαρανθεῖσα
(lit. *withered*, metaph.). The LXX. of Job vii. 9 (ἀποκαθαρθέν)
makes καθαρθεῖσα possible: as a mist is cleaned away from the sky
by the sun's heat, so the name perishes. This has the advantage of
being true to physical science, although the point may not be pressed
in dealing with an ancient writer: heat causes vapour to evanesce, but
what condenses it and precipitates it as rain is *cold.* If mg. *weighed
down* is retained (text does not face the difficulty), the idea is of *weari-
ness*: the cloud, chased by the sun's rays, is worn down with exertion.
Cp. St Matt. xx. 12 "the *burden* of the day."
   5.   *our allotted time*]   Text follows א, καιρός, Vulg. *tempus nostrum.*
For *shadow*, cp. 1 Chr. xxix. 15; Job viii. 9, xiv. 2; Eccl. vi. 12, viii. 13.
Probably the shadow is that of a sun-dial; cp. Ecclus. xlvi. 4, xlviii. 23
(ἀνεπόδισεν, *returned*, Is. xxxviii. 8). ἀναποδισμὸς occurs in the next *l.*,
and may help to determine the reference of *shadow* here.
   retreateth not]   Vulg. *non est reuersio*, so marg. which is preferable,
no putting back of our end (see prec. note).
   The line does not mean that there is no recurrence of death, because
man can only die once and one death exhausts his store; but that our
death cannot be put back, any more than under normal conditions the
shadow on the dial.

Because it is fast sealed, and none ¹turneth it back.
Come therefore and let us enjoy the good things ²that *now* 6
are;
And let us use the creation ³with all our soul ⁴as youth's
possession.
Let us fill ourselves with costly wine and perfumes;   7

> ¹ Or, *cometh again*   ² Or, *that are*   ³ Gr. *earnestly.*
> ⁴ Some authorities read *even as our youth.*

sealed] The end of man's life is *sealed* in the sense of certainty and
irreversible destiny, cp. Dan. vi. 17, xii. 9, as a document is sealed for
authentication.

turneth it back] better than marg. The Gk. verb is transitive in
ch. xvi. 14; cp. the parallel use in Is. xxxviii. 8 LXX. (ἀποστρ.). But
ἀναστρ. is intr. in 2 Sam. xii. 23, and Ecclus. xl. 11. For the sense,
cp. Ecclus. xxxviii. 21.

6. *Come therefore*] *vv.* 6—9 are an expansion of Is. xxii. 13 (cp.
1 Cor. xv. 32); cp. Is. lvi. 12, and Eccl. iii. 12, ix. 7. These verses
exemplify "the dregs of Epicurean theory" (Farrar). Epicurus himself could say (Diog. Laert. x. 140) "It is impossible to live pleasur-
ably, without living wisely and honourably and justly"; but pleasure,
however highly it may be conceived, when viewed as the chief good,
gives a false direction to the moral system.

that now *are*] mg. *that are*, i.e. that have real being. Either rendering is permissible: if the latter is adopted, it expresses the materialist's
sneer that spiritual blessings are either future or unseen and therefore
possibly imaginary, as contrasted with the pleasures of sense which at
least belong to the present and can be seen, handled, and tested. With
this as his standard of reality, the hedonist views sensual pleasures as
the things that really are, and thus falls under the condemnation of ch.
xiii. 1.

the creation] frequently in Wisdom and Ecclus. for the aggregate of
created things. Cp. Rom. viii. 19.

as youth's possession] So אA (νεότητος), Vulg. agrees with B ὡς
νεότητι, *tanquam in iuuentute*, i.e. as in youth when pleasure is keenest,
or energy is most abounding. A. H. McNeile suggests ὡς νεότης with
the same meaning. Neither text, nor marg. which follows B, provides
a satisfactory sense; an early error seems probable. I suggest a very
simple change, to read κτίσεως for κτίσει ὡς, and to follow B and keep
νεότητι; the sense will be "Let us use the youth of creation." This
is expanded in *vv.* 7, 8 "Let no flower of *spring* pass us by...rosebuds
before they be withered." Then, this call to enjoy the youthful elements
in creation is wilfully supplemented by the call to abuse that in it which
is past youth, *v.* 10, and the picture is complete. Self-indulgence tends
always to issue in intolerance towards the unfit.

7. *fill ourselves*] Text, by zeugma, makes the Gk. verb do double

And let no flower of [1]spring pass us by:
8 Let us crown ourselves with rosebuds, before they be
    withered:
9 Let none of us go without his share in our proud revelry:
    Everywhere let us leave tokens of *our* mirth:
    Because this is our portion, and our lot is this.
10 Let us oppress the righteous poor;

<hr>

[1] Some authorities read *air*.

<hr>

duty "*fill* ourselves with wine, and *anoint* ourselves with unguents." For
wine and perfumes, cp. Prov. xxvii. 9 LXX; Is. xxv. 6, 7; Amos vi. 6.
But (by hendiadys) *wine and perfumes* may stand for *perfumed wine*,
cp. Song viii. 2 LXX.
flower of spring] Text follows A, ἔαρος, cp. Vulg. *flos temporis*,
which is preferable to ἀέρος of אB "flower that scents the air."
For flowers at feasts, cp. Philo, *Somn*. i. § 20 in a similar passage
"couches strewn with flowers."
    8. *rosebuds, before they be withered*] and we with them. For the
idea, cp. Lam. v. 16; Judith xv. 13. Farrar quotes Anacreon "while
life lasts pour unguents over me, and crown my head with roses. For
life is like a swift revolving chariot wheel." Cp. Hor. *Od*. I. xxxvi.
15 "Neu desint epulis rosae." Cp. Becker, *Charicles*, vi. n. 10.
    After this *v*. Vulg. adds *nullum pratum sit quod non pertranseat
luxuria nostra:* "let there be no meadow untrodden by our riot." An
old glossary (in Cod. Coislin. 394, Paris) states that λειμών (meadow)
occurs in Wisdom, and therefore some would accept this line as authen-
tic. But it does not seem to have been noticed that Vulg. is simply a
rendering of the first *l*. of *v*. 9, with λειμών substituted for ἡμῶν. Either
this *l*. was introduced to complete the apparently unfinished *v*. 8, or it
is the original reading, and *v*. 9 *a* is the interpolation. *v*. 9 *a* as it
stands is somewhat pointless, and adds nothing to the sense.
    9. *our proud revelry*] The Gk. word (ἀγερωχία) is found nowhere
else in Gk. Bible except in 2 Macc. ix. 7 and 3 Macc. ii. 3, where it has
the meaning of arrogant dissoluteness. It represents a temper that
cannot live and let live: it must tyrannize over others.
    tokens] the plundered gardens, the trampled fields, the fading gar-
lands, and the oppressed poor.
    our portion, and our lot] Cp. Is. lvii. 6 LXX. "That is thy portion,
this is thy lot," and Eccl. iii. 22, ix. 9; Jer. xiii. 25. Let us enjoy
life while it lasts: we have nothing else to do, and nothing more to
expect (Grimm).
    10. *vv*. 10—21 contain a protracted tirade against the righteous
man. Like ch. v. 3—14, this passage betrays the literary rather than
the circumstantial character of the book. If Wisdom had been produced under the influence of very deep patriotic or religious feeling,
these passages could not have appeared in their present form. Besides

Let us not spare the widow,
Nor reverence the hairs of the old man gray for length of
    years.
But let our strength be *to us* a law of righteousness ;   11
For that which is weak is ¹found to be of no service.
But let us lie in wait for the righteous man,   12
Because he is of disservice to us,
And is contrary to our works,
And upbraideth us with sins against ²the law,

> ¹ Gr. *convicted*.   ² Or, *law*

being dramatically inartistic, they are cold and tedious: it would be
impossible to say of them *facit indignatio uersus*.

Let us oppress the righteous poor] Here a second result of unbelief
exhibits itself, in the form of tyrannical intolerance.   For the oppression
of the just, cp. Hab. i. 4; and of the poor, cp. Zech. vii. 10 ; Ezek. xviii.
12; St James ii. 6.   We may see in these verses a reference to wealthy
and apostate Jews, who persecuted their humbler fellow-countrymen
who would not deny their faith.   There is no doubt that both in Egypt
and in Palestine, apostasy for interested reasons was not uncommon:
Philo's nephew was among those who attained to high position as the
reward of embracing Paganism, and became procurator of Judaea, cp.
Philo, *Conf. l.* § 23 "Let us make laws to banish righteousness, that
cause of poverty and disgrace."

the widow]   Cp. Is. x. 2; Mal. iii. 5.   The widow, the orphan, and
the poor were particularly exposed to injustice.   Cp. Ps. x. 8, 9; Jer.
xxii. 3.

11. *our strength*] i.e. let might be right.

of no service]   The reason why strength should be the law: before it
weakness is convicted (ἐλέγχεται) of being ineffective.   It is futile, and
deserves only to exist on sufferance: superior strength is needed to
reduce it to its proper condition.

12. *lie in wait*]   Cp. Ps. x. 8, 9 LXX.   The source of this *l.* and
the next is the LXX. of Is. iii. 10, with which it is identical except for
lie in wait which replaces *bind*.   This is a passage that indicates Greek
as the original language of this book.   Is. iii. 10 (Hebrew) is altogether
different from LXX., and the agreement between the latter ("Let us
bind the righteous man, for he is of disservice to us") and this passage
points to a Greek source for the writer's quotations.   Clem. Alex. (*Str.*
v. 4) quoting this passage with reference to Christ has "let us remove."

of disservice]   Positively baneful.   A much stronger word than the
negative cognate word in *v.* 11.

the law]   Marg. *law*.   Grimm points out that in Jewish writings *law*
without the article stands always for the law of Moses, and urges that
this *l.* proves that the enemies of the righteous man are apostate Jews.

And layeth to our charge sins against our discipline.
13 He professeth to have knowledge of God,
And nameth himself ¹servant of the Lord.
14 He became to us a reproof of our thoughts.
15 He is grievous unto us even to behold,

¹ Or, *child*

But the argument is not conclusive: there were many professing Jews who were disobedient to the law.

—ἴζει ἡμῖν ἁμαρτήματα occurs both in this and the next *l.* It is unlikely that this repetition is the work of the author, who had sufficient literary sense to vary his phrases with almost ostentatious care. Some early corruption probably lies hidden under these lines which repeat one another in sound and sense.

sins against our discipline] This tr. makes the best of a difficulty, although it is not clear that the Gk. verb can bear the sense here given to it (see Liddell and Scott). Cyprian, quoting this passage (*Testim.* ii. 14) omits this line altogether. Nothing is lost by its absence: besides, *sins against our discipline* is a very clumsy way of expressing the idea suggested.

13. *knowledge of God*] of His will and requirements, what He rewards and what He punishes (Deane). Contrast Gk. with 1 Cor. xv. 34 "to have no-knowledge (ἀγνωσία) of God." *professeth*, Vulg. *promittit*, cp. 1 Tim. vi. 21.

servant of the Lord] Marg. *child*, Vulg. *filium*. But text is probably right. παῖς and υἱὸς are interchangeable, cp. ch. ix. 4, 7, xii. 19, 20. But as παῖς is the regular LXX. rendering for "*servant* of the Lord" in Is. xli. 8, 9 and often, and as *vv.* 16, 18 deal with the sonship of the righteous man, παῖς here probably points to the less intimate relation.

If Wisdom is a protest on behalf of the persecuted Egyptian Jews, the *righteous man* and the *servant of the Lord* (as in Isaiah), might be a collective formula standing for the whole community. Some see here a definite reference to the sufferings of Christ. Some of the Fathers regard it as a prophecy: cp. Cyprian, *Testim.* ii. § 14; Augustine, *de Civ. Dei* 17, 20 § 1 "In one of these books, known as the Wisdom of Solomon, the Passion of Christ is most definitely prophesied. His wicked murderers are even represented as saying 'Let us lie in wait.'" There is, no doubt, an extraordinary resemblance to the charges brought against Christ; and this has led some to treat the passage as a Christian interpolation, and others to argue that the whole book was the work of a Christian. But the truth seems to be that the picture is ideal, and that there will be a likeness between the charges levelled in all ages against men of God by men of evil life.

14. *a reproof of our thoughts*] Cp. St John vii. 7, and Ep. to Diognetus vi. 4 "The world hateth Christians, though it receiveth no wrong from them, because they set themselves against its pleasures."

15. *grievous unto us*] Cp. Prov. xxi. 15, xxix. 27 LXX.; Is. liii. 3.

Because his life is unlike other men's,
And his paths are of strange fashion.
We were accounted of him as base metal,   16
And he abstaineth from our ways as from uncleannesses.
The latter end of the righteous he calleth happy ;
And he vaunteth that God is his father.
Let us see if his words be true,   17
And let us try what shall befall in the ending of his *life*.
For if the righteous man is God's son, he will uphold him,   18
And he will deliver him out of the hand of his adversaries.

Philo quotes Antisthenes (*Quod omn. lib.* § 5) "The sober man is in-
tolerable."
   unlike other] lit. *other men*.   For the *comparatio compendiaria*,
cp. ch. vii. 3.
   of strange fashion] *mutatae* Cyprian.   Gk. literally means *changed*,
i.e. "abnormal" or "affected."   The sense probably is *mad*.   Cp.
Dan. iv. 15 (ἀλλοιοῦν) and 1 Sam. xxi. 13.   See also ch. v. 4, *madness*.
   16.   *as base metal*]   A.V. counterfeits.   For the Gk., cp. Is. i. 22
LXX.   They are not hypocrites, for they make no pretences.   The
righteous man assays their metal, and refuses to pass it for the currency.
   uncleannesses]   Cp. Is. lii. 11.
   the latter end]   Vulg. *nouissima*.   The righteous man's view of *the
latter things* is unfolded in ch. iii.   Cp. Numb. xxiii. 10.
   But *the latter end* may belong to this life, and not to the next.   Cp.
Job xlii. 12 LXX., and James v. 11 (Mayor's note).   The Book of Job
has many points of contact with Wisdom, and Job's prosperous end
may be before the writer's mind.
   In favour of this, note that the enemies of the righteous man challenge a visible interposition by God in his defence, if indeed he is what
he claims to be (*vv.* 17, 18).   No divine judgment would convince
them but one that operated on this side of the grave.
   vaunteth that God is his father]   Fervent prayers convey a sound of
unwarranted presumption to undevout ears.   Cp. Ecclus. xxiii. 1, 4;
St John v. 18; and see W. C. Allen, note on St Matt. v. 16.
   17.   *if his words be true*]   Cp. Jer. xx. 10 LXX.; St Matt. xxvii. 49.
   ending of his life]   Vulg. *quae uentura sunt illi*, i.e. the accompaniments of his end.   They are no longer punishing the righteous man out
of spite, but in order that God may have opportunity to vindicate his
claim.   They are bent now on experiment, not vengeance.   There is a
curious parallel in Jer. xviii. 18.
   18.   The likeness of this *v.* to St Matt. xxvii. 43 has led some to
suspect a Christian interpolation here, but that *v.* is couched in O.T.
language (Ps. xxii. 8 LXX.).   For this *v.* cp. Is. xlii. 1 "Jacob, my
servant, I will help him," LXX.; 3 Macc. vi. 11.   This line of argument on the part of the oppressors (if..., he will uphold him) points to
an interpretation of *latter end v.* 16 in terms of earthly life.

19 With outrage and torture let us put him to the test,
That we may learn his gentleness,
And may prove his patience under wrong.
20 Let us condemn him to a shameful death;
For ¹he shall be visited according to his words.

21 Thus reasoned they, and they were led astray;

¹ Gr. *there shall be a visitation of him out of his words.*

19. *with outrage and torture*] With a certain subtle cynicism the
writer delineates the change in the motives of the oppressors from
vindictive spite to a considerate anxiety that their victim should have
opportunity to draw succour from heaven and exercise his own noblest
qualities. They offer him *outrage* that he may respond with *gentleness*,
and by *torture* they hope to elicit *patience.*

put to the test] a somewhat euphemistic expression, cp. Acts xxii. 24.

learn his gentleness] Perhaps the source of St Paul's injunction,
Phil. iv. 5. The Gk. word (Vulg. *reuerentia*) means self-restraint in
relation to others. In 2 Cor. x. 1 it is used in conjunction with
"meekness," of our Lord.

may prove] Text rightly adopts reading of ℵA δοκιμάσωμεν. Vulg.
probemus.

For *patience under* [physical] *wrong,* cp. 2 Tim. ii. 24 and Epict.
Ench. § 10 "If insult be offered you, you will find patience a defence
against it."

20. *a shameful death*] Cp. James v. 6. It has been suggested that
Hegesippus had this passage in mind when he wrote the account of the
death of James the Just (Eus. *H. E.* ii. 23). But there the just man is
the victim of a sudden outburst of fanaticism. Further, Hegesippus
takes direct from Isaiah the passage which is found here (*v.* 12), as he
quotes the second half of the *v.* which does not appear in Wisdom.
For the just man's shameful death, cp. the famous passage in Plato,
Rep. ii. 5.

shall be visited] by God. This is made quite clear by *v.* 18. God
is so close to him, he affirms, that He will protect him (cp. Ps. cix. 31),
and therefore his oppressors need feel no compunction. For ἐπισκοπή,
cp. Job x. 12 LXX.

shall be visited may also be interpreted in a bad sense, and marg.
allows for this, cp. ch. xiv. 11. "Let us condemn him, and he shall be
punished for his prating," cp. Gen. xxxvii. 20. But Gk. (lit. *out of his
words*) is best rendered as in text.

COMPARISON I. (*a*, CONT.) *vv.* 21—24. THE MATERIALIST—HIS
BLINDNESS AND SPIRITUAL DEADNESS.

21. *reasoned they, and*] Cp. Jer. xviii. 18. Text suggests that the
being led astray was consequent upon their false reasoning. Rather,

For their ¹wickedness blinded them,
And they knew not the mysteries of God,   22
Neither hoped they for wages of holiness,
Nor did they judge *that there is* a prize for blameless souls.
Because God created man for incorruption,   23

¹ Or, *malice*

the verbs express simultaneous action "thus reasoned they in their error." Their false reasoning was the outcome of their evil deeds. They were not wicked because they were blind; they were blind because they were wicked. Cp. ch. v. 6.

blinded them] Through evil living they had lost the eye for spiritual things, cp. Is. lvi. 10. They could not conceive of a fellowship between God and man which could overleap death. This *v.* presents one of the leading ideas of Wisdom: the wicked are their own punishment, and are burdened with the reaction of their own misdoings, cp. ch. xvi. 1, xvii. 21, xviii. 4.

Farrar quotes :—

"For when we in our viciousness grow hard,
Oh! misery on't! the wise gods seal our eyes,
In our own filth drop our clear judgments, make us
Adore our errors, laugh at us, while we strut
To our confusion."

22. *mysteries of God*] Cp. ch. vi. 22 "The mysteries of Wisdom." What are God's mysteries? The truths which can be revealed to those alone who have the mind of God, and which bear upon God's prospective dealings with the righteous, cp. ch. iv. 17. The subjects of this revelation are God's triumph over the devil and death, and His inflexible pursuit of the great purpose of Creation, viz. life. God destined man for immortality, but seeing that many have chosen death, immortality has become the reward of sanctity, and the prize of blameless souls (cp. Bois, p. 297).

wages of holiness] Described in ch. iii. ὁσιότης leads some writers to see here a reference to the Hasidaeans, a religious body in Palestine, which took its name from Chasîdîm, the pious (ὅσιοι). This body is referred to in 1 Macc. ii. 42; vii. 13. But an allusion to them in a strictly Alexandrian work is improbable.

23. *for incorruption*] Vulg. *inexterminabilem.* "Incorruption" is primarily neither the life present nor the life to come, but that elevated life of the spirit for which man was created. It is the reward and the result of obedience to Wisdom. But inasmuch as wicked men have brought physical death into God's world, and have made it impossible for the righteous to live out the life of the spirit therein, death ushers the latter into a blissful immortality for which all were created, but which is now the reward for the faithful servants of God. See Introd. § 13.

And made him an image of his own ¹proper being;
24 But by the envy of the devil death entered into the world,

¹ Some authorities read *everlastingness.*

an image of his own proper being] The awkwardness of τῆς ἰδίας
ἰδιότητος has caused suspicion to fall on this line, although אAB and
Clem. Alex. *Str.* vi. 12 agree. They are unobjectionable on the ground
of sense, being a variation of Gen. i. 26. On the other hand Cod. 248,
Methodius, Epiphanius, and Athanasius, read ἀιδιότητος, *everlastingness,*
which though not theologically more true is more pleasing to the ear,
and defines the particular point of likeness that the author wishes to
impress, viz. immortality. Cp. Philo, *Opif.* § 13 "God gave them a
share in His *everlastingness*"; *Dec.* § 25.

It is impossible to decide finally between the two readings; if it
were not however for the strong MS. authority behind ἰδιότητος there
would be little room for hesitation. It evidently was suspected early,
as Syr. and Vulg. *similitudinis* presuppose a gloss ὁμοιότητος.

24. *But by the envy of the devil*] Quoted in Clem. Rom. *ad
Cor.* iii., in illustration of the havock wrought by envy. This passage
is there clearly interpreted of the murder of Abel by Cain : the words
immediately succeeding the quotation are "For thus it is written,"
followed by Gen. iv. 3—8, and the excerpt is summarized in the words
"Ye see, jealousy and envy wrought a brother's murder." This, the
earliest known interpretation of the words, is preferable to that which
interprets them of the serpent in the garden. (For the latter, see Jos.
Ant. i. i. 4.) Death, as a physical fact, entered into the world (according to Genesis) not with Eve, but with Cain, who was the first to take
human life. It is true that Ecclus. xxv. 24 has "From a woman was
the beginning of sin ; and because of her we all die." But she was
only the ultimate and indirect cause of the first physical death, however
responsible she may have been for the entrance of spiritual death.

Further, the murder of Abel by Cain was unquestionably prompted
by jealousy, the same motive which was at work in those who condemned and slew the righteous man (12—20). It is their action that is
traced to its source in this line, which would be pointless if referring
to Gen. iii.

This view is supported by 1 John iii. 12, which connects the act of
Cain with the prompting of Satan, a connection not definitely made
elsewhere in Scripture than in these two passages (and probably
St John viii. 44), which would thus seem to have a more than accidental mutual dependence. Theophilus (*ad Autol.* ii. 29) takes the
same view in a passage based on this : "Satan, being very jealous, when
he saw that Abel pleased God, worked in Cain his brother and caused
him to kill Abel, and thus the beginning of death came into this world."

Again, the identification of the serpent with the devil is not known
to Alexandrian literature of this date. Philo writing a century later
throws out no hint of it, nor does he treat the serpent as a type of
jealousy. In *Opif.* § 56 he handles the subject in his usual allegorizing

And they that are of his portion make trial thereof.
But the souls of the righteous are in the hand of God,   **3**

manner, but the serpent is for him a type of pleasure, because it goes
on its belly, eats dust, and has a poisonous bite. It is important to
observe that the author in ch. x. 1—4 makes the sin of Adam of small
importance, while Cain is the first "unrighteous man," the ancestor and
symbol of all who afterwards deserted Wisdom. *v.* 24 then is a return
to first principles. The tragedy of Cain and Abel is being reenacted in
every age: Cain inflicts physical death and chooses for himself spiritual
death, while Abel is the type of the just who suffer in the body, but are
heirs of immortality.

envy of the devil] διάβολος is the regular LXX. rendering of the Hebr.
Satan. Both words originally mean *enemy* with no metaphysical sense,
cp. Ps. cix. 6; 1 Macc. i. 36 (for διάβ. see Hatch, *Bibl. Greek*, 1889,
pp. 46, 7). *Satan* is used as a proper name only five times in O.T.,
Job i. 6, 12, ii. 1; 1 Chr. xxi. 1; Zech. iii. 1; and in each case LXX.
renders διάβολος (but cp. Ecclus. xxi. 27 σατανᾶ).

"The name and conception of Satan belong to the post-exilic age of
Hebrew development" (Whitehouse, Art. *Satan* in Hastings, *D. B.* iv.).
For the Palestinian Jews, with their strong sense of the supremacy of
God, sin and misfortune, and even the work of Satan and evil spirits,
could not be viewed as being outside the Divine causality. Satan is
regarded in O.T. as a subordinate agent of God, although not reflecting
the mind of God (see Whitehouse, *loc. cit.*).

This conception did not satisfy the Alexandrian mind. If on the
one hand God could not be supreme without being the ultimate cause
of evil, on the other hand the transcendence of God seemed violated if
He were conceived of as having any part in evil. Hence in Wisd. ii. 24
the devil is made the sole author of physical death, which according to
ch. i. 12—14 is neither God's creation nor according to the will of God.
Death and its agents are intruders.

death entered] i.e. physical death, the death inflicted upon Abel.
Death points back to *v.* 20 as well as to Gen. iv. 8, but there is a side-
reference to King Hades (i. 14, 16), the intruder into the world of men
designated for immortality.

entered into the world] Cp. Rom. v. 12. To be understood literally,
of death entering from without.

make trial thereof] "They that are of (the devil's) portion," like
Cain who "was of that wicked one" (1 John iii. 12), are goaded by
their envy to kill the righteous man.

COMPARISON I. (*b*) CH. III. 1—9. THE HOPE OF THE RIGHTEOUS.
IMMORTALITY IS NOW THE PREROGATIVE OF THE RIGHTEOUS
ONLY.

The writer does not teach a resurrection of the body, only an
immortality of the soul. But whether he has pious Gentiles in
view, or Israelites exclusively, it is impossible to say. There is a

And no torment shall touch them.

resemblance between this section and Enoch cii., ciii. (ed. Charles).
"Fear ye not, ye souls of the righteous, and be hopeful ye that
die in righteousness. And grieve not if your soul descends in grief
into Sheol, and that in your life your body has not fared as your
goodness deserved, but truly as on a day on which ye became like the
sinners, and on a day of cursing and chastisement. And when ye die
the sinners speak over you; 'As we die, so die the righteous, and what
benefit do they reap from their deeds? Behold, even as we, so do they
die in grief and darkness, and what advantage have they over us?
from henceforth we are equal.'...I swear to you, the righteous,...that
all goodness and joy and glory are prepared for them and are written
down for the spirits of those who have died in righteousness, and that
manifold good will be given to you in recompense for your labours....
And your spirits, (the spirits) of you who die in righteousness, will
live...and their spirits will not perish, but their memorial will be...unto
all generations: wherefore then fear not their contumely." The main
difference between the Alexandrine doctrine in Wisdom and the
Palestinian doctrine of the Book of Enoch is the absence of circumstantial detail in Wisdom, which is the natural outcome of a view
wholly spiritual. Spiritual conceptions need only a soul as their
theatre; an external judgment requires that time, place, actors, and
surroundings be definitely and vividly drawn.

iii. 1. *the souls of the righteous*] Freed from the body, the soul is
delivered from the pains that are inevitable in a material world. Cp.
Philo, *Jos.* § 43 "There is not one good man, but shall live hereafter
ageless and deathless, with a soul constrained no longer by the fetters of
the body"; and *Moses* iii. 39. The Alexandrine doctrine falls short of
the Christian doctrine of the immortality of the whole man.

in the hand of God] Under His protection. For the use of *hand*,
cp. Ps. lxxxviii. 5; Is. li. 16; St John x. 28. Contrast Hos. xiii. 14,
marg. This line furnished mediaeval art with one of its most striking
symbols.

And no torment shall touch them] Such as had touched their bodies,
ch. ii. 19. The introduction of torment here means nothing more than
this. It is more natural to regard the contrast as between the bliss of
the future life and the anguish of the earthly life, than as between future
bliss and future anguish (cp. ch. iv. 19). The latter contrast might be
called for if the writer was addressing an audience accustomed to all the
developments of the N.T. doctrine as elaborated in later ages. The
idea is very different from that in Is. lxvi. 24, where the indignities
inflicted on unburied corpses are in view. *Shall not touch* occurs in
Job v. 19 in a similar sense. Cp. ch. xviii. 20 marg.

them] The righteous, or their souls? Probably the latter, as the
emphasis is on the advantage possessed by the soul over the body. For
although this section deals mainly with the future life, *v.* 1 stands at a
transition point, and might refer to earthly life.

In the eyes of the foolish they seemed to have died;   2
And their departure was accounted *to be their* hurt,
And their journeying away from us *to be their* ruin: 3
But they are in peace.
For even if in the sight of men they be punished,   4

2. *In the eyes of the foolish*] i.e. the morally foolish who by their
vicious life have forfeited the capacity for spiritual judgment. They
can judge only by the eye.

they seemed to have died] *Seemed...was accounted...*(4) *in the sight
of men*. The writer emphasizes the paradox that in truth the visible is
only that which seems. The sensual man thinks that he touches reality
when he takes his stand on the visible, but he is the sport of shadows.
Cp. Philo, *Fuga* § 10 "Enquiry taught me that some living men are
dead and some dead men are alive : the wicked who live to be old men
are mere corpses devoid of the life of virtue, but the good, though they
are parted from the body, live for ever, enjoying an immortal destiny."
Cp. ibid. *Det. pot.* § 14 and Ep. to Diognetus x. (tr. Lightfoot, *Apost.
Fathers*) "the true life which is in heaven—the apparent death which
is here on earth—the real death reserved for those that shall be
condemned."

their departure...their hurt] *Hurt* (κάκωσις) indicates a process,
while *departure* means not merely death, but manner of dying, cp.
ch. ii. 17. *Departure*, the quitting of life, is contrasted with *journeying*
(*v.* 3), the loss of the familiar human surroundings. For *departure*
(ἔξοδος), cp. St Luke ix. 31.

3. *And their journeying*] Cp. Eccl. xii. 5; St Luke xxii. 22.

in peace] Cp. Is. lvii. 2. This may mean nothing more than is
intended in Isaiah, or in Job iii. 17, 18, where *peace* is purely negative,
implying rest from toil, and freedom from harassing care. There may
even be an unconscious identification of the self with the body instead
of with the soul, through a reminiscence of Ecclus. xliv. 14 "Their
bodies were buried in peace, and their name liveth to all generations."
But if the reference is to the *souls* of the upright, their peace lies in their
confident hope, *v.* 4.

4. *vv.* 4—10 have something of the character of Apocalyptic, the
object of which was "to solve the difficulties connected with the
righteousness of God and the suffering condition of His righteous
servants upon earth." (Charles, *Enoch*, p. 22.)

Apocalyptic was the refuge of those who found that the traditional
view of God's dealings with His people was unsatisfying. Earthly life
did not provide a full opportunity for justice and vengeance. It is not
to be wondered at that the inevitable rebound from a conception of life
limited to the earthly lives of a man and his descendants, to one in
which physical death was merely an incident, was accompanied by
wildly exaggerated promises and hopes. This passage exhibits unusual
reticence. It dismisses in one line the old view that suffering was an
indication of God's wrath and punishment. It is only "in the sight of

Their hope is full of immortality;
5 And having borne a little chastening, they shall receive
  great good;
  Because God made trial of them, and found them worthy
  of himself.
6 As gold in the furnace he proved them,
  And as a whole burnt offering he accepted them.

men" that the righteous are forsaken: what looks like punishment is
education.

Their hope] Not only when their bodies are in the grave, but even
during their earthly sufferings.

full of immortality] The succeeding *vv.* make it plain that this is a
personal life, and not a subjective resurrection in the memory of
descendants, cp. ch. iv. 1. Such an objective hope is found in
2 Macc. vii. 9; cp. Philo, *fuga* § 11 "This is the truest immortal
life, to be consumed with love and friendship for God, free from the
flesh and from the body." The word "immortality" (ἀθανασία) appears
several times in Wisdom, but in no other book of the Greek O.T.
St Paul uses it three times.

5. *chastening...good*] The thought recurs frequently, cp. Ps. cxix. 75;
Prov. iii. 11, 12; Rom. viii. 18; Heb. xii. 5—12; James i. 12.

God made trial of them] The Gk. word is used in the simple sense
of testing, cp. Ps. xxvi. 2. The idea of education through testing can
never be entirely absent, but in this line the thought is concentrated
upon the examination, while in the preceding line the preparation for it
is emphasized.

and found them] God's verdict. Again, God is viewed as testing
the righteous and passing judgment upon them, rather than training
them.

worthy] Cp. ch. vi. 16 "Wisdom goeth about seeking them that
are worthy of her." The idea suggested is of affinity rather than of
positive merit. Those who are worthy to be of the portion of Hades
make terms with him (i. 16), while God finds out those who belong to
Himself. This predetermined bias is one of the mysteries of the moral
world.

6. *As gold in the furnace*] Here again the thought is centred upon
the testing, and not the preparation to meet the test. The test (δοκίμιον)
is applied to see if they are genuine (δόκιμοι): if they are not, they are
rejected (ἀδόκιμοι). Cp. 2 Cor. xiii. 5; James i. 12. God proves that
they are not base metal, like the persecutors in ch. ii. 16. Mal. iii. 3
contains the metaphor of purifying the sons of Levi in the furnace, that
their offering may be acceptable.

as a whole burnt offering] The Gk. word (ὁλοκάρπωμα) has lost
entirely its etymological connection with fruits of the earth. It, and
its kindred word, are used of flesh offerings, cp. Is. xliii. 23. With the
sacrificial idea, cp. 2 Tim. iv. 6.

And in the time of their visitation they shall shine forth,   7
And as sparks among stubble they shall run to and fro.
They shall judge nations, and have dominion over peoples ; 8
And the Lord shall reign over them for evermore.
They that trust on him shall understand truth,   9

7. *in the time*] Vulg. *in tempore erit respectus illorum. Fulgebunt iusti.* The break seems to have been made deliberately, with the view of emphasizing both *visitation* and *shine. Visitation* in a good sense here, cp. *v.* 13, and ch. iv. 15. The impression that the writer wishes to convey is intentionally vague and indeterminate. He is not elaborating any systematized eschatological scheme such as appears in the Book of Enoch : the time and place of the fulfilment of his prophecies, whether he looks for a golden age on earth, or for purely spiritual joys hereafter, are left to the reader's imagination. (Introd. § 14.)

shine forth] Cp. Dan. xii. 3; St Matt. xiii. 43. For Gk., cp. Is. xlii. 4 LXX.

sparks among stubble] The effective vitality of the disembodied spirits of the just is suggested : brightness, swiftness, victorious power are theirs. The comparison with fire suggests not vengeance, but over-mastering energy; while the reversal of the relative positions of the righteous one and his many oppressors is indicated by the terrible power of a few sparks to consume a store of straw. Philo, *migr.* § 21, writes "Even the smallest spark,...kindles a vast conflagration : similarly the smallest fragment of virtue, when it has been nourished on good hopes and has been made to shine forth (ἀναλάμψῃ), gives sight to the blind, and causes the dry stock to flourish again. The tiny good, directed by the Divine counsel, becomes great, assimilating other things to itself." *Sparks* and *stubble* appear together in Is. i. 31 LXX., from which the simile is probably drawn. Cp. Jer. v. 14; Zech. xii. 6; Mal. iv. 1.

8. *They shall judge nations*] *To judge* is to govern : kingship, not vengeance, is the prospect held out by the verse. Cp. Prov. xxix. 9 LXX.; Ecclus. iv. 15.

the Lord shall reign over them for evermore] Except for the added *them*, a verbatim transcript from Ps. x. 16 LXX.

9. *They that trust on him*] Cp. Prov. xxviii. 5 LXX. "they that seek the Lord shall have understanding in everything" and St John vii. 17. Spiritual perception is closely associated with moral character and conduct, cp. Ps. cxi. 10. Contrast with this ch. i. 3. See Dr Pusey in (*Life of*) *Frederick Temple*, Vol. ii. p. 443, "The true way to study Divinity would be...to add to your duties a life of prayer and practical holiness."

But *the truth* here is more than intellectual truth. It may even be synonymous with Wisdom, and would certainly include some mystical knowledge of the God of truth. The understanding of truth suggests a heightening of the inmost moral faculties corresponding to the outward authority to be exercised hereafter by the just (*v.* 8).

And [1]the faithful shall abide with him in love;
Because grace and mercy are to his chosen.

10 But the ungodly shall be requited even as they reasoned,
They which lightly regarded [2]the righteous *man*, and revolted
from the Lord;
11 (For he that setteth at nought wisdom and discipline is
miserable;)

[1] Or, *they that are faithful through love shall abide with him*
[2] Or, *that which is righteous*

abide with him in love] i.e. shall be loved by God. The force of
in love is passive. The best, though not a complete parallel to this use
is in St John xv. 9, which means "Continue to be loved by Me," and 10
"I continue to be loved by Him." The faithful shall attain to fuller
perception, and shall be conscious of the Divine love embracing them.
Because grace and mercy] This *l.* is the same as ch. iv. 15. אAV
add here the second half of that *v.*, but the words are not found in B or
Vulg. They are doubtless an early interpolation. For *grace and mercy*
(Vulg. *donum et pax*), cp. the salutations in the two Epistles to Timothy.
Grace signifies the pleasure God takes in the just, and the bestowal of
His gifts upon them : *mercy*, His consideration towards their frailty,
and His pity for their sufferings.

COMPARISON II. (*a*) CH. III. 10—CH. IV. 6.

This section stands over against ch. iv. 7—14, in which the happier
lot of the righteous is set forth. Length of days and numerous posterity,
although possessed abundantly by the ungodly, are blessings certain to
be succeeded by an unhonoured age and a degenerate seed.

10. *requited even as they reasoned*] No arbitrary penalty : they
receive what belongs to them. Cp. Prov. i. 31 "the fruit of their own
way"; Ps. cix. 17—19; Job xxxiv. 11, for self-determined punishment.
For Gk. (ἐπιτιμίαν), cp. 2 Cor. ii. 6. *as they reasoned*, cp. ch. ii. 1.

lightly regarded] Contempt led to contumely. Not only did they
stop their ears to his crying, but they heaped indignities upon him.
the righteous man] Vulg. *iustum*, Aug. *iustitiam*. Cp. St Luke
xii. 57; Col. iv. 1; Job xxxiv. 10. Text is preferable, although the
adj. (τοῦ δ.) may be taken as masc. or neut. (marg.). The righteous
man has been the leading thought of ch. ii., to which this verse recalls
attention. Further, to make light of the righteous *man* is a more serious
charge to lay against the ungodly than to neglect abstract righteousness.
Again, it is more reasonable to couple the sin against God with sin
against man (cp. St Luke xviii. 4) than with neglect of the moral law.

revolted] Cp. ch. x. 3. Here not of apostasy from Judaism so
much as of the moral apostasy of sensuality, cp. ii. 10.

11. *setteth at nought*] This *l.* is an adaptation of Prov. i. 7.

And void is their hope and their toils unprofitable,
And useless are their works :
Their wives are foolish, and wicked are their children ;　12
Accursed is their begetting.　13
Because happy is the barren that is undefiled,

Wisdom is the quality of practical righteousness, *discipline* the path by which it is attained. The reasonings of the ungodly were a virtual repudiation of both. The personified Wisdom is called *a spirit of discipline* in ch. i. 5, but the meaning of the words here is determined by the quotation from Proverbs.

miserable] In a moral sense, in spite of outward circumstances. Used again in ch. xiii. 10, in connection with false hopes.

their hope] The prec. clause is rightly treated as a parenthesis, so that *their* refers directly to "those who revolted." *hope*, either absolutely in the conventional sense of "hope of posterity," or else the first term in a series *hope*, *toils*, *works*, which declares the futility of the wicked in respect of projects, labours, and results.

12. *foolish*] Vulg. *insensatae*. Probably as A.V. marg. "unchaste." Gk. bears its usual moral significance, cp. 2 Sam. xiii. 12, 13 ; Prov. v. 5 "The feet of foolishness," LXX. For the type, cp. Ecclus. xxiii. 26.

their children] In his effort to be logical, the writer embarks on a perilous generalisation. Hereditary taint is an undoubted fact, but not so its universality. Every new birth has the potentiality of a new beginning. If Ezekiel quotes in xvi. 44 the proverb "as is the mother, so is the daughter," in xviii. 1—18 he protests vehemently against any inflexible law of heredity. Ecclus. xvi. 1—4 is wiser, and argues that children *per se* are not a blessing : all depends on their character.

13. *Accursed*] Cp. Ecclus. xli. 5 "The children of sinners are abominable," and Philo, *Post. Cain* § 51 of the daughters of Lot "Cursed shall be their child-bearing." For the converse of this, cp. Is. lxv. 23 LXX. "They shall not labour in vain (*v.* 11), nor bear children for cursing ; for they are a seed blessed by God, and their offspring with them." Modern teaching emphasizes environment as against heredity. Though it is true to speak of a "bad stock," bad upbringing is a still more powerful factor.

Because] The argument is, Cursed is their sinful begetting, because blessing belongs to the sinless barren : "more are the (spiritual) children of the desolate than the children of the married wife." But the late Pss. cxxvii., cxxviii. show that the spiritual teaching of Is. liv. 4 and lvi. 1 did not command universal acceptance.

the barren] To the Hebrew mind, childlessness was a reproach to a woman (Gen. xxx. 23 ; Is. iv. 1 ; St Luke i. 25). Some editors have seen in this and the next *v.* a praise of asceticism as practised by the Therapeutae, based on the theory of the evil of the body. But if celibacy were in itself desirable, there would be no occasion to emphasize the compensations God offers. Further, στεῖρα does not mean "an un-

She who hath not conceived in transgression;
She shall have fruit when *God* visiteth souls.

14 And *happy is* the eunuch which hath wrought no lawless
   deed with his hands,
   Nor imagined wicked things against the Lord;

married woman": see St Luke i. 6, 7. The gist of the passage is that
sterility, if pure, is redeemed by a spiritual fertility. This *v.* and the
next are based on Is. liv. 1 and lvi. 4, which teach that parentage is not
to be treated as the criterion of human well-being. Such criterion must
be spiritual: "no list of *circumstances* can make a Paradise."

undefiled] The word is defined by the succeeding clause "she who
hath not conceived in transgression." She is contrasted with the
false wife in Ecclus. xxiii. 22. The thought is not the same as in
Ps. li. 5. There the infection of all human nature with sin is thought
of, here an act of unfaithfulness, which might take away the reproach
of barrenness at the cost of a secret and worse reproach.

fruit] The issue of a righteous life is *fruit*, a product enjoying
vitality; that of an ungodly life is "unserviceable *works*." The
contrast is (perhaps unintentionally) the same as in Eph. v. 9—11
between the "*fruit* of light" and the "unfruitful *works* of darkness."

when God *visiteth souls*] No very clear conception probably existed
in the writer's mind as to when and where there should be visitation.
Cp. Job xxxiv. 9 LXX. "Say not, there shall not be visitation of a man:
he shall have visitation from the Lord." Cp. 1 Sam. ii. 21; as there
was an earthly visitation of the childless Hannah, so there shall be a
spiritual visitation of those who preferred childlessness to sin. The
visitation may take place here or hereafter: it is a visitation of the soul,
the material aspects of which an Alexandrian writer was content to
ignore. See ch. iii. 7.

14. *And* happy is *the eunuch*] This is drawn from Is. lvi. 4, 5. The
eunuch was doubly unfortunate: he could leave no descendants, and so
his memory died with himself; and under the old covenant he was not
allowed within the congregation (Dt. xxiii. 1).

There is no advocacy here of voluntary celibacy (cp. Philo, *de Uita
Contempl.* § 8); the words refer to those who from natural causes find
themselves childless. Such men, if blameless in deed and thought
(cp. *v.* 13, *undefiled*), shall receive inner consolation.

which hath wrought no lawless deed] Physical infirmity is not, in
itself, a pledge of future Divine visitation: it must be accompanied by
clean hands, and a loyal heart. This qualification is very necessary,
since even under the Christian dispensation, it is often mistakenly
thought that poverty of circumstances e.g. is pronounced to be *per se*
blessed, and furnishes a claim upon material compensation hereafter.
But the soul that makes material poverty an excuse for spiritual
poverty is as far from the Kingdom of Heaven as they that trust in
riches. Philo, *det. pot.* § 48 writes "It is better to become an eunuch
than to indulge in lawless unions."

For there shall be given him for his faithfulness ¹a peculiar
favour,
And a lot in the sanctuary of the Lord more delightsome
than wife or children.
For good labours have fruit of great renown;   15
And the root of understanding cannot fail.
But children of adulterers shall not come to maturity,   16

¹ Or, *the grace of* God's *chosen*   Gr. *a chosen grace.*

given him for his faithfulness a peculiar favour]   Much better than
A.V. *special gift of faith.* πίστεως is no doubt unusual, perhaps gen. of
price. The idea of acquiring merit with God was very familiar to the
Jews: cp. ch. vii. 14; Phílo, *Abr.* § 46 "Loving the man for his faith
in Him, God gives him faith in return"; and id. *Post C.* § 43, a passage
which it is difficult not to connect with St John i. 16 "grace for grace."
    a lot in the sanctuary] Cp. Is. lvi. 5. To be interpreted in a
spiritual sense, cp. Ecclus. xlv. 22 "[Aaron] hath no portion among the
people : for [God] is thy portion and inheritance." Physical exclusion
from the congregation may even stimulate the pure soul to thirst after
God Himself, cp. Ps. lxxxiv. 5 R.V.
    than wife or children] The added words are supplied by analogy
with Is. lvi. 5. Gk. for *delightsome* (θυμήρης) is poetical, and not found
elsewhere in the Gk. Bible.
    15. *have fruit*] *Fruit,* cp. *v.* 13.
    of great renown] The thought of a subjective immortality cannot be
quite dismissed by the Jewish mind. It is not enough that his soul
should survive; his name and memory must obtain recognition. The
genitive in this line is objective, "the fruit which good labours *have*":
in the next line it is subjective, "the root which understanding *is*."
    root of understanding] Subj. gen., with a different sense from *root of
wisdom* in Ecclus. i. 6, where the gen. is objective. *Understanding* is
merely a poetical variation for the abstract quality of wisdom. For the
root, as an indication of permanence, cp. Prov. xii. 3, 12; and contrast
with Is. v. 24 "Their root shall be as rottenness."
    16. *children of adulterers*] The writer has *v.* 13 in his mind, and
singles out adultery as a typical sin, so that *adulterers* is almost identical
with "sinners." The expression recalls Is. lvii. 3—5: "adultery" is
often used metaphorically to express the unfaithfulness which leaves God
for the attractions of sin.
    shall not come to maturity] For the writer's wholesale condemnation,
cp. the malignant expressions in Jer. xviii. 21, 22. ἀτέλεστα (Vulg.
inconsummati) must not be translated in its secondary classical sense
of "uninitiated," as suggested by margin of A.V. "[shall not] be par-
takers of holy things." Such a rendering would be in this connection
superficial, and to support it by Dt. xxiii. 2 would be to confuse local
rules with universal principles. The writer may have the Mosaic rule
in his mind, but he is not reaffirming it.

And the seed of an unlawful bed shall vanish away.

17 For if they live long, they shall be held in no account,
And at the last their old age shall be without honour.

18 And if they die quickly, they ¹shall have no hope,
Nor in the day of decision *shall they have* consolation.

19 For ²the end of an unrighteous generation is alway grievous.

---

¹ Some authorities read *have*.   ² Gr. *the ends...are grievous.*

Text renders rightly *immature*, i.e. they shall die before reproducing
themselves. Unlike the godly, their life is limited to this world; therefore the judgment upon them is in terms of time and not of eternity.

seed of an unlawful bed] Cp. Is. lvii. 4 "a lawless seed" LXX.;
and Ecclus. xxiii. 24—26 "The children (of the unfaithful wife) shall
not spread into roots, and her branches shall bear no fruit. She shall
leave her memory for a curse."

vanish away] Cp. Bathsheba's child, 2 Sam. xii. 14. The judgment
upon the ungodly belongs to the writer's wish rather than to experience.
The tone is that of Pss. xxxvii., lxix. and cix., a retrogression from the
teaching of Ezek. xviii. 14—20.

17. *if they live long*] Lit. *be long-lived* (μακρόβιοι). The adj.
(masc.) refers by a sense construction to *children* and *seed* (neut.) in
v. 16. *They*, i.e. the children of adulterers, who shall die, either early
and without hope, or in old age and without honour.

at the last] Old age, usually reckoned an honour, shall in their case
be held in contempt. This lot will befall them in this world, a long
life in which is their desire, cp. Is. lxv. 20.

18. *quickly*] Vulg. *celerius*, either *early*, or *suddenly*. For Gk., cp.
ch. xvi. 11; Is. viii. 3 LXX.

shall have no hope] Text follows אA, which in view of next *l.* is
probably right: but if this *l.* stood alone, the reading of B *they have*
would be preferable. The meaning is, "If they die early, they have no
hope," hope i.e. of posterity. They are immature; their early death
precludes the possibility. Such is the earthly lot (side by side with
that of those who grow old only to find dishonour) of the children of
the ungodly who die young.

day of decision] For *day* as judgment-day, cp. 1 Cor. iv. 3. Gk. for
decision (διάγνωσις) is not used elsewhere in Greek O.T., and once
only in N.T., Acts xxv. 21, where it refers to the decision of the Roman
Emperor. Here it is used of the day of visitation of the righteous, cp.
v. 15—22, when the ungodly shall be winnowed with the storm. Gk.
word for *consolation* (παραμύθιον) is found in Phil. ii. 1; for the sense,
cp. St Luke vi. 24.

19. *For the end*] Marg. renders the Gk. better than text, *The ends...
are grievous.* Gk. word (τέλη) means more than "conclusion"; it denotes
finality, and includes the idea of completion. τέλη points back to
ἀτέλεστα *v.* 16, and suggests the paradox "their consummation which is

Better *than this* is childlessness with virtue;   **4**
For in the memory [1]of virtue is immortality:

> [1] Gr. *of it.*

no consummation." Every life-history may be conceived as leading up
to a certain fulfilment: the death of the wicked is grievous, because
they can say "It is ended," but not "It is finished." This *v.* is
expanded in ch. iv. 1—6.

iv. 1. *childlessness with virtue*] such as is spoken of in iii. 13, 14. *Virtue*
may mean general excellence, including manliness, cp. 2 Macc. vi. 31.
But it probably is only a variation for "wisdom," cp. Philo, *Cong.* § 3,
where they are convertible terms. Vulg. has by its translation, *O quam
pulcra est casta generatio cum claritate,* turned these words into a praise
of celibacy, and Philo, *de Uit. Cont.* § 8 has been adduced in support.
But the version in Cypr. *de Sing. Cler.* § 40 "melius est esse sine filiis"
gives the true rendering, showing that childlessness from natural or
accidental causes is intended, cp. Epict. iii. 22 "Were the Thebans
more advantaged by all their citizens who left children, than by Epami-
nondas who died childless (ἄτεκνος)? Did Priam with his fifty scourges
of sons, or Danaus, or Aeolus, contribute more to the public good than
Homer? Will a man refuse family life and the hope of children for
military service, and allow himself to be turned from his childlessness by
no hope of advantage or pleasure, and shall not Diogenes the Cynic
be equally applauded?" Cp. Ecclus. xvi. 4.

in the memory of virtue is immortality] i.e. of childless virtue. This
is the characteristic earlier Jewish conception of immortality, which,
side by side with the desire for physical immortalisation through an
unbroken line of descendants, preceded hopes which sprang up as
individualism developed. The Jew of O.T. was a part of a whole: his
conception of life hardly allowed him to ask, "What will become of
me?" A subjective immortality (such as in Ps. cxii. 6) was what he had
been taught to desire. It is strange how this doctrine has again come
to the front, with the revival of the corporate consciousness through the
teachings of Comte; cp. the lines of his English disciple, George Eliot:—

> "Oh may I join the choir invisible
> Of those immortal dead who live again
> In minds made better by their presence :...
> ....So to live is heaven:
> To make undying music in the world,
> ....This is life to come
> Which martyred men have made more glorious
> For us who strive to follow. May I reach
> That purest heaven."

So too, Campbell :—

> "And is he dead, whose glorious mind
>   Raised thine on high?
> To live in hearts we leave behind
>   Is not to die."

WISDOM

Because it is recognised both before God and before men.

2 When it is present, *men* imitate it;
  And they long after it when it is departed:
  And ¹throughout all time it marcheth crowned in triumph,
  Victorious in the strife for the prizes that are undefiled.

¹ Gr. *in the age.*

recognised both before God and before men] Cp. Ps. i. 6 "The Lord *knoweth* the way of the righteous," and note in this series, "Divine knowledge cannot be abstract or ineffectual. It involves approval, care, guidance." Cp. 1 Cor. viii. 3. Although here recognition is before men as well as God, this positive, effectual sense of "being known" by God is also present. To be "known" by God carries with it a measure of undyingness: a thing that has existed in the mind of God and has evoked His approval can never become as though it had not been. The argument is similar to that which our Lord used with the Sadducees, to prove the continued life of the patriarchs (cp. St Luke xx. 38). Forgetfulness, however, is possible to God, according to the old Jewish conception; see Ps. lxxxviii. 5. For *God and man*, cp. Prov. iii. 4; St Luke ii. 52; Rom. xiv. 18.

The two subjects of long life and posterity, and their inferiority to spiritual attainments, are dealt with in this passage very fully. The treatment would appeal to Greeks as well as Jews: posterity and long life appear in Zeno's system as good, though not so simply good as knowledge, Diog. Laert. vii. 58.

2. *When it is present, men imitate it*] This describes how virtue is recognised before men (see *v.* 1). Virtue reproduces itself, whether consciously as men set about to imitate it, or unconsciously as the inevitable law works itself out that men become like what they admire.

when it is departed] Grimm quotes Hor. *Od.* iii. 24, 31:—

"Uirtutem...sublatam ex oculis quaerimus inuidi."

throughout all time] See marg. But αἰών (cp. Vulg. *in perpetuum*) has no meaning apart from that of indefinite duration, which it possesses when used in this and similar phrases.

it marcheth] For the Gk. word, of a festival procession, cp. 2 Macc. vi. 7. The procession of Virtue is always along a Uia Sacra. Being immortal, she needs no slave to stand behind her in her progress and remind the conqueror that death must come (cp. Epict. iii. 24, 85). The conception is not Jewish, but Greek.

crowned] For the Greek crown of victory, cp. 4 Macc. xvii. 15; 1 Cor. ix. 25. The picture is very frequently found in Philo; στεφα-νηφορεῖν occurs in *Jos.* § 4, cp. *Quod Deus* § 29 "She is acclaimed as victor, and carries a palm in token of conquest."

Victorious in the strife] A common metaphor, cp. 1 Cor. ix. 25. Philo, *Somn.* ii. 21, speaks of the "conflict of life," cp. also *All.* ii. 26, and Epict. iii. 25 "The supreme conflict."

prizes...undefiled] ἆθλα, cp. 4 Macc. ix. 8 "the prizes of virtue,"

But the multiplying brood of the ungodly shall be of no 3
profit,
And [1]with bastard [2]slips they shall not strike deep root,
Nor shall they establish a sure hold.
For even if these [3]put forth boughs and flourish for a 4
season,
Yet, standing unsure, they shall be shaken by the wind,
And by the violence of winds they shall be rooted out.
Their branches shall be broken off before they come to 5
maturity,

[1] Gr. *from.*   [2] Or, *offshoots*   [3] Gr. *in boughs flourish.*

and xv. 29; Philo, *Migr.* § 6 "Thou hast proved thyself an invincible
athlete: thou hast won rewards and crowns in the conflict ordered by
virtue, who holds out to thee the prizes (ἆθλα) of victory."
undefiled] Philo, in writing of mundane rivalry, says it is a battle
in which the (moral) victor seems the loser. "Be slow" he says "to
enter upon it; if you can, run away; if you are compelled to stand and
deliver, then make haste to be beaten: the winner is the loser, and the
victors are the vanquished" (*Agric.* §§ 24, 25).
The prizes in the text are, of course, the moral prizes of enhanced
capacity and purified life which are the reward of moral effort. If man
is his own punishment, he is his own reward.
3. *shall be of no profit*] Cp. ch. iii. 12.
with bastard slips] Cp. ch. iii. 16. For the picture, cp. Philo, *Sobr.*
§ 8, where the process of planting is described. Vulg. renders μοσχεύ-
ματα, *uitulamina*, evidently connecting with μόσχος, *uitulus*, for which
Augustine, *Doctr. Christ.* ii. 12 censures it (Grimm).
shall not strike deep root] Cp. Ecclus. xxiii. 25 "Her children shall
not spread into roots," and Mal. iv. 1.
establish a sure hold] Cp. St Luke viii. 13, and contrast with
Ecclus. xxiv. 12.
4. *put forth boughs*] The picture of the tree with all its development above ground resembles in its meaning two of the N.T. parables,
the seed sown on stony ground (which, like the tree, had no root and
endured for a season), and the fig-tree, which had leaves but no fruit.
A false stock must develop falsely. Even though the large families of
evildoers deceive the eye, yet there is beneath them a hidden fundamental insecurity, which must betray them when the storm of God
arises.
standing unsure] This *v.* does not refer to outward prosperity, but
to apparently hopeful moral tendencies. Even the better dispositions
of the children of evildoers are insecure and will give way before
temptation (Grimm).
5. *shall be broken off*] The figure is slightly changed: the storm is

3—2

And their fruit *shall be* useless,
Never ripe to eat, and fit for nothing.
6 For children unlawfully begotten are witnesses of wickedness
Against parents when *God* searcheth them out.

7 But a righteous man, though he die before his time, shall
be at rest.

8 (For honourable old age is not that which standeth in
length of time,

now conceived of, not as uprooting the tree, but as breaking off the
branches.   For the language, cp. Rom. xi. 17.

before they come to maturity]   Cp. ch. iv. 18, and for "immature"
(ἀτέλεστοι), ch. iii. 16.

their fruit...useless]   Cp. Prov. xv. 6 LXX.; Ecclus. xxiii. 25 ; and
contrast Ps. lii. 8 "a fruitful olive" LXX.

Never ripe to eat]   The Gk. word (ἄωρος) is used of untimely death,
Job xxii. 16 ; Prov. xi. 30.

fit for nothing]   Contrast Prov. xi. 30 LXX. "Out of the fruit of
righteousness groweth a tree of life."   See also Ps. cxxix. 6—8.

6.   *For children unlawfully begotten are witnesses of wickedness*]
The sense is determined by "For": *v.* 6 is the corollary of *vv.* 3—5,
and the emphasis lies on *when God searcheth them out.*   It is when
children suffer misfortune, that they prove wickedness in their parents.
Cp. St John ix. 2 "Who did sin, this man, or his parents, that he should
be born blind?" and 34 "Thou wast altogether born in sins."   It is not
that the existence of the children is a reproof of the parents' lust, (for
the denunciation is directed neither exclusively nor chiefly against the
children of adulterous unions); but the misfortunes of children argue a
parental sin, cp. Ecclus. xli. 5—7.   This verse is without point, if it
does not lay stress upon the misfortunes threatened in *vv.* 3—5.

when God searcheth them out] i.e. the children ; cp., in connection
with the children of the wicked, ch. iii. 18 "the day of decision."
Searching out (ἐξετασμὸς) is a word somewhat like *visitation* (ἐπισκοπή),
whose meaning (for good or ill) must be determined by the context.
The word as used here connotes punishment.

COMPARISON II. (*b*) CH. IV. 7—14.

This section is complementary to the preceding one, contrasting the
hope of the righteous man with the destiny of the wicked.   As the
apparent prosperity of the wicked is no proof of stability, so the
premature death of the righteous is no proof of God's displeasure.

7.   *though he die before his time*]   The compensation of the righteous
man is the profound rest he enjoys : the wicked live on, although their
life is threatened for all its seeming prosperity, but the righteous man
has passed beyond the reach of care, cp. Job iii. 17; Is. lvii. 2.

8.   *old age...length of time*]   Cp. George Macdonald, *Within and*

Nor is its measure given by number of years :
But understanding is gray hairs unto men,   9
And an unspotted life is ripe old age.)
Being found well-pleasing unto God he was beloved *of him,* 10
And while living among sinners he was translated :
He was caught away, lest ¹wickedness should change his 11
    understanding,

¹ Or, *malice*

Without, Pt. II., Sc. 10 "Life is measured by intensity, not by the 'how
much' of the crawling clock." Illustrations might be cited from the
literature of all ages: cp. Seneca "Uita non quamdiu sed quam bene
acta refert," and "Exigua est pars uitae quam uiuimus." Epicurus in
Diog. Laert. x. § 126 "Men do not choose food for its quantity but for
its quality; so time is not reckoned by its length, but by its fulness."
Philo, *Quis rerum* § 58 uses words almost identical with the text. Cp.
Abr. § 46. Contrast Ecclus. xxxvii. 25.

its measure] Cp. Job xxxii. 7—9 LXX.; and

> "We live in deeds not years; in thoughts, not breaths;
> In feelings, not in figures on a dial:
> We should count time by heart-throbs."
>
> Bailey, *Festus.*

9. *But understanding is gray hairs unto men*] Cp. "The character
of some is aged by nature" (Menander), and Philo, *plant.* § 40
"Those who are gray, not through time, but in goodness of counsel."
Cp. Dt. xxx. 20.

an unspotted life...old age] Cp. Is. lxv. 20, which must be interpreted
in a moral sense, "The child shall die (ἔσται LXX.) an hundred years
old." Duration is not the measure of life, but inward character. For
a similar idea, cp. Ps. lxxxiv. 10.

10. *Being found well-pleasing*] Commentators hold that the case
of Enoch is cited, cp. Gen. v. 24 LXX. Cp. Ecclus. xliv. 16; Heb.
xi. 5. But the "righteous man" of *v.* 7 is still the subject, his death
being spoken of in terms used to recount the translation of Enoch, a
typical instance.

while living among sinners] Cp. Is. lvii. 1 LXX. "The righteous
is taken away from the presence of iniquity."

he was translated] Text renders as if Enoch was the subject. But
"transferred" would be more true to the sense of the passage than
translated. The righteous man of ch. ii. was not translated; he was
(*ex hypothesi*) killed. The writer is not concerned to say anything
about the righteous man, except that he was taken away (cp. Is. lvii.
1): accordingly he uses μετετέθη, which originally is a colourless word,
signifying "to change the place of." To render it "was translated"
is to bring in the idea of destination which is not in the writer's mind,
and lose sight of his main thought, viz. removal.

11. *He was caught away*] Cp. Acts viii. 39, Vulg. *raptus est.* The

Or guile deceive his soul.
12 (For the bewitching of naughtiness bedimmeth the things
which are good,

Gk. word shows that more than merely natural causes were at work in
his death. For although the words might be applied to any righteous
man who dies prematurely, the special reference is to the righteous man
who is murdered. In ch. ii. 20 the wicked say "Let us condemn him to
a shameful death"; here the writer points to the Divine interposition
which they had mockingly challenged the righteous man to invoke. If
in its physical aspect death is man's work, it has a spiritual and Divine
aspect as well.

wickedness] The context suggests that the marginal alternative
malice is the right rendering. If wickedness were in his heart, to
remove him from temptation would be ineffectual: God takes him away
lest he be *changed*, or *deceived*, both operations being the work of
external agents.

change his understanding] Cyprian plainly does not interpret this
passage of Enoch: for, having quoted Gen. v. 24, he adds (*de Mort.*
§ 23) "Sed et per Salomonem docet Spiritus sanctus *eos qui Deo
placeant maturius* istinc eximi, ne...polluantur: raptus est (inquit) ne
malitia mutaret." The idea is the exact reverse of St John xvii. 15.

change] *sc.* for the worse. Cp. use of ἀλλοιοῦν in Dan. iii. 94 (27), see
ch. ii. 15.

understanding] His *moral* insight.

Or guile deceive his soul] Cp. Eph. iv. 14. The writer only sees the
peril of temptation: cp. *The Christian Year*, 8th Sunday after Trinity,

"Death only binds us fast
To the bright shore of love."

But a higher truth is well stated by Browning:—

"Why comes temptation, but for man to meet
And master and make crouch beneath his feet,
And so be pedestalled in triumph? Pray,
'Lead us into no such temptation, Lord'!
Yea, but, O Thou whose servants are the bold,
Lead such temptations by the head and hair,
Reluctant dragons, up to who dares fight,
That so he may do battle and have praise."
The Ring and the Book. The Pope, 1185—92.

12. This *v.* is an expansion of *v.* 11. There are influences in the
world which are too strong for even the innocent of heart.

For the bewitching of naughtiness] In his note on Gal. iii. 1, Bishop
Lightfoot points out that βασκαίνειν in that passage involves two ideas;
(1) the baleful influence on the recipient, and (2) the envious spirit of
the agent. Both ideas are present here: naughtiness may overcome the
righteous man in spite of himself; it is jealousy which prompts the

And the giddy whirl of desire perverteth an innocent mind.)
Being made perfect in a little while, he fulfilled long ¹years ; 13

¹ Gr. *times.*

assault upon his fidelity. For (1) cp. Theocr. vi. 39, and for (2) Ecclus.
xiv. 3—10, and "envy of the devil" in ch. ii. 24.

naughtiness] Vulg. *nugacitas.* Plato makes the φαῦλος (the bad man)
the opposite of the σπουδαῖος (the good), and φαυλότης is probably used
in this sense here. Lightfoot mentions that bewitchment was held to
be especially potent in the case of children, and this idea is present
here. The righteous man is caught away early in life.

bedimmeth the things which are good] Among these things are the
innocent heart. The jealous influence of evil impairs and dulls the
spiritual vision. The *good things* are not those outside him: the influence of evil cannot spoil them, it can only spoil him for them.

And the giddy whirl of desire] The best commentary on these words
is Prov. vii. 12. ῥέμβεσθαι is there used of the roaming and prowling
habits of the strange woman. ῥεμβεύειν occurs with the same meaning
in Is. xxiii. 16. ῥεμβασμός then points to the insidious and persistent
solicitations of desire, which can make the flesh too strong for the innocent mind. Translate "the wandering allurements of desire."

If the text had linguistic authority for its rendering, the idea would
be that even the simple are liable to be fired by the sensuous dance of
desire, cp. Seneca, *de V. B.* 28. But the word denotes roving rather
than rapid movement.

Giddy is somewhat speciously used; there is in English a secondary use
in a moral connection of "giddy," but there is no such use in Greek.
The word-play is inadmissible as a translation.

perverteth] μεταλλεύει (which in class. Gk. means "to mine") is used
for μεταλλάσσει or μεταλλοιοῖ, recalling ἀλλάξῃ in preceding verse.
Possibly the writer supposed that it was derived from ἄλλος "other."
The meaning is plain, and the effort of A.V. to unite the sense intended
with the literal translation of the Greek in the rendering *undermine*, by
what Farrar calls a happy analogy, is, to say the least, unscholarly.
The mistake occurs again in ch. xvi. 25, and is due to a want of perfect
familiarity with classical Greek forms on the part of the writer. However, papyri yet to be discovered may prove this to have been a popular
Alexandrian use.

13. *Being made perfect*] In ecclesiastical Greek τελειοῦσθαι, "to
be made perfect," has the regular meaning of "attaining martyrdom."

fulfilled long years] For the vb., cp. 4 Macc. xii. 14, and Is. lxv. 20
"an old man who shall not fill his time" LXX. For the idea, cp.
Philo, *Post C.* § 17 "judging of old age rather by its worth than by its
length of years," and

"Sound, sound the clarion, fill the fife,
    To all the sensual world proclaim,
    One crowded hour of glorious life
    Is worth an age without a name."

14 For his soul was pleasing unto the Lord:
   Therefore ¹hasted he out of the midst of wickedness.
15 But as for the peoples, seeing and understanding not,
   Neither laying ²this to heart,
   That grace and mercy are with his chosen,
   And that ³he visiteth his holy ones :—
16 But a righteous man that is dead shall condemn the
   ungodly that are living,

> ¹ Or, *he hastened* him *away*   ² Gr. *such a thing as this.*
> ³ Gr. his *visitation is with.*

Prof. Jowett has a sermon (*Sermons, Biogr. and Misc.* p. 86 ff.) on
this text, crowded with illustrations, and Disraeli (*Coningsby*) writes in
a passage copiously illustrated "The history of heroes is the history
of youth."

14. *For his soul was pleasing*] Plaut. *Bacch.* iv. 7, 18 writes "whom
the gods love die young," translating from the Greek of Menander.

Therefore hasted he] R.V. marg. follows Vulg. *properauit educere
illum*, but text is probably right, as ἔσπευσεν is followed by no acc.
For this intr. use of σπεύδω, cp. Jer. xxxviii. 20 LXX. and Diog.
Laert. ii. 12, 7. See Ep. Barn. iv. 3 "that His loved one may make
speed."

COMPARISON III. (*a*) CH. IV. 15—CH. V. 14. THE REVERSAL
OF OPINION.

15. *But as for the peoples*] So the text of B, οἱ δὲ λαοί. But it can
hardly be right ; *v.* 17 of the text shows the word that is required, "the
ungodly." A has the variant reading ἄλλοι, which probably conceals
ἄνομοι "lawless," a very simple uncial confusion. ἄνομοι serves as a
substitute for ἀσεβεῖς, the key-word required for the beginning of the
new section. ἄνομοι is found in ch. iv. 6, and in this section it is echoed
in ἀνομήματα (iv. 20) and ἀνομίας (v. 7).

seeing and understanding not] These participles are held in suspense
over *v.* 16, which contains a comment of the same kind as *vv.* 8, 9,
and should perhaps follow *v.* 14; *v.* 17 is a parenthesis, and in it *seeing
and understanding not* (*v.* 15) are taken up and emphasised by the
corresponding *shall see...shall not understand*. Finally, *shall see* (*v.* 18)
takes up *seeing* (*v.* 15) and *shall see* (*v.* 17), and coordinates them with
shall despise, the main verb of the paragraph. There is thus no
anacoluthon, although the sentence is long and involved.

laying this to heart] For the phrase, cp. 1 Sam. xxi. 12 LXX.

grace and mercy] This line is almost identical with ch. iii. 9 *c.*

he visiteth] "Visitation" here in a good sense. See ch. ii. 20, iii. 7.

16. This *v.* would be more appropriate after *v.* 14. Where it
stands in the text, it interrupts sense and grammar.

a righteous man that is dead] By death his righteousness is sealed,

And youth that is quickly perfected the many years of an
unrighteous man's old age;
For *the ungodly* shall see a wise man's end,   17
And shall not understand what the Lord purposed concern-
ing him,
And for what he safely kept him :—
They shall see, and they shall despise;   18
But them the Lord shall laugh to scorn.
And after this they shall become a dishonoured carcase,

and placed beyond the possibility of being falsified by surrender to
temptation. The death which they rejoice over will establish his
witness, and the picture of his life will be a standing reproof to them.

condemn the ungodly] Not with final judgment, but by the daily
moral contrast between his life which they count as death, and their
moral death which they mis-call life. For the Gk. word, "to put in
the wrong," cp. Heb. xi. 7.

the many years] A touch of scorn. An old age that can boast of
nothing except that it has passed time, is an old age in name only.

17. This *v.* should be read in close connection with *v.* 15. The
italics of the text, by supplying a subject to the verbs, show what ought
to be the subj. of *v.* 15. Instead of "the ungodly" in this *v.* read
they, and in *v.* 15 for *the peoples* read *the lawless*. See n. on *v.* 15.

For...shall see] *shall see* takes up and expands *seeing*, in *v.* 15.
They shall see the wise man's early death, told of in *v.* 7. "Wise"
and "righteous" are interchangeable, just as are "wisdom" and
"virtue."

shall not understand] expands *understanding not* in *v.* 15. They
did not realise that God had any purpose concerning him.

safely kept him] Vulg. *quare munierit illum.* For the Gk. cp. Is.
xli. 10. God's method of safe-keeping is seen in *vv.* 11, 12.

18. *shall see...shall despise*] *shall see* takes up *seeing* of *v.* 15, and *shall
see* of *v.* 17. But the emphatic word of the paragraph is *shall despise*,
which is used absolutely, with no object expressed, and fixes attention
on the temper indulged in by the wicked.

But them the Lord] The pronoun is emphatic at the beginning of
the sentence, *them, in their turn.* With dramatic suddenness, another
scorn supervenes (cp. Hab. i. 5 "Behold, ye despisers, and wonder, and
perish" LXX.), and the despisers find themselves mocked. This *l.* is
an adaptation of Ps. xxxvii. 13 *a.*

after this] If πτῶμα is translated "carcase" as in text, *after this*
will mean "after this contempt of the righteous," or, "after the wicked
have ceased to despise" (Grimm). The verse evidently points to a
retribution beginning on earth.

dishonoured carcase] Cp. Ez. vi. 4 for the Greek word. *Dishonoured*
(ἄτιμος) has reference to the primitive idea (see Soph. *Ant.* 450 ff.) that
to be unburied involved dishonour, cp. Is. xiv. 19 " Thou shalt be cast

And ¹a reproach among the dead for ever :
19 Because he shall dash them speechless to the ground,
   And shall shake them from the foundations,
   And they shall ²lie utterly waste, and they shall be in
      anguish,

¹ Or, *be for outrage*   ² Or, *be a perpetual desolation*

out on the mountains, like a corpse accurst" LXX.; Is. lxvi. 24;
Jer. xxii. 19. This *l.* tells of the dishonour done to the memory of the
wicked in the eyes of their survivors, cp. Jer. ix. 22, xvi. 4.

reproach among the dead for ever] For δἰ αἰῶνος, cp. Dt. v. 29
LXX.; the phrase indicates indefinite duration.

The thought is Greek. Burial conferred a kind of franchise upon
the souls of the dead; the unburied were repudiated by those who
had predeceased them and had obtained burial. Cp. Verg. *Aen.* vi.
325 "inops inhumataque turba," and Conington's note; also Hor.
Od. i. 28.

The writer's meaning is vague, as no doubt was his intention.
Sufficient is said, however, to indicate his idea that in their death the
wicked would be dishonoured among both living and dead, and that
conscious retribution in some form would be their lot.

19. *Because he shall dash them*] The wicked are compared to the
children of a conquered city, cp. Ps. cxxxvii. 9; Is. xiii. 16. The
picture is drawn fiercely and mercilessly, and recalls the tone of
Job xviii., or of the imprecatory Psalms. No contemporary allusion
need be sought in the words : they are too vague and rhetorical. ῥήξει
seems to stand for ῥάξει, cp. Ps. cii. 10; Is. ix. 11; Jer. xxiii. 39 LXX.

speechless] Cp. the account of the Divine dealing with Heliodorus,
2 Macc. iii. 27, 29. Contrast the dumbness induced by terror with the
previous expressions of their arrogance.

shake them] The writer seems to have in mind Job ix. 6 LXX.
"who shaketh the earth from its foundations, and the pillars of it
tremble," thus comparing the judgments of God to an earthquake.

lie utterly waste] The Greek words recall Nahum i. 10 LXX. "it
shall be wasted to the foundation." The wicked are compared to a
parched land, cp. Is. xix. 5—10. That these three judgments do not
refer to final annihilation is seen from the following clause "they shall
be in anguish." Cp. Ps. lxxiii. 19.

be in anguish] The phrase is found in Is. xix. 10 LXX. "The
workers in them shall be in anguish." Direct speech takes the place
of metaphor : the plain fact is terrible enough.

memory shall perish] After the three vigorous metaphors drawn
from the destruction of captive children, the shaking of a city by an
earthquake, and the parching of a land by the failure of its rivers,
comes the final condemnation, "they shall be forgotten." The same
thought clinches the similar denunciation in Job xviii. 17. After all, it
is only what they had foreseen, ch. ii. 4 and Pss. Sol. xiii. 10.

And their memory shall perish.

They shall come, ¹when their sins are reckoned up, with 20
coward fear;
And their lawless deeds shall convict them to their face.
Then shall the righteous man stand in great boldness   5

¹ Or, *when they reckon up their sins*

20. *They shall come*]   After the vehement vagueness of *vv.* 18, 19,
the definite picture is suggested of the wicked being confronted after
death with their righteous victim of days gone by, now at length openly
justified for his manner of life.

sins are reckoned up]   The majority of commentators hold (though
Grimm disagrees) that this passage, though containing a vivid and
definite picture, is not meant to teach an objective judgment in time
and place, but only to suggest the reflections that follow upon the
clearer vision that death permits.   See Introd. § 13.

with coward fear]   Fear, partly of the unknown and partly of the
divine holiness.   Cp. Prov. xiii. 5 LXX.   "The wicked is ashamed, and
shall have no confidence"; Pss. Sol. xiii. 4, 5.

shall convict]   Their conscience is awakened, and they seem to meet
their sins once more.   Their sins, i.e. their sinful character, had always
been living with them, but the torpidness of their conscience had
enabled them to ignore their presence.   But now, the hideous truth of
the corruption of their own selves is apparent.

to their face]   Vulg. *ex aduerso.*   Cp. Ps. l. 21; St Luke xix. 22.
Although the writer is careful to abstain from any doctrine of a final
judgment, it is probable that he was not unfamiliar with such speculations as those of the Book of Enoch.   For the *reckoning up of sins,*
cp. Enoch 81, 4 "Blessed is the man who dies in righteousness,
concerning whom there is no book of unrighteousness written, and
(against whom) no day of judgment is found." *id.* 98, 8 "All your
oppression wherewith ye oppressed is written down every day till the
day of your judgment." *id.* 104, 7 "Ye sinners, though ye say 'Ye
cannot ascertain it, and all our sins are not written down,' still they
will write down your sins continually every day."   Cp. Daniel vii. 10.

v. 1.   Augustine (*Ep.* 185, 41; *Contr. Gaud.* 1, 51; *Serm.* 58, 7) treats
this passage as referring to the Day of Judgment.   But neither this
conception, nor that of a final triumph for the ideal Israel, and the
vindication of righteousness upon a renovated earth, seems to belong to
the book (Farrar).   The writer dislikes the local and definite, and
views the individual consciousness as the theatre of all rewards and
punishments.   Cp. Milton's

"The mind is its own place, and it can make
A heaven of hell, a hell of heaven."

Before the face of them that afflicted him,
And them that make his labours of no account.

2 When they see ¹*it*, they shall be troubled with terrible fear,
And shall be amazed at the marvel of *God's* salvation.

¹ Or, him

He postulates a continued consciousness after death (to be distinguished from immortality) in the wicked, who will be rendered
capable of seeing both themselves and the righteous man as they had
never done before, apart from the prepossessions of spite and sensuality.

The writer is impelled by a strong moral purpose : either he lacks
the imagination of the writer of Enoch, or else he writes for a different
public, and resolutely controls his inventive faculty.   He is much more
at his ease among abstract ideas, and prefers to dispense with the vivid
colouring and movement ordinarily to be found in Apocalyptic.   The
victory of Truth is his confident teaching, and he is indifferent as to
place and time.   He is concerned with principles, which are timeless.

Then]   The triumphant *then* finds an echo in St Matt. xiii. 43.

stand]   The posture denotes confidence, cp. St Luke xxi. 36.   With
boldness cp. 1 John ii. 28, iv. 17.   The boldness of the righteous stands
in sharp contrast with the speechlessness (iv. 19) and the fear (iv. 20) of
the wicked.   The wicked cannot have *boldness* before God, cp. Prov. xiii.
5 LXX.

afflicted]   Vulg. *angustiauerunt*.   The aor. part. points to the past
acts of cruelty which culminated in murder, while the pres. partic. *that
make...of no account* indicates an habitual attitude.   The meaning of
the latter Gk. verb stands midway between Vulg. *abstulerunt* (plun-
dered) and Eng. *despise*; cp. Heb. x. 28, of "disregarding" the law.
The wicked did not merely mentally despise his efforts after life (ch. ii.
15); they tried to negative his achievements by causing him to fall before
their temptations (ch. ii. 17, 19).

2.   *When they see* it]   Omit *it*; *see* is used absolutely (cp. *despise*,
iv. 18) and loses in suggestiveness if *it* or *him* (marg.) is supplied.

The ungodly "see" at last: they see the truth concerning the
righteous, they see his confidence, they see the contrast presented by
themselves.   Their self-confident challenge in ch. ii. 17 *let us see* is
dramatically recalled.

shall be troubled]   This passage recalls Is. xiii. 7, 8 LXX. where
shall be troubled, *shall be amazed* are found, while *v.* 3 *b* is suggested by
Is. xiv. 16. Cp. also Is. lx. 5 LXX.

God's *salvation*]   א has *his* salvation, i.e. either God's, or that
granted to the righteous man.   For the former, cp. Gen. xlix. 18,
although "salvation *from* the Lord" is the more natural expression
found in Ex. xiv. 13 ; for the latter, cp. LXX. frequently.   As however
the phrase is like that in 3 Macc. vi. 33 "their unexpected salvation,"
where there can be no doubt as to the meaning of *their*, it is better to
translate "the righteous man's salvation."   His salvation is his unexpected happiness, and the boldness of his bearing.

They shall say ¹within themselves repenting,   3
And for distress of spirit shall they groan,
This was he whom aforetime we had in derision,
And *made* a parable of ²reproach :
We fools accounted his life madness,   4
And his end without honour:
How was he numbered among sons of God?   5

¹ Or, *among*   ² Or, *reproach, we fools : we accounted*

vv. 3—14 contain the confession of the wicked.   The section forms a
tragic counterpart to their earlier utterance (ch. ii. 1—20), and by its refusal
to appeal to the emotions of readers, is marked by a dignified gravity.
   3.   *within themselves*]   Marg. *among*, which is better, cp. Is. xiii. 8
"they shall complain one to another," and Vulg. *dicentes inter se.*
   repenting]   In a non-religious sense, i.e. "changing their mind"; cp.
"repented himself," of Judas, St Matt. xxvii. 3.
   distress of spirit]   The Gk. word, meaning lit. "torturing confinement"
(Sanday and H. *Rom.* ii. 9), occurs four times in LXX. and in St Paul.
Cp. 4 Macc. xi. 11.
   This was he]   For *this*, cp. Is. xiv. 16.   There may be a reminiscence of these words in Ep. Barn. vii. 9 "Is not this he whom once we
mocked and spat upon?"
   in derision]   lit. *for derision*.   For the phrase, cp. Jer. xx. 7,
xlviii. 26, 39 LXX.
   a parable]   The word is coupled with "proverb" or "byword"
(cp. Hor. *fabula fies*) in Dt. xxviii. 37 ; 2 Chr. vii. 20 ; cp. Ps. lxix. 11.
It is found, as here, with "reproach" in Jer. xxiv. 9.   The righteous
man is a "taunt-song of reproach."
   4.   *We fools*]   *fools*, in the literal sense of intellectual incapacity.
Vulg. *insensati*; the irony is then seen of fools accusing others of
madness.   But the words go with *v.* 3, as the rhythm of the Gk. shows;
whom...we had in derision, fools that we were.
   madness]   A strong word, denoting frenzy.   Perhaps a reference to
ch. ii. 15, where see note.
   without honour]   Cp. ch. ii. 20, iii. 2, 3.   Farrar recalls how Savo-
narola, Huss, Cranmer died amidst the execrations of their enemies,
and yet accepted with perfect faith their apparently final failure.
   5.   *How was he*]   Exclamatory, rather than interrogative, cp.
Is. xiv. 12.
   numbered]   For the word, cp. Is. xiv. 10.   There is a word-play in
Gk. between *numbered* and *accounted* (*v.* 4).   For the sense, cp.
St Luke x. 20.   Just as there was a register of the citizens of the
theocratic community, entitling those enrolled to temporal blessings
(Ps. lxix. 28), so an analogous register is pictured as existing in the
eternal world.   This conversation among the dead may have been
suggested by Is. xiv.

And *how* is his lot among saints?

6 Verily we went astray from the way of truth,
And the light of righteousness shined not for us,
And the sun rose not for us.

7 We took our fill of the paths of lawlessness and destruction,

sons of God] The expression conveys no metaphysical meaning, but has the same moral bearing as "sons of God" in Hos. i. 10. The phrase here is purely a variant for "saints": it is not "angels" as in Job i. 6, ii. 1. They recognise that the claim of ii. 13, 18 is justified.

his lot among saints] The lot of Israel was the Promised Land, so called with allusion to its division by lot. 'Lot' (κλῆρος) is then used (and κληρονομία "inheritance") metaphorically, as the inheritance in God which the saints enjoy, cp. ch. iii. 14; Ps. xvi. 5; Ecclus. xlv. 22. See Acts xxvi. 18 and Col. i. 12. Here the scene of the *lot* is placed among saints; in Col. i. 12 the inheritance of the saints is placed in the kingdom of light.

6. *Verily*] ἄρα, Vulgate *ergo*. The inferential particle marks the conclusion drawn. "We counted him mad; we find him among sons of God: therefore we went astray." The inference is not "Therefore (we can now see that) we went astray," but "Therefore, because we judged so falsely, we went astray." If it had been the former, the wicked would be seen struck with surprise that they had, after all, missed the way of truth and had been wandering in darkness. But in their most confident moments they had never been hypocrites; they had never posed as searchers after truth: they were frankly materialistic, and now they see why they were so; they had misjudged the righteous life.

the way of truth] Either, *the true way*, as opposed to the false way, i.e. 'our own' way, cp. Is. liii. 6, and Ep. Barnabas xviii., "There are two ways, the one of light and the other of darkness," or, the way which leads to truth, moral and spiritual. *Way of truth* is found in Ps. cxix. 30, cp. James v. 19; 2 Pet. ii. 2.

the light of righteousness] Cp. Ps. cxix. 105. Righteousness is compared to light, Is. lxii. 1.

the sun rose not for us] For the picture cp. Mal. iv. 2 "The sun of righteousness shall arise." More is intended than the subjective "our eyes were blinded with sin": the objective "God hid His face, and in His disfavour is death" is meant. For this *v.* cp. Is. lix. 9.

7. *We took our fill*] *Paths* used in a metaph. sense can go with *took our fill*; there is no need to see here a mixture of two constructions. A similar use is found in Prov. xiv. 14 LXX. "He shall be filled with his own ways," and in a more expanded form in Prov. i. 31. Vulg. goes slightly beyond the Greek, in rendering *lassati sumus*.

paths] For the *paths of lawlessness* contrasted with the way of truth cp. Ps. cxix. 29 LXX., where "way of iniquity" provides the same contrast. *Paths of destruction*, cp. Job xxx. 12, and St Matt. vii. 13.

And we journeyed through trackless deserts,
But the way of the Lord we knew not.
What did our arrogancy profit us?	8
And what good have riches ¹and vaunting brought us?
Those things all passed away as a shadow,	9
And as a message that runneth by:
As a ship passing through the billowy water,	10

¹ Gr. *with.*

trackless deserts] Their life had no moral purpose, and led nowhere: like the wanderer in the dark, they moved in a circle. The Greek words occur in Jer. xii. 10 and Ps. lxiii. 1. *trackless* is explained in next *l.*
way of the Lord] Cp. Baruch iii. 20, 23 "The way of knowledge, of wisdom, they knew not," and Job xxiv. 13. Cp. Ps. xcv. 10 LXX. "They knew not my ways." With the whole *v.*, cp. Is. lix. 7, 8, 9.

8. *our arrogancy*] ὑπερηφανία, a very strong word implying pride of self and contempt for others. It is twice attributed in Apocr. to the people of Sodom, Ecclus. xvi. 8; 3 Macc. ii. 5.

riches and vaunting] *diuitiarum iactantia*, Vulg. 'Vaunting' (ἀλαζονεία) is the ostentatious display of the materialist, who knows no measure of value except money In 4 Macc. i. 26 it is ranked with covetousness, vain-glory, factiousness, and envy, as a sin of the soul. J. B. Mayor (*Ep. of St James*, iv. 6, 16) distinguishes between ὑπερηφ. defiant wickedness, and ἀλαζ. confidence in one's cleverness, luck, strength, skill, etc. Cp. Clem. Rom. *ad Cor.* lvii. 2.

vv. **9—12** contain a series of similes, gathered largely from O.T., expressing the elusive fugitiveness of life. The world moves on, and things are as though men had never been.

9. *Those things all passed away*] In the Gk. the vb. παρῆλθεν stands emphatically at the beginning of the sentence, "Past are all those things." Cp. 1 John ii. 17. Their self-conceit, their wealth, and the masterfulness that rested on it are gone, and so identified with them were they (*v.* 13), that the passing of their possessions is tantamount to the passing of themselves.

as a shadow] Cp. ch. ii. 5; 1 Chr. xxix. 15; Job viii. 9. The idea is not merely the unsubstantialness of a shadow: it is that a shadow cast by a cloud sweeps across the land, and is gone, and leaves no mark by which its passage can be traced.

as a message that runneth by] For the Greek verb, cp. Philo, *Quod Deus* § 37 "a shadow or a breeze that runneth by and will not stay." Vulgate *tanquam nuntius percurrens*, cp. Job ix. 25; 2 Sam. xviii. 22—24.

10. *a ship*] The picture would not be true of a modern steamer, whose wake is traceable for miles, but the writer is thinking of the light skiffs, mentioned in the source-passage, Job ix. 26; cp. note in this series, "These skiffs, constructed of a wooden keel and the rest of reeds are the 'vessels of bulrushes' of Is. xviii. 2. They carried but one or two persons, and being light were extremely swift." The swift-

Whereof, when it is gone by, there is no trace to be found,
Neither pathway of its keel in the billows:
11 Or as when a bird flieth through the air,
No token of *her* passage is found,
But the light wind, lashed with the stroke of her pinions,
And rent asunder [1]with the violent rush of the moving
    wings, is passed through,
And afterwards no sign of *her* coming is found therein:
12 Or as when an arrow is shot at a mark,
The air disparted closeth up again immediately,

[1] Or, *with the violent rush, is passed through by the motion of
her wings*

ness is not in question here, but the lightness: the skiffs glide over the
surface, and leave no impression.

pathway of its keel] An example of the author's poetic language.
See Introd. p. xvi., note 3.

11. *a bird*] Cp. again, Job ix. 26 and Prov. xxiv. 54 LXX. (xxx.
19 A.V.) "the track of a flying eagle, and the path of a sea-faring ship."
Again, the wonder of things which pass and leave no trace is pointed to.

lashed...rent asunder] The use of these vigorous words emphasizes
the complete absence of any corresponding visible impression.

pinions] ταρσοί, either *feathers*, or the flat of the wing.

rent asunder] Cp.

"Illa leuem fugiens raptim *secat aethera* pennis."
                              Verg. *Georg.* i. 410.

with the violent rush] Lit. with the force of the rush of the beating
wings. Gk. word denotes impetus, and not noise, cp. 2 Macc. ix. 7.

is passed through] The passive is well used, to illustrate the complete
absence of reaction on the part of the medium in which the violent
agitation takes place. What means so much to the actors is matter of
indifference to their surroundings. Similarly, the world "is passed
through" by men who are "such stuff as dreams are made of," and
who leave not even the phantom of a trace of their passage. For reasons
of rhythm, the rendering of the marg. is to be preferred to that in the text.

is found] The three aorists *is passed through, is found, closeth up*
possess a gnomic force, the particular actions recurring continually,
with a suggestion of rapid instantaneous movement.

12. *The air...closeth up again*] The meaning of the line is quite
clear, but it is doubtful if the reading is right. ἀναλύειν in xvi. 14
means *to release* or *restore*, but it is questionable if "the air is released
(or restored) upon itself" would be Greek. Again, it is used in Philo
for "resolving" a compound into its elements (*Quis Rerum* § 57), but,
"the air is immediately resolved into itself" (Bissell and Farrar) does
not even give sense. Of the two renderings, *is released* is the better.

So that men know not where it passed through:
So we also, as soon as we were born, [1]ceased to be;   13
And of virtue we had no sign to shew,
But in our wickedness we were utterly consumed.
Because the hope of the ungodly man is as chaff carried by   14
the wind,

[1] Gr. *failed.*

So that men know not] ὡς ἀγνοῆσαι has no subject; it is therefore gratuitous to supply *men.* Rather, "the air cut through by the arrow, closes up again, so that *it* (the air) knows not where it passed." The air is as unconscious of the flight of the arrow once it has passed, as the world is of the lives of men who leave no mark in the moral sphere.

13. *So we also...ceased to be*] In this line the similes of *vv.* 9—12 are applied, and the life history of the sensualist is seen to be "we were born, we died." The time between the two points of appearance and disappearance when viewed in a moral light, is foreshortened till it becomes negligible. The argument is that righteousness alone possesses vitality, and therefore non-moral life is non-existent. Accordingly, the instantaneous rebound of the air when the arrow has flown through it is analogous to the death of the wicked succeeding instantaneously (morally speaking) to their birth.

For the Gk. word *died,* lit. *failed* (Vulgate *desiuimus esse*), cp. Ps. xc. 9 LXX.

of virtue we had no sign to shew] For *sign,* cp. *v.* 11 "no sign of her coming." Virtue is the sole reality, and therefore it is the only thing in a life which can leave a sign of itself. Evil is negative, and its traces, like the passage of the bird, are negation. Their only "signs" were the tokens of their mirth, ch. ii. 9.

But in our wickedness] The particles μὲν...δὲ show that there is a contrast intended between this line and the preceding "while we had no virtue to shew, we had wickedness enough to destroy us." A little of that which they refused could have given them an element of positiveness: that upon which they spent their lives reduced them to a sheer nonentity.

14. It is not plain whether this *v.* is the writer's summary, or the final words of the speakers of the previous verses.

Because] Four similes illustrate the principle which establishes the truth of all that has been said.

the hope of the ungodly man] abstr. for concr. "that on which he rests his hope," i.e his wealth, pleasure, etc.

as chaff] A picture of the solidity of his achievements. For *chaff carried by the wind,* cp. Is. xxix. 5; also Ps. i. 4, xxxiv. 5. χνοῦς, Vulgate *lanugo,* denotes properly dust of chaff.

And [1]as [2]foam vanishing before a tempest;
And is scattered as smoke *is scattered* by the wind,
And passeth by as the remembrance of a guest that tarrieth
　　but a day.

15 But the righteous live for ever,
　And in the Lord is their reward,

---

[1] Gr. *as foam chased to thinness* : or, *as thin foam chased*.
[2] Most Greek authorities read *hoar frost* : some authorities, perhaps
rightly, *a spider's web*.

as foam vanishing] אAB read πάχνη, *hoar-frost*, but hoar-frost is
not blown by the wind. The R.V. "foam" follows the reading of a few
Gk. MSS. ἄχνη, and Vulg. *spuma*.
　R.V. marg. has "some authorities (read) perhaps rightly, *a spider's
web*." ἀράχνη is very likely to be right, cp. Job viii. 14 LXX., where
it is found in the verse immediately succeeding "the hope of the ungodly
shall perish." Cp. note in this series "The flimsiness of the spider's
house is proverbial in the East. Mohammed compares idolaters to the
spider: 'The likeness of those who take to themselves patrons beside
God is as the likeness of the spider who taketh to herself a house; and
verily the frailest of houses is the spider's house.'" Koran xxix. 40,
cp. Job xxvii. 18 LXX.; Ps. xc. 9 LXX.
　smoke] Cp. Ps. xxxvii. 20; Is. li. 6.
　a guest that tarrieth but a day] No picture could represent more
pathetically the unabidingness of the hold upon life of the wicked.
He is like the "lodger" at the wayside inn, cp. Jer. xiv. 8, and is
forgotten by the next night when a new traveller claims the attention of
the host. Cp. also Is. xxxviii. 12.

COMPARISON III. (*b*) CH. V. 15—23. THE RIGHTEOUS LIVE IN
　GOD'S CARE, BUT GOD WHO EXALTS THEM MANIFESTS HIS
　WRATH AGAINST THE WICKED.

　15. *live for ever*] For ever (εἰς τὸν αἰῶνα) is almost a qualitative
phrase, indicating an eternalness of character as much as of time, cp.
St John xvii. 3. The writer has got beyond the stage at which mere
extension of time counts as immortality, cp. ch. viii. 17. Here he
argues that the righteous live eternally, i.e. on the eternal plane, their
reward and the care for them being with God, cp. 2 Macc. vii. 9;
Ecclus. xli. 13; and Philo, *Jos.* § 43 "In my judgment no good man
dies, but will live for ever an ageless life with an immortal nature."
　their reward] A continued spiritualisation of material conceptions.
Fellowship with God is their reward; He is their portion, cp. Pss.
lxxiii. 26, cxix. 57. Or, *in the Lord* may mean "in His keeping,"
cp. Is. lxii. 11, a rendering made more possible by next line.

And the care for them with the Most High.
Therefore shall they receive the crown of royal dignity   16
And the diadem of beauty from the Lord's hand;
Because with his right hand shall he cover them,
And with his arm shall he shield them.
He shall take his jealousy as complete armour,   17

the care for them] Cp. Pss. xl. 17, lv. 22.
with the Most High] Cp. Is. xlix. 4 "My judgment is with the Lord."
16. *Therefore*] Because God cares for them.
crown] The Gk. word βασίλειον is not necessarily a *crown*, the meaning being determined by the context. It sometimes means *palace*, sometimes *kingdom*, cp. ch. i. 14. Here, with *dignity* (εὐπρέπεια), it should be "the royal *robe*," cp. Ps. xciii. 1 LXX. (εὐπρ. ἐνεδύσατο) and Bar. v. 1, where the comeliness [dignity] of the glory of God is to be put on in place of the robe of mourning.
diadem of beauty] The idea is borrowed from Is. lxii. 3 "A crown of beauty, and a diadem of royalty in the hand of thy God." The *diadem* was a "band of purple silk sown with pearls, the symbol of oriental royalty" (Farrar). The conception is purely figurative, and is explained in the following lines.
cover them] Cp. ch. xix. 8; Is. xlix. 2, li. 16.
shield them] The Greek word means *to champion*, to throw one's shield over another, cp. Zech. ix. 15; 3 Macc. vii. 6. Farrar quotes Browning, *Instans Tyrannus*, vii. :

> ..."From marge to blue marge
> The whole sky grew his targe
> With the sun's self for visible boss,
> While an Arm ran across
> Which the earth heaved beneath like a breast
> Where the wretch was safe prest!"

17. The defence of the righteous brings the writer to the punishment of the wicked, a theme which he seems able to handle only in terms of the concrete, and which gives free scope to the fierce Hebrew vindictiveness which all his philosophy could not tame. This vivid and eloquent passage is based on Is. lix. 16—18 (cp. Ps. vii. 11—13), and is intended to suggest wonder and terror, rather than any definite scheme of final judgment. The only means that the prophets found effective for arousing worldly men to spiritual realities was to picture the world they knew overwhelmed by physical catastrophes ; they were compelled to speak in the only language that their hearers could understand. Cp. the connection between the phenomena prophesied in Joel ii. 30, 31 and the Day of Pentecost, Acts ii.
jealousy as complete armour] For *jealousy* (ζῆλος) see Is. xlii. 13; it is the jealousy of love that is provoked by the oppression of the loved one.

And shall make the *whole* creation his weapons [1]for vengeance on *his* enemies:

18 He shall put on righteousness as a breastplate,
And shall array himself with judgement unfeigned as with a
helmet;

19 He shall take holiness as an invincible shield,

20 And he shall sharpen stern wrath for a sword:

[1] Or, *to repel* his *enemies*

The full soldier's equipment consisted of helmet, breast-plate, sword,
shield, greaves, and lance.   For the connection of Eph. vi. 13—17 with
this passage, see Introd. § 17. A similar passage occurs in Ign. *Polyc.* § 6.
make the whole *creation his weapons*]   This is a favourite thought of
the writer's. See *v.* 20 and ch. xvi. 17, 24; xix. 6. Cp. Judg. v. 20
"The stars in their courses fought against Sisera," and Ecclus. xxxix. 29.
Philo, *Moses* i. 17, of the plagues of Egypt, writes "God determined
that the land of the wicked should be devastated with the four elements
of which the world is composed; for He fashions the same things in
health-giving ways, and turns them when He wills to the destruction of
the wicked."
for vengeance on his *enemies*]   Mg. *to repel* his *enemies*, cp. xi. 3.
The alternative rendering is perhaps better, as the idea of vengeance
does not for certain belong to the passage.
    18.   *shall put on righteousness*]   Cp. Job xxix. 14; Is. xi. 5.   There
are two similar metaphors relating to moral qualities in 1 Pet. iv. 1
"Arm yourselves with the same mind," and 1 Pet. v. 5.
    with judgement unfeigned as with a helmet]   κρίσις ἀνυπόκριτος
presents the same kind of verbal oxymoron as 2 Cor. vii. 10 μετάνοια
ἀμεταμέλητος.   The meaning is "judgement without respect of persons."
Unfeigned occurs in ch. xviii. 16; Rom. xii. 9; 1 Tim. i. 5.   There
does not seem to be any definite connection between the symbol and
the thing symbolized; the breast-plate and the helmet, armour of
defence, represent righteousness and judgement, both of which are
capable of offensive action.
    19.   *holiness as an invincible shield*]   "That holiness of God against
which all reproaches and opposition are hurled in vain" (Farrar).
ὅσιος in O.T. is almost exclusively used of piety *towards God*, but it is
used of God Himself in Ps. cxlv. 17 and Deut. xxxii. 4.   The shield,
which in Eph. vi. symbolizes unassailable faith, stands here for the
impregnableness of the pure life.
    20.   *And he shall sharpen*]   *And* (δὲ) introduces the weapons of
offence.   Cp. Ez. xxi. 9 for a like simile.
    stern wrath for a sword]   The word for "stern" (ἀπότομος) is used
five times in this book, meaning "stern to inexorableness."   Here there
is a word-play between it and *sword*, which suggests that the passive
ἀπότομον (abscisus) should have almost an active value (i.e. scathing).

And the world shall go forth with him to fight against *his*
insensate *foes.*
Shafts of lightning shall fly with true aim,   21
And from the clouds, as from a well drawn bow, shall they
leap to the mark.
And *as* from an engine of war shall be hurled hailstones 22
full of wrath;
The water of the sea shall be angered against them,

shall go forth with him to fight] Cp. *v.* 17 and ch. xi. 15—20. A
further illustration of a fact repeatedly noticed in this book that all
God's good things may be turned into agents of punishment. For
the Gk. verb, cp. Rev. vi. 8.

against his *insensate* foes] A stronger word (παράφρονες) than that
used hitherto (ἄφρονες), meaning *perverse, distraught.* This line marks
a transition. Not only will God arm Himself with His own virtues, but
His created world shall take up arms for Him, the lightning, the clouds,
the hail, the waters. *vv.* 21, 22 are based upon Hab. iii., which
suggests this line also.

21. *Shafts of lightning shall fly*] From Hab. iii. 11 εἰς φῶς
βολίδες σου πορεύσονται, "Thy shafts shall go forth as light." For
shafts of lightning, cp. Zech. ix. 14, and for the picture (sword, bow,
shafts in God's hand) cp. Ps. vii. 12, 13. "Shafts of lightning,"
gen. of apposition, i.e. shafts which are lightning.

from the clouds, as from a well drawn bow] So A.V., but Vulgate
has *a bene curuato arcu nubium,* and Farrar writes "the figure is more
startling and more in accordance with the writer's style if we render
'from the well-drawn bow of the clouds.'" For God's bow, cp.
Zech. ix. 13; Hab. iii. 9. But does not the writer mean more than
this? Does he not mean that the rainbow, previously set in the clouds
as a token of Divine mercy (Gen. ix. 14) and always turned away from
the earth, shall now become an engine of wrath and be seen pointed
against the earth? If so, the picture is still more startling.

shall they leap] Grimm notes that *leap* is used of an arrow as early
as in Hom. *Il.* iv. 125.

22. For this verse cp. Is. xxviii. 2; Ez. xxxviii. 22.

as from an engine of war] The πετροβόλος was a siege-engine
used for hurling stones, differing from the catapult, which was a large
cross-bow. The Vulgate mistakenly treats it as an adjective, and
taking θυμοῦ with it translates *a petrosa ira.* Farrar is somewhat
misled by this rendering, and forgets that πετρ. is found as a subst. in
Job xli. 19, and that *full of wrath* is a phrase found in ch. xi. 18 and
Is. li. 20.

hailstones full of wrath] The elements are made to share the anger
of God who wields them. Deane compares Jos. x. 11; Rev. viii. 7.
He sees here a reference back to the Egyptian plague, Ex. ix. 23—25.

The water of the sea] Cp. Ps. xviii. 15; the whole Psalm is some-

And rivers shall sternly overwhelm them ;
23 A mighty blast shall encounter them,
And as a tempest shall it winnow them away :
And *so* shall lawlessness make all the land desolate,

what similar in tone to this passage. Grimm sees here a possible
allusion to Pharaoh and his host at the Red Sea.

rivers shall sternly overwhelm them] For the word-play in the Greek,
see Introd. p. xvi., note 3. God's wrath is compared to an angry river,
Is. lix. 19 LXX. The combination *rivers shall overwhelm* occurs in
two other places, Song viii. 7 ; Is. xliii. 2 LXX.

23. *A mighty blast shall encounter them*] Vulg. *spiritus uirtutis.*
It is best to translate as in the text, since "the spirit of His power"
would require the pron. αὐτοῦ, cp. ch. xi. 20. ἀνὴρ δυνάμεως, υἱὸς δυν.
are common in LXX.

as a tempest shall it winnow them] Cp. Is. xli. 16. Cp. again
ch. xi. 20, the idea in which corresponds to that here. The winnowing
out may be meant to suggest nothing more than the action of a high
wind ; or some catastrophe may be indicated such as in Is. xxxvii. 36.

And so] καὶ very rightly rendered as in the text. The two last lines
of the chapter stand altogether apart in sense and style from those
preceding. They clinch with a somewhat obvious aphorism all the
eloquent denunciation that has gone before, and bring the reader back
with some suddenness from cosmic and timeless flights to concrete
moralisings. They serve the purpose, however, of a connecting-link
between the three comparisons which have occupied chs. ii.—v. and
ch. vi. 1—11, which is a reaffirmation of ch. i., more directly and forcibly
pointed in view of the considerations brought forward.

make all the land desolate] In vv. 17—23 God's wrath has been seen
in operation, and yet when all is summed up the ultimate cause is not
God's wrath, but man's lawlessness. Cp. ch. i. 12, 13 "God made not
death : draw not upon yourselves destruction." This truth is recognised
to-day. "A large part of the physical evil in the world is simply the
result of moral evil, and therefore to be regarded as part of the human
foreground, not the divine background of the picture which the world
presents" (J. R. Illingworth, *Christian Character*, p. 135) ; cp.
Is. xiii. 9. The significance of "all the land" must not be pressed :
the words merely carry on the imagery of vv. 21, 22, and are equally
in place whether the whole picture tells of earthly retribution or of a
final Judgement.

overturn the thrones of princes] Cp. Job xii. 18, 19, 21 LXX. The
writer passes from the general to the particular, from the land to its
rulers, and so prepares the way for beginning ch. vi. with an address to
rulers and kings similar to that with which he began ch. i.

PART I. B.

Chs. vi.—ix. incl. form the core of the book : here its Sapiential and
professedly Solomonic character are clearly seen. Solomon sets forth

And their evil-doing shall overturn the thrones of princes.

Hear therefore, ye kings, and understand;   6
Learn, ye judges of the ends of the earth:
Give ear, ye that have dominion over much people,   2
And make your boast ¹in multitudes of nations.
Because your dominion was given you from the Lord,   3
And your sovereignty from the Most High;
Who shall search out your works,
And shall make inquisition of your counsels:
Because being officers of his kingdom ye did not judge aright, 4

¹ Or, *in the multitudes of your nations*

the essential nature of Wisdom and acknowledges his complete dependence upon her. This portion opens (vi. 1—11) with an appeal to the
great men of the earth to recognise their responsibility for the power
they have received; and closes (ix.) with a prayer by him for the gift of
the Heavenly Wisdom. In chs. i.—v. there was no allusion, direct or
indirect, to the professed Solomonic origin of the book.

CH. VI. 1—11.   AN APPEAL TO RULERS TO LEARN WISDOM.

1. *Hear therefore, ye kings*] Solomon speaks with authority to his
peers, cp. *v.* 11. The book opened with a similar address: the inter-
vening digressions were rather abruptly closed by ch. v. 23 d, which
prepared the way for a return to the original subject.
Learn, ye judges] To judge was to rule, and therefore kings are still
in the writer's view. The *v.* is a reminiscence of Ps. ii. 10 "and now,
ye kings, understand" LXX.
the ends of the earth] *sc.* the earth in all its extent, cp. Ps. ii. 8,
xxii. 27. For the phrase, cp. 1 Sam. ii. 10.
Farrar writes "The long sufferings of the Jews under heathen
autocrats made them feel a special interest in ideal warnings to kings.
The writer could not really expect that his book would be read by
heathen rulers: his appeal to kings as his special auditors belongs only
to the rhetorical form of the book, and his assumption of the rôle
of Solomon."
3. *Because*] The reason why Solomon demands their attention.
your dominion...from the Lord] This derivation of sovereignty is
clearly taught in the Bible. Cp. 1 Chron. xxix. 12; Prov. viii. 15, 16;
Dan. v. 18; St John xix. 11. See also 4 Macc. xii. 11; Enoch xlvi. 5
"He will put down the kings from their thrones...because they do
not...acknowledge whence the kingdom was bestowed upon them";
Clem. Rom. *ad Cor.* lxi. 1.
shall search out] Cp. Ps. xi. 4, 5, and notes on ch. i. 6 b, 8, 9.
4. *Because*] The ground of the charge laid against them.

Neither kept ye ¹law, nor walked after the counsel of God.
5 Awfully and swiftly shall he come upon you ;
    Because a stern judgement befalleth them that be in high
        place :
6 For the man of low estate may be pardoned in mercy,

¹ Or, *the law*

being officers] Although merely administrators and stewards, they
had acted with the caprice of irresponsible despots.
judge aright] Cp. Ps. lxxxii. 2. They did more than give unfair
judgements : they debased the moral currency, falsified the weights and
gave evil the validity of good. The king's precedents have a terrible
cogency, almost divine because of his borrowed divinity.
Neither kept ye law] The law of right and wrong, cp. Rom. i. 19;
ii. 14, and Philo, *Abr.* § 1. The Divine Law is to some extent a
matter of intuition. "Those who will may without difficulty live
according to the prescribed laws, since the laws that the patriarchs
easily observed were unwritten, not one of them having been formu-
lated : in fact we ought to say that the laws are nothing else than the
chronicled lives of the men of old."
nor walked] For the phrase, cp. Ps. i. 1, "walketh not in the
counsel of the ungodly."
    5. *Awfully*] They shall experience the terror they (cp. ch. viii. 15,
dread princes) had inspired in others.
swiftly] Cp. Prov. i. 27. *Shall he come upon you*, cp. 1 Thess. v. 3.
Because...befalleth] *Because* gives the reason for the prec. line.
There is an eternal principle that most shall be required from those
who have received most. *Befalleth*, the present tense shows the application of a law of unfailing validity.
For " stern " (ἀπότομος), cp. ch. xi. 10. *In high place*, the Greek
word is the same as in Rom. xiii. 1; 1 Pet. ii. 13.
    6. The sense of this *v.* is plain, but the Greek is difficult. It is
impossible to translate συγγνωστὸς ἐλέους "for pity's sake," taking ἐλέους
(with Deane) as gen. of cause. The contemporary use of συγγνωστὸς
with the genitive may be seen in Philo, *Jos.* § 10 συγγ. τῆς ἄγαν
ἀπαιδευσίας, where the genitive is that of the thing in respect of which
pardon is given; but this is plainly not the use here. Vulg. reads
" exiguo conceditur *misericordia*," thus suggesting the translation " is
pardoned of mercy," i.e. receives the pardon which mercy gives. Cp.
the bold gen. in 1 Cor. ix. 21. An easy correction would be μετ'
ἐλέους (substituting μετ' for ἐστιν) ; μετ' ἐλέους is found in Is. liv. 7.
For God's simultaneous mercy and judgement, cp. Ecclus. xvi. 11, 12.
    The thought is not that the poor man is compensated for his low
estate by a corresponding laxity on God's part, but that necessity presses
on the humble with an insistence special to their case, cp. Prov. vi. 30,
for which the Judge makes allowance.

But mighty men shall be ¹searched out mightily.
For the Sovereign Lord of all will not refrain himself for 7
  any *man's* person,
Neither will he reverence greatness ;
Because it is he that made *both* small and great,
And alike he taketh thought for all ;
But ²strict is the scrutiny that cometh upon the powerful.   8
Unto you therefore, O princes, are my words,   9
That ye may learn wisdom and ³fall not from the right way.

¹ Gr. *put to the test.*   ² Gr. *strong.*   ³ Gr. *fall not aside.*

mighty men...mightily]   For the assonance, cp. Zech. xi. 2 ; Prov.
viii. 16 LXX.
searched out]   For the Gk. verb, cp. Gen. xii. 17 LXX.   Deane
adduces examples of great men being severely punished for apparently
light faults, e.g. Moses (Num. xx. 12); David (2 Sam. xxiv. 12);
Hezekiah (2 K. xx. 17).
7.   This *v.* contains a reminiscence of Dt. i. 17 ; cp. also Job xxxiv. 19
and Ps. lxxxii. 2.
the Sovereign Lord of all]   For the title, cp. ch. viii. 3 ; Job v. 8
LXX.   For *refrain himself*, cp. Dt. i. 17 ; Ex. xxiii. 21 LXX.
reverence greatness]   Cp. Is. xl. 15, 17.
small and great]   Cp. Dt. i. 17.   The Sovereign Judge observes the
rules He lays down for earthly judges.   He, who made the small as
truly as the great, will not pay heed to the great things He has made any
more than to the small.   Furthermore, they all depend on Him ; is He,
to whom even the greatest must look, likely to quail before any creature
of His hand?   Cp. Ps. l. 10—12 ; Prov. xxii. 2.
alike]   In God's sight there is no distinction between great and small,
important and unimportant : whatever is from Him is sacred for Him,
Rev. xi. 18.   For God's universal care, cp. Ps. civ. 27, cxlv. 9.   προνοεῖ,
" provideth," is used here (as in xiii. 16) without any reference to the
philosophical doctrine of Providence (Pythagoras, Plato, the Stoics), cp.
Dan. vi. 18 LXX.   There is a similar passage in Jubilees v. 15, 16.
8.   *strict is the scrutiny*]   A verbally varied expression of 6 b : the
strong shall feel the strength of the searching God, cp. St Mark xii. 40.
This re-affirmation of *vv.* 5, 6 gives the writer one more opportunity of
introducing an appeal to kings to obey Wisdom.
9.   Cp. the call of Wisdom in Prov. viii. 4.
O princes]   τύραννοι in LXX. means simply *kings.*   For their dependence on Wisdom, cp. Prov. viii. 15, 16.
my words]   Solomon is the speaker.
fall not from the right way]   as in *v.* 4, by unjust judgements and
personal lawlessness.   The Gk. vb., παραπίπτειν, implies deviation
from the ordained path, cp. Ps. ii. 12.

10 For they that have kept holily the things that are holy
    shall *themselves* be [1]hallowed;
    And they that have been taught them shall find what to
    answer;
11 Set your desire therefore on my words;
    Long for *them*, and ye shall be [2]trained by *their* discipline.

12 Wisdom is radiant and fadeth not away;
    And easily is she beheld of them that love her,

<hr>

[1] Or, *accounted holy*   [2] Gr. *disciplined.*

<hr>

10. *shall* themselves *be hallowed*] Nothing will satisfy the divine
requirements save character, but character will stand where mere rank
counts for nothing. The rule is exemplified that men become like the
things they contemplate: "those who have observed the eternal
sanctities shall be sanctified."

they that have been taught them] To have kept the sanctities with
pious intention (ὁσίως) results in *having been taught them*, a state
implying not merely an intellectual acquaintance, but a vital inner
correspondence. The king's truest defence when on his trial is the man
that he has become.

11. *on my words*] Cp. the invitations of Wisdom in Prov. iv.
10, 20, v. I.

Long for them, *and ye shall be trained*] The same sequence appears
in Prov. iv. 6 "Love [Wisdom], and she shall keep thee." Ye shall
learn true wisdom, which is the daily practice of virtue (Deane).

CH. VI. 12—16. THE ACCESSIBILITY OF WISDOM: SHE
LOVES THOSE THAT LOVE HER.

12. Wisdom, the semi-personal being, is here spoken of, and not the
abstract quality of wiseness. See Introd. § 9. The praise of Wisdom
occupies the following chapters, and begins here with a tribute to her
luminosity and the imperishableness of her nature.

radiant] Cp. Philo, *Alleg.* iii. 59, "What could be more radiant or
more conspicuous than the Divine Logos?" The source of the radiance
of Wisdom is given in ch. vii. 25, 26.

fadeth not away] As righteousness is immortal, so is Wisdom. They
belong to the kingdom of God, two characteristics of which are light
and life. For the word, cp. 1 Pet. i. 4.

easily is she beheld] The law of affinity dominates this and the
succeeding *vv.* Virtue is to men as they are to her: they can only see
what they bring. Cp. Prov. iii. 15 "She is easily discerned by them
that draw near to her" LXX., and viii. 21; Ecclus. vi. 22 "not unto
many is she manifest," and xxvii. 8. The thought appears repeatedly
in St John's Gospel, x. 3, 14, xiv. 21, xviii. 37. Cp. St Matt. v. 8.

And found of them that seek her.

She forestalleth them that desire *to know her*, making herself 13
first known.

He that riseth up early to *seek* her shall have no toil,   14
For he shall find her sitting at his gates.

For to think upon her is perfectness of understanding,   15
And he that watcheth for her sake shall quickly be free
from care.

Because she goeth about, herself seeking them that are 16
worthy of her,

And found of them that seek her] There is overwhelming MS.
authority (B marg. ℵA) for the insertion of this *l.* which is a variant
of Prov. viii. 17 b. Cp. Ecclus. vi. 27 "seek and she shall be made
known unto thee."

13. *forestalleth*] Wisdom is ever making advances. She cannot
enter into men without their invitation, but she is ever seeking to dispose
them to welcome her. Cp. Is. lxv. 2, 24. Cp. Philo, *Cong.* § 22, of
knowledge, "she goeth out, putting envy away from her, and draweth
unto her them that are well disposed"; id. *Fuga* § 25 "God goeth out to
meet them, and showeth Himself unto them that desire to see Him."
For the Gk. verb with infin., cp. ch. iv. 7.

14. *riseth up early*] The verb occurs commonly in LXX. both in its
literal and metaphorical significance, cp. Ps. cxxvii. 2; Ecclus. iv. 12;
vi. 36.

sitting at his gates] For πάρεδρος (lit. *assessor*), cp. ch. ix. 4, and
Prov. i. 21, viii. 3. The man who rises early to seek for Wisdom will
find his task easy. Wisdom was seeking for him, and waiting for him
as he left his house.

15. *to think upon her...understanding*] Understanding (φρόνησις) is
not identical with Wisdom, as in iii. 15, iv. 9, nor is it one of the four
cardinal virtues mentioned in viii. 7 as one of the activities of Wisdom.
It is rather a moral than an intellectual quality, being the "insight into
the relations of life, and the power to turn circumstances to its own
profit" (Grimm). Through the contemplation of Wisdom, a man
perfects that moral understanding which enables him to make the most
of life, in the highest sense.

watcheth for her sake] Cp. Prov. viii. 34. *watcheth* in its old sense
of *waketh*, and so, metaphorically, of *vigilance*. There is a reminiscence
in this *v.* of Ps. cxxvii. 1, 2, where also *rise up early*, *labour*, *wake* occur.

free from care] Like Wisdom herself (vii. 23). Eus. (*Praep. Ev.*
667 b) records a saying of the Alexandrian Peripatetic, Aristobulus
(c. 150 B.C.). "They that follow Wisdom consistently shall be free
from trouble (ἀτάραχοι) all their lives." For *care*, cp. St. Matt. xiii. 22.

16. *she goeth about,...seeking*] Cp. ch. viii. 18; Acts xiii. 11.

them that are worthy of her] *worthy* is one of the characteristic words

And in their paths she appeareth unto them graciously,
And in every purpose she meeteth them.

of this Book, cp. ch. i. 16, xviii. 4.   Each human being determines his
own destiny.   He goes through the world finding that which belongs to
him, and never getting what he does not deserve.   "Our stars are in
ourselves."   Cp. Ecclus. xiii. 15, 16.   Philo elaborates this doctrine
in *Somn.* ii. §§ 5, 6 "Every man lays hold of his own"; cp. id. *Migr.*
§§ 10, 11 "God draws near to give help to those who are worthy to
be helped.   And who are they who are worthy to be so blessed?
Clearly all who love wisdom and knowledge."

in their paths]   Cp. Prov. viii. 2.   Deane thinks that this *l.* refers to
the experiences of outer life, while the next *l.* points to the inner life of
thought and purpose.   Cp. Philo, *Somn.* i. § 19 "The Logos that waits
upon the seeking soul anticipates it with welcomes when it despairs of
itself and awaits his invisible approach."

in every purpose]   Vulg. by its translation *in omni prouidentia*
assigns the words to Wisdom, but the balance of the lines is best
preserved by making *purpose* refer to human purpose.

she meeteth them]   Cp. Philo, *Alleg.* iii. § 76 "Some souls God goes
out to meet.   What grace it is that He should anticipate our slowness
and lead our soul forth into perfect well-doing!"   With *meeteth*, cp.
Prov. xxiv. 8 "death meeteth the simple" LXX.   Only they can meet
who belong to one another : for such, meeting is inevitable, cp.
Amos iii. 3.

CH. VI. 17—21.   WISDOM IS THE TRUEST TEACHER OF KINGSHIP.

vv. 17—20 contain a famous example of the logical figure, Sorites.
Sorites is a cumulative series of syllogisms, in which the conclusion of
each becomes the premiss of the next, until the main conclusion is
reached.   It is essential to the validity of the figure that each new
premiss should be identical with the preceding conclusion : in this
example however there is an apparent violation of the rule, since the
writer with his habitual desire to avoid wearisome repetitions varies the
wording of the premiss from its form as conclusion.   The variation however is purely verbal.   The series is :—

[Desire for Wisdom is] the beginning of Wisdom.
The beginning of Wisdom is care for discipline.
Care for discipline is love of her.
Love of her is the keeping of her laws.
The keeping of her laws is incorruption.
Incorruption brings near to God.
To be near to God is [to be a king].
Conclusion.   Desire for wisdom makes men kings.

The nearest approach to Sorites in the Bible seems to be Hos. ii.
21—23; Rom. iv. 3—5, x. 13—15 ; 2 Pet. i. 5—7.

For ¹her ²true beginning is desire of discipline;   17
And the care for discipline is love *of her*;
And love *of her* is observance of her laws;   18
And to give heed to *her* laws confirmeth incorruption;
And incorruption ³bringeth near unto God;   19
So then desire of wisdom promoteth to a kingdom.   20

> ¹ Or, *her beginning is the true desire*   ² Gr. *truest.*
> ³ Gr. *maketh to be near.*

17. *true beginning*] Cp. Ps. cxi. 10; Prov. i. 7, ix. 10. The requirements of the Sorites decide that *true* goes with *beginning*. For *discipline*, cp. Clem. Rom. § 56, which deals with the blessings which flow from the Divine discipline.

care] *Care* is merely a verbal variant for *desire*. The virile moral sense which welcomes correction answers, in the spiritual sphere, to the passion for Wisdom.

18. *observance of her laws*] This seems to be based on Ex. xx. 6: cp. Ecclus. ii. 15 "They that love [the Lord] will keep his ways," cp. id. vi. 26. The idea is reproduced in St John xiv. 15 "If ye love me ye will keep my commandments," and *vv.* 21, 24 and 1 John v. 3.

to give heed to her *laws*] *To give heed* is a poetic variation for *observance*. For the idea, cp. St Matt. xix. 17; St John viii. 12. Philo, *Cong.* § 16 "He lives the true life who walks in the...commandment of God, so that the practices of the ungodly would be death." Those who would have the assurance of incorruption must rest not on feeling which is often either absent or deceptive, but on the solid ground of moral fact. The validity of this argument is admitted in 1 John i. 9 and iii. 14, in both of which cases it is employed.

19. *incorruption bringeth near unto God*] The word ἀφθαρσία is used of moral incorruption. The argument of the preceding line is not that obedience to Wisdom confers incorruption, but that it gives assurance of its possession, showing the obedient to which Kingdom they belong, that of righteousness and the living God, as distinguished from that of sin and Hades. The Book of Wisdom postulates that men are born for life, and that only wilful sin brings them into the power of death. Similarly, in this line *incorruption* makes men near to God, not by making them what they were not by birth, but by realising itself naturally in them. Cp. Philo, *Fuga* § 11 "This is the glorious goal of a deathless life, to be held in a bodiless, fleshless passion and love for God."

One step in the Sorites must be understood, viz. *to be near God is to be a king*. Spiritual kingship involves such lordship over outward things as liberates the spirit permanently from the passions of fear, desire, regret, pride, which outward things arouse in hearts that are in subjection to them.

20. *So then*] The main conclusion of the Sorites is the premiss of the first syllogism combined with the conclusion of the last. The

21 If therefore ye delight in thrones and sceptres, ye princes of
    peoples,
   Honour wisdom, that ye may reign for ever.
22 But what wisdom is, and how she came into being, I will
    declare,
   And I will not hide mysteries from you;

kingship here in question is spiritual. Cp. Eccl. iv. 13, 14, and Philo,
Agr. § 10 "Moses gives the name of shepherd to the wise, who alone
are really kings," and *Post. C.* § 41 "The wise man is alone free and a
ruler, though his body may acknowledge a thousand lords." Cp. Zeno,
in Diog. La. ii. 7, 122 "The wise are not only free, but kings; their
kingship is an irresponsible rule, which could stand in no other case
than in that of the wise."

promoteth] Wisdom is called the path to God in Philo, *Quod D.*
§§ 30, 34.

21. *If therefore ye delight*] Solomon argues, "You love your external
kingship with its symbols of authority : honour Wisdom then, and you
shall enter upon a higher kingship." Ps.-Solomon is not urging the
cult of Wisdom, in order that kings may find their power consolidated,
but that they may covet a different class of power.

Honour wisdom] Cp. Prov. viii. 15, 16, and Philo, *All.* iii. § 58
"This is the Divine law, to honour virtue for her own sake."

for ever] With a moral rather than a temporal significance. Cp.
"way everlasting," Ps. cxxxix. 24.

CH. VI. 22—25. SOLOMON WILL UNFOLD TO HIS READERS
THE WHOLE TRUTH CONCERNING WISDOM.

It is uncertain what is the range of the writer's undertaking. Is he
pledging himself to a revelation of the nature and origin of Wisdom
absolutely, or is he concerned merely to show how Wisdom has
manifested herself in connection with him?

The promise of these verses sounds unconditional, but the perform-
ance is very limited. The difficulty has been widely felt, and variously
explained. Considering how little is said about the origin of Wisdom
(nothing except in ch. vii. 25, 26), attention being fixed upon the
secondary effects of her dealings with man; and seeing that Solomon
is occupied throughout chs. vii.—ix. with his own experiences and his
personal petitions, it is not impossible that *vv.* 22—25 contain a promise
by Solomon to disclose what Wisdom has been *for him*. But more
probably, ch. vii. 22—27 is a sufficient fulfilment of the undertaking of
v. 22 a.

22. *what wisdom is*] See vii. 22—27.

how she came into being] Vulg. *quomodo facta est.* Ewald would
understand μοι, *how she began for me*, thus accounting for the personal
history of vii.—ix. But see ch. vii. 25 ; cp. Prov. viii. 24.

mysteries] *sc.* the mysteries of Wisdom, cp. "the mysteries of God,"

But I will trace *her* out ¹from the beginning of creation,
And bring the knowledge of her into clear light,
And I will not pass by the truth;
Neither indeed will I take ²pining envy for my companion 23
    in the way,
Because ³envy shall have no fellowship with wisdom.
But a multitude of wise men is salvation to the world,   24
And an understanding king is tranquillity to *his* people.

¹ Or, *from her first beginning*   ² Gr. *wasted*.   ³ Gr. *this*.

ii. 22. The *mysteries* of Wisdom mean all the knowledge of her that
may be communicated to her initiated votaries (vii. 22—27); all the
teachings she possesses and imparts (vii. 17—22); all the blessings
including immortality which she mediates.

from the beginning of creation] See ch. x. for the operations of
Wisdom from the dawn of human history.

the knowledge of her] Cp. ch. viii.

23. *take...for my companion*] Note the assonance between συνοδεύσω
and παροδεύσω in *v.* 22.

pining envy] *Envy* (or *grudgingness*) is here personified, and is
depicted as suffering from the wasting complaint which attacks the
envious man. Solomon will not associate himself with the niggardly
spirit which withholds knowledge to the detriment of the hearer. In
this and the prec. *v.* there is a reference to the sophists, or paid
teachers who had recourse to obscurantism in order to safeguard their
prospective profits. For the practice of the sophists, cp. Philo, *Post. C.*
§ 44 "The sophists under the influence of greed and envy stunt the
natures of their pupils by keeping back much of what they ought to tell
them, and refusing to surrender their prospects of future gain: but
virtue is generous and open-handed, and would use every faculty she
possesses to give help."

envy shall have no fellowship with wisdom] Solomon is the companion of Wisdom : her nature is so opposed to greed, that if he would
continue with her, he must be free from even the suspicion of it. This
v. makes the nearest approach to a personal touch, the author, elsewhere veiled effectually behind the person of Solomon, stepping forward
to defend himself against charges such as those of Philo.

24. The writer has the public welfare at heart, and accordingly
refuses to regard himself as holding any private monopoly of truth.
If the world is better in proportion to the number of its wise men, and
a wise king is the security of his people, he will impart his knowledge
as widely as possible.

salvation to the world] A familiar idea with Philo, cp. *Sacr.* § 37
"the wise man is the ransom of the foolish"; id. *Migr.* § 21 "the
righteous man is the prop of the human race." Cp. St Matt. v. 13, 14.

tranquillity] Cp. Prov. xxix. 4 ; Ecclus. x. 2, 3. The Gk. word is

25 Wherefore be disciplined by my words, and *thereby* shall ye profit.

7 I myself also am [1]mortal, like to all,
And am sprung from one born of the earth, *the man* first formed,
2 And in the womb of a mother was I moulded into flesh in the time of ten months,

[1] Many authorities read *a mortal man*.

commonly used of stable conditions of government, cp. 2 Macc. xiv. 6; Clem. Rom. lxi. 1.   Grimm quotes Plato's dictum (*Rep.* v. 473) that philosophers should be kings and kings philosophers.

25. *be disciplined*]   Cp. *vv.* 9, 11.   The final appeal in what is practically the introduction to the central division of the book.

CH. VII. 1—6. SOLOMON, THE PROVERBIALLY WISE MAN, MIGHT HAVE BEEN THOUGHT TO HAVE BEEN SPECIALLY DISPOSED BY NATURE TOWARDS WISDOM. BUT HE WAS OF COMMON FLESH AND BLOOD. HE WAS THUS RICHLY ENDOWED ONLY BECAUSE HE PRAYED FOR WISDOM.

1. Solomon encourages his hearers by the thought that he started from precisely the same point as they do. He shows firstly that his place in the scale of creation was identical with theirs, and secondly that the circumstances attending his birth were completely normal.

mortal]   If marg. *a mortal man* (following B^ab and A) is right, Solomon declares himself to be (1) mortal, (2) man, (3) like to all, (4) child of Adam. It is interesting to note the contrast between the insistence upon Solomon's human origin and normal birth, and the teaching of the Gospels concerning the Divine origin yet normal birth of Jesus Christ.

sprung from...the man first formed]   The term *protoplast* (found also in ch. x. 1) seems to have been coined by the writer from Gen. ii. 7, "the Lord God formed...(ἔπλασεν)," and was used of Adam and Eve by Irenaeus and Clem. Alex., cp. 1 Tim. ii. 13.

born of the earth]   Adam is called "the first man, the earth-born" in Philo, *Opif.* § 47.

2. *in the womb...was I moulded*]   Cp. Ps. cxxxix. 15; Eccl. xi. 5. Solomon was *flesh*, i.e. material rather than sinful. See Davidson, *Theol. of O.T.* pp. 191, 192. The man is here identified with his body, which when formed in the womb, received the "loan" (ch. xv. 8) of an already existing soul.

in the time of ten months]   i.e. lunar months. Cp. Verg. *Ecl.* iv. 61 "Matri longa decem tulerant fastidia menses," and 4 Macc. xvi. 7, though in 2 Macc. vii. 27 the period is the more usual one of nine months. Nine calendar months are about equal to ten lunar months.

Being compacted in blood of the seed of man and pleasure
that came with sleep.
And I also, when I was born, drew in the common air, 3
And fell upon the ¹kindred earth,
Uttering, like all, for my first voice, the selfsame wail:
In swaddling clothes was I nursed, and ²with *watchful* cares. 4
For no king had any other first beginning; 5
But all men have one entrance into life, and a like de- 6
parture.

¹ Gr. of like qualities.   ² Gr. in.

in blood] Cp. Job x. 10, 11; 4 Macc. xiii. 19, and St John i. 13
"born, not of blood." The blood stands for all the material substance
contributed by the mother to the growth of the embryo.

3. *when...born*] The circumstances of his first moments were completely normal. *born* covers only *v.* 3, i.e. not in infancy and youth,
but first experiences only. Issuing from the womb, he drank in every
man's air, he "fell" upon every man's earth, he uttered every man's
panting cry.

fell upon] Cp. Is. xxvi. 18 (G. A. Smith in *Exp. Bible*) "neither
have inhabitants of the world been born" R.V. marg. (have fallen,
R.V. text).

the kindred earth] If *kindred* is right, Solomon means that Earth
was his mother no less than of others, and that he was only common
clay. But the sense of the prec. and succeeding clauses requires that
ὁμοιοπαθής should mean something like "that suffers the same thing
at the hands of all her children." The point of the adjective is not
to show that Solomon and the earth were related, but Solomon and
other men. ὁμ. occurs twice in N.T. Acts xiv. 15; James v. 17,
meaning "of like passions": the word is used here in a very strained
sense. Grimm's suggestion that it means "aequa tellus" (Hor. *Od.* ii. 18)
will not do, as the word must have a passive significance. "Impartial"
would require a different compound of ὅμοιος.

Uttering, like all,] Text reads with B, πᾶσιν ἴσα κλαίων. For ἴσα, cp.
Phil. ii. 6.

Farrar quotes Sir Wm Jones (from the Persian):

"On mother's knee, a naked new-born child
Sad thou didst weep, while all around thee smiled."

4. Note the quaint collocation of swaddling-clothes and cares.
Solomon in his infant years experienced the ordinary homely needs (cp.
St Luke ii. 7). The touch of humour recalls the famous speech of the
nurse in the *Choephori* of Aeschylus. Cp. 4 Macc. xvi. 8.

5. *no king*] i.e. no man however great.

first beginning] Vulg. *natiuitatis initium*, cp. ch. vi. 22, lit. "beginning of birth." There is a reference to *v.* 2.

6. *a like departure*] Cp. Eccl. ix. 3.

7 For this cause I prayed, and understanding was given me :
   I called upon *God*, and there came to me a spirit of wisdom.
8 I preferred her before sceptres and thrones,
   And riches I esteemed nothing in comparison of her.
9 Neither did I liken to her any priceless gem,
   Because all the gold *of the earth* in her presence is a little
      sand,
   And silver shall be accounted as clay before her.
10 Above health and comeliness I loved her,
   And I chose to have her rather than light,

CH. VII. **7—14.** SOLOMON'S ESTIMATE OF WISDOM.

7. Having no natural advantage over other men, he took the course
open to all alike, and prayed, see ch. viii. 21, and ix. Cp. James i. 5.

understanding] See 1 Kings iii. 11, 12. The Gk. word (φρόνησις)
is here merely a poetical variant for wisdom, cp. 1 Kings iv. 29: the
parallelism of the clauses does not contrast the ideas but repeats them.
Was given, came to me show how completely Solomon depended on
inspiration for his wisdom. *Was given*, cp. ch. viii. 21.

called upon God] For the Gk. verb without object expressed, cp.
Acts vii. 59.

spirit of wisdom] Cp. Ex. xxxi. 3; Lk. xi. 13; Eph. i. 17. Rightly
"*a* spirit of w.," wisdom being the subjective wisdom, answering to
understanding in prec. *l.*

8. *sceptres*] Solomon contrasts himself with the kings of ch. vi. 21.
Wisdom will brook no rivals: she must be placed first.

riches] Cp. 1 Kings iii. 11. See also Job xxviii. 15—19; Prov.
iii. 14, 15, viii. 10, 11; Ps. xix. 10, cxix. 72, 127.

9. *priceless gem*] lit. *unpriced*, 3 Macc. iii. 23; cp. Prov. iii. 15,
viii. 11. Farrar quotes *Richard III.* i. 2.

    "I thought I saw a thousand fearful wrecks,
       Inestimable stones, unvalued jewels."

all the gold of the earth] Cp. Philo, *Cong.* § 20 "Every deed wrought
according to wisdom is more precious than gold."

in her presence] ἐν ὄψει αὐτῆς, cp. ch. iii. 4, xv. 19. Vulgate has
in comparatione, not quite accurately.

silver...as clay] The comparison recalls the depreciation in the value
of silver in Solomon's reign, 1 Kings x. 21; 2 Chron. i. 15.

10. *Above health and comeliness*] I would rather be wise than well.
The sentiment has a flavour of asceticism hardly true in the mouth
of the real Solomon. On the importance attached to health, see Ecclus.
xxx. 15 "Health and a good constitution are better than all gold, and
a strong body than wealth without measure. There is no riches better
than health of body."

I chose] The Gk. verb is the classical word for deliberate moral
choice.

Because her bright shining is never laid to sleep.
But with her there came to me all good things together,   11
And in her hands innumerable riches :
And I rejoiced over *them* all because wisdom leadeth them; 12
Though I knew not that she was the ¹mother of them.
As I learned without guile, I impart without grudging ;   13
I do not hide her riches.

¹ Some authorities read first origin.

rather than light] Again an exaggerated profession, if literally
taken. The next *l.*, however, shows the meaning to be that he could
find nothing so stable and unvarying as Wisdom, not even the light of
day.

never laid to sleep] Cp. *vv.* 29, 30. There is no night that alternates
with Wisdom, as with the day. Wisdom needs no sleep as does the
wearied sun. Philo, *Migr.* § 8 "Wisdom is the archetypal light of God,
whose image and copy is the sun." φῶς in 10 b is the light-source,
contrasted with φέγγος in 10 c, the light-rays.

11. *with her there came*] Prov. viii. 21, x. 22. For the historical
reference, cp. 2 Chron. i. 12 ; Ecclus. xlvii. 18.

in her hands...riches] Cp. Prov. iii. 16.

12. What he sacrificed for Wisdom's sake, he received back with joy
in Wisdom's name. He loved what she brought him, and he had her
to direct him in the use of it. The ideal Solomon is seen here, but the
real appears in Ecclus. xlvii. 19, 20.

Though I knew not] i.e. when he prayed. There was no ulterior
motive in his cry for Wisdom : his sole desire was for spiritual benefits.

the mother of them] Text reads with A γενέτιν, while אB have
γένεσιν, as marg. *first origin*. The original may even have been the
masc. form γενέτην, which was changed by some over-sensitive scribe.
For Philo (*Fuga* § 9) has "Let us not pay too much heed to words, but
say that wisdom, the daughter of God, is male and a father, begetting
in souls learning, education, fair deeds." If γενέτιν ("mother") is read,
cp. Philo, *Ebr.* § 8, where Wisdom is called the bride of God, and
spiritual mother of all things, and of God's first-born son, the world.
Wisdom comes to Solomon, leading (ἡγεῖται) her children-blessings,
and giving them their value by letting them accompany her train.

13. *learned*] *learned* is in direct contrast with *knew not*, v. 12.
What he learnt was what he had been ignorant of, viz. that Wisdom
was the All-mother. *Without guile*. What he attained in this way, he
will count no robber's prize, but will transmit without grudging. He
will not exploit his spiritual privileges.

without grudging] Cp. ch. vi. 23, and 1 Pet. iv. 10. Philo (*Gig.* § 9)
writes "Is not their disgrace obvious, who call themselves wise, and
yet barter wisdom, like auctioneers in the market?"

do not hide] Cp. ch. vi. 22, and Ps. xl. 9, 10.

5—2

14 For she is unto men a treasure that faileth not,
   And they that use it ¹obtain friendship with God,
   Commended *to him* ²by the gifts which they through disci-
   pline present *to him.*

15 But to me may God give to speak ³with judgement,

¹ Gr. *prepare for themselves.*   ² Gr. *for the sake of the presents that
come of discipline.*   ³ Or, *according to* his *mind* Or, *according to*
my *mind*

14. Wisdom belongs to the spiritual sphere, and can purchase for
men the friendship of God, by the results she enables them to achieve.
There is a singular likeness of tone and language between this passage
and St Luke xvi. 9.
   that faileth not] Cp. St Luke xii. 33 ἀνέκλειπτον.
   they that use it] For the unusual acc. with χρῆσθαι, cp. 1 Cor. vii. 31,
and for the sense, cp. 1 Tim. iii. 13.
   obtain friendship] The Gk. verb (gnomic aor.) is a colourless word,
cp. ch. xiv. 1.   For friendship with God, see *v.* 27; Is. xli. 8; James
ii. 23.   Philo (*Abr.* § 46) has "God, loving a man for his faith in Him,
gives him a pledge in return, confirming by an oath His promise of
gifts, no longer speaking as God to man, but conversing with him as a
friend with an acquaintance."
   Commended] For the Gk. verb, cp. 1 Macc. xii. 43; Rom. xvi. 1.
   by the gifts which they through discipline present to him] lit. *gifts
from discipline.* Cp. ch. iii. 14.   They commend themselves to God by
deeds so prompted by discipline that they are God-like in character,
and accordingly are offerings to God well-pleasing to Him.   Such
spiritual gifts are compared to those which recommend a visitor to
an Eastern monarch.
   This seems to be the sense required by the prec. words, but the
more lit. translation of marg. offers another possibility.   "*Men are commended* to God *for the sake of* (i.e. that *they,* not God, may receive) *the
presents that* come *of discipline.*"   This rendering is more true to the
Gk., and emphasizes the bounty of God, cp. Philo, *Post. C.* § 43 "God
practises a certain economy with His gifts, withdrawing the earlier ones
before men can become surfeited with them, and substituting continually
new gifts for old.   He measures His gifts to suit the capacity of the
receivers."   For *discipline,* which is one aspect of Wisdom, cp. ch. i. 5.

CH. VII. 15—22a. SOLOMON'S ENCYCLOPÆDIC WISDOM, AND THE
           ACKNOWLEDGED SOURCE OF IT.

   15. *to me may God give*] So the best MSS. (δῴη). A.V. *hath
granted* follows an inferior reading.   As Solomon approaches the climax
of his task, in true classical style he invokes the aid of heaven.   Cp.
"Musa, mihi memora causas."

And to conceive thoughts worthy of what ¹hath been given
me;
Because himself is one that guideth even wisdom and that
correcteth the wise.
For in his hand are both we and our words;   16
All understanding, and *all* acquaintance with divers crafts.
For himself gave me an unerring knowledge of the things 17
that are,
To know the constitution of the world, and the operation
of the elements;

¹ Some authorities read *is said.*

to speak with judgement] The Gk. κατὰ γνώμην can in this connection bear several meanings, but the first marginal alternative is to be
preferred, *according to* his *mind*, i.e. God's.
thoughts worthy] Text does not quite represent the Greek, which is
"to think in a manner worthy of what hath been given," i.e. to use my
talents faithfully. The theme deserves to find a prophet adequately
prepared; an unfit medium can misrepresent the divinest subject. Text
follows B and Vulgate in reading δεδομένων; marg. *is said* gives the
reading of ℵA λεγομένων, which (though supported by the Syr., Arm.
and Ar. versions) Grimm shows to be a gloss.
Because himself is one] The reason why he appeals to God. God
is the ultimate source, even for Wisdom.
that guideth even wisdom] Cp. St John viii. 28, 29. For ὁδηγὸς
"guide" used literally, see ch. xviii. 3; 1 Macc. iv. 2; 2 Macc. v. 15.
that correcteth] Vulg. *emendator.* Wisdom only needs direction;
wise men make mistakes, which require correction.
16. *in his hand*] Derived from God and dependent on Him,
cp. 1 Chr. xxix. 12; Job xii. 10; Ecclus. x. 4, 5.
and our words] Cp. Ex. iv. 11.
All understanding] i.e. practical wisdom.
acquaintance with divers crafts] Ability to design and skill to
execute. Cp. Ex. xxxi. 3—5, of Bezaleel.
17. *For himself gave me*] A reiteration with special reference to
Solomon of the general truth enunciated in *v.* 15. *Himself* is again the
emphatic word.
knowledge of the things that are] i.e. of "the sum of things." "A
knowledge of nature" is roughly what is intended.
the constitution of the world] The Gk. (σύστασις) means the composition
of the world, i.e. the principles of its harmonious self-consistence (Plato,
Timaeus 32 E), or the organisation of the elements, cp. Philo, *Q. R. D. H.*
§ 57 "The four principles and powers of which the world is composed
(συνέστηκεν)."
the elements] i.e. earth, air, fire, water (cp. ch. xiii. 2, xix. 18), the
four elements into which substance was first resolved by Empedocles,

18 The beginning and end and middle of times,
   The alternations of the solstices and the changes of seasons,
19 The circuits of years and the ¹positions of stars ;
20 The natures of living creatures and the ragings of wild
   beasts,

   ¹ Or, *constellations*

who styled them "roots of all," see Zeller, *Outlines*, p. 72. Plato
was the first to suggest the name στοιχεῖα (*Theaet.* 201 E, *Tim.* 48 B),
which passed down through the Stoics into Judaeo-Alexandrinism
and the system of Philo. So familiar were all *literati* at Alexandria
with Greek philosophical terms, that the writer of Wisdom may have
used them freely, even if possessed of no first-hand acquaintance with
Greek philosophy.

   18. Chronology and astronomy. *Times* does not refer either to
historical periods or to eschatology, but to "days, months, and years,"
see Philo, *Opif.* § 19. *Beginning, middle*, and *end* occur together in
Philo, *Q. R. D. H.* § 25 in connection with the perfect number. The
study of the mystic properties of numbers was keenly pursued at
Alexandria, and accordingly a reference may be seen here to the relation
between the regulation of the calendar and mathematical calculations.
Philo points to this in *Opif.* § 19 "Time teaches the nature of number."

   solstices...seasons] The words for *solstices* (τροπαί, lit. turnings) and
changes of seasons (μεταβολαί) occur together frequently in Philo (*de Cong.*
§ 19; *Somn.* i. § 3; *Q. R. D. H.* § 50). The former is the classical
word for the *solstices* : Philo writes of the summer and winter solstices
in *Q. R. D. H.* § 27: for his explanation of the phenomenon, see § 29.

   19. *circuits of years*] The expression is used by Philo (*Somn.* i. § 3)
for the succession of seasons which complete the year. Grimm renders
by the indeterminate *Jahreswechsel*. Perhaps we should render "cycles."

   positions of stars] Probably as marg., their relative positions, i.e. as
constellations, cp. Philo, *Cong.* § 24 "the company of stars moving
round in their ordered ranks," although "their positions at various
times of the year" (as in text) is possible. Deane sees a reference to
solar and lunar cycles and methods of intercalation, whereby sacred
and civil reckonings were determined. Possibly there is a reference to
astrology, or to the predictions of eclipses (Cic. *de Nat. Deor.* ii. 61).

   20. Zoology, psychology, botany. Philo (*Q. R. D. H.* § 22) speaks
of plants and animals, as the natures which lie midway between heaven
and earth. Josephus writes "Solomon spoke parables about all sorts
of living creatures; for he was not unacquainted with any of their
natures."

   The natures of living creatures] He knew the habits and ways of
animals generally. Deane notes allusions to the life and habits of
animals in Prov. vi. 6—8, xxvi. 2, 11, xxx. 15, 19, 25—31.

   the ragings of wild beasts] *Ragings* plur. partly because of the plural
subject " wild beasts," partly to indicate the varying expressions of their
courage and ferocity.

The violences of ¹winds and the thoughts of men,
The diversities of plants and the virtues of roots:
All things that are either secret or manifest I learned,   21
For she that is the artificer of all things taught me, *even* 22
    wisdom.

    ¹ Or, *spirits*

The violences of winds] Vulgate *uim uentorum.* There can be little
doubt that text and Vulgate are right. Cp. ch. iv. 4 and a similar passage
in Diog. Laert. *Heraclitus* ix. 1, 6. The phrase itself occurs in Philo,
Opif. § 19, which suggests that the meaning here is that Solomon
could predict storms and tides.

Grimm makes an interesting suggestion that as Solomon is taking
various objects in pairs, πνευμάτων βίας should go with *thoughts of
men,* and mean (see marg.) *spirits* whether good or evil, including human
spirits. He quotes Jos. *Ant.* 8. 2. 5 "God enabled S. to learn that
skill which expels demons, a science useful and sanative to men."
Cp. R. Browning's *Abt Vogler,* which reflects the power over spirits
ascribed to Solomon by Eastern legends. But βίας would be an
unlikely word in combination with πν. in this sense.

thoughts of men] His intuition enabled him to forecast the working
of men's minds. Something less abstract than psychology (Deane) is
intended, viz. that sensitiveness of perception which enabled him to
decide perplexing cases (1 Kings iii. 16—28), or to tell the Queen of
Sheba "all her questions," 1 Kings x. 3.

diversities of plants] The phrase occurs in Philo, *Somn.* i. § 35.
The various species of plants, and their uses in medicine.

the virtues of roots] Josephus (*Ant.* 8. 2. 5) tells of a root (known
to Solomon) with which he saw a Jewish exorcist, in presence of
Vespasian and Titus, draw out an evil spirit through the nostrils of
a demoniac. For the virtues inherent in herbs, cp. Ecclus. xxxviii.
4—6, and for Solomon's legendary lore in botany and natural history,
cp. 1 Kings iv. 33.

21. *secret or manifest*] Facts and the true deductions from them ;
natural objects and their laws, properties and uses; the sequences of
cause and effect; portents and their obscure significance: Solomon
was made master of these, in all their subtle complexities.

22. *she that is the artificer of all things*] Cp. ch. viii. 6, xiv. 2;
Philo, *Det. Pot.* § 16 " Wisdom, through whom the sum of things was
completed." Two points should be noted, (1) God is represented as
making nothing directly : the agent of His creative will was Wisdom
(ch. ix. 1, 2), who is therefore called universal artificer. (2) In line
with this aloofness of God, this verse tells that *Wisdom* was Solomon's
teacher, although in *v.* 15 he writes "may God give me...for Himself
is guide," and in *v.* 17 " Himself gave me an unerring knowledge."
God thus is the teacher because *qui facit per alium facit per se* ; but the
writer rarely attributes unmediated action to God. A similar identification is seen in Acts vii. 30, 33. For Wisdom as teacher, see ch. ix. 17.

For there is in her a spirit quick of understanding, holy,

CH. VII. 22 B—CH. VIII. 1. THE NATURE OF WISDOM.

22—24, THE QUALITIES OF WISDOM: 25, 26, HER DERIVATION:
27—VIII. 1, HER ACTIVITIES.

Wisdom is described in a series of twenty-one epithets. The number
is no doubt intentional, 7 and 3 being sacred numbers: 7 symbolised
completeness, while 3 was the Divine number.   Similar series may
be seen in St James iii. 17, 18, of the "Wisdom from above";
and in Philo, *Sacr.* § 5 where 11 companions of pleasure and 34 of
virtue are named, and as many as 147 epithets are lavished upon the
lover of pleasure.   Cleanthes named 26 characteristics of "the good,"
Clem. Alex. *Protr.* 6. 72. It may be that this passage, which is the
heart of the book, won for it the name of Πανάρετος Σοφία, "the
Wisdom which comprises all virtues" (Introd. § 1).   Is Wisdom with her
many names to be identified with the "Logos of the many names" of
the Stoics?   Philo calls W. the "many-named" (*All.* i. § 14), but if there
is to be an identification, it must be for a different reason.   Bois,
Origines, pp. 230—260, argues that, although in the flux of Alexandrian
thought it is difficult to arrive at any definiteness, nevertheless Wisdom
is identified by Pseudo-Solomon with so many of the concepts (Justice,
Providence, Power) with which the Logos was identified by the Stoics,
that their provinces overlap and almost coincide.   But there is probably
no conscious identification : for the writer of Wisdom, Wisdom was the
rallying-point around which the floating conceptions gathered which in
Greek philosophy had made the Logos their centre (Introd. § 9).

22. *For there is in her a spirit*] *For* explains how it was that
Wisdom taught him.   The reading of text *in her* is that of אB, supported by four versions.   A reads αὐτὴ ("For she is a spirit"), but the old
Latin, which supports אB, shows that ἐν αὐτῇ is at least very early.   The
MS. evidence requires that ἐν should be retained.   ἐν αὐτῇ may either
be rendered as in text, the *spirit* being the essential life-principle of
Wisdom (cp. Job xxxii. 8) and therefore identical with her ; or it may be
read as ἐν αὐτῇ "Wisdom is in herself a spirit," cp. *v.* 27.   The former
rendering is to be preferred.

quick of understanding] The word νοερὸς is a technical Stoic term,
denoting "possessed of mind." It indicates (not degree of mental
capacity, but) the possession of mental faculty in distinction from non-
possession of it.   The Stoics taught that there was a "rational" world-
soul, the Logos, of which men are emanations.

holy] For *holy spirit* as synonym of Wisdom, see ch. ix. 17.   In
neither case is there any thought of the Third Person of the Trinity.

The original significance of *holy* was not ethical so much as metaphysical or ceremonial, so that anything divine was "holy."   But later,
as the ethical side of the Being of God became more clearly realized,

¹Alone in kind, manifold,
Subtil, freely moving,
Clear in utterance, unpolluted,
Distinct, unharmed,
Loving what is good, keen, unhindered,

¹ Gr. *Sole-born.*

holy gained in moral content until it came to denote especially the morally good. See Davidson, *Theol. of O.T.* p. 148. *Holy* has a moral significance here, cp. Philo, *Fuga* § 35. *Holy spirit* occurs only three times in O.T. (Ps. li. 11; Is. lxiii. 10, 11).

Alone in kind] The meaning of μονογενὲς must be determined by its contrast with *manifold*. Just as the Stoics believed in one world-soul with countless manifestations, so the author teaches that Wisdom is unique yet manifold. For the Greek word, cp. St John i. 14; and Clem. Rom. xxv. of the phoenix. Grimm renders "sole in its kind, existing only in one example," and cites the analogous antithesis of the One Spirit and His diverse gifts, in 1 Cor. xii. 11.

For *manifold*, cp. Heb. i. 1 and Philo, *All.* iii. 59, where the Logos is compared to a coriander seed, of which "gardeners say it can be cut into minute fragments, every one of which can be sown as successfully as if it were the original seed: so is the Logos, beneficial all through and in every part."

subtil] The Gk. λεπτὸν is used of the manna in Ex. xvi. 14 ff., meaning *thin, fine.* Philo (*All.* iii. 59) applies it to the Logos in the sense of minuteness, transparency, purity. The thought here is of a being altogether spiritual in essence.

freely moving] Cp. ὀξυκίνητος "swiftly moving" (of the Logos) in Philo, *Cher.* § 9; and *v.* 24. Farrar cites an old gloss, which makes it mean almost *ubiquitous.*

clear in utterance] Vulg. *disertus.* For τρανὸς, cp. ch. x. 21, and Is. xxxv. 6. Wisdom, who makes eloquent, is herself eloquent. Others render *penetrating.*

unpolluted] Being possessed of creative purity, she cannot contract impurity.

distinct] Giving no uncertain sound, as a moral guide.

unharmed] i.e. not liable to suffering or injury, cp. Zeno, in Diog. Laert. vii. 72, 147, "God can be touched by no harm," in contrast with Matter, which the Stoics called "passible," cp. Philo, *Opif.* § 2 παθητόν.

loving what is good] In Philo, *Sacr.* § 5, goodness is one of thirty-four qualities attending upon Virtue, who describes herself as a "hater of evil."

keen] Cp. Heb. iv. 12. Philo, *Q. R. D. H.* § 26, has "God cuts... with His Logos which acts upon all things like a knife."

Wisdom is keen like a knife, and therefore penetrating, and in her activities is *unhindered.* She divides, arranges, and unites Matter.

Beneficent, 23loving toward man,
Stedfast, sure, free from care,
All-powerful, all-surveying,
And penetrating through all spirits
That are quick of understanding, pure, most subtil:
24 For wisdom is more mobile than any motion;
Yea, she pervadeth and penetrateth all things by reason of
her pureness.

Beneficent] See ch. x. 10. Clem. R. § lix. calls God the one benefactor of spirits.

23. *loving toward man*] Cp. ch. i. 6, xii. 19. This quality is one of those named by Philo (*Sacr.* § 5), as attending on Virtue.

This and the preceding word form a pair: *philanthropic* denotes the inward disposition of good will, of which *beneficent* implies the practical manifestation.

free from care] Cp. ch. vi. 15. Wisdom is self-contained and self-sufficing, and is therefore free from worldly care. Her lofty interests make her *sure and steadfast*, leaving her undistracted by the appeal of created things. For a commentary on the word, cp. M. Arnold's lyric "Self-dependence."

all-powerful] Cp. ch. xi. 17, xviii. 15. The rest of *vv.* 23, 24 emphasize the universality of Wisdom.

all-surveying] Cp. ch. i. 6—10 and Prov. xv. 3. A similar word is applied to God in 2 Macc. ix. 5; Ep. Polyc. vii.; Clem. Rom. lxiv. Cp. Philo, *All.* iii. § 59 "The word of God is very keen of vision, so that he can survey all things."

all spirits] *spirits* in the widest sense, whether angelic or human, and the latter whether incarnate or discarnate.

Penetrating through indicates a very close spiritual intimacy: but Wisdom cannot enter into all spirits, but into those only which have the necessary affinity with her, viz. those which are *quick of understanding* (men, as self-determining and self-conscious agents), *pure* (angels, as immaterial beings), *subtil* (men, in so far as they are refined through purity).

24. *more mobile*] This clause is closely connected with the preceding, and explains the penetrating power of Wisdom.

She is like the air, whose omnipresence explained or suggested to the Stoics the Divine omnipresence. To *pervade* and to *penetrate* were technical words in Stoic philosophy for describing the diffusion of the world-soul, cp. Diog. La. vii. 70, 138, 139, 147. The reason for all this is her *pureness*, the simple uncompoundedness of her essence: there is in her nothing gross or of the earth. Her *pureness* is metaphysical rather than moral. For *mobile*, cp. Philo's description of the Logos in *Cher.* § 9, and Thales in Diog. La. i. 9, 35 "Mind is the speediest thing there is: it courses through all things."

For she is a ¹breath of the power of God,   25
And a clear effluence of the glory of the Almighty;
Therefore can nothing defiled find entrance into her.
For she is an effulgence from everlasting light,   26

¹ Gr. *vapour.*

vv. 25, 26. THE DERIVATION OF WISDOM.

The emphasis in these *vv.* lies not so much upon *breath, effluence, effulgence, mirror, image,* as upon *power, glory, light, working, goodness.* As that which is born of spirit *is* spirit, so Wisdom as emanating from the Divine possessor of these attributes, possesses them herself by inherent right. *Power, glory, light, working, goodness* are part of her very essence. Her origin only emphasizes her personal prerogatives: her derivation is of little importance, unless derivation connotes identity.

25. *a breath*] Cp. Ecclus. xxiv. 3. As an exhalation of the Divine power, Wisdom is and has Divine power, cp. ch. i. 3.

effluence] Cp. Philo, *Fuga* § 9 "Wisdom is the virgin daughter of God, of inviolate and stainless nature because of her own nobleness and of the honour of him who begat her." *Effluence* denotes the outflow of either water or light. For the former, cp. Ecclus. i. 9; Enoch xlix. 1 "Wisdom...poured out like water"; Philo, *All.* i. 19, of a stream flowing out of a river: for the latter, which is to be preferred (see Grimm, p. 160), cp. Ez. i. 13 (Aquila), and Athenag. (*Apol.* x.), who calls the Holy Spirit the "effluence of God," being to Him as its rays are to the sun. The word *clear* is used here, like *pure* above, to emphasize the immateriality of *Wisdom,* cp. Philo, *Opif.* § 8 "No sensible object is *clear.*" There is nothing in her to mar the *glory* (i.e. glory of light, cp. next *v.*) which she inherits. Wisdom has a glory of her own, cp. ch. ix. 11.

nothing defiled] Being immaterial, and also partaker of the divine glory, she has nothing in her that can contract stain. The Gk. verb denotes an insidious approach on the part of defilement: what cannot conquer her might seek to beguile her. But her nature, and not her mere habit is *unpolluted, v.* 22. Cp. Philo, *Fuga* § 9 on prec. *l.*

26. *effulgence*] It is natural to see here the source of the expressions applied to the Son in Heb. i. 3. But both *effulgence* and *image* (χαρακτήρ), cp. Philo, *Plant.* § 5, are words of common occurrence in Philo, and consequently the borrowing is hardly more certain in this case than in ch. v. 17—19. The meaning of ἀπαύγασμα here is disputed. It means either the light emitted from a luminary, or the reflection of the luminary. Philo, *Opif.* § 51, *Plant.* § 12, uses ἀπαύγ. as "reflection," and the context makes this rendering the more probable. In this *v.* it is coupled with *mirror* and *image,* with both of which "reflection" is more allied than "effulgence." Again, there is a contrast between *v.* 25 and *v.* 26, the former emphasizing a relation to God by emanation, the latter by reflection.

And an unspotted mirror of the working of God,
And an image of his goodness.
27 And she, being one, hath power to do all things;
And remaining in herself, reneweth all things :
And from generation to generation passing into holy souls

everlasting light] For God as light, see Is. lx. 19, 20, and 1 John i. 5.
Everlasting in its original sense of "unbeginning and unending," cp.
ch. ii. 23.   Wisdom was, before the world was created: accordingly
her light is superior to created light, *v.* 29.
   an unspotted mirror] Vulg. *speculum sine macula.* If Wisdom is
in her essence an emanation from the Divine power, *v.* 25, she is a
faithful representation of that power in its concrete manifestation.
Her operations do not belie her origin.
   image of his goodness] According to Philo, power and goodness are
the greatest attributes of God, and Wisdom shares the latter as well as
the former, *v.* 25.   She is the means of its manifestation, being its
image : through her God reveals His character as lover of men and
good.   *Image* (εἰκών) is frequently used of the Logos by Philo, *Fuga* § 19,
Conf. l. § 28.   For *image* as expressing representation and manifestation, see Lightfoot on Col. i. 15.   God's goodness was His motive in
creation, cp. ch. xi. 24—xii. 1, and accordingly His intermediary is
shown to exhibit the same characteristic.

v. 27—Ch. VIII. 1.   The activity of Wisdom in the
          physical and moral world.

   27.   *she, being one...all things*] The same contrast as in *v.* 22
"alone in kind, manifold."   Wisdom is one in essence, yet manifold in
effective operation.   The universality of her domain, dwelt on in 23 b
and 24, is again referred to: though she is but one, her influence is
felt everywhere.
   remaining in herself, reneweth] Wisdom is unchanging and unchangeable, yet the agent of all change.   She is the vital force by
which the world lives: she suffers no decrease, needs no increase, but
the world with its deaths and resurrections lives by her life.   Cp. Ps.
civ. 30.   Philo, *Q. R. D. H.* § 31, writes "God's art (Wisdom), wherewith
He fashioned all things, admits of neither tension nor slackening, but
abiding the same (μένουσα ἡ αὐτή) has fashioned perfectly each thing in
its degree."   Anaxagoras (Arist. *Phys.* 8. 5) taught that Mind (νοῦς) was
the cause of all change and movement in the universe: while producing
variation all around, itself remained constant and stable.   But the idea
is found in O.T.   See Ps. cii. 27, 28.
   passing into holy souls] As with things, so with men.   Her mobility
is exercised in all ages and on the spiritual no less than on the material
plane, see *v.* 23 b.   But her operations are limited by the worthiness of
men, see ch. i. 4, 5, vi. 16 : where there is no affinity, there can be no

She maketh *men* friends of God and prophets.

For nothing doth God love save him that dwelleth with 28
wisdom.

For she is fairer than the sun, 29

inspiration. Cp. St John xiv. 21, 23, and Prov. xxii. 11 LXX. "The
Lord loveth holy hearts."

friends of God] The phrase is practically without LXX. precedent:
it occurs in A.V. twice, where it is used of Abraham, 2 Chron. xx. 7
and Is. xli. 8, but in neither case is the phrase represented in LXX. by
'friend' (φίλος). But Philo, *Sobr.* § 11 quotes Gen. xviii. 17, with the
addition of the words "my friend." From St James ii. 23 the expression
passed into Christian literature, while a similar use is found in St John
xv. 14, 15. The origin of the phrase is perhaps to be sought in Greek
philosophy. In his note on St James ii. 23, J. B. Mayor quotes
examples from Xenophon, Plato (twice) and Epictetus. Philo,
Q. R. D. H. § 5 has "All wise men are friends of God," and "friend of
God" appears also in Epict. ii. 17; while Diogenes (Diog. Laert.
vi. 2, 37) playfully argued: "All things belong to the gods: the wise
are *friends of the gods*: the property of friends is common: therefore
all things belong to the wise."

maketh...prophets] The Gk. verb is the same as in ch. ix. 2 (R.V.
formedst). Wisdom has a creative effect upon holy souls: she adopts
them into the Divine relation which she herself has inherited. Probably
the writer has in mind not the ordinary prophet who fell into a trance or
experienced moments of half-frenzied inspiration, but the prophet of a
rare type such as Moses, who is (Numb. xii. 7) expressly differentiated
from the ecstatic prophet. It is perhaps from Moses and not from
Abraham (although the latter is currently known in the East as El
Khalil "the friend") that the phrase "friend of God" is drawn; see
Ex. xxxiii. 11. The prophet (e.g. Abraham, Gen. xx. 7, and Moses) not
only spoke from God to men, Ex. xx. 19, but to God for men, Ex. v.
22, 23, xxxii. 32. Philo, *Q. R. D. H.* § 5 has an interesting paragraph
on the boldness of Moses' speech with God, who "dared to speak to God
in a way that men would not speak to a king. But it was not insolence,
it was confident trust. Freedom of speech is the sign of *friendship*; to
whom might a man speak his heart if not to his friend?"

28. *save him that dwelleth with wisdom*] The metaphor is from
marriage, cp. ch. viii. 2, 9, 16. The thought is more strong and unqualified
than the writer allows elsewhere, cp. ch. xi. 24, although Philo, *Quod
Deus* § 34, writes of Wisdom "through her alone can suppliant souls
escape for refuge to the Unbeginning One." This *v.* is one of those
that seem to anticipate, if not suggest, teachings in the Fourth Gospel,
cp. St John xiv. 6 b, xvi. 27.

29. *For she is fairer*] Cp. Song vi. 9. Philo, *Ebr.* § 11 writes
"When the knowledge of Him who is shines forth, it illuminates all
around it till it darkens the things that seem to be most bright in
themselves." The sun as a single object of radiant glory, the stars in

And above [1]all the constellations of the stars:
Being compared with light, she is found *to be* before it;
30 For [2]to the light *of day* succeedeth night,
But against wisdom evil doth not prevail;
8 But she [3]reacheth from one end *of the world* to the other
with full strength,
And ordereth all things [4]graciously.

2 Her I loved and sought out from my youth,
And I sought to take her for my bride,

---

[1] Gr. *every arrangement of stars.*   [2] Gr. *to this.*   [3] Or, *reacheth*
from end onward unto end mightily   [4] Or, *unto good use*

---

their manifold groupings, cannot vie with her in beauty: while for
steadfastness the daylight is not to be compared with her.

30. *doth not prevail*] Philo, *Mos.* iii. 37 writes "He was grieved
that a fabricated tale should quench so bright a beam of that truth,
upon which the eclipse neither of sun nor of all the army of stars could
cast a shadow. For it shines with an immaterial light of its own, in
comparison with which physical light would be as night to day."
With this faith in the invincibleness of Wisdom, cp. St John i. 5 "The
light shineth in darkness, and the darkness overcame it not." Cp. also
R. Browning "One who...never dream'd, though right were worsted,
wrong would triumph."

viii. 1. *reacheth*] Grimm points out that the Divine activities were
viewed by Philo as an extension (or out-reaching) of the Being of God.
This *v.* therefore points to the function of Wisdom as an emanation from
Him. Cp. Philo, *Migr.* § 32 "This universe is held together by
unseen powers, which the demiurge *stretched* from the ends of the earth
to the uttermost part of heaven. Now these powers are chains that
cannot be broken." Plato, *Tim.* 34 B speaks of God making a kind of
world-soul, which He spread (or stretched) throughout the whole (ἔτεινε
διὰ παντὸς).

ordereth] The prec. clause points to the support of the world, this
to its government, by Wisdom. The Gk. word was in common use
among the Stoics, who debated the question, "Is the world *ordered*
(διοικεῖται) by providence?"

CH. VIII. 2—21. SOLOMON DESIRES TO TAKE WISDOM FOR
HIS BRIDE.

vv. 2—8. HER MORAL AND INTELLECTUAL SUPREMACY.

2. *from my youth*] Cp. Ecclus. vi. 18, li. 13.
my bride] Solomon is compelled to resort to the use of this image,
if he is to express adequately the intimacy and the fruitfulness of his

And I became enamoured of her beauty.

She glorifieth *her* noble birth in that it is given her to live 3
with God,

And the Sovereign Lord of all loved her.

For she is initiated into the knowledge of God,   4

relation to Wisdom. The picture is one which reverence would forbid
any but a mystic to employ, but it is to be found also in Philo, *Cong.*
§ 14, where it is extended, and Wisdom is seen as mother as well as wife.
Philo also describes himself as having in his youth loved one of the
handmaids of Wisdom, Grammar, who bore children to him, writing,
reading, and history. Philo's language shows clearly the danger of un-
seemliness, which always threatens the mystical use of sensuous images.

became enamoured] Cp. Plato, *Phaedrus* 250 D " O what marvellous
love would Wisdom cause to spring up in the hearts of men, if she sent
forth a clear likeness of herself also, even as Beauty doth ! " (tr. J. A.
Stewart).

3. her *noble birth*] Does a man look for noble birth in his bride?
Who fulfils his requirements more truly than Wisdom? she is the
offspring of God. Cp. vii. 25, 26, and Philo, *Fuga* § 9, where she is
called " daughter of God."

to live with God] Image is piled on image without regard to incon-
gruity, and Wisdom is called the Bride of God. The Greek word (Vulg.
contubernium) suggests this meaning unreservedly, and a similar idea is
found in Philo, *Ebr.* § 8 " We shall be justified in calling the Creator the
Father of the world, and His knowledge its Mother, with whom God
dwelt and whom He made mother of the Creation, yet not after the
manner of a man." In the O.T. the closeness of Jehovah's relation to
His people Israel is often expressed by the figure of marriage, cp.
Is. l. 1, lxii. 4, 5 ; Hos. ii. 19, 20. *vv.* 2, 3 illustrate the limitations of
symbolism. Symbolism can never view a situation as a whole, only in
detail : as one point after another catches its eye, it throws off a rapid
picture of each. Taken singly and without relation to each other, these
pictures are suggestive : in combination, they are grotesque and impossible. E.g. the characterisations of Wisdom as Bride of Solomon,
Daughter of God and Bride of God are mutually exclusive : taken
together, they present the *reductio ad absurdum* of symbolism.

And] Vulg. *sed et,* "yea, and."

loved her] Cp. Prov. viii. 30.

the Sovereign Lord of all] The same phrase is found in Job v. 8
LXX. and is expanded in Job v. 9 ff.

4. *For*] Considering her relation to the knowledge and the works
of God, she must be loved by Him.

she is initiated] This is the usual meaning of the Gk. word ($\mu\dot{\nu}\sigma\tau\iota\varsigma$),
but it sometimes has an active meaning "one who initiates," and so
Vulg. *doctrix.* The context however, which touches on the relations of
God and Wisdom alone, seems to show that the word refers to the

And she [1]chooseth out *for him* his works.
5 But if riches are a desired possession in life,
   What is richer than wisdom, which worketh all things?
6 [2]And if understanding worketh,
   Who more than [3]wisdom is an artificer of the things that are?
7 And if a man loveth righteousness,
   [4]The fruits of wisdom's labour are virtues,

---

[1] Some authorities read *deviseth* for him.   [2] The Greek text of
this clause is perhaps corrupt.   [3] Gr. *she.*   [4] Gr. *Her labours are.*

exceptional prerogative of Wisdom. The knowledge of God is the
knowledge which God possesses, and wherewith He searches out His
creation. Into the secret mysteries of this knowledge it pleased God to
initiate Wisdom.

chooseth out] Vulg. *electrix.* The idea seems to be that God allowed
her a voice in deciding the order in which His works should proceed.
"Through His Wisdom God knows what is best, and through the same
Wisdom He performs it" (Grimm).

5. Besides nobility, wealth is desirable in a bride. This Wisdom
possesses in preeminent degree.

worketh all things] She "chooses out God's works" for Him.
Possibly there is a play on the Greek word (ἐργάζεσθαι) which means
(1) to work at a trade, (2) to gain by trading. Wisdom accordingly
is rich, because she possesses the secret of all work and therefore of
all profit.

6. It is possible that there is a corruption in this verse. As it stands,
it does not add appreciable strength to *v.* 5: Vulg. however translates
it literally. The sense seems to be that Wisdom, if a worker at all, must
be supreme in any thing to which she puts her hand.

understanding] This is a variant for "Wisdom" in *v.* 5, but the
writer uses it with the deliberate intention of emphasizing the intellectual aspect of Wisdom. Can any thing be conceived, he asks, more
skilful in creative work than Wisdom in her aspect as Mind? cp. vii. 22.

If objection is taken to the identification between "Wisdom" in
v. 5 and "understanding" in *v.* 6, another rendering is possible, which
contrasts them. "If human wisdom is a worker, if who more than *she*
(the heavenly Wisdom) is artificer of the things that are?" Human
wisdom can produce results, but only the heavenly Wisdom can call
into being things having in themselves the quality of permanence and
self-existence. Philo, *Det. Pot.* § 16 speaks of Wisdom as the "mother
of the world, through whom the universe was brought to completion."

7. Nobility, Wealth, Intellect belong to Wisdom : she possesses
also Righteousness.

the fruits of wisdom's labour] lit. *her labours,* Vulg. *labores,* abstr.
for concr., cp. x. 10.

are virtues] Cp. Epicurus, "Prudence is the most honourable

For she teacheth soberness and understanding, righteousness
and courage;
And there is nothing in life for men more profitable than
these.
And if a man longeth even for much experience,   8

part of philosophy, because from it spring all the virtues : they teach
that it is impossible to live happily without also living prudently,
and righteously" (Diog. Laert. x. 132). Wisdom is shown to be the
parent of the four cardinal virtues of Greek philosophy; the same
teaching is given in Philo, *Alleg.* i. 19, where the garden of Eden is
made to represent Wisdom (which is identified with the Divine Logos);
the river stands for Virtue, and the four heads into which it parts are
Prudence, Justice, Temperance, Fortitude. Aristobulus had written
(c. 150 B.C.) "The whole constitution of our Law was arranged with
reference to piety, righteousness, temperance, and all other truly good
things" (Eus. *Praep. Ev.* 667 a).

For she teacheth etc.] This passage is one of the obvious points of
contact between the Book of Wisdom and Greek philosophy. Plato
was the first to establish and explain the principal virtues, which he
enumerated as four : (1) Wisdom, which consists in the right quality of
the reason, (2) Courage, when the spirit supports the reason against
desire for pleasure and fear of pain, (3) Self-control, when the soul is
conscious of harmony in all its parts on the question which is to command and which is to obey, (4) Justice, when every part of the soul
fulfils its mission (Plato, *Rep.* iv. 441 C ff.), cp. Zeller, *Outlines of
Greek Philosophy*, p. 157, and Diog. Laert. iii. 80, 91, where Prudence
takes the place of Wisdom, a change which was adopted by the Stoics
and which found general acceptance. These four virtues appear in
4 Macc. i. 6, 18, being called in the latter place the forms (ἰδέαι) of
Wisdom : in 4 Macc. v. 22, 23 Piety is substituted for Prudence. Piety
was counted as a cardinal virtue by Socrates, from whom Plato drew
his theory of virtue. "Righteousness" appears twice in this *v.* : in the
first case meaning the sum of human moral rectitude, as in ch. i. 1,
and in the second in a more restricted sense, although it is impossible
to say how far that sense is identical with the Platonic. Plato's
cardinal virtues are closely connected with his analysis of human nature
into reason, courage, and desire (Diog. Laert. iii. 67), but this trichotomy is not recognised by the author of Wisdom.

nothing...more profitable] This line seems to be recalled in Hermas,
Mand. viii. 9 "Faith, fear of the Lord, love, concord, works of righteousness,...nothing is better than these in the life of men."

8. *much experience*] The Greek word is used loosely of insight into
the future, as well as of experience of past events: Vulg. is therefore to
be preferred *multitudinem scientiae*. Wisdom possesses that mental
vigour which places all past experience at the service of the constructive
imagination, and enables her to anticipate the future.

She knoweth ¹the things of old, and ²divineth the things to
come:
She understandeth subtilties of speeches and interpretations
of dark sayings:
She foreseeth signs and wonders, and the issues of seasons
and times.

¹ Some authorities read *how to divine the things of old and the things
to come.*   ² Gr. *conjectureth.*

the things of old]   For knowledge of the past and future as a Divine
possession, cp. Ps. cxxxix. 5 LXX.; Prov. viii. 21 a; Is. xli. 22, 23,
xlv. 21; Ecclus. xxxix. 1; Ep. Barn. v. 3 "The Lord hath both revealed
unto us the past, and made us wise in the present, and as regards the
future we are not without understanding." Philo (*Mos.* ii. 39) argues
that past and future do not exist for God.

divineth]   Foreknowledge is not claimed for Wisdom, nor is it
stated that God communicates to her His own prevision.   God knows,
but Wisdom conjectures.   There is considerable MS. authority for the
marginal reading (εἰκάζειν), which is found in BC.

subtilties of speeches]   Cp. Ecclus. xxxix. 2, 3.   The wise man will be
a student of the past and of the future: "he will enter in amidst the
subtilties (στροφαί) of parables.   He will seek out the hidden meaning
of proverbs, and be conversant in the dark sayings (αἰνίγματα) of
parables."   The phrase appears in Prov. i. 3 LXX.   The Gk. word
(στροφή) is originally used of the twistings and turnings of the wrestler
in his effort to elude his opponent: the word was naturally applied to
the elaborated efforts of the wise men to mystify their rivals and outdo
them in the conflict of wits.

interpretations of dark sayings]   Cp. Prov. i. 6.   The "dark saying"
(αἴνιγμα) is properly a veiled, allusive, oracular utterance, cp. Num.
xii. 8; 1 Cor. xiii. 12.   The propounding of parables and riddles
and sphinx-like questions is not uncommonly alluded to in O.T., Judg.
xiv. 12; 1 Kings x. 1; Ezek. xvii. 3.   For Solomon's fame, cp. 1 Kings
iv. 32, and Ecclus. xlvii. 17; for Daniel's, Dan. v. 12.

signs and wonders]   These words are frequently found in combination both in O.T. and N.T., cp. St John iv. 48, and they appear also in
Dan. iv. 34 LXX. in conjunction with "seasons and times."   *Wonders*
are natural phenomena in their aspect as marvels, *signs* in their aspect as
witnesses to something not yet clearly manifested.   Philo in *Opif.* § 19
tells how the stars were used by men for foretelling storms and calms,
clear weather and cloudy, drought and plentiful rains, earthquakes and
thunder.   That this kind of fore-calculation is pointed to here is shown
by ch. vii. 17—19, and by *seasons and times* in the following line,
which probably has the same reference as in ch. vii. 18.   The normal
meaning of "seasons and times" is:—*seasons* are climatic periods of
uncertain length, *times* are fixed periods depending on the measured

I determined therefore to take her unto me to live with me, 9
Knowing that she is one who would ¹give me good *thoughts*
for counsel,
And ²encourage me in cares and grief.
Because of her I shall have glory among multitudes, 　　10
And honour in the sight of elders, though I be young.
I shall be found of a quick conceit when I give judgement, 11
And in the presence of ³princes I shall be admired.
When I am silent, they shall wait for me; 　　12

¹ Or, *hold counsel with me for good things, and...against cares and
grief* 　² Or, *exhort* Or, *advise* 　³ Or, *mighty men*

movements of sun and moon (Philo, *op. cit.*). Wisdom can foretell the
issues of the year in respect of harvests, etc., and no doubt some
prevision of human concerns is included.

vv. **9—16.** THE BENEFITS THAT SOLOMON'S BRIDE WILL CONFER
UPON HIM.

9. *to live with me*] i.e. to be my wife. The Greek word is the
same as in *v.* 3. Cp. Philo, *Cain* § 23 "The knowledge that dwells
with (σύμβιον) the wise."
give me good thoughts *for counsel*] σύμβουλος with the gen. of the
counsel given is found in 2 Chron. xxii. 3 LXX.
encourage me] παραίνεσις (Vulg. *allocutio*) is usually taken here in
this sense, though there is no other example of such a use.
10. *I shall have glory*] Cp. Prov. xxxi. 23 LXX. The people will
admire the king for his wise judgments (1 Kings iii. 28), and the elders
will applaud his wisdom in the council. *multitudes*, i.e. assemblies.
though I be young] Cp. 1 Kings iii. 7 "I am but a little child";
1 Chr. xxix. 1. Josephus says that Solomon died at ninety-four, having
reigned eighty years: this would make his age, on his accession, to be
fourteen. Grimm, arguing from 1 Kings xi. 4 suggests about twenty-
five. The writer has in view the ideal Solomon, and ignores throughout
the book the darker side of the later picture which is alluded to in
Ecclus. xlvii. 19, 20.
11. *of a quick conceit*] i.e. intelligence. The allusion is doubtless to
1 Kings iii. 16 ff. For "conceit," an archaism retained from A.V.,
Deane compares *Merchant of Venice* i. 1 :

　　"With purpose to be dressed in an opinion
　　　Of wisdom, gravity, profound conceit."

in the presence of princes] Either the chief men of his own people,
or the kings of other nations. For the latter, cp. 1 Kings iv. 34, v. 7
Hiram, x. 5—9 the Queen of Sheba.

And when I open my lips, they shall give heed unto me;
And if I continue speaking, they shall lay their hand upon
their mouth.

13 Because of her I shall have immortality,
And leave behind an eternal memory to them that come
after me.

14 I shall govern peoples,
And nations shall be subjected to me.

15 Dread princes shall fear me when they hear *of me*:
Among *my* ¹people I shall shew myself a good *ruler*, and in
war courageous.

¹ Gr. *multitude*.

12. *they shall give heed*] The passage recalls Job xxix. 21, 22.
their hand upon their mouth] A gesture expressive of respectful silence.
Cp. Job xxi. 5, xxix. 9, xl. 4; Ecclus. v. 12.

13. *Because of her*] For διὰ with acc. in this connection, cp. St John
vi. 57 "He shall live by Me" (ζήσει δι' ἐμέ).
immortality] Clearly of the subjective kind, i.e. undying fame, as
the context shews.
an eternal memory] Cp. Ps. cxii. 6 "The righteous shall be had in
everlasting remembrance." This is a reversion to the strict O.T. view
of the future life: the memory of his deeds and his name perpetuated
in his descendants, constituted the immortality that the early Hebrew
looked for.

14. *I shall govern peoples*] A reminiscence of the Messianic Psalm
lxxii. 8—11, which contains obvious allusions to the empire of Solomon.
As Wisdom caused Solomon to be honoured in his own land (*vv.* 10—13),
so she would win him renown in foreign countries (*vv.* 14, 15). There
is no occasion to distinguish between *peoples* and *nations*, the repetition
being due solely to the requirements of the poetic parallelism, cp. Ps.
lvii. 9 LXX. Cp. 1 Kings iv. 21 "Solomon reigned over all kingdoms
from the river unto the land of the Philistines... : they brought presents,
and served Solomon all the days of his life." See Kirkpatrick, *Psalms*,
pp. 420, 421 in this series. For *subjected*, cp. Ps. lx. 8 LXX.

15. *Dread princes*] Cp. Ps. lxxii. 10, 11 "The kings of Tarshish
and of the isles...the kings of Sheba and Seba. Yea, all kings shall fall
down before him." See 1 Kings x. 23—25 "King Solomon exceeded
all the kings of the earth for riches and for wisdom. And all the earth
(all kings of the earth LXX.) sought to Solomon, to hear his wisdom...."
when they hear of me] Cp. Ps. xviii. 44.
a good ruler, *and...courageous*] An effective combination of royal
qualities, the king being seen to be strong in domestic affairs as well as
brave on the field. Cp. Homer's description of Agamemnon, which
Plutarch says was frequently on the lips of Alexander:
ἀμφότερον βασιλεύς τ' ἀγαθὸς κρατερός τ' αἰχμητής
(Both a noble king and a mighty man of war).

When I am come into my house, I shall find rest with her; 16
For converse with her hath no bitterness,
And to live with her hath no pain, but gladness and joy.
When I considered these things in myself,   17
And took thought in my heart how that in kinship unto
    wisdom is immortality,
And in her friendship is good delight,   18
And in the labours of her hands is wealth that faileth not,
And in ¹assiduous communing with her is understanding,
And great renown in having fellowship with her words,

¹ Gr. practice of communion.

16. *shall find rest with her*] Cp. Philo, *Migr.* § 6 "Wisdom is the best dwelling-place of virtuous souls."
converse with her] For the Greek word, cp. 3 Macc. ii. 31. The word denotes merely social intercourse.
to live with her] *Life with her* (συμβίωσις, cp. *vv.* 3, 9) means life under one roof with her, while *converse* (συναναστροφή) in the preceding line refers to the intimacy of moral intercourse with her.
but gladness and joy] Philo (*Quis rerum* § 62) compares Wisdom to a river full of gladness and joy and all other blessings; again (*Plant.* § 40) he writes that "her features are not sour and austere, but cheerful and serene, full of mirth and joy."
This verse treats of the private life of Solomon with his bride, in contradistinction to his public life (*vv.* 10—15), in which she is the secret of his success. The Greek word for "find rest with her" has special reference to the intercourse of intimates, friend with friend, brother with brother, father with son, cp. Epict. iii. 13.

vv. **17—21.** SOLOMON, WEIGHING ALL THE ADVANTAGES CONFERRED BY WISDOM, PRAYS TO GOD TO GRANT HER TO HIM.

17. This and the succeeding verse are a recapitulation of the merits of Wisdom.
in kinship unto wisdom] Cp. Prov. vii. 4 "Say unto Wisdom 'Thou art my sister.'" For *immortality*, see Eccl. vii. 12 LXX. "The knowledge of Wisdom will give life to him that hath it." *Kinship* (συγγένεια) is used here of the spiritual affinity between himself and his bride which Solomon anticipates.
18. *in her friendship*] *v.* 16 end.
labours of her hands] *vv.* 5, 6.
assiduous communing with her] The thought is of the mutual interaction of the characters of Solomon and his bride, not merely in speech (as Vulg. *in certamine loquellae*), but in the exercise of mutual intercourse generally.
great renown] *vv.* 10—12. Wisdom will be his monitor.

I went about seeking how to take her unto myself.
19 Now I was ¹a child of parts, and a good soul fell to my lot;
20 Nay rather, being good, I came into a body undefiled.

¹ Or, *a goodly child*

I went about seeking] Cp. vi. 16 where Wisdom is the seeker, and, for the expression, Plato, *Symp.* 209 B.

19. *a child of parts*] "of good natural disposition," Vulg. *ingeniosus.* The Gk. εὐφυὴς is used of both spiritual and physical qualities, cp. Plato, *Rep.* iii. 409 E.

fell to my lot] The plain meaning of *vv.* 19, 20, is this, "I was a goodly child, well-endowed both in soul and body." But the writer, in stating the fact that he was well-endowed in soul, expresses himself in terms which do not altogether satisfy him, and he corrects himself. It might be expected that the correction would not appear in the final draft of his book, but it does appear; and hence the debate which has centred round this passage.

A good soul, he says, *fell to my lot*: we should expect him to add, "and a good body." But that would have suggested that he thought (i) that body and soul both came into being at the time of conception, and (ii) that his soul was something distinct from his Ego, and a possession not pre-ordained but obtained by chance. Accordingly, as a believer in the pre-existence of the soul, and in the identification of the Ego with the soul, he corrects himself, *nay rather, being good* (i.e. being a good soul), *I came into a body undefiled*. He finds himself unable to apply to the body a more generous epithet than *undefiled*, owing to his tendency as an Alexandrian towards dualism. This tendency is however controlled, and the nearest approach the writer makes to the extreme view of Philo is in ch. ix. 15 where he writes "the corruptible body presseth down the soul." He is in fact true to O.T. teaching in not asserting that the cause of man's moral frailty is to be found in his physical nature, or that the flesh is in itself sinful, or the seat of sin (Davidson, *Theol. of O.T.* p. 192). His body is unstained: he starts life without prejudice. For the body as receptacle of the soul, see ch. ix. 15; 2 Cor. v. 4; Barnabas, Ep. vii. 3; Lucr. iii. 441 "corpus quod uas quasi constitit eius."

If the question is asked, How does the doctrine of pre-existence agree with O.T. teaching? it must be replied that O.T. hardly considers the question. Gen. ii. 7 e.g. does not touch upon the endowment of man with a soul, i.e. an immaterial self-consistent element, but only with the granting of vitality to man. This vitality is not, even though it now belongs to man, a spiritual substance or soul: it is simply a spiritual principle, which God can withdraw and reabsorb into Himself. It has no existence as anything in itself. The doctrine of the pre-existence, like that of the immortality, of the soul, is not a Hebrew idea: O.T. thought deals with different categories. It is only in later books, when Jewish thought had begun to assimilate foreign elements,

But perceiving that I could not otherwise [1]possess *wisdom* 21
except God gave *her* me
(Yea and to know [2]by whom the grace is given, this *too* came
of understanding),
I pleaded with the Lord and besought him,

---

[1] This is the probable sense: the Greek text is perhaps defective.
  [2] Gr. *of whom is the grace.*

---

that this spirit is spoken of more as if it had an independent existence
of its own, Eccl. iii. 21, xii. 7 (Davidson, *Theol. of O.T.* p. 193 f.). But
even Ecclesiastes had no conception of souls that had sinned before
birth. Weber (*Altsyn. Pal. Theol.* p. 217) quotes from Midrash
Tanchuma to show that it was held that God had created all souls,
and created them good from the first. They dwelt in a heavenly
region, and were united with a body at the time of conception.
Predestination was an accepted theory among the Alexandrian Jews, see
Philo, *All.* iii. 28 "Some there are whom even before birth God moulds
kindly and disposes well, and chooses for them a goodly lot": but the
Divine method of effecting it was to give the individual a greater or less
inclination to the (invariably good) life of the soul. Even in *Gig.* § 3,
where Philo writes of the differing fortunes of souls after they have
become incarnate, although he acknowledges that some are enslaved by
the body, while others rise superior to it, he does not attempt to account
for this sensual tendency by any theory of pre-natal sin.

  21. *possess* wisdom] This rendering is suggested by the entire
context, and a similar use of ἐγκρατής (without the genitive of the thing
obtained) is found in Ecclus. vi. 27. Vulgate translates ἐγκρατής by
continens, a perfectly legitimate rendering of the word, but with nothing
to commend it except the occurrence of "a body undefiled" in *v.* 20.
With *except God gave*, cp. Prov. ii. 6; Jer. x. 23.

  this too *came of understanding*] He could not be seeking Wisdom, had
not Wisdom already found him. Cp. Tennyson, *Launcelot and Elaine*,

"In me there dwells
No greatness, save it be some far-off touch
Of greatness to know well I am not great."

  I pleaded with the Lord] What are the limits of Solomon's prayer?
why should it be restricted to ch. ix.? God is addressed in x. 20 and
from xi. 17—xii. 27, and again in some portion of each succeeding
chapter (except xiii.) of the book. The answer is that God is indeed
addressed, but is not supplicated: ch. ix. is the only one in which
Wisdom is asked for. In all the following chapters the use of the
second person is purely rhetorical, and the third person would suit
equally well. At the most, they might be described as a meditation.

And with my whole heart I said,

9 O God of the fathers, and [1]Lord who keepest thy mercy,
　Who madest all things [2]by thy word;
2 And by thy wisdom thou formedst man,
　That he should have dominion over the creatures that were
　　made by thee,
3 And rule the world in holiness and righteousness,
　And execute judgement in uprightness of soul;
4 Give me wisdom, her that sitteth by thee on thy [3]throne;

---

[1] Gr. *Lord of thy mercy.* Compare 2 Sam. vii. 15; Ps. lxxxix. 49.
[2] Gr. *in.*　　　[3] Gr. *thrones.*

CH. IX. SOLOMON'S PRAYER.

vv. 1—4. HE APPEALS TO GOD FOR THE GIFT OF WISDOM.

1. *O God of the fathers*] There are several reminiscences in this chapter of 1 Chr. xxviii., xxix. LXX. This invocation (cp. Dan. ii. 23) is based on 1 Chr. xxviii. 9 and xxix. 18, 20, the fathers being Abraham, Isaac and Israel.

Lord...mercy] God's mercy is a leading thought in the prayer in 1 Kings iii. 6 f., and in the Messianic passage 2 Sam. vii. 15, the promises of which are reaffirmed in Ps. lxxxix. 28, cp. Ex. xxxiii. 19.

Who madest...by thy word] There is no allusion here to Greek Logos-doctrine (see Introd. § 10). The tone of the passage is Hebrew, and the combination of *mercy* and *word* recalls Ps. xxxiii. 5, 6 "The earth is full of the mercy (margin and LXX.) of the Lord. By the word of the Lord were the heavens made," cp. id. *v.* 9 "He spake and it was done."

2. *thou formedst man*] i.e. didst form and equip. For the Greek word, which means *to organize* in relation to existing matter, cp. 4 Macc. ii. 21.

That he should have dominion] For the connection between the creation of man and his supremacy over the animal world, cp. Gen. i. 26, 28. See Ps. viii. 6—8; Ecclus. xvii. 2—5.

3. *holiness* and *righteousness* are the aspects of man's life as he maintains a right relation to God and to man, cp. St Luke i. 75. Man is not an irresponsible ruler; he is the servant of the moral law.

in uprightness of soul] An almost identical expression is found in 1 Kings iii. 6; Ps. cxix. 7. To *judge in uprightness* occurs in Ps. ix. 8, xcvi. 10, xcviii. 9. Cp. Ps. lxxv. 2. The idea is that clearness of vision cannot be dissociated from integrity of character.

4. *her that sitteth by thee*] *adsistricem* Vulg., cp. Prov. viii. 27—30, and Ecclus. i. 1.

Philo calls Justice the assessor (πάρεδρος) of God (*Mos.* ii. 10), and

And reject me not from among thy ¹servants:
Because I am thy bondman and the son of thy handmaid,   5
A man weak and short-lived,
And of small power to understand judgement and laws.
For even if a man be perfect among the sons of men,   6
Yet if the wisdom that cometh from thee be not with him,
    he shall be held in no account.

¹ Or, *children*

Greek classical poets apply the same metaphor to Righteousness, and
Themis, cp. Pindar, *Ol.* 8, 22. Cp. Soph. *Ant.* 451.
throne] Gk. *thrones*, cp. *v.* 12, and Ps. cxxii. 5. The plural of dignity.
and reject me not] A reminiscence of Ps. lxxxix. 38 f., which depicts
the Messianic king rejected and forsaken by God. Solomon deprecates
a fate which he knows must befall him, if he thinks to dispense with
Divine aid.

vv. 5—8. SOLOMON PLEADS HIS OWN WEAKNESS, AND THE
        MAGNITUDE OF THE TASK ASSIGNED HIM.

5. *bondman...handmaid*] Taken from Ps. cxvi. 16 and (with a
slight variation) Ps. lxxxvi. 16. The double expression indicates special
dependence. See note in this series on Ps. cxvi. 16, "'The son of thine
handmaid' is a synonym for 'thy servant,' denoting a closer relation-
ship, for servants 'born in the house' (Gen. xiv. 14) were the most
trusted dependents."
    weak and short-lived] Epithets characteristic, not of Solomon in
particular, but of the whole human race to which he belonged. Cp. 1 Chr.
xxix. 15 "We are strangers before thee, and sojourners...; our days on
the earth are as a shadow." Cp. also, however, 1 Kings iii. 7 "I am
but a little child."
    of small power to understand] Vulg. *minor ad intellectum*, cp.
1 Kings iii. 9, 11.
    Judgment points to political administration, *laws* to judicial equity.
    6. *perfect among the sons of men*] The same contrast between the
natural and the spiritual man is intended, as is referred to by our Lord
in St Matt. xi. 11. There may be a side-reference to the choice of
David in preference to the other sons of Jesse in 1 Sam. xvi. 6, 7.
Perfect, Vulg. *consummatus*. The word denotes not so much moral
perfection, as the full possession of all natural qualities. "Sons of
men" may be compared with "born of women" in Job xi. 3 LXX.,
xiv. 1, xv. 14, xxv. 4; both expressions emphasize the material side of
human nature.
    if wisdom...be not with him] Cp. Philo, *Post. C.* § 41 "Whence can
the thirsty heart of man be filled save from the inexhaustible spring of
the Divine Wisdom?" and *Quis rerum* § 12. See St John xv. 5.

7 Thou didst choose me before *my brethren* to be king of thy
     people,
And to do judgement for thy sons and daughters.
8 Thou gavest command to build a sanctuary in thy holy
     mountain,
And ¹an altar in the city of thy ²habitation,
A copy of the holy tabernacle which thou preparedst afore-
     hand from the beginning.

¹ Or, *a place of sacrifice*   ² Gr. *tabernacling.*

7. *Thou didst choose*] *Thou* is emphatic.   The responsibility does
not lie with Solomon.   Cp. 1 Chron. xxviii. 5 ; 2 Chron. i. 9.
     before my brethren] Cp. 2 Sam. iii. 2—5, and 1 Kings i. 5 and
28—31.
     thy sons and daughters] The expression is unusual, cp. Is. xliii. 6,
and "sons and daughters of Sion," Is. iv. 4.   The rarity of the occurrence of "daughters of God " is due, it has been suggested, to the
depressed condition of Eastern womanhood.   If the king is the son of
God (2 Sam. vii. 14), his people are, by a natural extension, called sons
and daughters of God.
     8. *command to build*] Cp. 2 Sam. vii. 13 ; 1 Chron. xxviii. 10 ;
Ecclus. xlvii. 13.
     thy holy mountain] Mount Moriah, traditionally associated with the
trial of Abraham's faith (Gen. xxii. 14) and with the vision of the angel
at the threshingfloor of Araunah (2 Chron. iii. 1).   The expression
occurs six times in the Psalms (LXX.) and in Is. lvi. 7.   "Holy, said
of things, cannot denote a moral attribute.   It can only express a
relation ; and the relation is belonging to Jehovah, dedicated to God-
head....Everything belonging to Jehovah, whether as His by nature or
as dedicated to Him, is called *holy*....In a wider way, the tabernacle,
the place of His abode, was holy ; Zion was the holy hill." (Davidson,
Theol. of O.T. pp. 152, 153.)
     the city of thy habitation] Lit. as marg. *tabernacling* (κατασκήνωσις),
cp. 1 Chron. xxviii. 2 ; Ps. lxxiv. 2 ; 2 Macc. xiv. 35.   For the "city of
God," cp. Ps. xlvi. 4, lxxxvii. 3.
     A copy] 1 Chron. xxviii. 11, 12, 18, 19.   The word is in app. to
sanctuary and *altar* earlier in the same *v.*   The Chronicler represents
David as having received from God a detailed account of the Temple
which he passed on to Solomon, thus imitating the account in Ex. xxv.
9, 40 of the instructions given by God to Moses with respect to the
Tabernacle.   But the "holy Tabernacle " which Solomon was meant to
copy is not the Tabernacle of Moses, but an ideal archetype which the
writer pictures as existing in heaven (see Westcott, Heb. viii. 5, addit.
note).   This, as existing in the timeless mind of God, he describes as
"prepared atorehand from the beginning."   Cp. the Talmudic treatise
Pesachim, which affirms that seven things existed before the creation,

And with thee is wisdom, which knoweth thy works,   9
And was present when thou wast making the world,
And which understandeth what is pleasing in thine eyes,
And what is right ¹according to thy commandments.
Send her forth out of the holy heavens,   10
And from the throne of thy glory bid her come,
That being present with me she may toil *with me*,
And *that* I may learn what is well-pleasing before thee.
For she knoweth all things and hath understanding *thereof,*   11
And in my doings she shall guide me in *ways of* soberness,

¹ Gr. *in.*

the law, hell, paradise, repentance, the throne of glory, the temple, and
the name of the Messiah (Etheridge, *Targums* p. 11). The writer is
possibly influenced by the Greek philosophical theory of ideas, which
was not without its influence upon Heb. viii., ix.: Plato argued that
ideas existed of all possible things, and accordingly the Alexandrian
author of Wisdom may have inferred that there must be an archetypal
idea of the Temple, as of the Tabernacle (Ex. xxv. 40).

vv. 9—12.   WISDOM CAN INFORM AND DIRECT HIS PUBLIC AND
PRIVATE LIFE.

9. *with thee is wisdom*]   Ecclus. i. 1, cp. St John i. 1—4.
present when thou wast making]   See ch. viii. 3, 4, notes.
in thine eyes] is a Hebraism corresponding to ἐνώπιόν σου in Dt.
xii. 8; Is. xxxviii. 3; 1 John iii. 22.
right according to thy commandments]   Right (εὐθὲς) is regularly used
in LXX. in the expression "He did that which was *right* in the sight
of the Lord."
10.   *Send her forth...bid her come*]   Cp. the Greek verbs in St John
xx. 21.   The distinction in sense between the two verbs, urged in
Westcott, St John, addit. note on xx. 21, does not apply here.   The
sentences are parallel, and the second is the repetition rather than the
complement of the first.
holy heavens]   Cp. Ps. xx. 6.   For *holy*, see note on *v.* 8.
throne of thy glory] upon which she sits as God's assessor, *v.* 4.   For
the expression, cp. Jer. xvii. 12 LXX.
being present with me]   Cp. Prov. viii. 27.   He desires that Wisdom,
who was present when God was creating (*v.* 9 a), should aid him in his
work.
11.   *she knoweth all things*]   Cp. vii. 21, 22, viii. 8.
guide me...guard me]   Cp. Ps. xxiii. 3, 4.   The Gk. vb. (ὁδηγεῖν) is
used in this Psalm and in many others of moral guidance.   See
Ps. lxxiii. 24.

And she shall guard me in her glory.
12 And *so* shall my works be acceptable,
And I shall judge thy people righteously,
And I shall be worthy of my father's ¹throne.
13 For what man shall know the counsel of God?
Or who shall conceive what the Lord willeth?
14 For the thoughts of mortals are ²timorous,
And our devices are prone to fail.
15 For a corruptible body weigheth down the soul,

---

¹ Gr. *thrones.*   ² The Greek text here is perhaps corrupt.

guard me in her glory] *in sua potentia* Vulg. If Vulg. is right, cp. Rom. vi. 4, "raised...by the glory of the Father." But the *glory* of Wisdom is probably the light which she possesses as an emanation from the eternal Light, and with which she illuminates his path.

12. *I shall judge*] Vulg. *disponam.* The Greek word refers to the general administration of the state.

throne] The plural of dignity as in *v.* 4.

vv. 13—19. MAN IS SO CLOSELY IMPLICATED WITH THE MATERIAL WORLD THAT, APART FROM SPECIAL GRACE, HE CANNOT CONCEIVE SPIRITUAL THINGS.

13. *For*] The reason why Solomon was so earnest in the search for Wisdom. The king is God's vice-gerent, and no king can interpret the will of God who orders his life upon purely natural principles.

what man] *Man* is emphatic. What human being?

shall know] The verse is based on Is. xl. 13, and is very similar to 1 Cor. ii. 11—16, in which the same quotation appears.

conceive what the Lord willeth] Vulg. *quid velit deus.* "What" introduces not a substantival clause, but an indirect question (τί not ὅ). The Greek suggests not that he cannot receive God's will into his mind, but that he cannot by searching find it out.

14. *the thoughts of mortals*] A reminiscence of Ps. xciv. 11, which is quoted with a slight change in 1 Cor. iii. 20, a passage similar in tone to 1 Cor. ii. 11, 16.

timorous] Marg. suggests that the reading may be corrupt. But the epithet *timorous*, properly applicable to *men*, is applied to their thoughts.

our devices] Vulg. *prouidentiae.* Prone to fail through human short-sightedness.

15. This famous passage has caused the writer to be charged with dualistic views of which he is not guilty. There is in this verse none of that dualism which pronounces matter evil : the writer goes no further than the Psalmist when he says "He knoweth our frame : He remembereth that we are dust," or St Paul in Gal. v. 17. It is a common-

And the earthy frame lieth heavy on a mind that ¹is full of cares.

¹ Or, *museth upon many things*

place of experience that the spirit is willing, but the flesh is too weak (or too strong): the writer does not go beyond this, either here, or in ch. viii. 20. For one to whom classical literature was open either at first hand or through Alexandrian teachers, it is remarkable how he has avoided an error into which Philo fell: this passage presents a typical example of the distinction between Philo with his speculative bent, and Pseudo-Solomon with his inflexible religious purpose.

Philo accepted Heraclitus' epigram σῶμα σῆμα "The body is a tomb," see *All.* i. 33, *Quod D.* 32, *Migr.* 3, *Cong.* 18, *Somn.* i. 22. A characteristic passage is *de Gig.* § 7 "The chief cause of ignorance is the flesh and association with the flesh. Nothing presents such a hindrance to the growth of the soul as the flesh, for it is a kind of foundation of ignorance and stupidity, on which all the (abovementioned) evils are built....Souls that bear the burden of the flesh are weighed down and oppressed till they cannot look up at the heavens, and have their heads forcibly dragged downwards, being rooted to the earth like cattle." In a more temperate passage (*Q. R. D. H.* § 18) he writes " It is not easy to believe in God because of the mortal companion with which we are yoked." The body is a prison (*Migr.* 2); a corpse (*Agr.* 5), cp. Epict. "You are a poor little soul carrying a corpse." Many passages might be quoted from classical authors in this strain. One whose language was not without influence on this passage is Plato, *Phaedo* xxx. 81 c "The body is burdensome, and heavy and earthy: by the possession of it such a soul is oppressed." Cp. βαρούμενοι, 2 Cor. v. 4. See Hor. *Sat.* ii. 2. 77—79; Verg. *Aen.* vi. 730—734. Christian thought has not altogether escaped dualism: St Francis called his body "Brother ass," perhaps misunderstanding Rom. vii. 23, 24. Browning gives the thought intended by the author in its truest form,

> " What hand and brain went ever paired?
> What heart alike conceived and dared?
> What act proved all its thought had been?
> What will but felt the fleshly screen?"
>
> (*The Last Ride together.*)

corruptible] Liable to change and decay, cp. 1 Cor. xv. 53. The soul is ever striving to soar upwards to its source, the Eternal God; but the corruptible body holds it bound to itself as with chains.

the earthy frame] The second clause adds nothing to what has been said in the first; the picture is slightly varied.

frame] Vulg. renders well *inhabitatio*. The original meaning is *tent*, cp. 2 Cor. v. 1, 4, and 2 Pet. i. 13 (σκήνωμα) and *Ep. to Diognetus* § 6 (which contains an extended contrast between body and soul). A similar expression is found in Plato. Cp. Edmund Waller "The soul's dark *cottage*, battered and decayed."

16 And hardly do we ¹divine the things that are on earth, .
And the things that are close at hand we find with labour;
But the things that are in the heavens who *ever yet* traced
out?

17 And who *ever* gained knowledge of thy counsel, except thou
²gavest wisdom,
And sentest thy holy spirit ³from on high?

18 And it was thus that the ways of them which are on earth
were corrected,
And men were taught the things that are pleasing unto thee ;

---

¹ Gr. *conjecture.*   ² Or, *hadst given...and sent*
³ Gr. *from the highest.*

mind that is full of cares] There is no antithesis between *mind*
and *soul* in the preceding line. The margin *that museth upon many
things* (Vulg. *multa cogitantem*) suits the context better than text, but
is not an exact translation of πολύφροντις (full of care). The idea is that
the mind, in spite of its superiority, is incessantly hampered and depressed by matter.

16.   This verse takes up *v.* 13, expatiating on the impossibility of
the natural fathoming the supernatural. The knowledge of the things
around him is largely conjecture for man; acquaintance with the most
necessary things of daily life is only acquired with toil : how entirely
then beyond mortal reach must be the things of God, cp. Is. lv. 9.
For τὰ ἐν χερσίν, *the things that are close at hand,* א reads ποσίν, "at
his feet," which causes a singular resemblance between this passage and
Diog. Laert. i. 8. 34 : Thales fell into a pit when he went out to look
at the stars, and an old woman cried out, "If Thales cannot see the
things at his feet, does he expect to learn the things in the heavens?"

17.   Cp. Is. xl. 13. No distinction must be pressed between *wisdom*
and *holy spirit,* cp. vii. 22. The variation of terms is due to poetical
parallelism, and the third Person of the Trinity is not thought of.
"The holy spirit (in O.T.) is the name for all godly aspirations, as
well as for the cause of them ; it is that quickened human spirit which
strives after God, and it is that Divine moving which causes it to strive,
and it is that God even after whom there is the strife" (Davidson,
Theol. of O.T. p. 233).

sentest] Inspiration is spoken of in similar terms, Is. lxiii. 14 LXX.
"a spirit came down from the Lord and guided them." Cp. Ps. civ. 30;
Bar. iii. 29, and Philo, *Q. R. D. H.* § 13 "inspired from above."

18.   *the ways...were corrected*] The same metaphor appears in Jer.
vii. 3, of the making straight of that which was morally crooked. For
the things that are pleasing to God, cp. Bar. iv. 4 LXX. The reference
is general, and not restricted to the illustrations in ch. x.

And through wisdom were they saved.

[1]Wisdom guarded to the end the first formed father of the 10
world, that was created alone,

[1] Gr. *She.*

were they saved] Saved, not in the theological sense, but in the
sense of "preserved" from dangers spiritual and bodily.   The manner
of the *saving* is of course relative, varying with the needs of each case.
Vulg., apparently without any Greek authority, supplies as subject to
the verb ἐσώθησαν, *as many as pleased Thee, O Lord, from the beginning.*

PART II.

Chapters x.—xix. form the second part of the book.   The unifying
idea is the beneficent action of Wisdom in history.   Attention is mainly
concentrated upon the contrast between the fortunes of Israel and their
heathen enemies whether in Egypt or in Canaan : idolatry is assigned as
the cause of the judgments of God upon heathenism.   Emphasis is laid
upon the Fatherhood of God, and upon the position of Israel as the
chosen people, towards whom God's mercy is shown with a constancy
which the writer's national sympathy enables him to justify while
exaggerating.   This Jewish philosophy of Israelitish history requires
considerable licence in the interpretation of Scripture, and the writer
does not confine himself to the authoritative records, but avails himself
of amplifications and traditions provided by Jewish teachers in their
midrashim (commentaries).   For the divisions of Part II., see Introduction § 15.

Ch. X.   The operation of Wisdom in the history of Adam
1, 2 ; Cain 3 ; Noah 4 ; Abraham 5 ; Lot 6—9 ; Jacob 10—12 ;
Joseph 13, 14 ; Israel under Moses 15—21.

1.   *Wisdom*]   Marg. *She,* with reference to ix. 18, of which *v.* this
ch. is the expansion.   The emphatic pronoun (αὔτη) is used throughout
this ch. in *vv.* 5, 6, 10, 13, 15.   Wisdom in this ch. appears as an
active principle of good, leading, saving, protecting men, and forsaken
at their peril.

the first formed]   See on vii. 1.

father of the world]   In accordance with the custom of the book,
which, though largely occupied with history, does not mention by name
any historical character, indirect allusion is made to Adam.   Since
familiarity with the Jewish Scriptures is thus presupposed on the part
of the reader, the book was evidently addressed to a Jewish circle.

that was created alone]   Vulg. *cum solus esset creatus.*   There are
two possible interpretations of the Greek, of which text contains one,
almost certainly right, while the other is *the alone-created,* i.e. Adam

And delivered him out of his own transgression,
2 And gave him strength to get dominion over all things.
3 But when an unrighteous man fell away from her in his
    anger,
He perished himself in the rage wherewith he slew his
    brother.

alone, of all the human race, can claim to have been created ; all others
were born, although they may be spoken of as created, in a derivative
sense, through him.   But this interpretation is somewhat strained : the
thought does not seem natural to the writer, nor has it any relevancy
to the sense of the passage.   In view of *guarded to the end*, it is plain
that the solitude of Adam is the writer's thought, and that he is telling
how, when the future of the race of men hung upon the single thread of
Adam's life, Wisdom watched over the destined father of mankind.
Grimm and others render μόνος *unprotected*, but it is better to take the
word literally.   Cp. Etheridge, *Targums* p. 169 "The word of the
Lord God said 'Behold, Adam...is sole in my world, as I am sole in
the heavens above.'"
    delivered out of...transgression]   The exact reference is not very clear,
but that any suggestion of Adam's final salvation is made, is out of the
question.   Such a discussion, besides its irrelevancy, has no place in a
pre-Christian work, the Incarnation being the indispensable presup-
position for such a restoration (cp. Irenaeus' attack upon Tatian's
doctrine of the final loss of Adam, *adv. Haer.* iii. 23).   Wisdom, the
writer suggests, gave him repentance, kept him humble, and caused the
curse to fall not upon Adam but upon the serpent and upon the earth.
The words probably allude to the penalty denounced upon disobedience
(Gen. ii. 17), which was not enforced at any rate literally.   Irenaeus
held that God caused Adam ultimately to die, not in wrath but in pity,
lest he should continue a sinner for ever : Tertullian (*de Paen.* § 12)
held that Adam was restored to Paradise after confession of his sin.
    2.   *And gave him strength*]   This verse refers to the authority given
to mankind over all living creatures (Gen. i. 26, 28, and again Gen. ix. 2).
Wisdom did not deny to Adam the aid which the Fall rendered more
than ever necessary.
    3.   *an unrighteous man*]   i.e. Cain.   His bearing is contrasted with
that of Adam.
    fell away from her]   Cain rejected Wisdom both by his crime against
his brother, and by his insolent behaviour subsequently ("am I my
brother's keeper?"), which aggravated his offence (Irenaeus, *Haer.* iii.
23. 4).
    perished himself in the rage]   The Talmud has two legends with
regard to Cain's death (1) that he was the man killed by Lamech, Gen.
iv. 23, (2) that he was crushed by a falling house (Jubilees iv. 31).
But συναπώλετο (*he perished with* his rage) makes a spiritual interpretation of the passage more probable.   Cain, in killing his brother, killed

And when for his cause the earth was drowning with a flood, 4
Wisdom again saved it,
Guiding the righteous man's course by a poor piece of wood.

Moreover, when nations consenting together in wickedness 5
had been confounded,
¹Wisdom knew the righteous man, and preserved him blameless unto God,

¹ Gr. *She.*

his own soul. This agrees with Philo's "Cain killed himself, not
Abel" (*Det. Pot.* § 14). With this use of the Greek verb, cp. Ep. of
Barnabas, xxi. (twice) and Prayer of Manasses, 13. Neither text nor
Vulgate recognise the force of *σύν* (with) in the verb.

4. *for his cause*] The wickedness which brought the flood upon
the earth is laid at the door of Cain and not of Adam, cp. ch. ii. 24.
Josephus (*Antiq.* i. 2. 2) tells of the wickedness of Cain in the years
after the murder of Abel, and of the wickedness of his posterity. Cp.
Gen. vi. 4—6.

was drowning] Cp. Gen. vi. 17 ff.

again saved it] Cp. ch. xiv. 6, where Noah is called *the hope of the
world*. The "earth" was saved in an indirect sense although it was
drowned, its interests being identified with the human stock preserved
through Noah in the ark. Wisdom watched over the ark, as she had
watched over Adam, thus preserving the race a second time.

Guiding] lit. steering, Vulg. *gubernans.*

the righteous man] Noah is the first man, Gen. vi. 9, to be called
righteous in the Bible (Philo, *Cong.* § 17). It is not an accident
(Philo adds) that he is tenth from Adam, but righteousness stands to the
conduct of life as the number ten to the number one.

by a poor piece of wood] Cp. 1 Pet. iii. 20 in which the instrument of
safety is, not the ark, but the water which bore it ; see ch. xiv. 5. In
both passages the inadequacy of the means to the end is pointed to.
The ark is not disparaged, for it is the work of Wisdom; but viewed
from the point of view of the deluge, it is insignificant.

5. *when nations...had been confounded*] *confounded* (συγχυθέντων)
recalls "confusion" (σύγχυσις, LXX. for Babel) in the account of the
"confusion" of tongues (Gen. xi. 1—9). The "consenting together
in wickedness" was the concerted action in building the tower, or
(Grotius) universal idolatry. The writer makes a point of concord
(ὁμόνοια) becoming confusion. The incident is introduced to bring out
by contrast the fact that there still existed a small righteous remnant.

knew] Text follows אAC and Vulg. B reads *found* (εὗρεν). The
reference is to Gen. xii. For the Divine knowledge of a man, cp. 1 Cor.
viii. 3.

blameless unto God] The same word is used in Gen. xvii. 1 LXX.
With this use of *unto God*, cp. Jon. iii. 3 LXX.; Acts vii. 20. For
Abraham's character before God, see Gen. xviii. 18.

And kept him strong when his heart yearned toward his child.

6 While the ungodly were perishing, [1]wisdom delivered a righteous man,
When he fled from the fire that descended out of heaven on [2]Pentapolis.

7 To whose wickedness a smoking waste still witnesseth,
And plants bearing fair fruit that cometh not to ripeness;

[1] Gr. *she.*   [2] That is, *the region of the five cities.*

when his heart yearned] lit. kept him strong against his compassion for his child : see Gen. xxii.; Ecclus. xliv. 20, Heb. xi. 17. Etheridge (*Targums* p. 226) quotes a *midrash* "While Sarah was yet sleeping, Abraham left in the early morning. Satana stood in his way as an aged man, and said 'Whither goest thou?' 'To pray.' 'But why with wood and knife?' 'I must needs prepare food.' 'Should a man like you kill his son who was given him in old age?' 'God has commanded.'"

6. *a righteous man*] For the escape of Lot from Sodom, see Gen. xix. 17 ff., cp. 2 Pet. ii. 7, 8, "righteous Lot."

Pentapolis] The group of five "cities of the plain," of which only Zoar was spared (cp. Gen. xiv. 2). "Provided it may be assumed that in Abraham's time what is now the shallow S. part of the Dead Sea was the 'Vale of Siddim,' and the morass es-Sebkha (on the S. of the Dead Sea) a fertile plain, it may reasonably be supposed that the other four cities were situated on this plain....The evidence that the post-biblical Zoar was at the S. end of the Dead Sea clearly cannot be resisted, and in the case of...a well-known place, it seems scarcely likely that the Zoar of Josephus was on a different site from the biblical Zoar" (Prof. Driver in Hastings, *D.B.* iv. 986 b).

7. *a smoking waste still witnesseth*] Philo (*Abr.* § 27, *Mos.* ii. 10) mentions this phenomenon as still in existence. Smoke may have issued from the bituminous soil as in the Lydian Catacecaumene, or the notion may be due to the dense mist which rises from the basin of the Dead Sea. In the Greek *Acts of Pionius* this passage occurs "I myself, on crossing the Jordan saw a land which to this day witnesseth to the wrath that fell from God upon it, because of the sins wrought by its inhabitants. I saw smoke arising from it even till now, and the land scorched with fire, destitute of all fruit and water."

fruit that cometh not to ripeness] Cp. Dt. xxxii. 32 and Josephus, *Wars* iv. 8. 4 "There are still the remainders of that divine fire...the ashes still grow in their fruits, which fruits have a colour as if they were fit to be eaten; but if you pluck them with your hands, they dissolve into smoke and ashes."

Cp. Tert. *Apol.* § 40; Tac. *Hist.* v. 7. See Curzon, *Monasteries of the Levant*, p. 189, and Tristram, *Nat. Hist. of Bible*, p. 482.

Yea and a ¹disbelieving soul hath a memorial *there*, a pillar
of salt *still* standing.

For having passed wisdom by,   8
Not only were they disabled from recognising the things
   which are good,
But they also left behind them ²for *human* life a monument
   of their folly;
To the end that ³where they ⁴went astray they might fail even
   to be unseen:

¹ Or, *distrustful*	² Or, *by their life*
³ Gr. *wherein.*	⁴ Gr. *stumbled.*

a disbelieving soul] Cp. Gen. xix. 17, 26. In Clem. Rom. xi. Lot's
wife is called "otherwise-minded and not in accord (with God)": her
pillar exists to this day as "a warning to the double-minded and those
who doubt the power of God."

hath a memorial] The Gk. word probably contains a double meaning (1) memorial, (2) tomb: according to the legend, her pillar was her
tomb. Cp. Heraclitus' σῶμα σῆμα (p. 93).

Josephus (*Ant.* i. 11. 4) claims to have seen the very pillar: Irenaeus
(*Haer.* iv. 31. 3) sees in its continued existence a picture of the Church's
life. The story is readily accounted for by the remarkable rock forma-
tions in the *Jebel Usdum*, a range of cliffs at the south-west end of the
Dead Sea, consisting of crystallised rock-salt. From the face of these
cliffs great fragments are occasionally detached by the rains, and appear
as "pillars of salt" (Sir G. Grove in Smith, *D. B.* iii. 1180). Prof.
Driver (Hastings, *D. B.* iii. 152) quotes an American traveller who
described one such pillar, which was about 40 ft. high, cylindrical in
form, and rested on a kind of oval pedestal, some 50 ft. above the level
of the sea. Such pillars are constantly in process of formation and
destruction.

8. This verse contains the philosophy of *v.* 7, and is a variation
upon Prov. i. 29—31. Those who reject Wisdom (like the men of
Sodom and Lot's wife, a woman of Sodom) incur a double loss: they
become spiritually blind, and they are held up to the reproach of future
generations, with an unenviable immortality. Philo (*Conf. l.* § 8) speaks
of them as "sterile in wisdom and blind in heart."

for human *life*] i.e. living men, Vulg. *hominibus.* Cp. 4 Macc.
xvii. 14 "The world and human life were looking on." Marg. suggests
by their life, their memorial corresponding to and springing out of their
life, cp. the smoking land, the bitter fruit, the pillar of salt.

their folly] The opposite of wisdom, "godlessness."

they might fail even to be unseen] Their self-inflicted punishments,
see xi. 16, springing out of the sins that produced them, proclaim
publicly the misdeeds of those whom they overtook.

9 But wisdom delivered out of troubles those that waited on
her.

10 When a righteous man was a fugitive from a brother's
wrath, [1]wisdom guided him in straight paths;
She shewed him God's kingdom, and gave him knowledge
of holy things;
She prospered him in his toils, and multiplied the fruits of
his labour;

11 When in their covetousness *men* dealt hardly with him,
She stood by him and made him rich;

12 She guarded him from enemies,
And from those that lay in wait she kept him safe,
And over his sore conflict she watched as judge,

[1] Gr. *she*.

9. So much for the cities of the plain and their ungodly inhabitants.
Turn now to the examples of those who cultivated Wisdom, and see
what a deliverer she is.

10. *When a righteous man*] See Gen. xxvii. 41—45. The writer
has applied the epithet *righteous* to Noah, Abraham, Lot, and *unrighteous* to Cain. Jacob here and Joseph (*v.* 13) are called *righteous*,
while the same epithet is given to Israel in *v.* 20, in contradistinction
to the Egyptians who are called *ungodly* (cp. *v.* 6 of the men of Sodom).
There is a touch of patriotic bias in the characterisation (cp. esp. *v.* 15),
which is very marked in the two succeeding chapters.

straight paths] Cp. Gen. xxviii. 20; Prov. iii. 6.

God's kingdom] Probably referring to Jacob's dream, Gen. xxviii.
10—17, in which God revealed to him some of the providential agencies
of the kingdom of God.

knowledge of holy things] i.e. of supernatural mysteries. This may
refer to the wrestling with the angel, Gen. xxxii. 24—32 "I have seen
God face to face," and to the prophetic visions of Gen. xlviii., xlix.

prospered him] This may include the reflected prosperity of Laban,
Gen. xxx. 30, as well as what accrued to himself, Gen. xxx. 43.

the fruits of his labour] lit. his labours, cp. viii. 7; Ecclus. xiv. 15.

11. See Gen. xxxi. 38—42. Wisdom helped him to prosper in
spite of Laban's churlishness.

12. *guarded him from enemies*] Such as Laban, who was warned in
a dream not to hurt Jacob (Gen. xxxi. 24, 29).

those that lay in wait] Esau (Gen. xxvii. 41, xxxii. 11, 20, xxxiii.).
Deane suggests also a reference to the Canaanite tribes on the way to
Bethel (Gen. xxxv. 5) upon which the "terror of God" had fallen.

over his sore conflict she watched as judge] Gen. xxxii. 24—30; Hos.
xii. 3, 4. Vulg. *certamen dedit ut uinceret*. The Gk. verb has the

That he might know that godliness is more powerful than ¹all.

When a righteous man was sold, ²wisdom forsook him not,   13
But ³from sin she delivered him;
She went down with him into a dungeon,
And in bonds she left him not,   14
Till she brought him the sceptre of a kingdom,
And authority over those that dealt tyrannously with him;
She shewed them also to be false that had mockingly
    accused him,

¹ Gr. *every one*.   ² Gr. *she*.
³ Or, *from the sin* of his brethren...*into a pit*

general sense of "acting as arbitrator, or umpire," cp. Philo, *Quis rerum* § 19: Vulg. goes beyond the meaning of the word. The writer suggests that not only has piety nothing to fear from men, but it actually prevails with God (Grimm).

That he might know] The wrestling with God was also a parable. To the writer every historic event has its value as a symbol of spiritual truth, cp. ch. xvi. 28. Like Robert Browning, he might say "My stress lay on the incidents in the development of a soul: little else is worth study."

more powerful] Even than Jacob's own astuteness, cp. 1 Tim. iv. 8.

13. *was sold*] See Gen. xxxvii. 27, 28.

from sin] Vulg. *a peccatoribus*. This interpretation is accepted by marg., which reads "*from the sin* of his brethren," and renders λάκκον in next *l. pit*, this being the LXX. word for "pit" in Gen. xxxvii. 24. But inasmuch as in the first *l*. Joseph was said to have been sold, it seems almost contradictory to say later "but delivered him from his brothers." The reference is more probably to the temptation of Joseph and his answer (Gen. xxxix. 9).

with him into a dungeon] Either this or marg. is possible. But in Gen. xl. 15 LXX. λάκκος stands for the dungeon of Potiphar, and so probably here. Cp. Dan. iii. 49 LXX. "The angel of the Lord went down with them (συνκατέβη) into the furnace."

14. *And in bonds*] See Gen. xxxix. 21 ff. and xl. "It was not needful for the captain of the prison to watch Joseph,...because he saw that there was no fault in his hands; for the Word of the Lord was his helper." Etheridge, *Targum of Palestine* p. 296.

sceptre] Gk. *sceptres*. Plural of dignity, expressing the idea of power generally, Gen. xli. 39—45. Philo, *Jos.* § 21 writes "Pharaoh made him second in the kingdom, or rather (to speak the truth) king."

authority over those that dealt tyrannously] i.e. the Egyptians generally (Gen. xli. 44), whose representatives had imprisoned him.

shewed them also to be false] Potiphar's wife, Gen. xxxix. 17, 18.

had mockingly accused him] Vulg. has *maculauerunt*, "defamed";

And gave him eternal glory.

15 ¹Wisdom delivered a holy people and a blameless seed from
a nation of oppressors.
16 She entered into the soul of a servant of the Lord,
And withstood terrible kings in wonders and signs.
17 She rendered unto holy men a reward of their toils;

¹ Gr. *She.*

"mockingly" is not in the Greek.   There may be a side-reference to
Gen. xxxvii. 8, cp. xlix. 23.
  gave him eternal glory]   For the phrase, cp. Is. xxii. 22 LXX. "I
will give him the glory of David."   "Eternal" indicates rather the
undying fame of Joseph, than his temporal reputation in Egypt and
lordship over his brothers.

v. 15—21.   WISDOM AS THE HELPER OF ISRAEL.

15. *holy people...blameless seed*]   The writer assumes that Wisdom
was on the side of Israel, and designates the people accordingly.   He
can only draw a convincing picture by isolating certain broad characteristics of the Israelite people: artistically he is correct, as the qualifications
necessary for literal accuracy would weaken the impression he desires to
convey, and are allowed for mentally by the Jewish circle he addresses.
The Jews are the people of God, cp. Ex. xix. 6; ideally they take their
character from the Name by which they are called: similarly the heathen
as not knowing God are stigmatised as the reverse of all that is godly
(*v.* 20, xii. 11).   Deane rightly remarks that the expression does not
point to any definite blamelessness in the Israelites, but is an official
designation.   That there were even traditions of idolatry among the
Israelites in Egypt is plain from Jos. xxiv. 14; Ezek. xx. 8, xxiii. 3.
  16. *She entered into the soul*]   Cp. Ex. iv. 12, vii. 1.
  a servant of the Lord]   Moses alone is known as the servant (θεράπων)
of the Lord in canonical books, although the word is applied to Aaron
in Wisd. xviii. 21.   The word carries a more honourable significance
than "bondservant" (δοῦλος).   Cp. Heb. iii. 5.
  terrible kings]   Possibly refers only to Pharaoh, the plural being
employed in a general sense, cp. Ps. cv. 30 (but LXX. reading is not
certain).   But the reference is almost certainly identical with that in
Ps. cxxxv. 9, 10, and includes kings outside Egypt, cp. Ps. cxxxvi. 17, 18.
  wonders and signs]   Cp. ch. viii. 8 and Ps. cxxxv. 9.
  17. *holy men*]   Again, the idealised Israel.
  reward of their toils]   The obvious reference seems to be Ex. xi. 2, 3,
xii. 35, 36, although the borrowed jewels could hardly have repaid the
people for their years of servitude.   Liberty, and the catalogue of
mercies recorded in *vv.* 17—19 should be included, as well as the

She guided them along a marvellous way,
And became unto them a covering in the day-time,
And a flame of stars through the night.
She brought them over the Red sea,   18
And led them through much water;
But their enemies she drowned,   19
And out of the bottom of the deep she cast them up.
Therefore the righteous spoiled the ungodly;   20
And they sang praise to thy holy name, O Lord,

"much substance" (Gen. xv. 14) gathered in Egypt which the people
took with them (Ex. xii. 32, 38).

a marvellous way] Ex. xiii. 21, 22. With the line cp. Ps. cxxxix.
24 LXX. Philo (*Mos.* ii. 34) speaks of the path through the sea as
"a marvellously wrought path" (μεγαλουργηθεῖσα).

became unto them a covering] The cloud was thought of not only as
guide (Ex. xiii. 21), but as protection from the heat, see Num. x. 34;
Ps cv. 39; cp. Is. iv. 5, 6. See chs. xviii. 3, xix. 7. Wisdom is here
identified with the cloud. Such identification might easily spring from
the language of Ex. xiv. 19, cp. the identification of the rock with
Christ, borrowed from Jewish speculation, 1 Cor. x. 4. In *Mos.* i. 29
Philo writes of the cloud, in its aspect as guide, that possibly it concealed
some ministering angel.

flame of stars] Cp. Ps. lxxviii. 14.

18. See Ex. xiv. Philo (*Mos.* ii. 34) amplifies the account of the
passage of the sea, but adds no important traditional details.

19. Ex. xiv. 26—28. Vulg. makes the second *l. from the bottom of
the deep she brought them up* refer to the Israelites, but Philo's use of
ἀπεβράσθησαν in connection with the casting up of the Egyptian corpses
(cp. ἀνέβρασεν *cast them up* here) makes it almost certain that text is
right. The Pal. Targum has "The sea and the earth had controversy
one with the other. The sea said to the earth, Receive thy children;
and the earth said to the sea, Receive thy murderers. But the earth
willed not to swallow them, and the sea willed not to overwhelm them....
Then God swore to the earth that He would not require them of her in
the world to come. Then did the earth open her mouth and swallow
them up." Etheridge, *Targums* p. 494.

20. *Therefore...spoiled the ungodly*] Because the Egyptians were
dead on the sea-shore, the Israelites could take their spoil. The Greek
word is the same as that in Ex. xii. 36 of the spoiling of the Egyptians
before the departure, but no doubt the reference is to the tradition
mentioned by Josephus (*Ant.* ii. 16. 6 and iii. 1. 4). "On the next day
Moses gathered the weapons of the Egyptians, which were brought to
the camp of the Hebrews by the current of the sea, and the force of
the wind assisting it; and he conjectured that this also happened by
Divine Providence, that so they might not be destitute of weapons."

sang praise] Ex. xv. 1—22.

And extolled with one accord thy hand that fought for them:
21 Because wisdom opened the mouth of the dumb,
  And made the tongues of babes to speak clearly.

11 She prospered their works in the hand of a holy prophet.

2 They journeyed through a desert without inhabitant,

extolled] Cp. 3 Macc. ii. 8.

with one accord] Philo (*Mos.* ii. 34) writes "Moses divided the people into two bands of men and women, to sing in harmony to the Creator-Father; for men's deep voices, and the clear tones of women, blend in a sweet and melodious strain. The many thousands of the people he persuaded to join together in singing with concerted voices of those marvellous works."

21. *the mouth of the dumb*] A clear reminiscence of Ex. iv. 11, 12. The plural, by a kind of poetic generalisation, first points to Moses, and then includes all the people.

tongues of babes] Cp. Ps. viii. 2.

speak clearly] Cp. Is. xxxv. 6 LXX. Wisdom gave articulate utterance to those who were but babes in eloquence. The language is general and rhetorical: no definite allusion is intended, unless perhaps to what Philo records (*Mos.* ii. 34), viz. that the two bodies of singers, with no previous rehearsal, found themselves joining in the same words of praise.

CH. XI. 1—CH. XII. 2. CONTRAST BETWEEN THE FORTUNES OF ISRAEL AND EGYPT IN RESPECT OF WATER. REFLECTIONS ON THE PURPOSE FOR WHICH THE PLAGUES OF EGYPT ASSUMED THEIR PARTICULAR FORMS. GOD'S DEALINGS WITH ISRAEL FOR ITS PRESERVATION AND WITH EGYPT FOR PUNISHMENT.

vv. 1—3. WISDOM PRESERVED ISRAEL DURING THE WANDERINGS.

1. *She prospered their works*] Wisdom is still the subject. For a similar phrase, see Gen. xxxix. 23 LXX. *In the hand* is a common Hebraism (cp. Ps. lxxvii. 20; Neh. ix. 14), signifying "by the agency of."

a holy prophet] Moses, cp. Dt. xviii. 15; Hos. xii. 13. For the expression, cp. St Luke i. 70. Philo (*Mos.* ii. 23) writes of Moses, that as he was the greatest king, lawgiver, and high priest, so he was also the most famous prophet, cp. Dt. xxxiv. 10. *vv.* 2, 3 are an expansion of this *v.*

2. *desert without inhabitant*] Cp. Dt. xxxii. 10; Ps. cvii. 4. The idea is not that they came upon no tribes inhabiting the desert, but that the desert had no established city-life. For ἀοίκητος (uninhabited) cp. Hos. xiii. 5.

And in trackless regions they pitched their tents.
They withstood enemies, and [1]repelled foes.   3
They thirsted, and they called upon thee,   4
And there was given them water out of [2]the [3]flinty rock,
And healing of their thirst out of the hard stone.
For by what things their foes were punished,   5
By these they in their need were benefited.
[4]When *the enemy* were troubled with clotted blood instead of 6
a river's ever-flowing fountain,

[1] Or, *took vengeance on foes*   [2] Or, *the steep rock*   [3] See Deut.
viii. 15; Ps. cxiv. 8.   The text of this verse is perhaps corrupt.

in trackless regions] For ἄβατος, cp. Ps. lxiii. 1 LXX. Hobab was
their guide, Num. x. 29—32.
pitched their tents] Perhaps a reference to Succoth (Tents), the first
encampment of the Israelites after leaving Egypt, Ex. xii. 37. Cp. the
institution of the feast of Tabernacles, Lev. xxiii. 43.
3. There is probably no distinction to be observed between *enemies*
and *foes*: poetical variation accounts for the reduplication. Among the
enemies in the wanderings were the Amalekites, Ex. xvii.; Arad, Sihon
and Og, Num. xxi.; the Midianites, Num. xxxi.

vv. **4—10.** HOW WATER WAS USED TO BLESS THE ISRAELITES
AND TO PUNISH THE EGYPTIANS.

4. *They thirsted*] Ex. xvii. 1—7; see also Num. xx. 8—11. The
people could only be said to have called upon God for water indirectly,
through Moses, cp. Ps. cvii. 5, 6. The writer ignores their murmurings.
water out of the flinty rock] ἀκροτόμου, Vulg. *altissima*, marg. *steep*.
The Gk. word (ἀκρότομος), properly "steep," "precipitous," is the
LXX. rendering of the Heb. word for "flinty" in Dt. viii. 15; Job
xxviii. 9; Ps. cxiv. 8. Philo (*All.* ii. 21) writes, "The 'rock of flint'
is the Wisdom of God, from which He feeds the souls that love Him";
cp. 1 Cor. x. 4.
healing of their thirst] For the phrase, cp. 4 Macc. iii. 10, and
Philo, *Mos.* i. 38, *Post. Cain* 41, *Somn.* ii. 9.
5. Thus water was a boon to the Israelites, but to the Egyptians
it was the medium of great misery. Water was miraculously provided
to relieve the thirst of the Israelites, but water was transformed into a
plague for the Egyptians (Ex. vii. 19, xvii. 6). There is a certain
resemblance between this contrast and that in 1 Pet. iii. 20, where
the drowning of the world by water is contrasted with the saving of
the ark by the water which carried it on its waves.
6. *When the enemy were troubled*] Text translates B. This rendering,
adopted by Vulg., causes an anacoluthon. AC read ταραχθέντος, in

7 To rebuke the decree for the slaying of babes,
  Thou gavest them abundant water beyond all hope,
8 Having shewn *them* by ¹the thirst which they had suffered
  how thou didst punish the adversaries.
9 For when they were tried, albeit but in mercy chastened,

¹ Gr. *the then thirst.*

which case the rendering is "Instead of the ever-flowing fountain of
a river now troubled with clotted blood, Thou gavest to Israel abundant
water." The sense is unaffected in either case, although the clauses are
better balanced in text.

clotted blood] Cp. Ex. vii. 19—25. Philo (*Mos.* i. 17) writes that
God determined to plague the Egyptians by water before anything else,
because they exaggerated its worth, and viewed it as the source of
all creative power. Josephus (*Ant.* ii. 14. 1, iii. 1. 4) writes that the
Nile water was sweet for the Irsaelites, all the time that it was blood
for the Egyptians.

7. *To rebuke the decree*] Ex. i. 15, 16, 22. A double punishment for a twofold sin is here set forth. Pharaoh was punished with
scarcity of water because he had sinned through water; and, secondly,
the Nile was turned to blood because he had sinned by the blood of the
firstborn. Cp. Etheridge, *Targums* p. 448 "The king of Mizraim was
struck (with disease), and he commanded to kill the firstborn of the
sons of Israel that he might bathe himself in their blood." This incident,
not recorded in Scripture, is held to have occurred while Moses was in
the land of Midian. Farrar points out that Scripture does not allude
to the notion that the plagues were related by any causal connection to
the sins of the Egyptians: they are set forth as signs of power, to urge
Pharaoh to obedience to God.

8. This *v.* shows that the writer has no thought of the tradition quoted
from Josephus (see *v.* 6), but is contrasting the gift of water to Israel in
the wilderness with the failure of water experienced by the Egyptians.
Confident in his thesis that what punished Egypt benefited Israel, he
argues that the Israelites were allowed to thirst for a little, in order
that they might be able to measure the proportionately worse sufferings of the Egyptians when their water had been turned into blood.
According to the writer, no moral purpose was served by the scarcity of
water experienced by Israel: the main reason was that their imagination
might be whetted to appreciate the tortures endured by the Egyptians.
Needless to say this is not the Scriptural account, which for moral
sublimity is unsurpassed, Dt. viii. 2, 3.

9. *when they were tried*] The Israelites, though chastened by
mercy, could nevertheless argue from the known to the unknown, and
conceive what the chastenings of anger might be. The writer is hardly
consistent in these utterances with those humane sentiments at the end
of the chapter which are the beauty of the Book of Wisdom, *vv.* 23—26.
God is represented here as arbitrarily restricting His mercy to Israel,

They learned how the ungodly were tormented, being
  judged with wrath:
For these, as a father, admonishing them, thou didst prove; 10
But those, as a stern king, condemning them, thou didst
  search out.
Yea and whether they were far off *from the righteous* or near 11
  them, they were alike distressed;
For a double grief took hold on them,   12
And a groaning at the remembrance of things past.

and His wrath to Egypt, but a truer version of the facts may be seen in
Ex. xxxii. 28; Num. xi. 33.

the ungodly] The writer's national particularism shows itself in his
use of *ungodly* for the Egyptians (cp. xii. 11) in contrast with the "holy
people and blameless seed," x. 15.

A.V. introduces here without any warrant from MSS. or versions
the third clause of *v.* 14. The change has nothing to recommend it,
and spoils the carefully arranged parallelism of the three consecutive
contrasts in *vv.* 8, 9, 10.

10. The writer affirms that God's purposes towards Israel were
educative, and towards Egypt retributive. The two contradictions of
God as avenger and as forgiver, and of God as God of Israel and
God of all, though reconciled in the Incarnation, were for the writer
irreconcilable, and yet caused him but slight perplexity. This verse
belongs to the same dispensation that produced the imprecatory Psalms,
cp. Mal. i. 2, 3 "I loved Jacob, and I hated Esau."

as a father] Cp. Dt. viii. 5; 2 Sam. vii. 14. Contrast with this
verse Acts x. 35; Rom. ii. 9.

vv. **11—14.** THE EFFECT OF THE MIRACLE OF THE WATER FROM
            THE ROCK UPON THE EGYPTIANS.

11. *far off...or near*] When Israel was in Egypt and the Nile was
as blood, the Egyptians suffered: but when Israel was in the wilderness, and the Nile was once more water, the Egyptians suffered no
less. This time mentally: for it galled them to hear the report that
water, which had been so hostile to themselves, had befriended the
escaping Israelites.

12. *a double grief*] (1) The objective tortures of thirst, now past;
(2) the subjective annoyance at the good fortune of the Israelites.

and a groaning] The news from the wilderness revived the slum-
bering memories of the water-famine. To be reminded of Israel was
to be reminded of the stricken Nile. Vulg. *gemitus cum memoria prae-
teritorum* supports text in following אA παρελθόντων for παρελθουσῶν
of BC.

13 For when they heard that through their own punishments
    the others [1]had been benefited,
    They felt *the presence of* the Lord;
14 For him who long before was [2]cast forth and exposed they
    left off mocking:
    In the last issue of what came to pass [3]they marvelled,
    Having thirsted in another manner than the righteous.

[1] Some authorities read *were being*.   [2] Some authorities read *cast
forth in hatred they*.   [3] Or, *they marvelled* at him

13. *For*] What made the annoyance of the Egyptians more intoler-
able, and so doubled their grief, was the realisation that Jehovah, the
God of Moses whom they had despised, had triumphed over the gods
of Egypt, cp. Ex. xii. 12.

their own punishments] i.e. the "medium of their own punishment,"
water. Perhaps the punishment of the Egyptians by water, when Israel
escaped and their own forces were destroyed, is also in the writer's mind.

had been benefited] Marg. following B *were being*; so Vulg. *bene
secum agi*. It would be a worse blow to the Egyptians to know that
Israel was being *continuously* benefited by water.

They felt...the Lord] Cp. xii. 27; Ex. v. 2.

14. *cast forth and exposed*] Text adopts the reading of B ἐν
ἐκθέσει, which has the support of xviii. 5. Marg. *cast forth in hatred*
follows ℵAC ἐν ἐχθεσει (σι) : for ἔχθος in pl., cp. Hom. *Il.* iii. 416. The
latter is to be preferred. The exposure of Moses in his infancy is not
germane to the topic in hand, nor has it any connection with the
"mocking" of the Egyptians: on the other hand, *cast forth in hatred*
refers plainly to Ex. x. 11, 28. πάλαι (long before) has a purely relative significance, and is as applicable to Pharaoh's rejection of Moses as
to Moses' exposure in infancy.

they left off mocking] The writer adds this touch from his own
fancy: there is no doubt that the attitude of the Egyptians towards
Moses must have been allied to mockery, when some of the plagues
were matched by the enchantments of the magicians. The attitude of
contempt for Moses the spokesman of Israel is not incompatible with
considerable regard for him as a man, Ex. xi. 3.

In the last issue] The time to which this clause refers is fixed by
the succeeding one. The writer postulates that news reached Egypt
of the miracle of the smitten rock, and that the tidings caused Egypt to
marvel at the man whom for so long it had flouted. This clause rests
on as little Scriptural authority as the one before.

of what came to pass] τῶν ἐκβάσεων refers not to the ten plagues
(Grimm) but to the whole series of events which reached its climax at
Massah, Ex. xvii.

Having thirsted in another manner] A mild way of saying "with
sufferings far beyond those of the Israelites." This sentence, which

But in requital of the senseless imaginings of their un- 15
righteousness,
Wherein they were led astray to worship irrational reptiles
and wretched vermin,
Thou didst send upon them a multitude of irrational
creatures for vengeance;
That they might learn, that by what things a man sinneth, 16
by these he is punished.

A.V. transferred to end of *v.* 9, is rightly kept in its place by Vulg.,
containing as it does the reason why the contempt of the Egyptians was
turned into respect.

vv. 15—20. THE PLAGUES OF FROGS AND LICE.

15. *in requital of...*] A new idea unfolds itself. The Egyptians
were unrighteous not only in their actions, but in their worship. If they
did not know God, they were to be blamed for not knowing Him.
Their ignorance was not intellectual, it was moral. Unrighteousness
was the character of their creed and cult. This unrighteousness gave
birth to "senseless imaginings" (again, moral rather than intellectual,
ch. i. 3), cp. Rom. i. 21—23. And as they thought in their hearts,
so did God visit them: as they loved the creature more than the
Creator, God gave them their desire.
irrational reptiles] *Reptiles* includes all creeping things. Not only
did Serpent-worship exist in Egypt, but also the worship of creatures of
all kinds from the crocodile to the beetle.
wretched vermin] κνώδαλα is as vague a word as our "creatures."
For *wretched* (lit. cheap), cp. Philo, *Mos.* i. 19 "If God desires
to employ instruments for His punishments, He does not use the
largest and strongest, for He thinks little of their prowess, but He
furnishes the small and wretched (εὐτελῆ) with invincible powers and
punishes the wrongdoers by their means" (referring to the lice,
Ex. viii. 16 ff.).
irrational creatures] The plagues of frogs, lice, flies (Ex. viii.),
locusts (Ex. x.). For the flies, see Philo's imaginative description in
Mos. i. 23. With this use of the creatures venerated by the Egyptians,
for their punishment by God, should be contrasted their use by Him
for the benefit of Israel. As lice and flies were sent to plague the
Egyptians, so quails were sent to feed the Israelites, ch. xv. 18 ff.
16. The Egyptians received punishment in the particular forms which
it took, in order that they might be forced to recognise a great moral
law "As a man sins, so is he punished." This law acts with unfailing
certainty in the spiritual sphere alone, where there is no exception to
the rule that a man reaps as he sows. The penalty for an untruth is
untruthfulness. If the writer had confined himself to the inward sphere,
his doctrine could not be challenged. For in the external world,

17 For thine all-powerful hand,
   That created the world out of formless matter,

although physical sins often entail physical consequences, it is by no
means universally true that the sinner suffers by his own sin. There
are instances of dramatic justice, but it is their rarity which makes them
striking, cp. Adoni-bezek, Judg. i. 7; Saul, 1 Sam. xv. 23; see Rev.
xvi. 6. But these examples do not correspond completely to the idea
of "hoist with his own petard": the true illustration is Ps. vii. 15
"He is...fallen into the ditch which he made," cp. Ps. lvii. 6. But
the application of the law to the plagues of frogs and lice and flies
is very artificial. There is no inevitable causal connection between
the Egyptian gods and the plagues. The most that can be said is that
the Egyptians saw the lesson of their folly emphasised when they were
plagued through their deities. See xii. 23, xvi. 1, xviii. 4, xix. 13; Job
iv. 8; Ps. cix. 17; Prov. v. 22; Is. xxx. 3, 16; Ez. xxxv. 6; Obad. 15;
2 Macc. ix. 6; cp. Philo, *Q. R. D. H.* § 22; Jub. iv. 31; Test. xii
Patr. *Gad* v, and Etheridge, *Targums* p. 505.

   17. *thine all-powerful hand*] Some would identify the *hand* of
God with Wisdom, cp. ch. xiv. 6. Deane observes that in Is. xlviii. 13
"hand" is rendered "word" by the Chaldee paraphrast: but cp. "the
finger of God" in connection with the plague of lice, Ex. viii. 19. For
the epithet, cp. xviii. 15.

   created...formless matter] *Formless matter* is a Greek philosophical
expression, belonging to a system of speculation altogether different
from that of the Jews. The Jews believed in a creation out of nothing;
the Greeks believed in the eternity of matter (ὕλη) and the arrangement
of matter by mind, cp. Anaxagoras, Diog. La. ii. 3.   There was a
conflict, therefore, between philosophic dualism and religious monism:
the Greeks conceived of two preexisting eternals, God and matter, while
the Jews held that God created all things either out of nothing or out
of Himself. It is impossible to say with certainty which view was held
by the writer of Wisdom: even Philo was not consistent, and oscillated
between the two positions, and the writer of Wisdom was far more of a
Hebraist than Philo. It is quite possible that *formless matter* (ἄμορφος
ὕλη) stands as a convenient Greek symbol for the Hebrew of Gen. i. 2,
which is rendered by LXX. ἀόρατος καὶ ἀκατασκεύαστος (invisible and
unorganised). Further the use of κτίζειν (create) here is non-committal:
it leaves the origin of matter out of sight, and deals merely with the
arrangement of matter. Cp. xiii. 3, where ἔκτισεν is equivalent to
κατασκευάσας in xiii. 4.

   The extreme fluidity of thought on this subject may be seen by
contrasting Philo, *Somn.* i. 13 "God not only brought the world into
visible manifestation, but He made things which before were not,
seeing that He is not only demiurge but creator" with his affirmation
of Aristotle's dictum, "It is impossible for anything to be made out of
that which is not," *de Incorr. Mundi* § 2. In *Cher.* § 35 he lays down
four causes of Creation, God the agent (ὑφ' οὗ), the Logos the instru-

THE WISDOM OF SOLOMON XI. 17—20.   111

Lacked not means to send upon them a multitude of bears,
  or fierce lions,
Or ¹new-created wild beasts, full of rage, *of* unknown *kind*,   18
Either breathing out a blast of fiery breath,
Or blowing forth *from their nostrils* noisome smoke,
Or flashing dreadful sparkles from their eyes;
Which had power not only to consume them by their 19
  ²violence,
But to destroy them even by the terror of their sight.
Yea and without these might they have fallen by a single 20
  breath,
Being pursued by Justice, and scattered abroad by the
  breath of thy power.

¹ Some authorities read *unknown wild beasts, full of new-created rage.*
² Gr. *harmfulness.*

ment (δι' οὖ), matter the source (ἐξ οὖ), and God's goodness the final
cause (δι' ὅ). This analysis plainly puts matter on a footing of pre-
existence. For a very clear statement of the rival theories of Creation,
see P. N. Waggett, *Scientific Temper in Religion* pp. 165—169, 170, 171.
Bois (*Orig. J. A. Phil.* pp. 265 ff.) concludes that *formless matter* means
for the writer what it would have meant for a Greek philosopher, and
that he uses κτίζειν (create) in the sense of "arrange." He admits
however that in a transition-document like Wisdom, it is quite possible
that both the Greek and Hebrew ideas are found with no attempt made to
reconcile them, and that κτίζειν here might have the sense of "create."

Lacked not means] Cp. xii. 9. God who can do the greater, can do
the less.

bears or...lions] Philo (*Mos.* i. 19) asks "Why did God visit the land
with such insignificant creatures, and omit to send bears or lions or
leopards or other kinds of fierce animals?" The noisome beast was
one of God's four sore judgments, Ezek. xiv. 21; cp. Lev. xxvi. 22;
2 Kings xvii. 26; Jer. viii. 17.

18. *new-created...full of rage*] The epithet applied to the divine
hailstorm, ch. v. 22. God who created the world, might have created
special instruments of punishment. Some would render *full of poison*
(θυμός). Philo (*Mos.* i. 19) asks further "Why did not God send even
the Egyptian asps, whose bite is fatal?" cp. Dt. xxxii. 33 LXX.

19. God could have sent creatures the very sight of which might
have destroyed the Egyptians. The thought is hardly (as Farrar thinks)
of the basilisk which was reputed to kill with its glance.

20. *by a single breath*] Cp. 2 Kings xix. 7; Job iv. 9; Is. xi. 4.

Justice] Cp. Acts xxviii. 4. Vulg. *persecutionem passi ab ipsis
factis suis* suggests comparison with ch. xiv. 31. See *v.* 16.

scattered abroad by the breath of thy power] The figure is the same
as in ch. v. 23. Cp. Is. xl. 24.

But by measure and number and weight thou didst order all things.

21 For to be greatly strong is thine at all times;
And the might of thine arm who shall withstand?
22 Because the whole world before thee is as ¹a grain ²in a balance,

> ¹ Gr. *that which* just *turneth*.   ² Gr. *from.*

by measure and number and weight thou didst order all things] God is a God of order : force is not His distinguishing attribute (*Ep. to Diogn.* vii. 4): inflexible purpose and unfailing mercy are His most notable characteristics. Hence, the sins of the Egyptians did not divert God from His settled will. In the beginning, God had imprinted on the universe a uniform and harmonious order : by this He was Himself bound as He estimated the offences of men, and dealt out their punishments in proportion. For the collocation of *measure, number,* and *weight,* cp. Job xxviii. 25; Is. xl. 12, 26; Philo, *Somn.* ii. 29 "God and not the mind of man measures, weighs and numbers all things, and circumscribes them with bounds and limits"; and Charles, *Enoch,* p. 132 "In apocryphal literature historical events are methodically arranged under artificial categories of measure, number, weight (Wisdom xi. 20; 4 Esdr. iv. 36, 37)." "He hath weighed the world in the balance ; and by measure hath He measured the times, and by number hath He numbered the seasons ; and He shall not move nor stir them, until the said measure be fulfilled," 4 Esdr. l.c. Cp. Philo, *Mut.* § 40 for *measure* and *weight,* and Test. xii Patr. *Napht.* ii, for *weight, measure,* and *rule.*

> *v.* 21—xii. 2.   GOD IS LOVE, AND IS MERCIFUL AS WELL
> AS MIGHTY.

21.   *For to be greatly strong*]   The reason why God might have punished the Egyptians with the terrors set forth in *vv.* 17—20. Cp. 1 Chr. xxix. 11 and Philo (*Mos.* i. 19) "God is the highest and greatest power."

who shall withstand?]   Cp. xii. 12.   A conflation of these two passages appears in Clem. Rom. xxvii. "Who shall say unto Him, What hast thou done? or who shall resist the might of His strength?" This and ch. ii. 24 are the earliest known patristic quotations from Wisdom.

22.   There is a reminiscence in this *v.* of Is. xl. 12—24, in which the insignificance of man by the side of God is set forth; cp. 2 Macc. viii. 18.

grain in a balance]   Vulg. *momentum staterae,* lit. (as marg.) *that which* just *turneth the balance,* and so the tiniest atom that makes the scale-pan dip. Cp. Is. xl. 15.   The figure of weights and scales (*v.* 20) is resumed, and enables the writer to combine the two thoughts of the exceeding smallness of the world and the refined delicacy of God's equity.

And as a drop of dew that at morning cometh down upon
the earth.
But thou hast mercy on all men, because thou hast power 23
to do all things,
And thou overlookest the sins of men to the end they may
repent.
For thou lovest all things that are,   24
And abhorrest none of the things which thou didst make;
For never wouldest thou have formed anything if thou didst
hate it.

drop of dew] A type of man's littleness and transitoriness. See Hos.
vi. 4, xiii. 3. Cp. Is. xl. 6, 7.
23. *mercy on all*] Ecclus. xviii. 13 "The mercy of the Lord is on
all flesh."
power to do all things] Job x. 13 LXX., xlii. 2; Philo, *Opif.* § 14. The
combination of mercy and power is brought out in xii. 16, 18, 20. The
summit of strength is self-control. For the two great attributes of God,
His goodness and His power, see Philo, *Sacr.* § 15. The Gelasian
Collect for the 11th S. after Trinity is founded on this *v.* "O God, who
declarest Thy almighty power most chiefly in showing mercy and pity."
The combination is first seen in Ps. lxii. 11, 12 "Power belongeth unto
God; also unto Thee, Lord, belongeth mercy," cp. Ex. xxxiii. 17 ff.
Farrar quotes *Merchant of Venice,* iv. 1.

"It is an attribute to God Himself,
And earthly power doth then shew likest God's
When Mercy seasons Justice."

thou overlookest] Cp. Acts xvii. 30; Rom..iii. 25 R.V.
they may repent] Rom. ii. 4; 2 Pet. iii. 9. Cp. Ecclus. xvii. 29 and
Philo, *Mos.* i. 19 "God willed rather to admonish the inhabitants of
Egypt than to destroy them," and id. *Fug.* § 18 "God is not inexorable,
but kind because of the gentleness of His nature; whoso knows this,
though he have sinned, may turn and repent with full hope of amnesty
(ἀμνηστία)."
24. *thou lovest all things*] Ps. cxlv. 8, 9. For God's goodness as
the final cause of Creation, see Philo, *Cher.* § 35.
abhorrest none of the things] Cp. the Collect for Ash Wednesday,
and the third Collect for Good Friday, and Philo, *Fug.* § 18 "Mercy,
whereby the Creator hath pity upon His own work."
never wouldest thou have formed] This utterance is hardly consistent
with xii. 11 a, but it is truer. For whatever may be said of the mercies
of a corrective discipline (xii. 10), it is hard to see how a seed "accursed
from the beginning," and "with wickedness inborn" (xii. 10, 11) is other
than the victim of pre-reprobation.

25 And how would anything have endured, except thou hadst
willed it?
Or that which was not called by thee, *how would* it have
been preserved?
26 But thou sparest all things, because they are thine,
O Sovereign Lord, thou lover of *men's* [1]lives;
12 For thine incorruptible spirit is in all things.

[1] Or, *souls*

25. *except thou hadst willed it*] Ps. cxix. 91 LXX.
called by thee] i.e. into existence. Cp. Is. xli. 4 and Rom. iv. 17 (see
Sanday and Headlam *in loc.*).
have been preserved] The word (διετηρήθη) is the LXX. word used
of Pharaoh in Ex. ix. 16, recalled here no doubt purposely.
26. *because they are thine*] This *v*, and xii. 1 must be taken
together. They furnish an additional reason why God spares such as
the Egyptians. God's mercy is the outcome of more than love: they
are in the world by His decree, *v.* 25; they are His. The meaning of
"His" is explained in xii. 1. To have God as Father, i.e. to have
been created by God, is to have God's spirit within. God's spirit is an
indissoluble link between God and them; a true immanence is a
principle of unity. That can never be beyond the help of God which
has God's spirit within it: therefore, God who breaks not the bruised
reed, spares in hope. *Thou sparest, because,* cp. xii. 16, xv. 2;
Ps. ciii. 13.
O Sovereign Lord] This title follows naturally on the acknowledgment of God's ownership of the souls He has made. Cp. Ep. of Jer.
(Bar. vi.) 5; Clem. Rom. lxi. 1, 2.
thou lover of men's *lives*] Or as marg. *lover of* men's *souls*. The
author gives a new meaning to the word (φιλόψυχος) which in class.
Gk. means "fond of life," "cowardly." Cp. i. 13; Ezek. xviii. 4;
St Matt. xviii. 14; St Luke ix. 56.
xii. 1. *thine incorruptible spirit*] All things, wicked men included,
live by the breath of the Divine. Even though they refuse the moral
indwelling, yet the physical dependence still survives, cp. Job xxxiii. 4;
Ps. civ. 30. The writer was no doubt aware of the Greek conception of
a "soul of the world," and was probably influenced by it in the expressions
he employs regarding Wisdom, i. 7, vii. 24, viii. 1; but there is nothing
to decide whether in this passage his thought is Hebrew or Greek. If
Greek, *spirit* must be identified with Wisdom, as the agent of the
immanence of God; if Hebrew, spirit stands not for a Being distinct
from God, but for the characteristic conception of "God in operation"
(Heb. *ruach*). On this see Davidson, *Theol. of O.T.* p. 193. "All
life, whether in man, or in the lower creatures, or in the world, is an
effect of the *ruach*, the spirit of God. God's spirit is merely God
in His efficiency—God exercising power, communicating Himself, or

Wherefore thou convictest by little and little them that ¹fall 2
from the right way,
And, putting them in remembrance by the *very* things
wherein they sin, dost thou admonish them,
That escaping from their wickedness they may believe on
thee, O Lord.

For verily the old inhabitants of thy holy land,   3
Hating *them* because they practised detestable works of 4
enchantments and unholy rites

¹ Gr. *fall aside.*

operating. This power may be simply vital power, physical life; or it
may be intellectual, moral, or religious life."
    2. *Wherefore*] Because there is a germ of the Divine nature even
in the heathen.
    convictest by little and little] By letting their own sins recoil upon
them rather than by instant destruction.
    admonish] In *v.* 10 Israel was admonished, while Egypt was
condemned; but here the writer agrees with Philo, *Mos.* i. 19 (see note
on *v.* 23), that God's purpose was educative. Plagues of animals were
sent that Egypt might learn that it had sinned through animals.
    may believe on thee] The writer regards idolatry as due to moral
rather than intellectual deficiency, and holds that moral correction
would lead the heathen to the acknowledgment of the true God.

CH. XII. 3—27.

God, though His power is absolute, was as forbearing in the use of it
towards the Canaanites as towards the Egyptians. His judgments are
altogether righteous. His bearing is a lesson to Israel.

vv. **3—11.** THE CANAANITES EXCITED THE WRATH OF GOD WITH
    THEIR DEBASING CULTS, BUT HE WAS PATIENT WITH THEM.

    3. *the old inhabitants*] The writer passes from the Egyptians to
the Canaanites, and emphasizes the new topic by placing it at the
beginning of the long sentence which covers *vv.* 3—6. The governing
verb is found at end of *v.* 6. (*Thy*) *holy land* is first found in Zech.
ii. 12, cp. 2 Macc. i. 7.
    4. *Hating* them] Cp. Hos. ix. 15. This is not more than a formal
contradiction of ch. xi. 24; *qua* sinner, a man is bound up with the
sins which God detests, cp. xiv. 8, 9. The writer expressly says
hating them on the ground that, a qualification which limits *hating* more
narrowly in the Greek than in the English.
    works of enchantments] The enchanter, or sorcerer (Dt. xviii. 10),
was one who, by means of the superstitious use of drugs, herbs, spells,

8—2

5 ([1]Merciless slaughters of children,
And sacrificial banquets of men's flesh and of blood),
6 Confederates in an impious fellowship,
And murderers of their own helpless babes,
It was thy counsel to destroy by the hands of our fathers;

[1] The words rendered *slaughters* and *impious* in verses 5 and 6 differ but slightly from the readings of the Greek text, which here yield no sense.

produced magical effects. See Driver, *Deut.* p. 225. For the superstitions of the Canaanites, see Dt. xii. 29—31, xviii. 9—14.

5. *slaughters of children*] Reading φόνους. This was the principal enormity of the Canaanites, whose example Ahab followed (2 Kings xvi. 3), cp. Ps. cvi. 34—38. The object of child-sacrifice was for the purpose of averting calamity or obtaining an oracle, see Lev. xviii. 21, and Mesha's sacrifice, 2 Kings iii. 27.

sacrificial banquets] Easier than MS. would be σπλαγχνοφάγον, an Aeschylean type of compound with gen.; lit. "the banquet gorging itself with human flesh and blood." No corroboration seems forthcoming for this charge against the Canaanites, but cp. Ezek. xvi. 20. Religious feasts, in which the flesh of enemies is consumed, are not uncommon in primitive tribes. How easily such charges obtain credence may be seen from the accusations laid against the primitive Christians of "Thyestean banquets," and those even in modern times brought against the Jews in Russia.

6. *Confederates*] A discussion of the Greek reading which has baffled all elucidators would be out of place. Text follows Grimm (1837) in reading ἐκμυσοῦς μύστας θιάσου.

The phrase, which is in apposition to the subject of the sentence (*v.* 4) beginning *because they practised*, points to some associated act of worship of an esoteric kind.

murderers] For the sacrifice of a child by its parent, as being the most precious offering to be found, cp. Abraham, Jephthah, Mesha, Ahab, Hiel the Bethelite(?), and in Greek literature, Agamemnon and Iphigenia. On this subject very interesting light has been thrown by the recent discoveries at Gezer, see Quarterly Statement of Pal. Expl. Fund, Oct. 1903. The reference in 1 Kings xvi. 34 to the foundation of the rebuilt Jericho seems to point to child-sacrifices, the traces of which have been brought to light by Mr Macalister. When a house or public structure was to be erected, an infant, probably alive, was laid underneath the wall; or else (later) the child was killed, and its body placed in a jar which was then buried, either at the corner of the house, or under the door. If the reference in the text is not to this particular practice, it at least serves to throw light on the class of sacrifice enjoined by Canaanitish religions. Cp. Jer. xix. 4, 5.

It was thy counsel to destroy] Two reasons are assigned in Dt. for the expulsion of the Canaanites (*a*) because God loved Israel,

That the land which in thy sight is most precious of all *lands* 7
Might receive a worthy colony of God's [1]servants.
Nevertheless even these thou didst spare as *being* men, 8
And thou sentest [2]hornets as forerunners of thy host,
To cause them to perish by little and little;
Not that thou wast unable to subdue the ungodly under the 9
    hand of the righteous in battle,
Or by terrible beasts or by *one* stern word to make away
    with them at once;

---

[1] Or, *children*   [2] Or, *wasps*

Dt. iv. 37, 38; (*b*) because of the wickedness of the Canaanites,
Dt. ix. 5; cp. Gen. xv. 16. Israel was God's instrument, Ex. xxiii.
23; Dt. vii. 2.

7. *the land...most precious*] Cp. Dt. xi. 12. Farrar quotes several
Jewish sayings in honour of the holy land: e.g. "He who traverses so
much as four ells in the land of Israel is sure of eternal life" (*Kethuboth*,
f. iii. 1).

a worthy colony] Colony (ἀποικία) was the classical word for a party
proceeding from the motherland and settling in a new country. Here,
Egypt is viewed as the starting-point, while Canaan is being colonized
by the emigrants from Egypt. The more proper use of the word by Jews
is that found in 3 Macc. vi. 10 of the Dispersion in Egypt, and in
Jer. xxix. 1 and 2 Esdr. i. 11 of the captivity in Babylon. *Worthy*:
the land that was most precious in God's eyes did not possess inhabitants worthy of their dwelling-place, as long as rites involving
human sacrifice endured.

8. *as being men*] Cp. Gen. vi. 3, and Ps. lxxviii. 39, ciii. 14, 15.

hornets] Marg. (as Greek) *wasps*, see Ex. xxiii. 28; Dt. vii. 20;
Josh. xxiv. 12. There have always been two views of the promise to
expel with the hornet. Metaphorical interpretations rely on the use of
the simile of bees in Dt. i. 44, and on Ex. xxiii. 27 "the terror."
Wisdom however takes the promise literally.

Driver (*Deut.* p. 104) writes that four species of hornet exist in
Palestine, two of which construct their nests underground or in
cavities of rocks: the combined attack of a swarm has been known
to be fatal.

by little and little] See Ex. xxiii. 29, 30.

9. *Not that thou wast unable*] The same argument as in xi. 17 ff.

in battle] As in the case of Ai (Josh. viii.), and Amalek (Ex. xvii.).

beasts] Cp. Dt. xxxii. 24, and note on xi. 17.

by one stern word] Cp. xviii. 15, where the same epithet (ἀπότομος)
is applied to the Logos "a stern warrior." Cp. also Ex. xxiii. 27 "My
fear," and Is. xxxvii. 7 "a blast, a rumour."

at once] Vulg. *simul*, in contrast with *by little and little*, next *v*.

10 But judging them by little and little thou gavest them a
place of repentance,
Not being ignorant that their nature by birth was evil, and
their wickedness inborn,
And that their manner of thought would in no wise ever be
changed,
11 For they were a seed accursed from the beginning:
Neither was it through fear of any that thou didst leave
them *then* unpunished for their sins.

12 For who shall say, What hast thou done?

10. *judging them*] In Ex. xxiii. 29, 30 the reason assigned for the
gradual expulsion of the Canaanites is not that given here, but the good
of the land : if uncultivated for any length of time, it would deteriorate,
and be overrun with pests.

place of repentance] Cp. *v.* 20. The phrase is found in Heb. xii. 17
and Clem. Rom. vii. The verb in Greek is imperfect, not *thou gavest*,
but *thou offeredst*. For the idea, cp. Rom. ix. 22, 23.

their nature...evil] Cp. iii. 12 b.

wickedness inborn] The writer does not attempt to reconcile the contradiction between this proposition and ch. i. 12—14. Again, contrast
this teaching of an innate bias towards evil with the self-determination
of ch. i. 16 "Ungodly men *called* death unto them."

manner of thought] Cp. Gen. vi. 5. For the word (λογισμός) in a
bad sense, cp. i. 3.

11. *a seed accursed from the beginning*] The reference is probably
to the curse of Canaan, Gen. ix. 25. Cp. iii. 13 a; 2 Pet. ii. 14
"children of cursing" (R.V.). Writing on Gen. vi. 8, Philo (*Quod. D.*
§ 15) has "Evil men were made in the wrath of God, good men in His
favour....Now anger is the fountain of sins: whatever we do under
the influence of any passion is faulty." Contrast Is. lxv. 23 "My
elect...shall not bring forth children for a curse, for they are a seed
blessed by God, and their offspring with them" (LXX.).

Neither...through fear] God was absolutely disinterested in His
patience. The Canaanite stock was doomed, but God hoped that
individuals would repent. Cp. the deliverance of Rahab and her
family, and the virtues of faith, hospitality and prophecy discovered
in her (Clem. Rom. xii.). Grimm places *v.* 11 b in the following section.

leave them then *unpunished*] Vulg. *ueniam dabas*, lit. *offer freedom
from fear* (ἄδεια, amnesty) *in respect of their sins*. The fact that God
did not cut them off precipitately might look as though He winked at
sin. Cp. Ex. xxxiv. 7.

vv. **12—18.** GOD'S SUPREME POWER DELIGHTS IN BENEVOLENCE.

12. *For*] It was not fear that dictated God's leniency; rather, it
was God's position of unassailable supremacy.

Or who shall withstand thy judgement?
And who shall accuse thee for the perishing of nations
    which thou didst make?
Or who shall come and stand before thee as an avenger for
    unrighteous men?
For neither is there any God beside thee that careth for all, 13
That thou mightest shew *unto him* that thou didst not judge
    unrighteously:
Neither shall king or prince be able to look thee in the face 14
    to plead for those whom thou hast punished.
But being righteous thou rulest all things righteously,   15
Deeming it a thing alien from thy power
To condemn one that doth not himself deserve to be
    punished.

who shall say...judgement?] These two clauses are taken direct
from Job ix. 12, 19 LXX. A conflation of this line and of xi. 21
appears in Clem. Rom. xxvii. (see xi. 21). For similar questions, cp.
Eccl. viii. 4; Dan. iv. 35; Rom. ix. 19.
who shall accuse thee] There is no one in a position to criticize God,
for fear of whose protests God abated the severity of the judgments
which of Himself He would have inflicted, *v.* 11.
nations which thou didst make] Ps. lxxxvi. 9.
come and stand before thee] There may be some allusion to the
pursuit of a murderer by the avenger-kinsman (Num. xxxv.). There is
a word-play between ἔκδικος (avenger) and ἄδικος (unrighteous).
God is an absolute irresponsible autocrat: He knows no check
upon His power, save His own nature. Nothing but revelation, which
affirms that the All-powerful is all-merciful, could make men accept
with submission and satisfaction the teaching that man is without
appeal in the hands of God.
13. *any God beside thee*] Deut. xxxii. 39   There is no God beside
Jehovah, to whom He might have to justify His actions.
14. *look thee in the face to plead for*] The Gk. verb is found in
Acts xxvii. 15 of a ship facing the wind, in Clem. Rom. xxxiv. of an
idle workman not looking his employer in the face, cp. Ep. Barn. v. 10.
15. There is no one to remonstrate with God who can require that
God shall listen to him. God is His own critic; His standard is
within Himself. He *is* righteous. Man has no ground of confidence
to compare with this.
being righteous] Gen. xviii. 25; Ex. ix. 27.
a thing alien] The Greek phrase is found in Philo, *Abr.* § 44,
Conf. l. § 23.
To condemn] God possesses arbitrary power, but never uses it
arbitrarily. He does not make sport with His creatures. Condem-

16 For thy strength is the beginning of righteousness,
And thy sovereignty over all maketh thee to forbear all.

17 For when men believe not that thou art perfect in power,
thou shewest thy strength,
¹And ²in dealing with them that know *it* thou puttest their
boldness to confusion.

18 But thou, being sovereign over *thy* strength, judgest in
gentleness,
And with great forbearance dost thou govern us;

---

¹ The Greek text here is perhaps corrupt.   ² Or, *in them*

nation rests with men: they judge themselves, and are their own
penalty. Cp. Ps. lxii. 12 "Unto thee belongeth mercy; for thou ren-
derest to every man according to his work." Browning's "Caliban
upon Setebos" provides an interesting study of the subject of arbitrary
power.

16. *thy strength*] The context gives these words a singularly
different significance from that borne by the almost similar words in
ii. 11. There, righteousness is to give way to power; here righteousness and power are declared to be fundamentally an unity. The writer
suggests that there is a causal connection between God's justice and
IIis power. *Because* He is so strong, He is so just. It may be that
the temptation to men to use their strength tyrannically arises solely
from their limitations, which dictate a corresponding self-assertion:
where there is no challenge, there may be an undisturbed moral
equilibrium, which precludes all desire for misuse or display. Ante-
cedently, apart from human experience, why should power make for
wrong and confusion rather than right and order? Does not essential
power presuppose power over itself?

thy sovereignty] A repetition of xi. 23, 26; cp. Ps. lxii. 11, 12;
see Philo, *Quod. D.* § 16, for God's preference of mercy to judgment.

17. *when men believe not*] Ex. v. 2, Pharaoh had said "who is the
Lord? I know not the Lord."

shewest thy strength] This expression is used with reference to
Pharaoh in Ex. ix. 16 LXX.; cp. Ps. cvi. 8.

them that know] B probably retains the right reading, being supported by Cod. Amiatinus *hos qui sciunt.*

Those who know God's power are distinguished from those (in prec. *l.*)
who disbelieve in it. When men know God's power, but insolently
disregard it or even defy it, God puts them to confusion.

18. *being sovereign*] Vulg. finely translates as a title, *Dominator
uirtutis*, but text is probably right. For the sense, cp. Ps. lxxviii. 38,
39 and Chilo (Diog. La. i. 3, 69) "The strong man should be gentle."

forbearance] The next *l.* shows that it is forbearance, and not indifference, or fear of reproach that dictates God's gentleness. The
power to strike is ready, though in reserve: the only law of God's

For the power is thine whensoever thou hast the will.

But thou didst teach thy people by such works as these,   19
How that the righteous must be a lover of men;
And thou didst make thy sons to be of good hope,
Because thou givest repentance when men have sinned.
For if on them that were enemies of thy ¹servants and due 20
    to death
Thou didst take vengeance with so great heedfulness and
    indulgence,

¹ Or, *children*

power is His good will.   For *gentleness* (ἐπιεικία) used of Christ, cp.
2 Cor. x. 1.

vv. **19—22.**   GOD'S MERCIFUL FORBEARANCE WAS A LESSON TO
                    THE ISRAELITES.

19. *thou didst teach*]   The writer sums up chs. xi., xii.—18. God
sought to teach the chosen people two lessons: (1) that righteousness
is merciful, *v.* 22 b, (2) that repentance finds forgiveness, *v.* 22 c. If
mercy was shown to the Canaanites, *v.* 20, how much more mercy
was shown to Israel, and accordingly how merciful ought the Israelites
to be: again, if Israel was disciplined, and the Canaanites were chastised
a thousandfold more (but still chastised and not instantly annihilated),
the repentant may always hope for mercy.   For the writer, the world
revolves round the chosen people: Egypt and Canaan are brought upon
the scene only to provide object-lessons for Israel.   For other examples
of the writer's interpretations of history, see xvi. 11, 26, 28, and cp.
Philo, *Fuga* § 14.

by such works]   See xi. 15, xii. 8.

righteous...a lover of men]   One of the writer's truest anticipations
of N.T. teaching, see 1 Cor. xiii.; 1 John iv. 20.   Cp. ch. i. 6, vii. 23
and Philo, *Mut.* § 22 "It is the province of God to be a benefactor";
Abr. § 37 "It belongs to the same nature to be pious and philanthropic"; *Fuga* § 6 "Be known first by your virtue among men, that
you may be commended for your virtue before God."   That philanthropy
is part of righteousness in man is shown by the "philanthropy" (Tit.
iii. 4) of a righteous God.

to be of good hope]   The writer makes no allusion to the sins of
Israel; in fact the "holy and blameless seed" has not once been
criticized for the sins in the wilderness which brought down heavy
chastisements upon the people.   The sins whose forgiveness causes
them to be of good hope are those of the Canaanites.

20. *due to death*]   lit. *owed*, on account of their wickedness and
impenitence.

and indulgence]   So ℵ διέσεως.   B reads "entreaty" (δεήσεως), cp.
Is. lxv. 2.   *liberasti* Cod. Am. represents the διέσωσας of some MSS.
The last is quite inadmissible.   For the idea, cp. Rom. ix. 22.

Giving them times and place whereby they might escape
from their wickedness;

21 With how great carefulness didst thou judge thy sons,
To whose fathers thou gavest oaths and covenants of good
promises!

22 While therefore thou dost chasten us, thou scourgest our
enemies ten thousand times more,
To the intent that we may ponder thy goodness when we
judge,
And when we are judged may look for mercy.

23 Wherefore also the unrighteous that lived in folly of life

times and place] For *place*, see *v.* 10. For *times*, Rev. ii. 21; Philo,
All. iii. 34 "God will not proceed even against sinners immediately, but
gives time for repentance, and the healing and correcting of their error."
Cp. Rom. ii. 4. Philo, *Mos.* i. 24, writes of Egypt "God did not pro-
pose to devastate the land, but only to admonish it."

21. If God's vengeance on the heathen was so carefully tempered,
what must have been the attention He bestowed on the judging (i.e.
disciplining) of His sons!

To whose fathers] Abraham, Isaac and Jacob, see Ex. xxxii. 13.
Oaths and covenants, cp. ch. xviii. 22.

22. *chasten us*] Cp. Dt. viii. 5.

scourgest our enemies] The contrast between *chasten* (παιδεύειν) and
scourge (μαστιγοῦν) is not necessarily very strong, cp. Prov. iii. 11,
but it is intentionally emphasized here. For an interesting philosophy
of the calamities which befel the Jews of the Maccabaean age, see
2 Macc. vi. 12—17. God forbore to punish the heathen, till they had
filled up the measure of their sins; the Jews, however, were corrected
for the slightest sin, that a delayed vengeance might not be necessary.

that we may ponder] That God while disciplining the Jews was
content to administer chastisement, however severe, to their enemies,
was for the writer a mark of God's mercy. The lesson of mercy, apart
from the way of reaching it, anticipates St Matt. xviii. 33, cp. James ii. 13.

when we are judged] Cp. Ps. lxxviii. 38.

vv. 23—27.   The Writer reverts to the Egyptians, and
reaffirms the law of xi. 16.

23. *Wherefore*] The writer now views the sufferings of Egypt apart
from any moral teaching for Israel, and solely in the light of disci-
plinary chastisement. *Wherefore* takes up *v.* 22 a "Thou *scourgest* our
enemies."

folly of life] Cp. i. 3, xi. 15. The moral folly that issued in virtual
atheism, Ps. liii. 1. By *the unrighteous* are meant the Egyptians, as is
clear from the reference to animal worship in *v.* 24.

Thou didst torment through their own abominations.
For verily they went astray very far ¹in the ways of error,   24
Taking as gods those ²animals which even among their
enemies were held in dishonour,
Deceived like foolish babes.
Therefore, as unto unreasoning children, thou didst send 25
thy judgement to mock them.
But they that would not be admonished ³by a mocking 26
correction as of children
Shall have experience of a judgement worthy of God.

¹ Or, *even beyond*   ² Gr. *living creatures*: and so elsewhere in
this book.   ³ Or, *by a correction, which was as children's play*   Gr.
by child-play of correction.

through their own abominations] The reference is to the visitation
upon the sacred Nile, the murrain upon the cattle, the plagues of frogs,
lice, flies, cp. ch. xi. *Abominations* (βδελύγματα) is of course a technical
use, and stands for a Hebrew word applied almost exclusively as a
contemptuous designation of an idol (Is. xliv. 19), or of heathen deities
(1 Kings xi. 5). The argument of xi. 15 is recalled.

24. *very far in the ways*] This rendering is preferable to that of
the marg. *even beyond*, which would be somewhat exaggerated.

those animals which even among their enemies] Philo (*Dec.* § 16), in a
description of Egyptian animal worship, writes that they worship oxen,
rams, and goats, which indeed might have some show of reason. But
then they worship wild animals like lions, crocodiles, and asps; and he
adds dogs, cats, wolves, the ibis, hawks, and fishes or even parts of
fishes. Farrar recalls the scornful tirade against Egyptian worship in
Juv. *Sat.* xvi.

25. If they were children, they should be treated as such. If they
worshipped animals, their animals should make sport of them. The
writer does not speak of a mock-punishment, for he admits it was real
enough: but the character of the punishment was such that it made
both gods and people ridiculous. Cp. Ex. x. 2 R.V. marg. "how I
have mocked the Egyptians."

26. *a mocking correction*] *Mocking* imports an idea not in the
Greek, see marg. *child-play of correction.* There is similarity of sound
in Greek, but not of sense, between ἐμπαιγμός (mockery) *v.* 25, and
παιγνίοις (child-play) *v.* 26. The connection is with *babes* (*v.* 24) and
children (*v.* 25). As child's play is to men's work, so were the earlier
chastisements to God's real judgments. For "play" in connection
with God, see Philo, *Mos.* i. 38 "The miracle of the smitten rock
was God's play, compared with His creative works which are really
great."

Shall have experience] The writer throws himself back in imagination
to the time between the earlier plagues and the Exodus, and pictures

27 For through the sufferings whereat they were indignant,
Being punished in these creatures which they supposed to
be gods,
They saw, and recognised as the true God him whom before
they ¹refused to know:
Wherefore also the last end of condemnation came upon
them.

13 For verily all men by nature ²*were but* vain who had no
perception of God,

¹ Or, *denied that they knew*　　　　² Or, are

himself waiting with prophetic certainty for the death of the firstborn
and the destruction of the Egyptian hosts in the Red Sea.

27. *For through*] lit. For being punished in respect of those things,
concerning which they suffered and were indignant—concerning those
creatures, I mean, which they supposed to be gods, they saw...

They saw, and recognised] They were grieved that their gods should
be touched; but it was the very touching of their *gods*, which proved
the operation of a greater God, Ex. vii. 5.

refused] or, as marg., *denied that.* Cp. xvi. 16; Ex. v. 2.

the true God] Ex. ix. 28, x. 16.

Wherefore] supply "when they recognised the true God, and still
refused to let the people go."

the last end] The death of the firstborn, and the drowning in the
Red Sea. This is the "judgment worthy of God," cp. 1 Thess. ii. 16.

CHAPTER XIII.

The thought of the false gods of the Egyptians leads the writer on
to a disquisition on false worship in general, in chs. xiii.—xv. He
divides false worshippers under two heads—those who rest in nature
and deify it (*vv.* 1—9), instead of looking through it to God; and those
who make to themselves idols, or worship animals. For the former
class he can see some excuse; for the latter he feels nothing but
contempt and abhorrence.

The argument in *vv.* 1—9 would seem to be directed chiefly against
the Greeks. They were lovers of beauty, but they failed to infer from
the beauty around them the Author whose works they enjoyed. In so
far also as the Egyptians practised solar worship, the scope of the
argument includes them.

vv. 1—9. NATURE-WORSHIP IS THE LEAST REPREHENSIBLE FORM
OF FALSE WORSHIP.

1. The *v.* begins with *vain* in Greek, which answers to *miserable*
at beginning of *v.* 10. For *vain* of idolatry, cp. Jer. ii. 5 LXX.;
3 Macc. vi. 11; Rom. i. 21.

And from the good things that are seen they gained not
power to know him that is,
Neither by giving heed to the works did they recognise the
artificer;
But either fire, or wind, or swift air,   2

no perception] They ought to have had knowledge, but had it not.
They were vain *by nature* (xii. 10), thus differing from those illuminated
by Wisdom, cp. ch. ix. 13, 17. Philo, *Conf. l.* § 28, writes of men
"who, like incapable archers, assigned countless causes (all of them
wrong) for the origin of things, but had no perception of the one Maker
and Father of all."

that are seen] Cp. Acts xiv. 17; Rom. i. 20. The argument from
the created world to the character of its Creator is found in Ps. xix. 1 ;
Is. xlii. 5; Job xxxvi. 22 ff. LXX. Liddon quotes, on Rom. i. 20, Arist.
de Mundo 6 "The unseen God is to be seen in His very works." Cp.
Kant "The starry sky above me and the moral law within me fill my
soul with ever increasing reverence."

him that is] God is either "the Existent," in the sense that no
other quality than pure existence may be attributed to the Unconditioned
and Absolute One (cp. Philo, *Quod Deus* § 11 "Pure being without
attributes"; or the one, true, self-existent God, cp. Ex. iii. 14 LXX.
"*I am He that is*" (ὁ ὤν, as here). Philo calls God "that which truly
is" (τὸ πρὸς ἀλήθειαν ὄν), "Him who really is" (τὸν ὄντως ὄντα). They
were too feeble to rise to the knowledge of the Absolute from the
phenomena of common observation.

the artificer] At least they might have taken the logical step of
inferring that a thing made postulated a maker. For God as *artificer*,
cp. Philo, *Quod Deus* § 6, and *All.* iii. 32 "Those who thus argue
apprehend God through a shadow, perceiving the artificer through his
works." See id. *Ebr.* § 22.

2. For the worship of the elements, cp. Philo, *Dec.* § 12 "Some
have deified the four elements, earth, water, air, and fire, and others the
sun and the moon and the stars; others the heaven only, and some
the whole universe ; and the Creator, Governor, and Director they
have obscured behind their false ascriptions. For they call the earth
Demeter, the sea Poseidon, the air Hera, the sun Apollo, the moon
Artemis, and fire Hephaestus," and id. *Conf. l.* § 34. Bois (p. 293)
suggests that not only is polytheism in the writer's mind, but certain
Greek philosophic conceptions. Heraclitus referred everything to fire,
Thales (Diog. La. i. 1, 27) to water. Anaximenes (Diog. La. i. 2, 2)
suggested air, while Pythagoras, who regarded heat as the source of life,
reckoned sun, moon and stars as gods (Diog. La. ii. 8, 27).

fire] Diog. La. (*proem.* vi. 6) writes that the Magi count fire, earth,
and water as gods, but condemn the worship of images. Cp. Herodotus
i. 131 for the Persians as worshippers of natural forces. Among the
Greeks Hephaestus was god of fire, and patron of all arts needing
the aid of fire.

Or ¹circling stars, or raging water, or ²luminaries of heaven,
They thought to be gods that rule the world.
3 And if it was through delight in their beauty that they took
them to be gods,
Let them know how much better than these is their
Sovereign Lord;
For the first author of beauty created them:

---

¹ Gr. *circle of stars.*   ² Or, *luminaries of heaven, rulers of the world, they thought to be gods*

wind] Cp. the Greek cult of Aeolus. The Egyptians worshipped the winds in connection with the annual overflow of the Nile. The Persians offered sacrifices to the winds, Hdt. i. 131.
swift air] Personified by the Greeks as Hera.
circling stars] Cp. Dt. iv. 19, xvii. 3. Diog. La. (*proem.* vi. 8) writes that Zoroaster sacrificed to the stars. The *circling stars* are so called because the stars seem to revolve in relation to the earth: the expression almost means the vault in which the stars are set.
raging water] The Egyptians worshipped water, Philo, *Mos.* i. 17; the Greeks personified it as Poseidon.
luminaries of heaven] The Egyptians worshipped the sun and moon (Isis and Osiris), Jer. xliii. 13. That the Israelites before the exile did so is plain from Jer. vii. 18; xliv. 17; cp. Ezek. viii. 16. See Job xxxi. 26—28, and note in this series.
gods that rule the world] This is better than (as marg.) to isolate *rulers of the world* and make it apply to sun and moon only. Gen. i. 16 at first sight seems to support marg., but the balance of the sentence is thereby destroyed.
3. *their beauty*] A Greek touch. Plutarch (*Philos.* 3) says that the Stoics inferred the beauty of the divine character from the beauty of creation. The aesthetic sense was repressed among the Israelites: in the endeavour to throw them back on the spiritual sense, and to deaden them to the attractions of nature-worship or the worship of representations of natural objects, the Mosaic system rather turned their eyes away from the external world in its aspect of beauty. Contact with Greek thought was required before such a passage as Ecclus. xliii. 9—12 could be written. The Israelite was conscious of the majesty of nature and of its symbolism, but delight in beauty for its own sake seemed dangerous to the non-Hellenized Jew. The passage recalls the *Symposium* myth concerning the discovery of the Absolute Beauty (Plato, *Symp.* 211 B, C "'Tis when a man ascendeth from these beautiful things by the Right Way of Love, and beginneth to have sight of that Eternal Beauty—'tis then, methinks, that he toucheth the goal. For this is the right Way...beginning from the beautiful things here, to mount up alway unto that Eternal Beauty, using these things as the steps of a ladder" (tr. Stewart, *The Myths of Plato*).
first author of beauty] Cp. Philo, *proem. et poen.* § 7 "They con-

But if it was through astonishment at their power and 4
  [1]influence,
Let them understand from them how much more powerful
  is he that formed them;
For from the [2]greatness of the beauty [3]even of created things 5
[4]In like proportion [5]does man form the image of their first
  maker.
But yet for these [6]men there is but small blame,   6
For they too peradventure do *but* go astray
While they are seeking God and desiring to find him.

---

[1] Gr. *efficacy.*   [2] Some authorities read *greatness and beauty of.*
[3] Some authorities omit *even.*   [4] Or, *Correspondently*   [5] Gr. *is
the first maker of them beheld.*   [6] Or, *things*

---

cluded that all these beauties so admirably ordered did not come into
being of themselves, but are the work of some Maker, the Creator of
the world."
  4. *if it was through*] Supply *that they took them to be gods* from *v.* 3.
Some who are not affected by the world's beauty are struck by its power
and vital resources. The artificer must be greater than his work, cp.
Philo, *Dec.* § 14.
  he that formed them] For the Greek word and the idea, see note on
ix. 2, and cp. Heb. iii. 3.
  5. *from the greatness*] Read with mg. *and beauty of created things.*
vv. 4 and 3 are united in the one argument from the phenomenal
manifestation to the hidden Reality. The word ἀναλόγως, *in like proportion*, marg. *correspondently*, does not occur in LXX., but the cognate
subst. is used in Rom. xii. 6. The limits of the inference from the
creation to the Creator are here seen. From it man can learn that
power and beauty may be ascribed to Him. But His possession of the
higher moral qualities, righteousness and love, must be revealed.
  does man form the image] lit. as marg. *is beheld.* The Greek word
implies the use of the imaginative faculty (not necessarily, as Farrar,
"adoring vision"), whereby man sees the invisible. Shakespeare
speaks of "the soul's imaginary eye."
  6. But nature-worshippers are in a measure, although not altogether
(*v.* 9), excusable. They are aroused by the world's beauty, and set out
to seek God: but they are arrested midway and fail to attain to the end.
  for these men] *things* marg. Either rendering is possible, but text is
preferable, as *they* (αὐτοί) in next *l.* takes up *these*. The worshippers
of nature at least take what God has provided them ; they do not *make*
Gods.
  seeking God] Cp. Acts xvii. 27. To the followers of the less
debasing and reprehensible nature-cults he extends the benefit of the
doubt: no doubt they are seekers after God, but have lost the way.

7 For ¹living among his works they make diligent search,
And they ²yield themselves up to sight, because the things
that they look upon are beautiful.

8 But again even they are not to be excused.

9 For if they had power to know so much,
That they should be able to explore ³the course *of things*,
How is it that they did not sooner find the Sovereign Lord
of these *his works*?.

10 But miserable ⁴*were* they, and ⁵in dead things ⁴*were* their
hopes,

¹ Or, *being occupied with*   ² Or, *trust their sight that the things*
³ Or, *life* Or, *the world* Gr. *the age.*   ⁴ Or, are   ⁵ Or, *amongst*

7. *living among his works*] The Greek verb refers to the daily
affairs of life rather than, as marg. *being occupied with*, to scrutiny of
natural phenomena.   While occupied with the duties of life, they *make
diligent search* after God.   The thought is of practical men, who try to
find light upon their life, but by their very externality are liable to be
victims of sense-impressions.

8. *not to be excused*] Cp. vi. 6; Rom. i. 20.   Whatever apology
may be found for them, they are really inexcusable: in the last resort,
they failed to use the faculties they had been endowed with.

9. *if they had power*] Recalls *gained not power to know* in *v.* 1.   This
v. returns to *v.* 1: there it was stated that men did not rise up to God
through His works; here the question is asked, If they could scrutinize
God's works, why did they not rise up to God?

be able to explore] Certain faculties, mental and moral, are required
for a reasoned attitude towards the world: these doubtless beckoned
nature-worshippers to go farther, but must have been disregarded.
Philo, *Abr.* § 15, writes of the Chaldaeans "They referred everything to
the movements of the stars, and conjectured that the world was
governed by powers connected with numbers; and they magnified the
visible creation, taking no thought of the invisible: but making
numerical calculations with the help of the heavenly bodies...they
conjectured that the world itself was God, unwisely likening the
creation to its Creator."

the course of things] αἰών is the sum of things in their time-aspect,
cp. xiv. 6; Eccl. iii. 11.   On this word Westcott writes (*Heb.* i. 2,
note) "The universe may be regarded...as an order which exists
through time developed in various stages."

did not sooner find] There was a moral failure involved.   Men who
had advanced so far as to conclude that the world was God, or that
natural forces were divinities, ought to have had insight enough to infer
that the works they saw around them postulated a Worker outside and
above them.

Who called them gods which are works of men's hands,
Gold and silver, wrought with careful art, and likenesses of
 animals,
Or a useless stone, the work of an ancient hand.
Yea and if some [1]woodcutter, having sawn down a [2]tree that 11
 is easily moved,
Skilfully strippeth away all its bark,

[1] Gr. *carpenter* who is *a woodcutter.*   [2] Gr. *plant.* The Greek
word, slightly changed, would mean *trunk.*

vv. 10—19. THE FOLLY OF IDOLATRY.

The writer displays no originality in this section. It recalls the
argument and phraseology of Is. xl., xli., xliv., xlvi. ; Jer. ii. 26—28
(cp. Ps. cxv., cxxxv.), and resembles the apocryphal Epistle of Jeremiah
(Baruch vi.), written probably in Egypt in the 1st. cent. B.C.

10. *miserable*] Answering to *vain* in *v.* 1.

in dead things were *their hopes*] The contrast is not with Jehovah,
the Living God, but with the physical life of the forces of Nature, the
worshippers of which were the subject of the prec. section. Nature is
at least alive. Vulg. renders *among the dead.* Cp. xv. 17 and Ep. Jer.
(Bar. vi.) 27 "They offer gifts to them as to (the) dead," id. 71 "Their
gods of wood are like a dead man cast into darkness."

works of men's hands] Prec. by *silver and gold*, the words are taken
from Ps. cxv. 4, cxxxv. 15, cp. Dt. iv. 28 ; 2 Kings xix. 18 ; Dan.
v. 4 ; Ep. Jer. often.

wrought with careful art] lit. the product of the exercise of art. Cp.
Acts xvii. 29. The expression is in app. with *gold and silver.*

likenesses of animals] Cp. the Golden Calf of Aaron and the calves
of Jeroboam, 1 Kings xii. 28, and the beast-headed gods of Egypt.
For the animal worship of Egypt, see Philo, *Dec.* § 16.

useless stone] Either a stone idol, or a sacred aerolite. Cp. W. M.
Ramsay (Art. *Religion of Greece* in Hastings, *D.B.* vol. v.) "A rude
and shapeless stone, which had fallen from heaven (διοπετής), doubtless
a meteorite, existed originally at Pessinus,... ; it is a type of many other
similar stones at Orchomenos, Thespiae, etc. Many of these stones
had some approximate regularity of shape, sometimes perhaps accidental,
in other cases distinctly due to human workmanship." Cp. Acts xix. 35.

work of an ancient hand] See prec. quotation.

11. *Yea and if*] This long conditional sentence finds its apodosis in
the last clause of *v.* 13. "Then *he giveth it.*" For the whole passage,
cp. Is. xliv. 9—20 ; Jer. x. 3—5 ; Baruch vi.

a tree] Cp. Hor. *Sat.* i. 8. 1

"Olim truncus eram ficulnus, inutile lignum,
    Cum faber incertus scamnum faceretne Priapum
    Maluit esse deum."

And fashioning it in comely form maketh a vessel useful for
the service of life;

12 And burning the refuse of his handywork to dress his food,
eateth his fill;

13 And taking the very refuse thereof which served to no use,
A crooked piece of wood and full of knots,
Carveth it with the diligence of his idleness,
And shapeth it by the skill of his ¹indolence;
² *Then* he giveth it the semblance of the image of a man,

14 Or maketh it like some paltry animal,
Smearing it with vermilion, and with ³paint colouring it red,
And smearing over every stain that is therein;

¹ Or, leisure   ² Or, And   ³ Gr. rouge.

fashioning it] The workman first takes a handy piece of timber,
picks out the best part of it, and turns it to account. The household
vessel is the object of his effort, the image is an after thought.

useful for...] Cp. Baruch vi. 59 "a vessel useful in the house."
There is doubtless a reminiscence of this passage in *Ep. to Diognetus* c. 2
"Is not one idol bronze, no better than the vessels forged for our use,
is not another earthenware, not a whit more comely than that which is
supplied for the most dishonourable service (ὑπηρεσία)?"

12. *burning*] Cp. Is. xliv. 15, 16. For *eateth his fill*, cp. ch. v. 7.
The workman turns his tree to further account before he concerns himself with the disposal of the remaining fragment.

13. *the very refuse*] lit. the refuse of the refuse. *Which served to no
use* is in contrast with *easily moved* (εὐκίνητος) in *v.* 11, which conveys
the impression of "serviceable and handy."

diligence of his idleness] So אB (ἀργίας). Vulg. *per uacuitatem
suam*. A has ἐργασίας *labour*; but this reading misses the sarcasm of
the paradoxical expression. Deane interprets "Such industry as a man
uses when enjoying his leisure."

skill of his indolence] So אAB Ven. ἀνέσεως. Another contradictory
expression, the point of which, as a complement to the prec. line, is
lost if *intelligence* (συνέσεως) with some Gk. MSS. and Vulg. is read
instead. Deane interprets "Such skill as carelessness gives."

14. *vermilion*] Farrar quotes Pliny, *H. N.* xxxv. 45, who speaks
of the statue of Jupiter as being coloured red on festal days, and Ovid,
Fasti i. 415, of the statue of Priapus "at ruber hortorum decus et
tutela Priapus"; Pausanias says that the images of Dionysus, Hermes,
and Pan, were painted vermilion. Verg. *Ecl.* x. 25—27, describes
Pan as *red with vermilion*. Not only was Bacchus painted red, but
(Tibullus ii. 1. 55) his rustic worshipper painted himself with vermilion.

every stain] A touch of sarcasm: the blemishes are matter of

And having made for it a chamber worthy of it,   15
He setteth it in a wall, making it fast with iron.
While then he taketh thought for it that it may not fall 16
    down,
Knowing that it is unable to help itself;
(For verily it is an image, and hath need of help;)
When he maketh his prayer concerning goods and his 17
    marriage and children,
He is not ashamed to speak to that which hath no life;
Yea for health he calleth upon that which is weak,   18
And for life he beseecheth that which is dead,
And for aid he supplicateth that which hath least experience,

indifference. They are covered over with paint, just as the marks on
white animals brought for sacrifice were chalked over.
    15. *a chamber*] Either a small shrine, cp. Tibull. i. 10. 19 "Stabat
in exigua ligneus aede deus"; or a niche in the wall.
    making it fast] For safety. Cp. Bar. vi. 18 "the priests make fast
their temples with doors, with locks, with bars, lest they (the images)
be carried off by robbers"; Is. xli. 7, Jer. x. 4.
    16. *may not fall down*] Cp. Bar. vi. 27 "If they fall to the ground
at any time they cannot rise up again of themselves." This sentence,
describing the helplessness of the image, in sarcastic contrast with the
universal Providence of God (vi. 7), is shown by the Greek particles to
be in antithesis to *v.* 17, which tells of the demands made upon it.
    unable to help itself] Cp. Bar. vi. 49 "which can neither save
themselves from war, nor from plague," and 58 "neither shall they be
able to help themselves," and for the phrase Job iv. 20 LXX., and Philo,
All. iii. 9. Cp. the fall of Dagon, 1 Sam. v.
    hath need of help] Cp. Bar. vi. 27 "If they fall they cannot rise
up again of themselves; neither, if they be set awry, can they make
themselves straight."
    17. *maketh his prayer*] He will actually petition a dead thing to
give him a good marriage and a large family. See Is. xliv. 17; Jer. ii.
26—28. Philo (*Dec.* § 14) writes "I know that some who have made
images pray and sacrifice to the things they have themselves made,
when it would be much better to worship one of their hands, or even
their hammers or anvils or tools."
    18. *for health*] Bar. vi. 36, 37 "They can save no man from
death...they cannot restore a blind man to his sight." Diog. La. (vi. 28)
writes that Diogenes was provoked at the idea of people offering sacrifices on behalf of their health, and then destroying their health by over-
eating at the sacrificial banquet.
    for life...that which is dead] *vv.* 18, 19 present a finely balanced
series of paradoxes, cp. 2 Cor. vi. 8—10.
    which hath least experience] Cp. 3 Macc. iv. 16 "praising gods

And for a *good* journey that which cannot so much as move
a step,

19 And for gaining and ¹getting and good success of his hands
He asketh ability of that which with its hands is most
unable.

14 Again, one preparing to sail, and about to journey over
raging waves,
Calleth upon a piece of wood more rotten than the vessel
that carrieth him;

¹ Or, *handywork*

which were dumb, and could not speak to them or help them," and Is.
xlvi. 7; Jer. xiv. 22; Bar. vi. 13, 14.

cannot...move a step] Cp. Bar. vi. 26 "Having no feet, they are
borne upon shoulders," and Ps. cxv. 7.

19. *getting*] Vulg. *de operando*. The Greek word means lit. *craft*,
business, cp. Ecclus. xxxviii. 34; but in Acts xix. 24 *gain*. The two
senses seem to meet in the verb in ch. viii. 5.

with its hands...unable] Cp. Ps. cxv. 7, and Bar. vi. 15 "He hath
a dagger in his right hand and an axe: but cannot deliver himself from
war and robbers."

CHAPTER XIV. IDOLATRY—ITS FOLLY, ITS ORIGIN, AND ITS
DISASTROUS EFFECT UPON SOCIAL LIFE.

vv. 1—11. THE FOLLY OF IDOLATRY ILLUSTRATED BY THE
SEAFARER, WHO TRUSTS IN HIS PIECE OF WOOD. THE DIVINE
PROVIDENCE ALONE PRESERVES MEN FROM THE PERILS OF THE
SEA. IDOL AND WORSHIPPER SHALL BE PUNISHED TOGETHER.

1. *a piece of wood*] An idol was carried at the prow or the stern of
ancient ships. In Acts xxviii. 11 the "sign" of the ship was Castor
and Pollux. Epict. (ii. 18) speaks of voyagers invoking the Dioscuri,
cp. Hor. *Od.* i. 3. 2 "sic fratres Helenae, lucida sidera (te, nauis,
regant)." Herodotus (iii. 37) explains what the image of Hephaestus
was like, by comparing it to the dwarf images of the Pataeci (their
tutelary deities) which the Phoenicians carried on their warships.

more rotten] For the word, used in a secondary sense, meaning
"more worthless," cp. secondary use of *cheap*, xiii. 14. The sailor
secures sound wood for his ship; any refuse will do for an idol. For
the practice of invoking the gods in a storm, cp. Jonah i. 5 and Bias
(Diog. La. i. 5, 86). Bias was sailing once with certain wicked men,
when the ship was caught in a storm. They all cried to the gods, and
Bias said "Be silent, else the gods will know you are sailing in this
ship."

For that *vessel* the hunger for gains devised,   2
And an artificer, *even* wisdom, built it;
And thy providence, O Father, guideth it along,   3
Because even in the sea thou gavest a way,
And in the waves a sure path,
Shewing that thou canst save out of every *danger*,   4
That *so* even without art a man may put to sea;

2. *the hunger for gains*] The ship has two advantages over the idol:—commercial enterprise called it into being, and it was made under the guidance of the Divine Wisdom.

artificer, even wisdom] All the best MSS. give this reading, which ch. vii. 22 shows must refer to the Divine Wisdom. But would the author allow that the work of a heathen craftsman was produced under the immediate direction of Wisdom? On the other hand, Vulg. has *artifex sapientia sua*, which represents τεχνίτης σοφίᾳ "the artificer, by his intelligence." σοφίᾳ κατεσκ. appears in ch. ix. 2. If (with Vulg. and Grimm) we accept the masc. τεχνίτης, a pointed antithesis is suggested between the *craftsman* who builds the ship, and the mere *wood-cutter* (ch. xiii. 11) who in an idle hour hacks a log into an idol. In this case *wisdom* is the human quality.

3. *thy providence*] For the philosophic sense of *thy care*, cp. "O God, whose never-failing providence ordereth all things" (8th S. after Trinity). The word *Providence* (πρόνοια) occurs here for the first time in the Gk. Bible, although of very early occurrence among class. Gk. writers. Pythagoras taught the providence of God (Diog. La. ii. 8, 27), also Plato (id. i. 3, 24). Philo (*Opif.* § 61) writes "From the Creation-story we learn fifthly that God exercises a providence over the world. By the laws of nature the maker must always care for the thing made, even as parents take thought for their offspring." Herodotus (iii. 108) says that Divine Providence displays, in certain physiological matters, great wisdom. But if the word is new to the O.T., the idea is not, cp. Ps. cxlv. 9. Bois (pp. 238, 264) sees in πρόνοια only another designation of Wisdom. He identifies it with the *hand of God* in *v.* 6, with Wisdom the pilot in x. 4. Cp. ch. vi. 7; xvii. 2.

in the waves a sure path] Cp. Ps. lxxvii. 19, cvii. 30 LXX.; Is. li. 10. Refers to the passage of the Red Sea, cp. Grimm, p. 242.

4. *out of every* danger] Contrast with xiii. 17—19.

without art] If God so desired, nautical skill would not be required for the trader, any more than for the escaping Israelites. Some MSS. of Vulg. (incl. Amiatinus) read *sine rate* "without a ship," which is no doubt a felicitous false reading for *sine arte*. There is a Greek iambic line, "With the will of God, you might go for a voyage on a mat." But although the writer has in mind the sea-passage of Israel, he suggests nothing so paradoxical as that God could carry men *on* the sea without vessels.

5 And it is thy will that the works of thy wisdom should not
be idle;
Therefore also do men intrust their lives to a little piece of
wood,
And passing through the surge [1]on a raft are brought safe *to
land.*
6 For [2]in the old time also, when proud giants were perishing,
The hope of the world, taking refuge on a raft,
Left to [3]the race of men a seed of generations *to come,*
Thy hand guiding the helm.
7 For blessed [4]hath been wood through which cometh
righteousness:

[1] Gr. *by.*   [2] The Greek text here is perhaps corrupt.
[3] Or, *future time* Gr. *age.*   [4] Or, *is*

5. *should not be idle*] The existence of ships makes commerce
possible: otherwise the fruits of the earth (*works of thy wisdom*) would
accumulate in the countries of their origin, and be wasted for lack of
the means of distribution.   There is a word-play in the Greek between
works and *idle* (lit. *workless*).
little piece of wood] Diog. La. (i. 8, 103) records how the Scythian
philosopher Anacharsis, having learnt that the thickness of a ship's
sides was four fingers' breadth, said "That is all the distance between
the passengers and death."
on a raft] Half depreciatingly of the ship that, compared to the
waves, is so frail. In *v.* 6 the word is used of the Ark. *are brought
safe,* the gnomic aorist in Greek.
6. *proud giants*] See Gen. vi. 4.
were perishing] See Gen. vi. 17, cp. 3 Macc. ii. 4, "Thou didst
destroy the sinners of old time, among whom were giants."
hope of the world] Noah and his family. Deane quotes Verg. *Æn.*
xii. 168 "Ascanius magnae spes altera Romae."
to the race of men] Rather, *to the world* (αἰών). Cp. note on xiii. 9.
αἰών is Creation as it unfolds itself in time.
a seed of generations to come] Cp. Philo, *Mos.* ii. 11 "Noah, counted
worthy to be the beginning of a new generation": *Migr.* § 22 "Noah
having escaped put forth from himself strong and goodly roots, from
which the race of wisdom sprang up like a plant." The expression
properly means *a seed of begetting,* Vulg. *semen natiuitatis.*
Thy hand guiding] *Hand* is perhaps synonymous with Providence,
v. 3. *guiding,* lit. *steering.* For the word applied to the Divine government, cp. Epict. ii. 17. 25.
7. *blessed hath been wood*] *Blessed* stands forcibly contrasted with
accursed, v. 8 : for through a ship once the will of God was done, and
the human race preserved. This is probably the sense to be given to

But the *idol* made with hands is accursed, itself and he that 8
  made it;
Because his was the working, and the corruptible thing was
  named a god:
For both the ungodly doer and his ungodliness are alike 9
  hateful to God;
For verily the deed shall be punished together with him that 10
  committed it.
Therefore also ¹among the idols of the nations shall there be 11
  a visitation,
Because, though formed of things which God created, they
  were made an abomination,
And stumblingblocks to the souls of men,

¹ Or, *upon*   Gr. *in*.

righteousness, but cp. Heb. xi. 7; 2 Pet. ii. 5. It is not surprising that
these words were interpreted with reference to the Cross, which is often
called "wood" or "tree" (ξύλον) in N.T., cp. Acts x. 39. See also
note on Ps. xcvi. 10 in this series on the curious addition to that verse
"The Lord hath reigned *from the tree.*" Many Fathers quote this *v.*
as a prophecy of the Cross (see Deane).

8. *the* idol *made with hands*] The Greek adjective is used in
LXX. to render the Heb. word for *idol*, Is. ii. 18, x. 11, xix. 1. This
sentence beginning with *cursed* stands in antithesis to *v.* 7 beginning
with *blessed*, while the *idol* is contrasted with the *ship* in *v.* 2 (ἐκεῖνο μέν).

accursed...and he that made it] Drawn from Dt. xxvii. 15. The
man is accursed for making the idol; the idol because the name of
God is given to it (*v.* 21), cp. Rom. i. 23.

9. *the ungodly doer and his ungodliness*] The abstract word stands
almost for the concrete *idol*, cp. "abomination" in xii. 23. For doer
and deed, cp. Hos. ix. 10 "They became abominable like that which
they loved." For God's *hatred* of sin, see Ps. v. 5.

10. *the deed*] Strictly speaking, a "thing done" cannot be
punished, neither can a sin. *Punishment* can only alight on a
personality. Hence τὸ πραχθέν (the thing done) must be interpreted
of the idol (the concrete result of human action) which is almost
personified.

11. *Therefore*] Explains prec. *v.* Cp. Ex. xii. 12; Jer. x. 15.

though formed of things] Cp. Rom. i. 25. The sense is that wood
and stone, which exist in God's creation and by God's decree, are
turned into representations of beings (or rather non-entities) which
dispute God's supremacy with Him. An idol is a misapplication of
created (i.e. divine) things, and therefore must be destroyed.

an abomination] in the eyes of the Creator.

stumblingblocks...a snare] to men. The two words occur together in

And a snare to the feet of the foolish.

12 For the devising of idols was the beginning of fornication,
And the invention of them the corruption of life:
13 For neither were they from the beginning, neither shall they
be for ever;
14 For by the vaingloriousness of men they entered into the
world,
And therefore was a speedy end devised for them.
15 For a father worn with untimely grief,
Making an image of the child quickly taken away,

Josh. xxiii. 13 and Ps. lxix. 22, cp. Ps. cvi. 36. The things that have
perverted human souls cannot but be viewed with indignation by the
" Lover of souls."

vv. 12—21.   The origin of idolatry.

12.   *the beginning of fornication*]   i.e. as A.V. *spiritual fornication.*
This is a common O.T. figure for the spiritual levity which can forsake
Jehovah for another deity, cp. Ex. xxxiv. 15, 16 ; Ps. cvi. 39 ; Hos. ii. 2.
the corruption of life]   Morally, see *v.* 27.   Cp. 2 Pet. i. 4 ; ii. 19.

13.   *from the beginning*]   Existence is not inherent in them, as in
God (Ex. iii. 14 ; Ps. xc. 2).   Cp. Dt. xxxii. 17 " New gods that came
newly up, whom your fathers feared not."   For *neither shall they be*
cp. Is. lxv. 3 LXX. " They burn incense upon the bricks to gods
which are not " (will not be, A).

14.   *vaingloriousness*]   Rather, *through the foolish fancy of men*, cp.
4 Macc. v. 9. Grimm points out that there is no vaingloriousness in
" untimely grief " (*v.* 15).
they entered into the world]   Idols, like death (ch. ii. 24), are intruders into God's world.   Like death, men brought them in (ch. i. 16).
" Coming into the world" is a phrase expressive of crossing the frontiers
of a kingdom : the idea is not so much metaphysical as moral : where
they came from is not so important as that they have been introduced
in violation of God's order of things.
was a speedy end devised]   If man can devise idols (*v.* 12), God can
devise a speedy ending of them.   When the end shall be is left as
indefinite as in *vv.* 10, 11.

15.   *untimely grief*]   i.e. grief for an untimely death.   This trans-
ference of adjectives is known as *hypallage.*
the child quickly taken away]   The classical instance of this is to be
found in Cicero's memorial to his daughter.   Lactantius (*Inst.* i. 15)
represents him as saying " With the approbation of the gods, I will
place you the best and most learned of all women in their assembly,
and will consecrate you to the estimation of all men."   But the more
natural process undoubtedly would be (as Mr Herbert Spencer argued),

Now honoured him as a god which was then a dead man,
And delivered to those that were under him mysteries and
solemn rites.
Afterward the ungodly custom, in process of time grown 16
strong, was kept as a law,
And by the commandments of princes the graven images
received worship.
And when men could not honour them in presence because 17
they dwelt far off,

for children to venerate their deceased ancestors (cp. 2 Macc. xi. 23),
as is seen in China.   Fulgentius (quoting from Diophantus) tells of an
Egyptian named Syrophanes, who, overcome with grief for the loss of
his son, erected a statue of him in his house.   To please the master of
the house, the members of the family decked it with flowers, and slaves
even fled to it for sanctuary.   And thus the statue gradually became an
idol.

Now honoured him as a god] The essential connection between death
and deity is well brought out by Prof. Ramsay in his Art. on *Rel. of
Greece* in Hastings, *D.B.* Vol. v. p. 131 (Burial).   He writes "It was
probably on the worship of the dead that the worship of Divine personal
beings was built up.   The dead parent links the family with the Divine
nature....Among the Greeks the special sacrifice to the dead hero took
place on his birthday."

16.   *custom...grown strong*] Cp. Philo, *Dec.* § 26 "Custom in
process of time becomes stronger than nature."   Custom becomes
prescription, and prescription is almost stronger than law.   *V.* 16 refers
to *v.* 15, to the child-worship now grown from custom into law: what
was begun by a father among his servants is now enforced by a tyrant
upon his subjects.   There is no connection between *v.* 16 and *v.* 17:
the dictated worship is contrasted with the voluntary.   *Princes* however
serves as a link between the verses.

17.   The reference in this *v.* is to divine honours paid to kings in
their lifetime, not after death.   W. M. Ramsay writes (Art. on *Rel. of
Greece* in Hastings, *D.B.* Vol. v. p. 154) "It was an easy step to
identify the man of surpassing excellence, physical or mental, with a
god either after his death or during his lifetime, when the perfection of
human nature was regarded as Divine....According to Plutarch, the
first man to whom worship was paid as a god during his lifetime was
Lysander (*Lys.* 18)....The Thasians honoured Agesilaos in a similar
way.   From the time of Alexander the deification of kings was customary, as a mere recognition of 'divine right.'·   Roman generals
were often honoured by Greek cities with festivals and games, which
implied deification.   Every Roman emperor in succession was worshipped; and it was inscribed on the coins and the engraved decrees
of the greatest Greek cities as a special honour that they were temple-

Imagining the likeness from afar,
They made a visible image of the king whom they honoured,
That by their zeal they might flatter the absent as if present.

18 But unto a yet higher pitch was worship raised even by
them that knew *him* not,
Urged forward by the ambition of the artificer:

19 For he, wishing peradventure to please one in authority,
Used his art to force the likeness toward a greater beauty;

20 And the multitude, allured by reason of the grace of his
handywork,

wardens of the emperors." Farrar mentions that Augustus was
hardly able to prevent the worship of himself in his lifetime : he could
only insist that temples in his honour should be associated with temples to Roma.   On the rise of Emperor-worship, cp. Westcott, *Epp. of
St John*, pp. 268 ff.

Imagining the likeness from afar] lit. the-from-afar-likeness. For
the *flattery* which elevates a living man into a god, cp. Acts xii. 22
"It is the voice of a god and not of a man."

18.   R.V. treats this *v.* as closely connected with the preceding, in
which case *them that knew him not* refers to the same people as those
"who dwelt afar off" (*v.* 17), while *worship* is the exaggerated form
of the *flattery* of the same *v.* But the *v.* may be viewed as altogether
distinct from *v.* 17, and the Gk. be rendered as A.V. "the ignorant"
(abs.), i.e. those who do not know what deception is being practised
upon them. But καί ("even") makes the R.V. rendering almost certain.
In that case, desire to flatter is seen passing into worship, on the part
of those who could only know the prince at second-hand. The workman, desiring to secure favour, produced so exquisite a statue, that he
captivated the hearts of a people ever ready to deify any surpassing
human excellence. And so those who began with grovelling subser-
vience were seduced by beauty into actual worship.

ambition] The artificer's ambition is not that of the artist, but of the
place-seeker. A.V. renders *singular diligence* with Vulg.

19.   *For he*] In *v.* 17 distant subjects make a representation of a
distant king : in this *v.* the court-sculptor makes the statue.

wishing...to please] Painters and sculptors were not the only artists
who lived by pleasing. Cp. Plut. *Lysander* "L. always kept the
Spartan poet Choerilus in his retinue, that he might be ready to add
lustre to his actions by the power of verse." The story of the painter
who desired to depict Cromwell without the wart on his face illustrates
how painters "force the likeness to greater beauty."

20.   *allured by...the grace*] Herodotus records (v. 47) that Philip of
Crotona was after his death worshipped as a hero and honoured with
sacrifices, because of his extraordinary beauty. The cases are not
exactly parallel, but in both beauty leads to deification.

Now accounted as an object of devotion him that a little
before was honoured as a man.
And this became ¹a hidden danger unto life,   21
Because men, in bondage either to calamity or to tyranny,
Invested stones and stocks with the incommunicable Name.

Afterward it was not enough for them to go astray as 22
touching the knowledge of God;
But also, while they live ²in ³sore conflict through ignorance
of him,

¹ Gr. *an ambush.*   ² Or, *for*   ³ Gr. *a great war of ignorance.*

him that a little before] This seems to point to the connection
between *vv.* 17, 18, assumed in text.
    21. *And this*] This looks back to all recounted in *vv.* 15—20.
With the line cp. 1 Kings xii. 30, xiii. 34.
    unto life] Either "the world" as Vulg. *mundo,* or "the life of man"
as Cod. Amiatinus *uitae humanae.* The latter seems better, cp.
4 Macc. xvii. 14, but see x. 8.
    in bondage] By syllepsis the same verb is used with two substantives
of dissimilar character, in a sense varying slightly with each. For
calamity see *v.* 15, and *tyranny, vv.* 16—18.
    the incommunicable Name] not of Jehovah, but of God. The sin lay
in giving the name of deity to things essentially beneath God, cp. Is.
xlii. 8 "neither will I give My praise to graven images," and Philo,
Ebr. § 28 "They actually made unreasoning animals and herbs par-
takers in the glory of things incorruptible."

vv. 22—31. THE INEVITABLE SEQUEL OF FALSE WORSHIP IS
FALSE LIFE.

    22. *it was not enough*] A truth of psychology. Conduct follows
creed. Cp. Rom. i. 28 "Even as they refused to have God in their
knowledge, God gave them up unto a reprobate mind."
    in sore conflict] Vulg. *inscientiae bello.* They live in a state of war
arising from ignorance of God, cp. xiii. 1, and yet call it *peace.* A
society infested with the social evils enumerated in *vv.* 23 ff. may have
no external enemies, but is really in a state of internal war. The life
of mutual antagonism dictated by self-seeking is pictured by Philo
in a curiously similar passage (*Conf. l.* § 12) "All that is done in war
they do in time of peace....Every man sets before him as his goal
wealth or honour, and directs the doings of his life at it as if he were
shooting arrows at a mark: he neglects fairness, and pursues inequality;
he refuses community of interests, and struggles to acquire the property
of all for himself alone: he hates his fellowmen, while professing good-
will; is a companion of bastard adulation while an enemy of legitimate
friendship; he hates truth and champions falsehood; he is slow to help

That multitude of evils they call peace.
23 For either slaughtering children in solemn rites, or celebrating
   secret mysteries,
Or holding frantic revels of strange ordinances,
24 No longer do they ¹guard either life or purity of marriage,
But one brings upon another either death by treachery, or
   anguish by adulterate offspring.
25 And all things confusedly are filled with blood and murder,
   theft and deceit,
Corruption, faithlessness, tumult, perjury, 26 ²turmoil,

¹ Or, *keep unstained either life or marriage*
² Or, *troubling of the good, forgetfulness of favours*

and swift to injure; foremost in slandering and a laggard in defending:
a clever cheat, a perjurer, a breaker of agreements, a slave to anger, a
servant of pleasure, a guardian of things evil, and a destroyer of things
good. All these things are the appanage of that widely sung and
highly vaunted *peace*; things which the idolatrous mind of the foolish
admires and adores." Similarly, the writer in this *v.* is complaining of
the social and intestine conflict of interests which is possible while a
state is said to be at peace. Cp. Jer. vi. 14 " Peace, peace, when there
is no peace."

   23. *slaughtering children*] Cp. xii. 5 and Is. lvii. 5.
   secret mysteries] The writer had the Jew's instinctive hatred of the
pagan mysteries. The standard of moral purity which was required for
participation in the mysteries was "consistent with habitual disregard
of some of the elementary moral rules of the...Hebrew religion."
   frantic revels] e.g. the Bacchanalian orgies such as those by which
the Temple was polluted in the time of Antiochus, cp. 2 Macc. vi. 1—7.
The Phrygian mysteries, the Babylonian worship of Aphrodite (Hdt. i.
199), and orgies of Bacchus-worship were typical instances of the
strange ordinances which flourished where God was unknown.
   24. Neither the sacredness of the individual life, nor the sanctity of
the marriage tie, is observed; treacherous murders, and children born
of adulterous unions are a commonplace.
   25. *blood and murder*] For the catalogue of sins in *vv.* 25, 26, cp.
Rom. i. 29; Gal. v. 19—21; 1 Tim. i. 9. See also Jer. vii. 9, Hos. iv. 2,
and the citation from Philo, *Conf. l.* on *v.* 22.
   Corruption] Moral corruption generally, cp. 2 Pet. ii. 10.
   faithlessness...perjury] These two sins go together in *Conf. l.* § 12.
The former is like " covenant-breakers " in Rom. i. 31, cp. Jer. iii. 7
LXX.; the latter is dealt with in *vv.* 28—31.
   tumult] Disorders of all kinds. Cp. 2 Cor. xii. 20.
   26. *turmoil*] Text takes θόρυβος alone, Vulg. joins with ἀγαθῶν,
tumultus bonorum, so marg. If "turmoil" must be taken alone, it
seems much the same as "tumult." If, however, marg. is possible,

Ingratitude for benefits *received*,
Defiling of souls, confusion of [1]sex,
Disorder in marriage, adultery and wantonness.
For the worship of [2]those [3]nameless idols   27
Is a beginning and cause and end of every evil.
For *their worshippers* either make merry unto madness, or 28
  prophesy lies,
Or live unrighteously, or lightly forswear themselves.
For putting their trust in lifeless idols,   29
When they have sworn a wicked oath, they expect not to
  suffer harm,

[1] Or, *kind*   [2] Or, *idols that may not be named* See Ex. xxiii. 13;
Ps. xvi. 4; Hos. ii. 17. [3] See ver. 21.

and the sense of "trouble given to good men" is allowed, the expression refers to such cases as that of ch. ii. The balance of the line
favours marg., cp. 2 Tim. iii. 3 ἀφιλαγαθοι, "no lovers of good."
   Ingratitude for benefits] or, if αγαθῶν is taken with θόρυβος, *forgetfulness of favours* marg., cp. 2 Tim. iii. 2 "unthankful."
   Defiling of souls] Cp. Jer. v. 26; 2 Pet. ii. 14 "beguiling unstable
souls," and 2 Tim. iii. 6.
   confusion of sex] Cp. Rom. i. 27.
   Disorder in marriage] Farrar quotes Seneca on the frightful preva-
lence of divorce in the Imperial epoch: women reckoned their years by
their discarded husbands. Philo (*Cher.* § 27) writes of μεθημεριυοὶ
γάμοι, "marriages of a day."
   wantonness] Philo, *Cher.* § 27, with his customary fulness, details a
long list of wantonnesses commonly indulged in.
   27. *nameless*] Vulg. *infandorum*. But ἀνώνυμος hardly means
"unnameable," as the marginal references to the prohibition of Ex.
xxiii. 13, etc. would suggest, but "without a name." The name of
anything was the symbol of its existence; hence *nameless idols* means
idols which represent no real gods, cp. Gal. iv. 8.
   beginning...and end] Philo (*Plant.* § 18) uses the same Greek words
of God, whom he calls "beginning and end of all things." The
insertion here of *cause* only intensifies the causal meaning of the words
(as distinguished from the temporal).
   28. Four results of idolatry: madness (μεμηνασιν, with a side-
reference to Bacchanalian revellers, μαινάδες, "mad women"), false
ideals, injustice, perjury. All these may be traced in Jer. v., which is
a typical denunciation of idolatry (1) *v.* 8, (2) *v.* 31, (3) *v.* 1, (4) *v.* 7.
   29. The writer implies that it was convenient to believe in false
gods, because it was possible to swear by them and yet have no fear of
breaking the oath. But it is a wrong inference that perjury, however
universal, proves the falsity of the gods whose name is taken in vain.

30 But for both *sins* shall the just doom pursue them,
  Because they had evil thoughts of God by giving heed to
    idols,
  And swore unrighteously in deceit through contempt for
    holiness.
31 For it is not the power of them by whom men swear,
  But it is ¹that Justice which hath regard to them that sin,
  That visiteth always the transgression of the unrighteous.

15 But thou, our God, art gracious and true,

¹ Gr. *the Justice of them that sin.*

It only proves scepticism, or want of sense of responsibility in the per-
jurers. Just as among the Jews the oath by the living God was binding
upon all but the worst, so among the heathen there were some deities in
whose name very few would dare to swear falsely, e.g. the Cabiri, cp.
Juv. iii. 144. ἀδικηθῆναι (suffer harm) loosely for δίκην δοῦναι (be
punished); or should we read ἐκδικηθῆναι (suffer vengeance)?

30 *for both* sins] *Pursue* governs double acc. The double sin was
(*a*) giving the name of God to idols, and (*b*) venturing to despise the
sanctities of life. With (*a*) cp. *v.* 21 c, an argument which would appeal
to Jews. With (*b*) Deane compares Ez. xvii. 18, 19. *Holiness* stands
for whatever measure of truth and honour the perjurer might be expected
to possess. Plutarch, quoting a saying of Lysander "children were to
be cheated with cockalls, and men with oaths," writes "He who over-
reaches by a false oath, declares that he fears his enemy, but *despises
his God.*" The writer's argument is that even if idols cause no fear,
every man ought to carry a fear within him : punishment awaits the
man who has stifled that sacred instinct.

31. *Justice which hath regard*] The writer views Justice in an
objective light, so that (whatever false gods men may acknowledge and
perjure themselves by) God's avenging minister will find them out,
as in Acts xxviii. 4 or Philo, *Jos.* § 29 "The Justice that watches over
human affairs, who displays the inexorableness of her nature against
those that deserve punishment," cp. id. *Conf. l.* § 24 fin. For the idea
of vengeance following on perjury, cp. Aristoph. *Pax* 277 "If any of
you were initiated in Samothrace, now would it be well to pray that the
feet of the avenger (the Cabiri) be turned away from pursuit of you."

CHAPTER XV.

vv. 1—6. THE PURIFYING AND RESTRAINING INFLUENCE OF THE
  WORSHIP OF JEHOVAH UPON THE LIFE OF ISRAEL.

1. The writer turns away from the appalling picture of the results of
idolatry to the character of the true God with its influence on the
national life, "But Thou, *our* God...."

Longsuffering, and in mercy ordering all things.
For even if we sin, we are thine, knowing thy dominion;   2
But we shall not sin, knowing that we have been accounted
thine:
For to be acquainted with thee is ¹perfect righteousness,   3
And to know thy dominion is the root of immortality.

¹ Gr. *entire*.

gracious, etc.] The four attributes of God here named are based on
the revelation of Ex. xxxiv. 6, cp. Dt. xxxii. 4 LXX. "God, His works
are true, and all His ways are judgments: God is faithful and there
is no unrighteousness (in Him); righteous and holy is the Lord." For
gracious (χρηστός), cp. St Luke vi. 35 and Rom. xi. 22. God is *true*,
not only because He alone is God, but because He keeps His promises
to His people.
   ordering all things] Cp. xii. 15.
   2. The first clause of this *v.* is to be interpreted by the second of the
next *v.*, and the second clause of this by the first of next *v.*
   For...we are thine] The clause, introd. by *For*, illustrates God's
mercy spoken of in the preceding *v.* Even sin cannot frustrate God's
goodness to His people, cp. Rom. iii. 3. *Thine, knowing thy dominion*
is explained by *v.* 3 b as "Thine, possessing the root of immortality,"
i.e. even though we sin, yet our faith in the effective power of the
true God saves us from the licentiousness of the heathen, which is
spiritual death. For *we are thine*, cp. Ex. xxxiv. 9 fin. LXX.
   But we shall not sin] He rejects the hypothesis of sin in those who
are named as God's. The point of view is ideal, but it is only an
anticipation of 1 John iii. 6, v. 18. Cp. also Ecclus. x. 2.
   3. *to be acquainted with thee*] Text suggests a difference of sense
between ἐπίστασθαι (be acquainted) in 3 a and εἰδέναι (know) in 3 b.
No distinction can be safely pressed. There is a natural tendency to
variation. "To know God is perfect righteousness"; the aphorism
contains the principle of which *v.* 2 b is the application: the knowledge
of God is not a matter of intellect, but of moral apprehension. Just as
St John writes (1 John iv. 8) "He that loveth not knoweth not God," i.e.
To know God is to love, so the writer lays down the principle "To
know God is to be wholly righteous." Cp. Jer. ix. 23, 24.
   to know thy dominion] As in the prec. *l.*, the emphasis is on *thy*.
Even the intellectual possession of a right theology has its value. On
the assumption that he who knows is guided by his knowledge, such
knowledge may be described as the root, the beginning, the first
element of immortality. If righteousness is immortal (ch. i. 15), the
first step to immortality is the discovery of Him who is righteous. For
the use of *root*, cp. iii. 15 and Ecclus. i. 20, and 1 Tim. vi. 10 (cp. Prov.
ix. 10). Life is frequently explained in moral terms, cp. Dt. xxx. 20
(as the love of God), St John xvii. 3 (as the knowledge of God), and
Philo, *Fuga* § 15 (as the taking refuge in Him who is).

4 For neither were we led astray by any evil device of men's
   art,
  Nor yet by painters' fruitless labour,
  A form stained with varied colours;
5 The sight whereof leadeth fools into ¹lust:
  Their desire is for the breathless form of a dead image.
6 Lovers of evil things, and worthy of such hopes *as these,*

        ¹ Some authorities read *reproach.*

4. *For*] See *v.* 2 " We are thine, for...."

evil device of men's art] κακότεχνος (evil...art) recalls τεχνίτης
(artificer) and τέχνη (art) xiv. 18, 19 : the writer makes it plain that he
thinks art evil, and the cause of idolatry. επινοια (device) is used in a
bad sense as in xiv. 12. Israel as a nation was never seduced into
idolatry; there was always a remnant, which stood ideally for the whole
people, cp. 1 K. xix. 18. But the writer is more probably thinking of
contemporary Judaism in contrast to the nations among whom the Jews
of the Dispersion were settled. The effect of the Captivity was to
confirm the post-exilic Jews in their antagonism to idolatry.

painters' fruitless labour] Philo (*Gig.* § 13) writes "Moses banished
from his polity the noble arts of sculpture and painting: they made a
counterfeit presentment of the true, and consequently deceived human
souls by deluding the eye." For *fruitless labour,* cp. Eph. v. 11, and
ch. iii. 13 (note on *fruit*).

stained with varied colours] Cp. xiii. 14. Statues and images were
habitually coloured. The use of the word *stained* is contemptuous.
While God never displayed Himself under any form or shape (Dt. iv.
12), the gods of the heathen not only *were* forms, but stained ones.

5. *lust*] Text reads rightly with אAC ὄρεξιν, Vulg. *concupiscen-
tiam.* B has ὄνειδος *reproach,* which is accounted for by εἰκόνος εἶδος
immediately below. Sight passes into desire, and desire into worship.
In his essay on Art in *Religious Thought in the West,* Bp. Westcott
suggests the true function of art. As it is through the senses that
temptation chiefly comes, the service of art is to teach the senses true
enjoyment, so that their taste may be spoiled for mean things, and they
may learn to find satisfaction only in that which elevates.

the breathless form] See xiv. 19, 20. The story of Pygmalion of
Cyprus and his ivory statue is quoted by Grimm from Arnobius *Adv.
nat.* vi. 22.

6. *worthy of such hopes*] Cp. i. 16. *Hopes* may be the futile trust
in idols, cp. xiii. 10, or else the idols themselves, which are such delusive
objects of trust. The writer's doctrine of affinity appears again : men
find the gods that suit them. *They that do,* see *v.* 4.

desire...worship] See *v.* 5.

Are both they that do,' and they that desire, and they that
worship.

For a potter, kneading soft earth,   7
Laboriously mouldeth each several *vessel* for our service :
Nay, out of the same clay doth he fashion
Both the vessels that minister to clean uses, and those of a
     contrary sort,
All in like manner ;
But what shall be the use of each *vessel* of either sort,
The ¹craftsman *himself* is the judge.
And also, labouring to an evil end, he mouldeth a vain god 8
     out of the same clay,
He who, having but a little before been made of earth,

¹ Gr. *worker in clay.*

vv. 7—13.   THE CONTEMPTIBLE FOLLY OF THE MAKER OF
                          CLAY IDOLS.

Hitherto the idols have been his mark, now he attacks the idol-
maker. For a man of clay to make gods of clay—for one who works
with a material which is a perpetual reminder to him of his own origin
and futility, both to make counterfeits of metal images and to forget the
lessons he might have learnt from his craft, is foolishness of mind and
character. Further, he impeaches the motives of the idol-maker: he is
led on by rivalry and the desire for gain, *vv.* 9, 12.

7. *potter*] The idol-maker is contemptuously called a potter ; cp.
the "carpenter" of xiii. 11. It is part of the writer's method of
contempt to suggest that the making of idols takes its place in the day's
work with the making of tables and pots. For the potter's work, see
Is. xlv. 9, lxiv. 8 ; Ecclus. xxxviii. 29, 30; Test. xii Patr. *Napht.* ii.
     out of the same clay] Cp. Rom. ix. 21.
     clean uses, and...contrary] St Paul seems to recall this passage in
2 Tim. ii. 21.
     is the judge] Cp. Jer. xviii. 4, and Hor. *Sat.* i. 8. 1 ff. "Once I
was a useless log, and a carpenter, after hesitating whether to make a
stool of me or a figure of Priapus, decided to make me into a god."
     8. *labouring to an evil end*] The word κακόμοχϑος takes up *laboriously*
(ἐπίμοχϑος) of *v.* 7 ; it has much the same meaning as "evil-devising"
(κακοτεχνος), *v.* 4. κακόμοχϑος almost means "unconscionable." The
clay-worker is engaged in a sham creation. God made man out of clay ;
the clay turns round and makes a god.
     made of earth] Gen. ii. 7 ; Job x. 9.

After a short space goeth his way *to the earth* out of which
   he was taken,
When he is required to render back the [1]soul which was lent
   him.
9 Howbeit he hath anxious care,
   Not because his powers must fail,
   Nor because his span of life is short;
But he matcheth himself against goldsmiths and [2]silver-
   smiths,
And he imitateth moulders in [3]brass,
And esteemeth it glory that he mouldeth counterfeits.

[1] Or, *life*   [2] Gr. *silver-founders.*   [3] Or, *copper*

to the earth *out of which*] Gen. iii. 19; Job xxxiv. 15, see also
Ecclus. xvii. 1, 2, xl. 1, 11, xli. 10.

to render back the soul which was lent him] Man's spirit is received
as a loan (*v.* 16); the loan must sooner or later be called in (cp. St Luke
xii. 20). See Introd. § 12. The idea is seen in Lucretius iii. 971
"Life is granted to none in fee-simple, to all in usufruct." Cp. Ambr.
(*de Bon. Mort.* 10) "The soul is required, but it is not destroyed."
Philo is very familiar with the idea, see *Abr.* § 44; *Q. R. D. H.* § 22
"Strive to count what you have received as worthy of all care, that
He who placed it in your keeping may have no fault to find with your
guardianship," and *Post C.* § 2 "Each man has to pay back his loan
to nature, whenever she chooses to call in the debts outstanding to her."
This conception is due to Greek influence. A. B. Davidson (*Theol. of
O. T.* p. 197) writes "While in earlier books the question is not raised
as to what becomes of the life-spirit in man when he dies, in later books
this spirit is spoken of more as if it had an independent being of its own.
That is, the immaterial element in man is identified with the spirit of life
or principle of vitality in him. 'The spirit shall return unto God who
gave it' (Eccles. xii. 7)"

9. The workman's misplaced anxiety. He is not thinking of his
own human frailty, but of competition with metal workers, and of his
success in imposing counterfeits on the market.

powers must fail] κάμνειν, Vulg. *laboraturus est*, i.e. grow sick and
weary.

span of life] Cp. ch. ii. 1; Job x. 20.

matcheth himself against] This is probably an exaggeration on the
writer's part. Clay images were no doubt made to look as much like
the precious metals as possible: but that they were deliberately palmed
off as gold and silver there is no reason to believe. Farrar writes that
in the Egyptian tombs have been found many scarabs and idols of clay,
gilded, or bronzed, or covered with a vitrified covering.

esteemeth it glory] Not only does he make a counterfeit god, but

His heart is ashes,   10
And his hope of less value than earth,
And his life of less honour than clay :
Because he was ignorant of him that moulded him,   11
And of him that inspired into him ¹an active ²soul,
And breathed into him a vital spirit.

¹ Gr. *a soul that moveth to activity.*   ² Or, *life*

by his spurious imitations he produces a counterfeit of a counterfeit ;
and this his shame, he counts his glory.

10. *His heart is ashes*] Another abrupt characterisation as in *v.* 6.
The expression is drawn from Is. xliv. 20 LXX. (see Introd. § 2), where
through confusion of Hebrew letters the words for "he feedeth on ashes:
a heart" are wrongly rendered "know that their heart is ashes." Cp.
Ezek. xi. 19, xxxvi. 26.

his hope of less value] If his god is a piece of baked clay, then the
hope he reposes upon his god is still more worthless. Cp. Eph. ii. 12.

his life...clay] In the idol-maker's life there is no upward look, no
acknowledgment of God as his Maker. Therefore his life has less
honour than even the clay. For all created things (including earth)
praise the Lord, cp. Song of the Three Children, *v.* 52: and the giver
of praise is himself elevated by his tribute.

11. He wilfully ignores his Maker, cp. Is. i. 3; Rom. i. 28.

moulded him] Gen. ii. 7. He moulds a god (*v.* 8), ignoring the fact
that he himself was moulded by God.

an active soul] It would seem as though the commonly accepted
trichotomy of body, soul, and spirit were present in this *v.*, cp.
Heb. iv. 12, 1 Thess. v. 23. But in *Theol. of. O.T.*, p. 186, Prof. Davidson
argues that the analysis is rhetorical and not to be taken literally.
With regard to "soul" and "spirit," the Jews viewed the immaterial
part of man in various lights: soul was not for them distinct from spirit,
but "the same thing under different aspects. 'Spirit' connotes energy,
power, especially vital power ; and man's inner nature in such aspects,
as exhibiting power, energy, life of whatever kind, is spoken of as
spirit. The soul on the other hand is the seat of the sensibilities. The
idea of 'spirit' is more that of something objective and impersonal; that
of soul suggests what is reflexive and impersonal." Cp. *op. cit.*, the
whole of section VI. The Doctrine of Man, pp. 182—203. For the
later and not strictly Jewish doctrine of the tripartite nature of man in
N.T., see Lightfoot, *Notes on Epp. of St Paul*, p. 88.

a vital spirit] The phraseology is very similar to that in Gen. ii. 7,
on which passage Prof. Davidson writes (*op. cit.* p. 194) "All that seems
in question here is just the giving of vitality to man. There seems no
allusion to man's immaterial being, to his spiritual element....Vitality is
communicated by God....The anthropomorphism of the author is very
strong. He represents God Himself as having a breath which is the

12 But ¹he accounted our *very* life to be a ²plaything,
And our ³lifetime a gainful ⁴fair;
For, saith he, one must get gain whence one can, though it
be by evil.
13 For this man beyond all others knoweth that he sinneth,

¹ Some authorities read *they accounted.*   ² Or, *sport*
³ Or, *way of life*   ⁴ Or, *keeping of festival*

sign or principle of life in Himself; and this He breathed into man, and
it became the same in him."

The writer practically identifies "soul" and "spirit" *vv.* 8, 16, and
the distinction lies between the two epithets of the one life-principle.
For vital (ζωτικὸν), cp. Philo, *Det. Pot.* § 22, where he says that man is
animal as well as human.   As animal he possesses "vital" (ζωτική)
faculty, while as man he enjoys "rational" (λογική) faculty as well.

12.   *he accounted*]   *They* (marg.), i.e. the idol-maker and the heathen
generally.

our very *life*]   ζωη, i.e. the life-principle, that which differentiates
between mineral and animal (cp. note on *v.* 11).   It is treating life
as a trifle, when man, who is clay, but clay suffused with vitality, sets
before himself for worship a piece of clay unredeemed by any trace of
life, that might be made into household utensils.   It has been suggested
that ζωη and βίος (next *l.*) are merely poetical variations, and should not
be distinguished; but in each case the predicates are quite different, and
accordingly the subjects may be treated as distinct.

And our lifetime]   Better, *way of life*, marg., Vulg. *conuersationem
uitae*.   βίος in this sense is the practical life, the life of affairs.   The
idol-maker's view of daily life is that it is like a public market, where
every man makes the best bargain he can.   The Gk. word (πανηγυρισμὸς)
includes the two ideas of festival and fair.   Pythagoras (Diog. La. viii.
8) used to "compare life to a festival, to which some went to contend,
others for commercial purposes, and the best in order to look on: so in
life (he said) some are slavish, pursuing honour and lucre, while others,
the philosophers, look for truth."   Epictetus (ii. 14) expands these
words of Pythagoras.   Cp. the account of the commerce of Tyre,
Ezek. xxvii. and St James iv. 13—15.

gain whence one can, etc.]   Cp. Hor. *Ep.* i. 1, 65 "rem facias rem Si
possis recte—si non quocumque modo rem."   Farrar quotes Juv. *Sat.*
xiv. 204 "lucri bonus est odor ex re Qualibet."

though it be by evil]   The idol-maker in this *v.* is distinguished from
the idolater of xiii. 17, in that he has no belief in the idols he makes.
He crowns his greed with chicanery.

13.   *knoweth that he sinneth*]   To all his other enormities he adds this
that he refuses to obey the truth that his own senses should bear in upon
his mind.   He makes household vessels out of clay, things which will
break with the slightest fall (εὐθραυστα), and then he makes gods out of

Out of earthy matter making brittle vessels and graven
images.

But most foolish ¹*were* they all, and ²of feebler soul than 14
a babe,

The enemies of thy people, who oppressed them ;

Because they even accounted all the idols of the nations 15
to be gods ;

Which have neither the use of eyes for seeing,

Nor nostrils for drawing breath,

Nor ears to hear,

Nor fingers for handling,

And their feet are helpless for walking.

¹ Or, are   ² Gr. *more wretched than the soul of a babe.*   The
Greek text here is perhaps corrupt.

the same material, and worships gods which are subject to precisely
similar risks: he worships a brittle, breakable god.

vv. **14—17.** WHATEVER MAY BE THE WICKEDNESS OF THE MAKER
OF CLAY IDOLS, THERE IS NO ONE TO COMPARE FOR STUPIDITY
WITH THE OPPRESSORS OF ISRAEL, WHO RECKONED ALL HEATHEN
IDOLS AS GODS.

14. *The enemies...who oppressed*] The reference would seem to be to
the Egyptians.   The writer has made a digression of three chapters
(beginning from xii. 27, where the Egyptians were in question), and in
ch. xvi. he will be found speaking of them again. *vv.* 14—17 form the
link between digression and main argument.   This view is supported
by *oppressed them,* which points to a past persecution; cp. also the
reference in *v.* 18 to animal worship.   But it is not clear how *v.* 15
refers to the Egyptians, for it was not they, but the Romans of imperial
times, who were the true religious eclectics.   But even the Romans did
not receive the full tide of Phrygian, Egyptian, Persian, and Syrian
cults until long after the latest date at which Wisdom could have been
written. See Gregg, *Decian Persecution,* p. 49.   The Egyptians may
have practised a general tolerance of foreign deities (cp. the worship of
Perseus at Chemis, Hdt. ii. 91), while adhering strictly to their own
national cults. The chief Egyptian persecutions of the Jews were
under Ptolemy Philopator c. 217 B.C., and Ptolemy Physcon, who
persecuted for seven years (145—138), though later becoming pacified,
while the oppression of Exodus was never allowed to be forgotten.
The writer forgets that he is writing as Solomon, unless *oppressed them*
is taken to refer to no oppression except the earliest.

15. This *v.* is a free imitation of Ps. cxv. 4—7, cxxxv. 15—17, cp.
also Philo's version in *Dec.* § 15. For the first *l.,* cp. also Ps. xcvi. 5.

16 For a man made them,
   And one whose own spirit is borrowed moulded them ;
   For no one hath power, *being* a man, to mould a god like
      unto himself,
17 But, being mortal, he maketh a dead thing by the work of
      lawless hands ;
   For he is better than the objects of his worship,
   [1] Forasmuch as he indeed had life, but they never.

18 Yea, and the creatures that are most hateful do they wor-
      ship,

[1] Most authorities read *Of which, he indeed.*

16. *whose own spirit is borrowed*] See *v.* 8, and cp. Ps. civ. 29;
Eccl. viii. 8.

For no one hath power] Man's life is not inherent, but derived:
accordingly, though he can transmit life by natural processes, he cannot
implant life in the works of his hands.   No man can make a god which
is even on a level with himself: however much the workman may call
his work his god, the workman must always be superior to his work.
On the other hand, spiritually "they that make them are like unto
them" (Ps. cxv. 8): their heart is ashes.

17. *a dead thing*] Cp. xiii. 10, 18, xiv. 8.

he is better] He is mortal, and will have to die one day; but his idol
has never even been alive.   The contrast explains why the worker's
hands are lawless: it is impiety for the animate, possessing the image of
God, to bow to the inanimate.   Philo (*Dec.* § 14) writes "The workman
is better than his work both in time (for he is older and in some sense
its father) and in faculty.   And although (if they were going to sin) men
ought to have deified their painters and sculptors, they have actually
left them in obscurity, and given the name of gods to their statues and
paintings."

Forasmuch as] So א (ανθ' ων) Vulg. *quia*, "because."   Other MSS.
read ὧν, *of which, he indeed*, etc.

but they never] Cp. Hab. ii. 18, 19.

vv. **18, 19.**   The folly of Egyptian animal worship.

18.   *vv.* 18, 19 form an introduction to ch. xvi., and must be taken
closely with it.

creatures...most hateful] Cp. xii. 24.   Diog. La. (*proem.* vii. 11)
writes that the Egyptians honour the useful animals as gods.   Philo
(*Post. C.* § 48) writes that they deify bulls and rams and goats.   This
(*Dec.* § 16) is quite intelligible ; they are useful and tame.   But they go
further and deify wild beasts, lions, crocodiles, poisonous asps, and
besides these dogs, cats, wolves, the ibis and the hawk, and fishes

¹For, being compared as to want of sense, these are worse
than all others;
Neither, as seen beside *other* creatures, are they beautiful, 19
so that one should desire them,
But they have escaped both the praise of God and his
blessing.
For this cause were *these men* worthily punished through 16
creatures like *those which they worship,*

¹ The Greek text here is perhaps corrupt.

(whole or in part); see note in F. C. Conybeare, *Vit. Cont.* p. 261.
Juvenal (*Sat.* xv. 1 ff.) writes of the crocodile, ibis, monkey, cat, fish as
Egyptian deities; "in fact, while you may not kill a kid, you may eat
the flesh of man."
  as to want of sense] The Egyptians worship deities which have neither
intelligence nor beauty to recommend them.   *Want of sense* points to
the less intelligent members of the pantheon, the fish, the crocodile,
the serpent.
  19. *Neither...beautiful*] These unintelligent creatures cannot even
appeal to beauty to commend them as objects of worship.   The crocodile e.g. is a revolting monster, devoid of grace and comeliness.
  should desire them] Cp. *v.* 5.
  have escaped both the praise] But Gen. i. 21, 25, 30, 31 show that
originally the entire animal creation was "good."   Even the serpent
was not cursed till after the Fall (Gen. iii. 14).   Perhaps the serpent
(under which form the Egyptians worshipped Kneph) is the chief, or
sole object of the attack in these two *vv.*

Ch. XVI.

The Egyptian animal-worshippers were punished by an animal plague,
while on the other hand animals were used to benefit Israel.   Even
when the Israelites were plagued with fiery serpents, they merely tasted
suffering by way of teaching, while the Egyptians were severely chastised,
when beset with flies and locusts (1—14).   Similarly, fire and water,
heat and cold, fought against the Egyptians and for the Israelites.   The
elements, in so doing, not only carried out the will of God, but taught
the Israelites lessons concerning both God as the source of all blessing,
and the duty of thanksgiving (15—29).
  These form the first two of a series of five comparisons between the
fortunes of Israel and Egypt, which occupy the remaining chapters of
the book.

vv. **1—4.** THE EGYPTIANS WERE PUNISHED THROUGH THE ANIMALS
        THEY WORSHIPPED.
  1. *For this cause*] See xv. 18, 19.
  worthily punished] As in i. 16, men get what, by their own choice,

And tormented through a multitude of vermin.

2 Instead of which punishment, thou, bestowing benefits on
    thy people,
  Preparedst quails for food,
  Food of ¹rare taste, to *satisfy* the desire of *their* appetite;
3 To the end that ²thine enemies, desiring food,
  Might for the hideousness of the *creatures* sent among them
  Loathe even the necessary appetite;
  But these, *thy people*, having for a short space suffered want,
  Might even partake of *food of* ¹rare taste.

          ¹ Gr. *strange*.   ² Gr. *those*.

they show to belong to them. The writer reverts to the principle of
compensation laid down in xi. 16, and reaffirmed in xii. 23, 27, cp.
Philo, *Mos.* i. 17.

vermin] For the Greek word, cp. xi. 15, of the plagues of locusts,
frogs, flies, etc.

2. *Instead of which punishment*] As animals were used to plague
Egypt, so were they made the instruments of blessing to Israel, cp.
Ex. xvi. and Num. xi.

quails for food] Quails "migrate in vast flocks, crossing the Arab.
desert. They always fly with the wind. Their bodies are so heavy in
comparison with the power of their wings that many perish even in a
short passage across the sea, and those which arrive safe are excessively
fatigued....Quails, when migrating, begin to arrive at night (Ex. xvi. 13),
and are found in large numbers in the morning (Num. xi. 31, 32)....
The quail is brown, shaded and mottled with rufous and grey. Its
length is 7½ inches. Its flesh is succulent." G. E. Post (Art. *Quails* in
Hastings, *D. B.* iv. p. 179), cp. Philo, *Mos.* i. 37.

rare taste] i.e strange, unaccustomed, because the people had
latterly been living on a non-flesh diet.

desire of their *appetite*] God gave them the flesh they cried out for,
cp. Ps. lxxviii. 29. There is no thought of God pandering to their
appetite by giving any special delicacy, as A.V. "quails to stir up their
appetite": their appetite was for flesh, and God gave them flesh.

3. The reason why the Egyptians were punished with animal-plagues
was, the writer states, in order that they might be made to loathe the
sight of animal food.

the hideousness] C preserves the right reading (the rare word
εἰδέχθειαν), against BNA and Vulg.

the creatures *sent*] The frogs in the ovens and kneading-troughs,
Ex. viii. 3.

suffered want] The same argument as in xi. 8. The Israelites
are to suffer want, in order that their appetite may be stimulated and
then proportionately satisfied. There is no scriptural authority for this
fancy.

For it was needful that upon those should come inexorable 4
want in their tyrannous dealing,
But that to these it should only be shewed how their
enemies were tormented.
For even when terrible raging of wild beasts came upon ¹thy 5
people,
And they were perishing by the bites of crooked serpents,
Thy wrath continued not to the uttermost;
But for admonition were they troubled for a short space,   6
Having a token of salvation,
To put them in remembrance of the commandment of thy
law :

¹ Gr. *them.*

4. *upon those*] i.e. the Egyptians.
to these...be shewed] i.e. the Israelites, see xi. 9.

vv. 5—14. THE PLAGUE OF SERPENTS CONTRASTED WITH
THE PLAGUES OF EGYPT.

In these *vv.* the plague of the fiery serpents is interpreted as being
sent for a brief space only, in order to warn and remind Israel, and to
teach two lessons to the Egyptians (*a*) that God was the Saviour of
Israel, and (*b*) that the reason why the Egyptians had suffered in a
worse degree, was because they deserved it.
5. *terrible raging*] See Num. xxi. 6.
crooked serpents] Cp. Is. xxvii. 1.
Thy wrath continued not to the uttermost] This *l.* explains the impf.
were perishing. Cp. xviii. 20, and xix. 1. See Ps. ciii. 9 LXX.
6. *But for admonition*] The writer does not consider that the
chosen people were chastised in punishment. They touched only the
fringe of suffering (πρὸς ὀλίγον), and that, with a view to future instruction. For the writer's love of didactic interpretation, cp. xi. 16, xvi. 28;
see also Judith viii. 27; 1 Cor. x. 11.
Having a token] The Israelites were not given over to the plague of
serpents : the writer implies that the Brazen Serpent was all the while
in reserve, ready to check the invasion as soon as its lesson had been
taught. אA read *counsellor* (σύμβουλον), which recalls Philo, *Agr.*
§§ 21, 22, where the serpent which deceived Eve is called her
"counsellor."
To put them in remembrance] Cp. Num. xxi. 8, 9, and *v.* 11. For
Philo's distinction between *memory* and *recollection*, see *Cong.* § 8.
The symbol was to remind the people of God and His law : the writer
refuses to allow any virtue to the Serpent : God saved the people by
reminding them of Himself.
Deane quotes the Jerusalem Targum on Num. xxi., in which the

7 For he that turned toward it was not saved because of that
   which was beheld,
   But because of thee, the Saviour of all.

8 Yea, and in this didst thou persuade our enemies,
   That thou art he that delivereth out of every evil.

9 For them verily the bites of locusts and flies did slay,
   And there was not found a healing for their life,
   Because they were worthy to be punished by such *as these*;

10 But thy sons not the very teeth of venomous dragons overcame,
   For thy mercy passed by where they were, and healed them.

11 For they were ¹bitten, to put them in remembrance of thine
   oracles,
   And were quickly saved, lest, falling into deep forgetfulness,

---

¹ Gr. *pricked.*

---

divine voice says " Now shall the serpent who has not complained of
his food, come and bite the people who complain. So the Word of the
Lord sent fiery serpents among the people."

7. *because of...beheld*] Cp. *v.* 12. It was a reminder, but not a
sacrament, much less an agent in its own right. Cp. St John iii. 14.

Saviour of all] Cp. 1 Tim. iv. 10. For God as Saviour, cp. Is.
xlv. 21, and Philo, *Quod D.* § 34, *Sacr.* § 19.

8. *persuade our enemies*] The writer argues, as in xi. 13, on the
assumption that the news was carried to Egypt of the fortunes of Israel
in the wilderness, cp. Ex. xxxii. 12; Num. xiv. 13; Dt. ix. 28.

9. *locusts and flies*] See Ex. x. 4—15, viii. 16—24, and ch. xi. 15,
cp. Philo, *Mos.* i. 21, 23, 26, for the intensified power of annoyance
supposed to be specially conferred upon these creatures. Cp. Jos. *Ant.*
ii. 14, 3; Philo, *Mos.* i. 19.

did slay] Cp. Ex. x. 17.

they were worthy] Cp. Rev. xvi. 6; Philo, *Conf. l.* § 36.

10. *venomous*] The same word is used of the serpents in Philo,
Mos. i. 35, *Agr.* 22. Many of the Egyptians were killed by creatures
usually harmless; the Israelites did not succumb to those habitually
deadly. Num. xxi. 6 however says "much people of Israel died."

11. *they were bitten*] Cp. *v.* 6. Memory is not uncommonly symbolized as using whips or stings, cp. Philo, *Somn.* ii. 44. Here her
stings are not metaphorical, but the actual bites of serpents.

thine oracles] The law of Sinai is called the "living oracles" in Acts
vii. 38.

quickly saved] The suffering was only allowed to last long enough
to awaken them.

They should become ¹unable to be ²roused by thy benefi-
cence:
For of a truth it was neither herb nor mollifying plaister 12
that cured them,
But thy word, O Lord, which healeth all things;
For thou hast authority over life and death,   13
And thou leadest down to the gates of Hades, and leadest
up again.
But though a man *may* slay by his ³wickedness,   14

¹ Some authorities read *bereft of help from thy beneficence.*   ² Gr.
distracted, or, *drawn away.*   The meaning is somewhat obscure.
³ Or, *malice*

unable to be roused] Vulg. *ne...non possent tuo uti adiutorio.* The
sense is plain, but it is not clear whether marg. *bereft of help from*
(ἀπερίστατοι) should be read for ἀπερίσπαστοι. Marg., with support of
Vulg., seems more probable.   For a short space they must be deprived
of the sense of God's beneficence, that they might learn to value it more.
   12. *neither herb nor...plaister*] Cp. *v.* 7, and *v.* 26.   Philo, *Sacr.*
§ 19 writes "Men do not trust God the Saviour completely, but have
recourse to the aids which nature offers, doctors, herbs, medical com-
pounds, rigid diet."   But for a different view, cp. Ecclus. xxxviii. 1—8.
For *plaister* (μάλαγμα), cp. Is. i. 6 LXX.
   thy word,...which healeth] Cp. Ps. cvii. 20 "He sent His word and
healed them."   There must be no confusion between the Logos of this
passage and the Alexandrine Logos (of Philo).   The thought is borrowed from the Psalms, and the Logos here means what is meant by
Logos there (see Introd. § 10)   It is unlikely that it contains even all
that is to be found in the Logos of ch. xviii. 15.   God's "word" heals,
because it is God's *expressed will* that there should be healing; see note
in this series on Ps. cvii. 20.   God's "word" is merely a periphrasis
for God in active relation with men.
   13. *vv.* 13, 14 bear traces of connection with Dt. xxxii. 39; 1 Sam.
ii. 6, while *v.* 15 is also connected with the former.
   authority over life and death] i.e. the right and the power to give life
and to take it away.
   the gates of Hades] A variation of the preceding line, except that the
order is significantly reversed, "Thou takest away life and givest it
back."   "*To* the gates" is not πρὸς (towards), but εἰς (into): God kills,
but He can restore.   Gates involve keys, which God, as overlord, possesses, cp. Rev. i. 18; and the holding of the keys implies the right to
unlock.   For "gates oₗ Hades," cp. Job xxxviii. 17; Is. xxxviii. 10;
3 Macc. v. 51; also Ps. ix. 13, cvii. 18, "gates of death."   For God's
power to bring down and lift up, see Job v. 18.
   14. This *v.* does not belong to the argument, being only an appendix
to the declaration of God's power in *v.* 13.   God is a life-giving power;

Yet the spirit that is gone forth he turneth not again,
Neither giveth release to the soul that *Hades* hath received.

15 But thy hand it is not possible to escape;
16 For ungodly men, ¹refusing to know thee, were scourged in
the strength of thine arm,
Pursued with strange rains and hails and showers inexorable,
And utterly consumed with fire;

¹ Or, *denying that they knew thee*

He can kill and restore: but man only controls life so far as to be able
to take it away. The point of the contrast is that, while man in his
weakness can only deal out death, God can both inflict death and
restore to life.

spirit] For the probable identity of *soul* and *spirit*, see ch. xv. 11.

he turneth not again] The vb. ἀναστρέφειν is transitive as in ii. 5, but
Vulg. *non reuertetur*. For man's powerlessness in face of death, see
Job vii. 9, 10.

giveth release] Vulg. *reuocabit*; ἀναλύειν, transitive here, is probably
intr. in ii. 1.

that Hades *hath received*] Cp. Tob. iii. 6. King Hades receives
the dead soul. Man cannot rescue his brother, Ps. xlix. 7, 8, but God
can redeem from the "hand" of Hades, id. 15 LXX.

vv. 15—29. How heat and cold, ignoring the laws that
usually govern them, punished Egypt and served Israel.

15. *thy hand*] i.e. thy power. This *v.*, following on *v.* 13, has
close affinity with Dt. xxxii. 39 (cp. Is. xliii. 13). Is. x. 14 LXX.
has "There is none that shall escape Me (My hand)," while in Tob.
xiii. 2, a passage occurs which is either the model or the reproduction
of this. Cp. Amos ix. 1—4.

16. *ungodly men*] Allusively as usual for the Egyptians.

refusing to know] Cp. xii. 27; Ex. v. 2 supports the marginal
alternative.

Pursued with strange rains] Cp. Ex. ix. 18—22, and 24 "hail, such
as there was none like it in...Egypt since it became a nation." Philo
(*Mos.* i. 20) writes that rain is not needed in Egypt, where the Nile
takes its place: consequently on this occasion the air was torn with
revolution (ἐνεωτέρισεν), rain, hail, winds, clouds, thunders, lightning
all falling upon the land with unparalleled severity. For the absence of
rain in Egypt above Memphis, see Dt. xi. 10, 11; Zech. xiv. 18;
Philo, *Mos.* iii. 24.

inexorable] Also in *v.* 4. C reads as adv. *inexorably*, perhaps to
contrast with *without toil* in *v.* 20.

utterly consumed] Ex. ix. 19, 25.

For, what was most marvellous *of all*,   17
In the water which quencheth all things the fire wrought
    yet more mightily;
For the world fighteth for the righteous.
For at one time the flame lost its fierceness,   18
That it might not burn up the creatures sent against the
    ungodly,
But that *these* themselves as they looked might ¹see that
    they were chased through the judgement of God :
And at another time even in the midst of water it burneth 19
    above the power of fire,
That it may destroy the ²fruits of an unrighteous land.
Instead whereof thou gavest thy people angels' food to eat, 20

¹ Some authorities read *know*.   ² Gr. *products*.

17. See Ex. ix. 24. In the plague of lightning and hail, it seemed
as though the hostile elements of fire and water were reconciled for the
punishment of the Egyptians. It is futile to speculate as to whether
the "fire that ran along the ground" signifies ordinary lightning, or
St Elmo's fire or some unusual manifestation. Philo (*Mos.* i. 20) writes
"Compact thunderbolts, of appalling appearance, ran hither and thither
through the hail : and for all the variance between their natures, the
rain did not quench the fire, nor the fire melt the hail."
    the world]   i.e. the whole order of nature.
    fighteth for the righteous] Cp. ch. v. 17, 20 and esp. *v.* 24, and xix.
6. There is a strong resemblance between this line and "All things
work together for good to them that love God" (Rom. viii. 28).
St Paul may be recalling this passage when he writes " We know that
all things, etc." With ὑπέρμαχος (fighteth for), cp. Clem. Rom. xlv.
    18.   The writer, with no Scriptural warrant, affirms that the frogs and
flies lasted until the plague of hail and fire, but see Ex. viii. 13, 31 :
the special reference shows that the writer is not thinking of the frogs
in the ovens, Ex. viii. 3.
    19.   If in one case the fire lost its power, in another its power was
intensified. There was no hail in the land of Goshen. Cp. Ex. ix. 25, 31.
For γενήματα, *fruits* (mg. *products*), cp. St Luke xii. 18, Ps. cv. 32, 33.
    20.   From this *v.* to the end, the miraculous properties of the manna
(metaphorically termed snow and ice, *v.* 22) are recorded and interpreted.
    gavest...to eat] Cp. Dt. viii. 3, 16. The word (ψωμίζω) is appropriate
to the daily dole, Ex. xvi. 4, 13, 14.
    angels' food] Cp. Ps. lxxviii. 25 LXX., and Vulg. The expression
is probably a correct rendering of the Hebr. *bread of the mighty*. Cp.
the Targum "The sons of men ate bread which came down from the
dwelling of the angels."

And bread ready *for their use* didst thou provide for them
from heaven without *their* toil,
Bread having the virtue of every pleasant savour,
And agreeing to every taste ;

21 For ¹thy ²nature manifested thy sweetness toward *thy*
children ;
While *that bread*, ministering to the desire of the eater,
Tempered itself according to every man's choice.

22 But snow and ice endured fire, and melted not,

¹ Some authorities read *the substance* thereof.
² Or, *creation* Gr. *substance.*

didst thou provide] In Ex. xvi. 4 God "rains" bread from heaven :
Philo (*Mos.* i. 36) calls the manna "an abnormal rain," cp. xix. 21,
and Ps. lxxviii. 24.

without their *toil*] Philo (*Mos.* ii. 36) calls the manna a food "that
cost no labour," as contrasted with corn which must be cultivated.

having the virtue of every pleasant savour] Vulg. *omne delectamentum
in se habentem.* It is said to have tasted like honey cakes (Ex. xvi.
31), or fresh oil (Num. xi. 8). But the Jewish legend to which apparently the writer alludes, told that it tasted for each man like grapes
or figs or whatever he desired. Aug. (*Retr.* ii. 20) refers to the tradition as being supported by this passage only.

21. *thy nature*] The Gk. word (ὑπόστασις) has caused great difficulty. Two translations are possible (1) God's *Nature* (as in text), not
absolutely, but as communicating itself to and through the manna; (2) as
marg., "*the substance* thereof," i.e. the manna. The adversative particles
μέν and δὲ show that *v.* 21 a is contrasted with *v.* 21 b, c; on the Divine
side the manna was a revelation of God, while on the human side it
ministered to the pleasure of man. The Gk. word perhaps combines
the two meanings, and is the manifestation, itself real and substantial,
which witnessed to the unseen God. For God's *sweetness*, cp. Ps.
cxix. 103, and Ps. xxxiv. 8 "Taste and see."

ministering] Cp. *v.* 24. A new subject is required to agree with
the partic. which is masc. Text rightly supplies "that bread."

the eater] For the Gk. (τοῦ προσφερομένου), cp. Judith xii. 9, Philo,
Mos. i. 37, and Diog. Laert. i. 2. 68.

Tempered itself] Vulg. *conuertebatur.* The Greek word means lit.
"to pour from one vessel to another and so mix." The idea is probably the same as that in *v.* 25 "converting itself," and in xix. 18
"changing their order." The four elements were supposed to possess
the power of mutual interchange, see Philo, *Mos.* ii. 36, and Pythagoras
in Diog. Laert. ii. 8. 25, and the author seems to be endeavouring to
supply the Jewish legend with a basis of philosophy.

22. *snow and ice*] The writer's way of describing the manna, cp.
xix. 21 "the ice-like grains, apt to melt." Philo (*Mos.* i. 36) speaks

That *men* might know that fire was destroying the fruits of
the enemies,
Burning in the hail and flashing in the rains;
And ¹that this *element* again, in order that righteous men 23
may be nourished,
Hath even forgotten its own power.
For the creation, ministering to thee its maker,   24
Straineth its force against the unrighteous, for punishment,
And slackeneth it in behalf of them that trust in thee, for
beneficence.
Therefore at that time also, converting itself into all forms, 25

¹ Some authorities omit *that*.

of it "as a dew which had been snowed from heaven, which was neither
water, nor hail, nor snow, nor ice," i.e. a thing like all of these, but
not actually any one of them. Cp. Ex. xvi. 14 "like hoar frost," and
Num. xi. 7 LXX. "the appearance of ice." By identifying manna with
that which it resembled, the writer is able to suggest a striking miracle.

melted not] By fire he means not sunlight (but see *v.* 27), but
hearth-fire. The miracle is that this ice-like substance could be placed
in ovens (Num. xi. 8) and yet not melt. Thus the writer shows that
fire, which abated or intensified its power to the detriment of the
Egyptians, mysteriously accommodated itself to serve the Israelites.

That men *might know*] Cp. *v.* 26. The writer must needs see a
moral purpose in every circumstance.

Burning in the hail] Almost a reproduction of the LXX. rendering
of Ex. ix. 24, which represents Hebr. "fire taking hold of itself, i.e.
flashing incessantly, in the hail," cp. *v.* 17.

23.   This verse is still governed by *know that* in last *v.*; so Vulg.
"*This* element" refers to the *fire* of last *v.*

Hath even forgotten] This verse rests on a seemingly fanciful identification of the manna with that which it resembled: any truth that there is
in the writer's argument lies in the fact that manna exposed to the sun
melted (*v.* 27), while it was capable of being baked with artificial heat.

24.   A general principle is enunciated. For the Jew there was no
conception of a purely physical, non-moral world. The universe was in
league with the righteous, and the enemy of the wicked; cp. Judg. v. 20.

ministering to thee its maker] Cp. Philo, *Mos.* i. 36 "Not one part of
the universe but the entire world is subjected to God, and the parts of it
are prepared for His service in any direction He may desire, like slaves
waiting on their master."

Straineth...slackeneth] A metaphor from stringed musical instruments,
cp. Philo, *Mut.* § 13 ; Diog. La. vii. 101. For nature, as opposing the
wicked, cp. ch. v. 17, 20; and ministering to the righteous, ch. xvi. 17,
xix. 6.

25.   *Therefore*] In accordance with the principle laid down in *v.* 24.

It ministered to thine all-nourishing bounty,
According to the desire of them that ¹made supplication ;
26 That thy sons, whom thou lovedst, O Lord, might learn
That it is not the ²growth of *the earth's* fruits that nourisheth
a man,
But that thy word preserveth them that trust thee.
27 For that which was not marred by fire,
When it was simply warmed by a faint sunbeam melted
away;

¹ Or, *had need*   ² Gr. *generations.*

converting itself]   The creation, composed of the four elements, was
held to be unchangeable in mass, but (as between the several elements)
there was unlimited mutual interchange, cp. Philo, *Mos.* ii. 36.   Hence
the creation, while in one aspect constant, was able to undergo perpetual
variation, as God willed.   *At that time also,* a particular illustration of
the general law.   The Greek verb is employed in an unusual sense,
cp. iv. 12.

ministered...bounty]   Cp. Philo, *Ebr.* § 28 "Ye are instruments to
minister to God, in His deathless acts of grace."

all-nourishing bounty]   Vulg. *omnium nutrici gratiae tuae,* i.e. the
manna.   For God as the All-sustainer, cp. Ps. civ. 27, cxxxvi. 25, cxlv. 16.

26.   *thy sons, whom thou lovedst*]   Cp. Hos. xi. 1.

might learn]   Nature was allowed to respond to the prayers of God's
people, in order that they might learn to look behind nature to the
Divine will that expresses itself through nature.

That it is not the growth...but]   These two lines are an expansion of
Dt. viii. 3, where LXX. renders the less definite Heb. by "every *word*
that proceedeth out of the mouth of God"; cp. St Matt. iv. 4 and
St John vi. 32.   For the Hebrew idiom, cp. "mercy *and not* sacrifice,"
i.e. rather than.

The teaching of this *v.* is the same as in *vv.* 7, 12 : God uses means,
but the means only obtain their vitalizing power from God, and more
important than their physical efficaciousness is the constraint they lay
upon men to remember God.

But that thy word]   Lit., *utterance* (ῥῆμα, not λόγος).   Philo identifies
the manna with the divine Logos (*Q. R.* § 15) "He has been trained to
fix his gaze on the manna, the divine Lógos, the heavenly incorruptible
food of the soul that loves vision."   So also in *Fuga* § 25 "Seeking
what it is that feeds the soul, they discovered it to be the utterance
(ῥῆμα) of God and the divine Logos, from which all disciplines and
wisdoms flow unfailingly," cp. id. *All.* iii. 56.

27.   From nature as a witness to the creative power of God, the
writer passes to symbolism.   The fact that manna, which did not melt
in the oven (*vv.* 22, 23, cp. Num. xi. 8), yielded readily to the sun's rays,
is interpreted as a symbol of the duty of early prayer.

That it might be known that *we* must rise before the sun to 28
give thee thanks,
And must plead with thee at the dawning of the light:
For the hope of the unthankful shall melt as the winter's 29
hoar frost,

warmed by a faint sunbeam] Cp. Ex. xvi. 21, Philo, *Mos.* ii. 35
"Whatever remained over after the people had gathered the manna
melted under the sun's rays and perished." A curious tradition is given
in the *Jerus. Targum* (Etheridge, p. 500), "At the fourth hour when the
sun waxed hot upon it, it liquefied and made streams of water, which
flowed away into the great sea; and wild animals that were clean and
cattle came to drink of it, and the Israelites hunted and ate them."

28. As the manna melted in the sun, so prayer that is later than the
dawn loses spiritual substantialness. "A beautiful precept, founded on
precarious exegesis" (Farrar). H. Vaughan has the same thought:—

"Yet never sleep the sun up; prayer should
Dawn with the day: these are set awful hours
'Twixt Heav'n and us; the manna was not good
After sun-rising; far day sullies flowers:
Rise to prevent the sun; sleep doth sins glut,
And Heaven's gate opens when the world's is shut."

rise before the sun] Cp. vi. 14, 15; Ps. cxix. 147; Is. xxvi. 9;
Ecclus. xxxix. 5.

to give thee thanks] Cp. Epict. ii. 23 "Be not thankless, my friend,
or forgetful; but for sight and hearing, yea for life itself and all that
contributes to it, for fruits, for wine, for oil, thank God." See
Ps. lxiii. 6 "in the night watches" (ἐν τῷ ὄρθρῳ μου); Ps. cxix. 62;
Acts xvi. 25.

at the dawning of the light] Rightly, although the Greek could mean
towards the East. But this rendering would have no connection with
the symbolism of the manna. Some, who have ignored this, have seen
in the verse an indication that the writer belonged to the Egyptian sect
of the Therapeutae who, like the Persians, prayed towards the rising
sun, or to the Jewish sect of the Essenes, of whom Josephus writes
"Before sun-rising they speak not a word about profane matters, but
put up certain prayers which they have received from their forefathers,
as if they made a supplication for its rising" (*B. J.* ii. 8. 5). The
Jewish daily prayer known as the *shema* beginning "Hear, O Israel;
the Lord our God is one Lord" (Dt. vi. 4) was to be recited (according to the Mishna) when the sun's rays lighted up the tops of the
mountains. Cp. Ps. v. 3, lvii. 8; Ecclus. xxxii. 14.

29. *the hope of the unthankful*] The writer is inconsequent. The
argument should be that the melting manna signifies the need of early
rising for purposes of thanksgiving, and that the man who fails to rise
early to give thanks finds his hope evaporate. But it is quite gratuitous

And shall flow away as water that hath no use.

17 For great are thy judgements, and hard to [1]interpret;
Therefore souls undisciplined went astray.

2 For when lawless men had supposed that they held a holy
nation in their power,
They *themselves*, prisoners of darkness, and bound in the
fetters of a long night,
Close kept beneath their roofs,
Lay exiled from the eternal providence.

[1] Or, *set forth*

to say as he does that it is impossible to thank God except at dawn, and
that therefore the late riser is thankless.
water that hath no use] Cp. Ps. lviii. 7.

CH. XVII.—CH. XVIII. 4.

A THIRD COMPARISON BETWEEN THE FORTUNES OF ISRAEL
AND EGYPT, IN RESPECT OF LIGHT AND DARKNESS.

1. *For*] The writer's use of *for* is loose : eight out of the first twelve
vv. of this ch. begin with " for." If there is any definite reference back
to ch. xvi., it is to the general teaching of the whole ch. as summed up
in xvi. 15.

thy judgements] i.e. principles of justice, and not judicial acts, cp.
Ps. xcii. 5—7; Rom. xi. 33.

Therefore] The principles of divine justice only commend and reveal
themselves to those who are taught by Wisdom. There is no understanding of God and His ways where there is no spiritual conformity.
With *undisciplined*, cp. ch. vi. 9—11 in a religious-moral connection.

went astray] The Egyptians lost their way in their effort to perse-
cute the chosen people.

2. *For*] Explains *v.* 1.

lawless men] i.e. the Egyptians.

prisoners of darkness] Cp. Ex. x. 21—23, and 2 Pet. ii. 4, and *v.* 17
"one chain of darkness."

a long night] Philo (*Mos.* i. 21) writes "It counted as nothing else
than one long night, equal to three days and three nights in length."

Close kept] They were prisoners even in their own houses : Ex. x. 23
"No man rose from his bed for three days" (LXX.).

lay] See prec. note. *Exiled*, i.e. like runaway slaves, cowering in
secret places. The Egyptians were punished with darkness, which
typified their self-banishment from God's presence and care.

the eternal providence] Cp. vi. 7, xiv. 3; 4 Macc. xiii. 19. *Provi-*
dence, cp. xiv. 3, is used almost as in English. The writer treats the
darkness as if it actually had the effect of screening them from God.

For while they thought that they were unseen in *their* secret 3
sins,
They were ¹sundered one from another by a dark curtain of
forgetfulness,
Stricken with terrible awe, and sore troubled by spectral
forms.
For neither did ²the dark recesses that held them guard 4
them from fears,
But sounds ³rushing down rang around them,
And phantoms appeared, cheerless with unsmiling faces.
And no force of fire prevailed to give *them* light,   5

¹ Gr. *scattered by*.   ² Gr. *the recess*.
³ Some authorities read *troubling them sore*.

3. *unseen in* their *secret sins*] Cp. xiv. 23. Another instance of the
principle set forth in xi. 16. They loved darkness (for their misdeeds),
therefore it came upon them, cp. Job xxiv. 14. For secret sins, cp.
Ps. xix. 12.

sundered one from another] So אB Vulg. lit. *scattered* (ἐσκορπίσθη-
σαν). This is not likely to be a corruption of the reading of AC ἐσκο-
τίσθησαν (*were darkened*), and is to be preferred. The word is very
commonly used of the demoralisation of an army, which becomes scattered like the sheep of a flock. The Egyptians were disorganised, each
man hiding in his own house. The *dark curtain of forgetfulness* must
mean God's forgetfulness. They had exiled themselves from His providence: they desired to be unseen, now they had their wish. Ps. x. 11;
Is. xxix. 15. If God "knows" the way of the righteous, He may be
said to ignore that of the wicked.

spectral forms] The writer, seeking to enhance the terror of the
darkness, either supplements the Scriptural account from Midrashic
sources by telling of ghostly apparitions, or is merely recording the
hallucinations of the terrified Egyptians. But whether he thinks of
demons or of the products of the Egyptian imagination is immaterial.

4. Their own houses were no security against the universal terror.
Sounds and shapes pursued them everywhere.

sounds rushing down] This, the bolder and more difficult reading
of B marg. AC, is far superior to that of B (see marg.), cp. *descendens*,
Vulg. Sounds like the roar of rushing cataracts are intended.

cheerless with unsmiling faces] Euphemistically for "grim with
savage faces."

5. *no...fire prevailed*] Philo (*Mos.* i. 21) writes that the darkness
was so oppressive that it put fires out, or else engulfed them so completely as to neutralize all their light. Jos. (*Antiq.* ii. 14. 5) writes
"By this darkness, the sight of the Egyptians was obstructed, and their
breathing was hindered by the thickness of the air, so that they died
miserably." Cp. Ex. x. 21 a "darkness which may be felt."

Neither were the brightest flames of the stars strong enough
to illumine that gloomy night:
6 But only there appeared to them the glimmering of a fire
self-kindled, full of fear;
And in terror they deemed the things which they saw
To be worse than that sight, on which they could not gaze.
7 ¹And they lay *helpless*, made the sport of magic art,

¹ Some authorities read *And the mockeries of magic art lay low, and
shameful* was *the rebuke &c.*

Neither...the stars] "There was darkness in Egypt three days. No
man saw his brother and none arose from his place for three days. But
among all the sons of Israel was there light that the wicked among
them who died might be buried, and that the righteous might be
occupied with the precepts of the law in their dwellings." Etheridge,
Targums p. 471.

6.   *the glimmering of a fire*] There is no indication what the writer
refers to, unless with poetic licence (cp. xvi. 18) he anticipates the
appearance of the pillar of fire, which darkened upon the Egyptians,
but shone upon Israel. The effect of this phenomenon, which gave
light in such a way that it could be seen by the Egyptians without their
deriving any benefit from it, was to increase their terror. The fire was
self-kindled, in the sense that its light seemed to originate from no
material or obvious source.

in terror they deemed]   R.V. in this and following *l.* departs from the
sense suggested by the rhythm of the sentence, and adopted by the
Vulg. "Terrified by that appearance which they saw not, they reckoned
the things they saw to be worse [than they really were]." What is the
sight (ὄψις, Vulg. *facies*) which they saw not? That of the angel of the
cloud, cp. Ex. xiv. 19, and the *Jerus. Targum*, Etheridge, p. 489 "The
Lord looked forth with anger from the column of fire, to hurl upon [the
Egyptians] flakes of fire and hail, and from the column of cloud."

It is possible to take the *v.* quite differently, and to view the
glimmering of fire as some supernatural globe of flame, which flashed
in every direction without disclosing the source of the flashes. This
flashing fire lit up common objects of vision, which, when thus illuminated, seemed so terrible that the Egyptians were more afraid of them
than of the fire itself, which, all unseen, produced these lurid effects.
τὰ βλεπόμενα ("the things seen") might be the phantoms of *vv.* 3, 4.

7.   *they lay* helpless] So AC, while אB Vulg. have sing. κατέκειτο.
Text renders ἐμπαίγματα as referring to the Egyptians, *the playthings*
of the sorcerers, or else, made a laughing-stock by reason of the failure
of the magicians. But marg. gives a better sense, and a more pointed
reference to the failure of the magicians, who after some success in Ex.
vii. 11, 22, viii. 7, not only failed in viii. 18, but were miserably dis-
comfited in ix. 11: cp. 2 Tim. iii. 8.

And a shameful rebuke of their vaunts of understanding :
For they that promised to drive away terrors and troublings 8
from a sick soul,
These were *themselves* sick with a ludicrous fearfulness :
For even if·no troublous thing affrighted them, 9
Yet, scared with the creepings of vermin and hissings of
serpents, 10 they perished ¹for very trembling,
Refusing even to look on the air, which could on no side
be escaped.
²For wickedness, condemned by a witness within, is a 11
coward thing,

¹ Or, *trembling, and refusing to*   ² This is the probable sense :
the Greek text is perhaps slightly corrupt.

a shameful rebuke] Rather, as marg. The magicians were as powerless as the people against the darkness and the phantoms.
8. *they that promised*] Cp. Gen. xli. 8.
a sick soul] Cp. 1 Tim. vi. 4 (marg.).
9. *even if no troublous thing*] Complete demoralisation had
wrought in the magicians all the effects of panic. During the protracted
darkness, when there was nothing really terrible near them save the
darkness, memory of past plagues caused their imagination to people it
with terrors.
scared] Perf. part. not present, lit. *having been scared*, i.e. when the
plagues of the insects and the frogs were in process. These plagues did
not continue till the plague of darkness, but during that plague there
was a recrudescence of the horror they had engendered. For *vermin*
as applied to the lice, flies, and locusts, see xvi. 1, while the reference
of *serpents* (ἑρπετά) to the frogs may be argued from xi. 15. The Greek
word for *scare* properly means "shooing" a bird. ἐκσεσοβημένοι does
not mean "scared *out of their retreats*" (Grimm), for *ex hypothesi* no
man moved from his place: ἐκ has an intensifying force.
10. *perished...trembling*] Cp. St Luke xxi. 26.
Refusing even to look on the air] They kept their eyes shut for fear of
unknown horrors. *The air in no wise to be escaped* is generally viewed
as being the "all-surrounding" air, in which case the epithet is very
forceless. May it not rather be the air *that needed no escaping from*?
It was innocent of all harm, and contained no terrors. The only terrors
were to be found in the minds of the Egyptians. This rendering would
fall in completely with that suggested for *v.* 9. All other terrors, beside
the objective darkness, were hallucinatory.
11. This and the next two *vv.* are concerned with the effects of inner
distraction, as the result either of fear or of sin. There are two readings
of 11a. (1) That of B, followed by Vulg. "For wickedness is a thing
innately craven, and bears witness to its own condemnation." (2) That

And, being pressed hard by conscience, always ¹forecasteth
the worst *lot* :

12 For fear is nothing else but a surrender of the succours
which reason offereth ;

13 And from within *the heart* the expectation *of them* being less

¹ Most authorities read *hath added.*

based on אA, *ἰδίῳ* (אc.a) *πονηρία μάρτυρι*, "Wickedness, condemned by
its own witness, is a craven thing." R.V. adopts (2), and this rendering
represents a smoother Greek text than (1), the general sense being
"Conscience doth make cowards of us all," and especially of the
guilty man.

being pressed hard by conscience] For the Gk. vb. of strong emotional
pressure, cp. St Luke xii. 50; 2 Cor. v. 14. *Conscience* is thought of as
a second self, standing over against the sinful self. This is the earliest
occurrence in the Greek O.T. (in its technical sense) of a word appearing
repeatedly in N.T. The word is borrowed from the Stoics, and in their
system stands for a man's judgment upon his act when done, rather
than for the principle which dictates his action. It means *con-scientia*,
his "co-knowledge" existing, as the result of reflection, by the side of
his knowledge of the act as done. The idea (*σύνοιδα*) is found in
Euripides (*Or.* 396), and the word in Menander "To all of us conscience
is a God," and in Epictetus, who compares it to a *paedagogus*. The
idea of conscience is, as might be expected, very prominent in Philo.
Cicero, *pro Milone* 23 has "Magna uis est conscientiae in utramque
partem."

forecasteth the worst] אABC have *προσείληφε* "hath added." A
very much better sense (as in text) is obtained by reading *προείληφε*
"hath forecast" with א (second hand) and Vulg. *praesumit.*

12. Fear is nothing but the surrender of reason. A guilty conscience
disturbs the inner equilibrium, and forbids a man to look out upon the
world with calm eyes. So close is the connection between the moral
and the rational faculty, that "the succours that reason offers" vanish
when conscience becomes apprehensive. Vulg. renders thus. It is not
surprising that א reads *προσδοκία* from following line. There was no
commoner definition of fear than that it was *προσδοκία*, "anticipation,"
cp. Zeno (Diog. La. ii. 7, 112); Epict. ii. 18. 30, iv. 1. 84. Philo
(*Mut.* § 30) writes "The presence of evil is pain, and the expectation of
it is fear"; and again in *All.* iii. 37.

For the mind as a source of strength, cp. Antisthenes (Diog. La.
i. 6. 13) "The mind is an impregnable fortress: walls should be provided in one's own unassailable thoughts." Farrar quotes Verg. *Georg.*
ii. 490 "Felix qui potuit rerum cognoscere causas Quique metus omnes
et inexorabile fatum Subiecit pedibus."

13. This *v.*, together with *v.* 12, explains *v.* 11 b. Fear surrenders
the supports of reason : when hope, whose ally is reason, is thus
inwardly disabled, its reckoning is all awry : it magnifies its ignorance

Maketh of greater account the ignorance of the cause that
bringeth the torment.

But they, all through the night which was powerless indeed, 14
And which came upon them out of the recesses of power-
less Hades,
All sleeping the same sleep,
Now were haunted by monstrous apparitions, 15
And now were paralysed by their soul's surrendering;
For fear sudden and unlooked for ¹came upon them.

¹ Some authorities read *was poured upon them.*

of the source of the evil that besets it; and the ignorance which is
always bewildering, now becomes overpowering.

In the Egyptian darkness, the source and extent and nature of the
attendant horrors were all unknown: and if "panic is caused by the
surrender of the imagination to ignorance," darkness only made the
panic worse by intensifying the ignorance. Cp. "omne ignotum pro
magnifico."

The gist of the three *vv.* is this. Moral guilt, when brought home
to a man, paralyses his reasoning faculties. Thus fear is engendered:
for, where reason has not full play, ignorance with its power of exaggeration takes the place of which reason is dispossessed; and the guilty
man is proclaimed a coward.

14. *the night which was powerless indeed*] Vulg. *impotentem.*
The darkness was really powerless to hurt, and came from the realm of
powerless Hades. Hades is the place of death and impotence:
accordingly the night in which it shrouded the earth partook of the
same character.

recesses of powerless Hades] Vulg. *ab inferis et ab altissimis inferis*
seems to point to βαθυτάτου (deepest), which by confusion with ἀδύνα-
του in the *l.* above has become ἀδυνάτου. If text is followed *powerless
Hades* either is the place whose inhabitants have no strength, or must
be interpreted by reference to ch. i. 14 "Hades, who has no dominion
on earth." The horror of the great darkness might well be described
as hell-born, cp. Job x. 21; Ps. lxxxviii. 6.

sleeping the same sleep] The only way of describing the enforced rest
of the Egyptians during a period of seventy-two hours is to be found in
terms of night, i.e. sleep. The subject of the sentence, *they*, is now not
the magicians, but the Egyptians generally. The *sleep* was shared by
all: the experience of each was different.

15. *apparitions*] *vv.* 3, 4.

their soul's surrendering] An evident reference to *v.* 12. Vulg. takes
it absolutely of the *treachery* of the soul, *animae traductione.*

fear sudden and unlooked for] The *fear* is expanded in the next four
verses. For the sense, cp. xviii. 17; St Luke xxi. 34.

16 So then *every man*, whosoever it might be, sinking down [1]in
   his place,
   Was kept in ward shut up in that prison which was barred
   not with iron :
17 For whether he were a husbandman, or a shepherd,
   Or a labourer whose toils were in the wilderness,
   He was overtaken, and endured that inevitable necessity,
   For with one chain of darkness were they all bound.
18 Whether there were a whistling wind,
   Or a melodious noise of birds among the spreading
   branches,
   Or a measured·fall of water running violently,

[1] Gr. *there*.

16. *So then*] Explains "fear" in prec. *l.* When the darkness suddenly swept over the land, every man fell where he was, and stirred not
in his terror.
   in his place] lit. *there*, i.e. on the spot ; where he was.
   kept in ward] Same word as in *v.* 2.
   prison...barred not] With the ironical contradiction between subst.
and adj., cp. Is. xxix. 9 "drunken, but not with wine." If Lovelace,
singing of liberty, can say

           "Stone walls do not a prison make,
               Nor ironbars a cage,"

the author, writing of fear, can conversely tell of a prison made without
fetters.
   17. *He was overtaken*] Same word as in Gal. vi. 1.
   that inevitable necessity] Necessity is used not technically of fate, but
of a compelling circumstance, as in 2 Cor. vi. 4 (plur.). *necessity* is
explained in the next *l.*
   chain of darkness] Cp. *vv.* 2, 16; 3 Macc. vi. 19; 2 Pet. ii. 4.
All slept the same sleep, *v.* 14; all were bound with the same chain.
   18. *a whistling wind*] All the sounds of nature continued as usual,
but for the Egyptians every sound was discordant and terrifying.
Farmer, shepherd, field-labourer heard the sounds to which they were
accustomed, but with changed ears. The sighing of the wind became
like the hissing (συριγμός, cp. *v.* 9) of some reptile. Cp. Lev. xxvi. 36.
   noise of birds] The birds' song became a shriek. It shows how
subjective the writer thinks the darkness to be, if the birds continued
their song. But, of course, he is here giving free play to imagination.
The Scriptural account undoubtedly suggests objective darkness.
   fall of water] The trickling stream became a "sound rushing down,"
v. 4.

Or a harsh crashing of rocks hurled down,   19
Or the swift course of animals bounding along unseen,
Or the voice of wild beasts harshly roaring,
Or an echo rebounding from ¹the hollows of the mountains,
All these things paralysed them with terror.
For the whole world *beside* was enlightened with clear light, 20
And was occupied with unhindered works;
While over them alone was spread a heavy night,   21
An image of the darkness that should afterward receive
    them;
But yet heavier than darkness were they unto themselves.
But for thy holy ones there was great light;   18
And *the Egyptians*, hearing their voice but seeing not their
    form,

¹ Or, *a hollow*

19. *crashing of rocks*] Falling stones would give forth a sound as of thunder.
swift course of animals] A sudden movement among the flocks or herds, not seen but only heard, was enough to suggest the horrors of xi. 17—19.
an echo rebounding] Skilful use is made of the terrifying effect of echo in an enclosed space in the dark in Judg. vii. 20.
paralysed them] Vulg. has *deficientes faciebant*, cp. Ps. liii. 5.
20. *the whole world*] The darkness was local, not universal. The writer oscillates between the two conceptions of a darkness moral rather than physical, and one local rather than universal. It is undoubtedly difficult to explain the distinction between the circumstances of the Egyptians and the Israelites in Ex. x. 23 on physical grounds, although some would see in the darkness the effect of the electrical wind called *hamsin*.
was occupied] συνέχεσθαι as in Acts xviii. 5.
21. *the darkness that should...receive them*] i.e. in Hades. For the phrase, cp. vii. 30. For darkness in connection with death, see *v.* 14; Ps. lxxxviii. 12. Hades *receives* souls, ch. xvi. 14 c, Tobit xiv. 10.
heavier than darkness were they unto themselves] Cp. Dt. xxviii. 28, 29. Contrast with Philo, *Mut.* § 1 "The things of the mind are their own light," and cp. id. *Somn.* i. 19. Conscience made the Egyptians to be their own darkness.
xviii. **1.** *thy holy ones*] The Israelites, cp. x. 15.
great light] Ex. x. 23; cp. Is. ix. 1. See Philo, *Somn.* i. 19, and the *Targum* quoted in note on xvii. 5.
hearing...seeing not] Cp. Dt. iv. 12; St John v. 37. The Egyptians could not see how the Israelites were faring, but they could hear their voices, and inferred that the same calamities had befallen them. That

Counted it a happy thing that they too had suffered,
2 Yet for that they do not hurt them *now*, though wronged *by them* before, they are thankful;
And because they had been at variance *with them*, they made supplication *to them*.
3 Whereas thou didst provide *for thy people* a burning pillar of fire,
To be a guide for *their* unknown journey,
And withal a [1]kindly sun for *their* [2]proud exile.

[1] Gr. *unharmful*.   [2] Or, *aspiring*

they, no less than themselves, had been plagued, gave the Egyptians their one ray of comfort: "they counted it a happy thing that they too had suffered." This must be the interpretation, if ὅτι μὲν οὖν (אBC) is accepted as in text; but in that case οὖν is untranslated. It is better with A and Vulg. to read οὐ "The Egyptians congratulated the Israelites that they had not suffered." The contrast suggested by μὲν, δὲ is more forcible if A is followed; in this case, it is assumed that the Egyptians knew that the experiences of the Israelites were different from their own.

2. *they are thankful*] Historic present, graphically used. While the Egyptians were glad the Israelites had suffered, they were thankful they did not make reprisals for the ill-treatment of many years. Under the cover of the protracted night, they might have inflicted serious damage.

because...at variance] This is the best rendering of a doubtful phrase. Others are (1) Vulg. *ut esset differentia, donum petebant*. (2) Besought them (the Israelites) the favour of departing, cp. Ex. xi. 8, xii. 33. Ex. x. 24 is in favour of (2), but this rendering strains the Greek.

3. *Whereas*] i.e. instead of all the terrors of darkness. Vulg. *propter quod* wrongly.

burning pillar of fire] Ex. xiii. 21, xiv. 24; Ps. lxxviii. 14, cv. 39.

To be a guide] "The sons of Israel were protected by seven clouds of glory on their four sides: one above them, that neither hail nor rain might fall upon them, nor that they should be burned by the heat of the sun: one beneath them, that they might not be hurt by thorns, serpents or scorpions: and one went before them, to make the valleys even, and the mountains low, and to prepare them a place of habitation." *Jerus. Targum*, Etheridge, p. 478. Cp. x. 17, and Philo, *Mos.* i. 29 "A cloud, in form like a massive pillar, went before the people, with a light as of the sun by day and as of fire by night, that they might not wander, but might follow an unerring *guide*."

a kindly sun] It gave light, but no smiting heat, cp. Is. xlix. 10. See quot. from Targum in prec. *v.* Vulg. takes ἀβλαβῆ as governing the genitive, quite legitimately, *sine laesura boni hospitii*, "a sun that harmed them not in their honourable banishment." Banishment, usually a disgrace, was in this case an honour.

For well did [1]the Egyptians deserve to be deprived of light 4
and imprisoned by darkness,
They who had kept in close ward thy sons,
Through whom the incorruptible light of the law was to be
given to [2]the race of men.

After they had taken counsel to slay the babes of the holy 5
ones,
And when a single child had been cast forth and saved [3]to
convict *them of their sin,*

[1] Gr. *they.*   [2] Or, *future time* Gr. *the age.*
[3] Or, *to be* to them *a rebuke*

proud] (marg. *aspiring*) perhaps in relation to God, cp. Ex. xiv. 4, 17.
4. *well did...deserve*] Another illustration of the principle in ch.
xi. 16. Those who had sinned by shutting Israel in the darkness of
captivity, must be punished with physical darkness.
thy sons] See Ex. iv. 22.
incorruptible light of the law] The law in its widest sense (cp. Is. i.
10, ii. 3), "including all Divine revelation as the guide of life." See
Introd. to Ps. cxix. in this series. *incorruptible* in the moral sense,
without reference to duration, cp. Ps. xix. 7. For *light* in a similar
sense, cp. Is. ii. 5; Ps. xxxvi. 9; Eph. v. 8.
given to the race of men] Or, the *world.* For αἰών (the world
regarded in its time-aspect), see notes on iv. 2, xiv. 6. This line
recognises the world-wide mission of the Jewish nation, cp. Ps. xxii. 27;
Is. ix. 2, xlii. 6, xlix. 6; Micah iv.; Tobit xiii. 11. Philo (*Abr.* § 19)
writes that he considers the Jewish people to hold the office of priest
and prophet on behalf of all the human race. Cp. id. *Mos.* i. 27.

CH. XVIII. 5—25. A FOURTH CONTRAST IS PRESENTED BETWEEN
THE FORTUNES OF ISRAEL AND EGYPT, THE SUBJECT BEING
DEATH. THE DISCIPLINE PROVED EFFECTIVE FOR ISRAEL
IMMEDIATELY THE SCOURGE BEGAN TO OPERATE.

vv. 5—19. THE DEATH OF THE FIRSTBORN.

Gutberlet notes a threefold contrast. (1) The Egyptians who had
killed the male children of Israel, lost their firstborn. (2) Those who
had used the Nile to drown Israel's children, were themselves drowned
in the Red Sea. (3) The rescue of one child resulted in widespread
destruction for his would-be murderers.

5. *to slay the babes*] Ex. i. 16. *the holy ones,* see *v.* 1.
a single child...cast forth] Moses, see Ex. ii. 3. Cp. perhaps ch.
xi. 14. Josephus (*Ant.* ii. 9) writes that at the time of the birth of
Moses a wise man had warned Pharaoh that a child would be born in

Thou tookest away from them their multitude of children,
And destroyedst all *their host* together in a mighty flood.
6 Of that night were our fathers made aware beforehand,
That, having sure knowledge, they might be cheered by the
oaths which they had trusted :

Israel who, "if he were reared, would bring the Egyptian dominion
low, and would raise the Israelites." With the policy adopted by
Pharaoh, cp. that of Herod, St Matt. ii. 1 ff. Farrar is wrong in
suggesting that the writer holds that Moses (*one child*) was the only
child exposed : he was the only one exposed and saved.

to convict] See marg. *to be* to them *a rebuke*. Grimm prefers to
connect these words with *saved* rather than with the succeeding clause.

tookest away...children] Ex. xii. 29, 30. The rescue of one led to
the death of many. The Gk. vb. governs a double acc.

together] Vulg. renders *pariter*, but the word means *wholesale*.
Destroyedst has for its object the acc. which stands at the beginning of
the *v.* in the Gk., *them having taken counsel to kill.* The point of this
line is that as the Israelite children perished by water, so the Egyptians
died by the same element, Ex. i. 22. Another example of the principle
in xi. 16. For the punishments by water, cp. ch. x. 19, xi. 6.

Charles (*Jubilees*, p. lxxiv) has an interesting note on this *v.*, and
would correct thus, "In retribution for even a single child that was
exposed Thou didst take away ten thousand Egyptians." He holds
that either Jub. xlviii. 14 was before the writer, or the two passages
are based on a common tradition, that for every Hebrew child exposed, a thousand Egyptians were doomed to be drowned.

6. *that night*] *That* points dramatically to a night so well known as
to need no further definition. Cp. Ex. xii. 42 LXX.

our fathers] The writer in a way most unusual for him identifies himself
with the Israelites. He has been strictly impersonal hitherto except in
xv. 1—4. The fathers are either the Israelite heads of families, who
were forewarned of the death of the firstborn, Ex. vi. 6, xi. 4 ff., xii. 21 ff.
or (perhaps better) the patriarchs, to whom the deliverance from bondage
was revealed, see Gen. xv. 14, xxvi. 3, cp. Ps. cv. 8 ff. "The fathers"
is a term not applied in this book to the people generally, but to the
patriarchs three times, ix. 1, xii. 21, xviii. 22. Further, *v.* 7 would be
an otiose repetition of this *v.*, if *people* in that *v.* were identical with
fathers in this. For the interest of the patriarchs in the future, cp.
Heb. xi. 39, 40; 1 Pet. i. 11.

having sure knowledge] Cp. Acts ii. 30, where David, in the spirit
of prophecy, "knows."

might be cheered] Vulg. *animaequiores essent.* The prospect
afforded the patriarchs a kind of Pisgah-gladness, cp. St John viii. 56.

oaths...trusted] They could rejoice, because God's oath was as sure
a ground of satisfaction as the accomplished fact.

So by thy people was expected salvation of the righteous 7
and destruction of the enemies;
For as thou didst take vengeance on the adversaries, 8
¹By the same means, calling us unto thyself, thou didst
glorify us.
For holy children ²of good men offered sacrifice in secret, 9
And with one consent they took upon themselves the
covenant of the ³divine law,
That ⁴they would partake alike in the same good things and
the same perils;

¹ Gr. *By this.* ² Or, *of blessing* Gr. *of good* men, or, *of good*
things. ³ Gr. *law of divineness.* ⁴ Some authorities read *the saints
would partake...perils; already leading the fathers' songs of praise.*

7. *of the righteous*] i.e. the Israelites, cp. "the holy," *vv.* 1, 5.
There is a resemblance in *vv.* 7, 8 to a passage in Philo's *Uit. Contempl.*
The dance of the Therapeutae, he says, recalls the wonders of the Red
Sea. "By the command of God the sea became author of safety for
these, and of extermination for those."

8. *calling us unto thyself*] God's intervention on behalf of Israel in
the death of the firstborn was an appeal to the people.

9. *holy children*] Note contrast with *children* in last *l.* of *v.* 10.
For the epithet, conventionally used, cp. *vv.* 1, 5, x. 17, and x. 20, xii. 9
(the righteous).

of good men] The adj. ἀγαθῶν may be masc. or neut.; see the marginal
alternatives. But the writer's habit of seeing good only in his own
people raises the presumption that it refers to the patriarchs of *v.* 6,
whose praises (see end of *v.*) the Israelites sang that night. If the adj.
were neuter, *children of blessing,* παῖδες would be very unusual for
τέκνα or υἱοί.

offered sacrifice in secret] The Passover is called a sacrifice in Ex.
xii. 27; Dt. xvi. 5; cp. Num. ix. 7. There was no secrecy in the
keeping of the first Passover, so far as is recorded. The feast was
celebrated in the privacy of the Israelite dwellings, Ex. xii. 46; but
that was in order that the family-idea might be emphasized.

with one consent...divine law] This clause governs the acc. and inf.
in the next *l.*: it seems better therefore to render "with one consent
they covenanted *by* the divine law" (i.e. by the common Passover feast
at which they were pledging their mutual fellowship). *the divine law*
(lit. as in marg.) is a strange phrase. Vulg. has *iustitiae legem,* standing
for ὁσιότητος, which is the reading of ℵ. The precise significance of
θειότης in this place is not clear: θειότητος νόμου may be merely a
periphrasis for τὸν θεῖον νόμον, i.e. the Divine institution of the Passover.

That they would partake] It is better to read "that the saints
would," as in marg. The rhythm of the Greek suggests this arrangement. With "the saints," cp. *vv.* 1, 20. It has been suggested that

The fathers already leading the sacred songs of praise.
10 But there sounded back in discord the cry of the enemies,
¹And a piteous voice of lamentation for children was borne abroad.
11 And servant along with master punished with a like just doom,
And commoner suffering the same as king,
12 Yea, all *the people* together, under one form of death,

---

¹ Some authorities read *And was piteously borne abroad in lamentation for children.*

---

fellowship in prosperity and adversity was symbolised by the common partaking of the dish of bruised fruits (ḥarôṣeth) and of the bitter herbs. But the former does not seem to have been part of the primitive ritual.

The fathers already leading] If this is correct, a contrast is suggested between the exultation of the Israelite fathers, and the woe of the Egyptian, see *v.* 10. But there is no reason given why the sons should sacrifice, and the fathers lead the singing: consequently, the reading of א (second hand) A, followed by Vulg., may be right, see marg. "already leading the fathers' songs of praise." *The fathers* are the patriarchs, see *v.* 6: their *songs of praise* are either the songs they sang, or songs in honour of them. The writer is attributing to those who partook of the first Passover a practice which grew up in later days, but of which there is no trace in Egypt, see 2 Chr. xxx. 21, xxxv. 15. The Hallel, Ps. cxiii.—cxviii., came to be sung at stated times in the course of the Passover celebration, but obviously such a Ps. as cxiv. could not have been sung by the Israelites in Egypt: accordingly the writer pictures them as singing either their fathers' songs, or songs in their honour. Farrar wrongly suggests that *already* is intended to show that the later practice of singing the Hallel had its counterpart in the first celebration: ἤδη defines a point of time in the celebration itself, "while now the singing was in progress."

10. *there sounded back*] Rather, *sounded in answer.* *in discord*, not "clashing with Isr. songs" (Farrar) but "discordant in itself." The Israelites were all harmonious (*v.* 9 a, b), while the Egyptians were distracted. Every house had its own sorrow.

a piteous voice] Text reads with אA φωνή, followed by Vulg. Cp. Ex. xi. 6, xii. 30. *children* is contrasted with *children* in *v.* 9. Marg. follows B, which omits φωνή.

11. See Ex. xii. 29. Etheridge (*Targums* p. 477) gives from the Jerus. Targum "From the firstborn son of Pharaoh...to the sons of the kings who were captives in the dungeon as hostages; and who, for having rejoiced at the servitude of Israel, were punished as the Egyptians." LXX. however makes the captives feminine, and Philo (*Mos.* i. 24) writes "down to the most obscure grinding-maid."

12. *all* the people *together*] Same Greek word as *v.* 5 d. Philo

Had *with them* corpses without number;
For the living were not sufficient even to bury them,
Since at a single [1]stroke their [2]nobler offspring was consumed.
For while they were disbelieving all things by reason of the 13
 enchantments,
Upon the destruction of the firstborn they confessed the
 people to be God's son.
For while peaceful silence enwrapped all things, 14
And night in her own swiftness was in mid course,
Thine all-powerful word leaped from heaven out of [3]*the* 15
 royal [4]throne,
A stern warrior, into the midst of the [5]doomed land,

[1] Gr. *turn of the scale.* [2] Or, *more cherished* [3] Or, thy
   [4] Gr. *thrones.*   [5] Or, *destroying*

(*Mos.* i. 24) writes "By reason of the universality of the blow all joined in one common lamentation (ὁμοθυμαδόν, as here), and one outcry rang throughout the land from end to end."

the living were not sufficient] A rhetorical amplification of Num. xxxiii. 4. Philo (*Mos.* i. 17) says that this was the case when the Egyptians died of the thirst which resulted from the smiting of the Nile.

their nobler offspring] "the chief of all their strength," Ps. cv. 36. Cp. Ex. iv. 23.

13. This *v.* is loosely joined to the preceding by *For.* The greatness of the calamity was evidenced by its effect.

disbelieving all things] Pharaoh was influenced by the fact that the magicians could do as Moses had done, Ex. vii. 13, 22. But the writer ignores the change in Ex. viii. 19, which affected the magicians themselves.

enchantments] Cp. Ex. vii. 11, viii. 7. For the word, see ch. xii. 4.

God's son] See Ex. iv. 22. Cp. ch. ii. 13, 18. It is not recorded in the Bible that the Egyptians made this acknowledgment, but the writer amplifies Ex. xii. 31.

14. *while peaceful silence*] The coming of the mysterious visitation is described in terms which recall Job iv. 13—15.

in mid course] Ex. xi. 4, xii. 29.

15. *all-powerful word*] For the epithet, see vii. 23, where it is applied to Wisdom. For the meaning of Logos here, see Introd. § 10.

royal throne] lit. *thrones*, plural of dignity. Cp. ix. 4; Dan. vii. 9.

A stern warrior] For the epithet, cp. v. 20, xii. 9. The Logos is called *a warrior* as bearing a sword and being sent on an errand of destruction. The passage is drawn from 1 Chr. xxi. 15 ff. Cp. Hab. iii. 5 "Before Him shall go the word" LXX.

doomed] For the adj. in a pass. sense, see 1 Kings xx. 42.

16 Bearing as a sharp sword thine unfeigned commandment;
And standing it filled all things with death;
And while it touched the heaven it trode upon the earth.
17 Then forthwith apparitions in dreams terribly troubled them,
And fears came upon them unlooked for:
18 And *each*, one thrown here half dead, another there,
Made manifest wherefore he was dying:
19 For the dreams, perturbing them, did foreshew this,
That they might not perish without knowing why they were
afflicted.

20 But it ¹befell the righteous also to make trial of death,

¹ Gr. *touched.*

16. *Bearing as a sharp sword*] The sword of 1 Chr. xxi. 16 is
introduced here, and allegorized as God's commandment.
unfeigned] Almost has the meaning of "inflexible." Cp. v. 18
and Heb. iv. 12.
filled...with death] Contrast with Ps. cxlv. 16 LXX.
while it touched] A variant of "between the earth and the heaven,"
1 Chr. xxi. 16. Grimm quotes a similar description of Discord from
Hom. *Il.* iv. 443, and the version of it applied to Fame in Verg. *Aen.*
iv. 177. The same description is found of the pillar of cloud in Philo,
Dec. § 11; of man in id. *Opif.* § 51; and of a tower of evil in id. *Conf. l.*
§ 23.
17. *apparitions...and fears*] Cp. Job iv. 13—15; Prov. i. 26, 27.
terribly] So B; and the rhythm makes it probable that this is right:
but אA followed by Vulg. have *terrible* agreeing with "dreams."
fears] Almost abstract for concrete. Cp. R. Browning, *Prospice*,
"The Arch Fear in a visible form."
18. *one thrown here*] The firstborn in each house.
Made manifest wherefore] The next *v.* makes it plain that this *l.*
means more than that the dying detailed the mental suffering they were
experiencing. They declared that the cause of their death was the
wrath of Jehovah.
19. *did foreshew*] Vulg. *praemonebant*, i.e. shewed before they died.
without knowing] Not only were the survivors to recognise God's
hand (*v.* 13), but the victims also. The incident of the dreams of the
firstborn before death is due to the writer's desire that the guilty should
drink the full measure of the cup of judgment, and that none should be
excused from acknowledging the hand of God. A painless and unexpected death in sleep would seem to him a futile judgment.

vv. 20—25. DEATH VISITED ISRAEL, BUT ONLY TO BE
DISMISSED AT ONCE.

20. *it befell the righteous*] i.e. the Israelites, as in xviii. 1, 9. The
incident referred to is the plague which followed the murmuring against

And a multitude were stricken in the wilderness:
Howbeit the wrath endured not for long.
For a blameless man hasted to be their champion: 21
Bringing the weapon of his own ministry,
Even prayer and the propitiation of incense,
He withstood the indignation, and set an end to the
   calamity,
Shewing that he was thy servant.

Moses and Aaron after the destruction of Korah, Dathan, and Abiram,
Num xvi. 44—50. Philo comments on the passage in *Somn.* ii. 35,
and *Q. R. D. H.* 42.
   trial of death] Cp. *v.* 25. The word implies that the mere taste of
death was enough to teach the Israelites the desired lesson.
   were stricken] lit. *a breaking* (θραῦσις, the word used of the plague
in LXX. Vulg. *commotio*) *took place*, Num. xvi. 47, and Ps. cvi. 30.
   the wrath endured not] Cp. xvi. 5. *The wrath* means "a distinct
manifestation of the righteous judgment of God," see Bp. Westcott's
note on St John iii. 36. The plague was indeed stayed, though not till
14,700 had died.
   21. *a blameless man*] Aaron. He is styled *blameless* for official
reasons, because he represented God, cp. *a blameless seed*, x. 15. Possibly, there is also a personal reference, as Aaron was unassociated with
the sin of Korah and the subsequent murmuring.
   hasted] He ran, Num. xvi. 47. Philo (*Q. R. D. H.* 42) allegorizes
Aaron into the divine Logos, who stands in human hearts between
holy and unholy thoughts.
   their champion] Cp. Job xlii. 8; Ps. xcix. 6, where intercession is
spoken of. See note on the intercession and mediation of Moses and
Aaron, Ps. xcix. 6, in this series.
   the weapon of his own ministry] Not "shield," as Vulg., but,
rather, an aggressive weapon, *a sword.* Cp. 2 Cor. x. 4, and Eph.
vi. 17, 18 "the sword of the spirit,...praying always." "Ministry"
(λειτουργία) is the regular word (cp. Ex. xxxviii. 21) for the ministrations
of the priesthood.
   prayer] Cp *Jerus. Targum* (Num. xvi.), Etheridge, p. 397 "Aaron
stood in the midst,...with the censer, and interceded in prayer."
   propitiation of incense] See Num. xvi. 47, and cp. 4 Macc. vii. 11.
For the supposed atoning efficacy of incense, cp. the ritual of the Day
of Atonement, when the high priest, on entering into the holy place,
was safeguarded by incense, Lev. xvi. 12, 13.
   withstood the indignation] Aaron's act was counted as one of heroism.
He withstood God, but with God's own weapons. Wrapped in the
smoke of the incense, he was secure in the midst of the divine wrath.
For *the indignation*, cp. Rom. xii. 19.
   thy servant] Aaron proved to the destroyer that he was God's

WISDOM   12

22 And he overcame the ¹anger,
Not by strength of body, not by efficacy of weapons;
But ²by word did he subdue ³the minister of punishment,
By bringing to remembrance oaths and covenants made
with the fathers.
23 For when the dead were already fallen in heaps one upon
another,

¹ The word rendered *anger* differs only by the transposition of two
letters from the reading of the Greek text, which here yields no sense.
² Or, *to a word did he subject*　　³ Gr. *him who was punishing.*

servant (θεράπων, a term of greater distinction than δοῦλος) by the
sacred ornaments of his office, see *v.* 24. For *servant*, applied here
only to Aaron, see x. 16. Cp. 1 Kings xviii. 36.

22. *overcame the anger*] MSS. ὄχλον, Vulg. *turbas*, which seems to
give no sense. R.V. accordingly adopts the conj. emend. χόλον, *anger*,
which only involves a transposition of letters. But in 4 Macc. vii. 11 it
is said that Aaron conquered the angel of the Burning, while in the *l.*
below this occurs "the minister of punishment." Why should not τὸν
ὀχλοῦντα ("the harasser") be read? This word is used of the visita-
tions of evil spirits in Tob. vi. 7; cp. St Luke vi. 18. To "conquer
the harassing angel" is at least as likely to be right as to "conquer the
wrath," anger having already been referred to in *v.* 21. If it were not
that the writer says practically nothing about angels, we might emend
ὄχλον to ἄγγελον ("angel") from 4 Macc. vii. 11.

by word did he subdue] His weapons were spiritual and not physical,
cp. 2 Cor. x. 4. Philo curiously calls Phinehas Logos (*Conf. l.* § 13)
and calls his javelin Logos (*Mut.* § 18), but he does not apply the same
term to Aaron. *Word* here means the word of intercession, see next *l.*
and cp. Ex. xxxii. 13.

the minister of punishment] Called an angel in 4 Macc. vii. 11. See
note on *word*, *v.* 15. There is some indeterminateness of language
in the passage: Aaron withstood "the anger"; he subdued "the
punisher." It is plain that the distinction between God and His Logos
(see *v.* 25) is quite undefined.

bringing to remembrance] For a typical example of intercession, see
Ex. xxxii. 13. The writer probably has in mind something more than
the promises of God to the fathers (Ex. ii. 24; Lev. xxvi. 42): he
thinks of Aaron pleading the merits of the fathers. Developed Rabbinic
teaching exalted the merits of the fathers till they served for the whole
nation. Cp. Sanday and Headlam, *Romans* pp. 330—332, from which
the following quotation is taken "As the vine supports itself on a
trunk which is dry, so Israel supports itself on the merit of the fathers,
although they already sleep" (Wajjikra rabba c. 36).

23. *fallen in heaps*] For σωρηδόν, cp. Philo, *Mos.* i. 17.

Standing between he stopped the *advancing* wrath,
And [1]cut off the way to the living.
For upon *his* long *high-priestly* robe was the whole world,   24
And the glories of the fathers *were* upon the graving of the
    four rows of [2]precious stones,
And thy majesty *was* upon the diadem of his head.

    [1] Gr. *cleft asunder*.   [2] Gr. *stone*.

between]   i.e. between living and dead, Num. xvi. 48.
he stopped]   The Greek word is used in Thuc. iv. 12 for *beating back*
an assailant.
    cut off]   He cut through it (lit.) as if he were breaking down a
bridge, so that the destroyer could not pass.
    24.   his *long* high-priestly *robe*]   Aaron's robes were symbolic, and
caused his intervention to be successful.   The *robe down to the feet* is
the long high-priestly robe of blue, fringed with bells and pomegranates.
Strictly speaking this robe was not quite ποδήρης (i.e. reaching to the
feet), but this is the word applied to it in Ex. xxviii. 4 LXX.   The real
full-length robe was the white linen garment of 1 Sam. ii. 28, there
called *ephod*.   But the *ephod* proper was the very elaborate "waistcoat"
described in Ex. xxviii. 6—12.
    was the whole world]   The blue "robe of the *ephod*" allegorically
represented the world for Jewish commentators.   Cp. Philo, *Mos.* ii.
12 "The whole robe is blue, a picture of the air.   The air is naturally
deep-coloured, and is a full-length robe, for it flows from sky to earth.
The flowers on it symbolize earth, and the pomegranates water, and
the bells the fusion of earth and water....Of the three elements, earth,
air, water, of which and in which created beings have their being, the
long robe with its hangings is a true representation.   As the robe is one,
so the three elements are of one category: and as the flowers and the
pomegranates hang from the robe, so in some fashion earth and water
hang from the air, for it is their vehicle."   See also id. *Somn.* i. 37, and
Jos. *Ant.* iii. 7. 7.   The interpretation is fantastic, and is not the same
in Philo as in Josephus, but the connection between their accounts is
sufficient to show that they represent traditional views as to the meaning
of the priestly garments.
    the glories of the fathers]   For the high priest's breast-plate, see Ex.
xxviii. 15—21, 29; Jos. *Ant.* iii. 7. 5.   Philo (*Mos.* ii. 12) sees in it a
symbol of the zodiac, which represents four seasons of three months;
Josephus, on the earth, which is in the middle of the world.   On each
of the twelve stones was inscribed the name of one of the tribes of
Israel: the names of the patriarchs are *the glories of the fathers*, whose
doings were symbolised by their names.
    the diadem of his head]   Over the linen mitre of the high priest was
fastened a golden crown (πέταλον, a plate), on which was inscribed
(Ex. xxviii. 36) "Holiness to the Lord."   Philo (*Mos.* ii. 11 and 14)
writes that the four letters of the sacred tetragrammaton were upon it,

25 To these the destroyer gave place, and these ¹*the people*
feared ;
For it was enough only to make trial of the wrath.

19 But upon the ungodly there came unto the-end indignation
without mercy;

¹ Some authorities read *he feared*.

in order that the name of "Him who is" might symbolize that the
world can only be sustained by the will of God. God's Name is *His
majesty*.

25. *To these the destroyer gave place*] The high priest thus stood
before the destroying angel clothed in the symbols of the world, the
fathers, and God, and prevailed over the destroyer. Just as the
Psalmists plead with God "for His Name's sake," that God would
remember what He is and has proclaimed Himself to be, so here Aaron
confronts God's agent with God's creation, God's chosen, and God
Himself (in symbol), cp. Ex. xxviii. 38.

the destroyer] Probably the Logos, as in *v*. 15; cp. Num. xvi. 45
"that *I* may destroy them"; see Ex. xii. 23; Heb. xi. 28.

these the people *feared*] R.V. rightly follows BC, lit. *they feared*.
א (second hand) A and Vulg. have *he* feared, whence it is argued that
the destroying angel must have been an evil spirit or he would not have
feared. But the order of the words is against this rendering: it would
be "He feared and yielded." The double *these* is unnecessarily rhetorical
with only one subject for the two verbs. For *feared*, cp. Ex. xiv. 31:
the sight of the sacred symbols upon the high priest brought the people
back to their allegiance. Just as (ch. xvi.) they were stung in order
that they might be reminded of God's oracles, and God's mercy passed
by and healed them, so here they were punished for forgetfulness of
God, and saved when Aaron had recalled to them God's name and His
oath.

enough only to make trial] Cp. *v*. 20, and xvi. 5, 6. The people
feared, because no more was needed to awaken them than the mere
preliminary taste of death. They were not like the Egyptians, who
needed to drain the cup to its dregs.

CH. XIX. 1—21.

THE FIFTH COMPARISON BETWEEN THE ISRAELITES AND EGYP-
TIANS, THE SUBJECT BEING THE PASSAGE OF THE RED SEA.

vv. 1—5. THE INCAPACITY OF THE EGYPTIANS TO LEARN
THE LESSON OF EXPERIENCE.

1. *the ungodly*] i.e. the Egyptians: contrast with xviii. 20 "the
righteous."

came unto the end] Cp. xvi. 5, and 1 Thess. ii. 16.

For their future also *God* foreknew,
How that, having changed their minds to *let thy people* go,   2
And having speeded them eagerly on their way,
They would repent themselves and pursue them.
For while they were yet in the midst of their mourning,   3
And making lamentation at the graves of the dead,
They drew upon themselves another counsel of folly,
And pursued as fugitives those whom with intreaties they
    had cast out.
For ¹the doom which they deserved was drawing them ²unto 4
    this end,

¹ Or, *their desert by necessity was*
² Some authorities read *unto this at last.*

without mercy] In ch. xii. 10 God's knowledge of the wickedness of
the heathen is given as a reason for His mercy: here, His foreknowledge of their future wilfulness is the reason why He put no check upon
His wrath.

God *foreknew*] The subj. is supplied out of *indignation* in prec. *l.*
  2. *changed their minds to* let thy people *go*] So אB, reading ἐπι-
στρέψαντες. ἐπιτρέψαντες, *having allowed*, the reading of א (second
hand) A and Vulg. *cum permisissent*, is probably a correction. Grimm
would render "having thought anxiously over their departure."
  speeded them eagerly] Cp. Acts xx. 38, xxi. 5. An allusion to the
presents which the Egyptians showered upon the Israelites at their
departure, Ex. xii. 35, 36. Philo (*Mos.* i. 24) pictures the distracted
Egyptians urging their rulers to hasten their going out.
  repent themselves] Ex. xiv. 5.
  3. *in the midst of*] lit. *having it in their hands*, cp. ix. 16. For
the embalming process, see Herodotus ii. 85—88. Cp. ch. xviii. 12.
  drew upon themselves] same Gk. verb as in i. 12.
  counsel of folly] For *counsel* in a (bad) moral sense, cp. i. 3 note on
thoughts. The natural revulsion of feeling, consequent upon the
realisation of the departure of Israel, was perhaps supplemented by the
hope that ignorance of the country would lead them into a trap.
Josephus (*Ant.* ii. 15. 3) explains the tactics of the Egyptians in their
pursuit, and the *Jerus. Targum* (Etheridge, p. 485) has: "Pharaoh
said, The people of the house of Israel are bewildered in the land: the
idol Zephon hath shut them in close upon the desert."
  pursued] Ex. xiv. 8.
  they had cast out] Same word, implying haste, as in Ex. xii. 39
LXX. *with intreaties*, cp. Ex. xii. 33.
  4. *the doom which they deserved*] "Necessity" here is not a fate
predetermined, and laid upon men by an arbitrary exterior power, but
the inevitable sequence of cause and effect, cp. *v.* 13. Such necessity
can only be "deserved," for by its law no man reaps or can reap other

And it made them forget the things that had befallen them,
That they might fill up the punishment which was yet
wanting to their torments,
5 And that thy people might ¹journey on by a marvellous road,
But they *themselves* might find a strange death.

6 For the whole creation, *each part* in its several kind, was
fashioned again anew,

¹ Some authorities read *make trial of*.

harvest than he has sown. For the law of affinity, cp. i. 16, vi. 16, xi.
16. The marginal rendering has little probability.

made them forget] What they were was the cause of their forgetfulness: the justice that sinners cannot escape from (ch. xiv. 31) blinded
them to consequences as it had deadened their memory. *The things
that had befallen them* are the plagues generally, and the death of the
firstborn in particular. It was not vengeance that prompted the pursuit,
says the writer; it was greed (see Ex. xiv. 5 end). Egypt could not
afford to lose the forced labour of a nation of serfs.

That they might fill up] Cp. Phil. ii. 30; Col. i. 24. Deane quotes
excellently 2 Macc. vi. 14 "when they have attained unto the full
measure of their sins." Farrar writes "The problems of predestination
and freewill presented themselves to the Jews more often in a national
than an individual aspect; and when the ruin of another nation tended
to the advantage of Israel, the sense of national, and much more of
individual, pity was modified, if not obliterated, by patriotic gratitude.
The Jew had so intense a conviction that his own people were the firstborn of Jehovah, that he could hardly keep steadily in view the impartial
love of God."

5. *a marvellous road*] Cp. xviii. 3, lit. *wayfaring*: same Greek
word as in St John iv. 6. If the journeying of the Israelites was unpre-
cedented, so was the death that awaited the Egyptians.

vv. 6—12. AN IMAGINATIVE ACCOUNT OF THE EXODUS.

6. *For*] Introduces the section which is an expansion of *v.* 5.

was fashioned again anew] Vulg. *refigurabatur.* The writer explains the miracle of the passage of the Red Sea by the philosophical
doctrine of the mutual interchange of the elements. As in xvi. 21, 25,
nothing new came into being when a miracle occurred: there was only
a transmutation of elements, in some ways comparable to that which is
now suggested by physicists between radium and helium. Epict. (iii.
24) writes "This cosmos is one city, and its constituent substance is
one, and there must needs be a certain periodicity and surrender of one
thing to another, some things being dissolved and others combining,
some things standing still and others moving"; and again (fr. viii.)
"This variability is partaken of by both men and animals; and not

Ministering to *thy* several commandments,
That thy ¹servants might be guarded free from hurt.
Then was beheld the cloud that shadowed the camp,   7
And dry land rising up out of what before was water,
Out of the Red sea an unhindered highway,
And a grassy plain out of the violent surge ;
²By which they passed over with all their hosts,   8
These that were covered with thy hand,
Having beheld strange marvels.
For like horses they roamed at large,   9

---

¹ Or, *children*   ² Or, *Through*

---

only they but the gods and the four elements are turned *up and down*
in their transmutations, so that earth becomes water, and water air,
and air *again* turns into aether : and the same process of transmutation
takes place in the reverse way (ἄνωθεν κάτω)." *The whole creation* (for
the phrase, cp. Rom. viii. 22) is involved in one miracle, because the
writer regards the quantity of matter as constant. Any partial disturb-
ance is followed by a corresponding reaction throughout the whole
mass.

again anew] For the pleonastic phrase, cp. Gal. iv. 9. ἄνωθεν also
contains the philosophic sense of "from top to bottom": but "from
above," in the theological sense of St John iii. 31, is plainly not the
sense here.

thy *several commandments*] So text with BC, reading ἰδίαις, i.e. the
law laid upon each part of the creation. But אA foll. by Vulg. have
σαῖς ("thy"), which might have been replaced by ἰδίαις through a confusion with ἰδίῳ in the *l.* above. This makes a simpler sense "ministering to thy comm.," cp. xvi. 24; xviii. 16.

free from hurt] Same Greek word (in pass. sense) as in xviii. 3
(active).

7. *that shadowed*] Num. ix. 18, 22; Ps. cv. 39.

dry land rising up...unhindered highway...grassy plain] Various
legendary embellishments of the Scriptural narrative grew up among
the Jews. Grimm quotes a Passover prayer, which speaks of springs
of sweet water, fruit-laden trees, and fragrant odours cheering the path
through the waters. Philo has only (*Mos.* ii. 34) "They walked
through the sea on a dry path and a stone paved road : for the sand
grew dry, and its seed-like substance coalesced."

8. *with all their hosts*] So אB, but AC (foll. by Vulg.) have *the
whole people* (πᾶν ἔθνος), in appos. to the subj. of the verb.

covered with thy hand] Cp. v. 16 c, and Is. li. 16 "I will cover
thee under the shadow of my hand" LXX.

9. *like horses*] Cp. Is. lxiii. 13. *roamed* more correctly as Vulg.
depaverunt (*escam*), they "roamed at pasture."

And they skipped about like lambs,
Praising thee, O Lord, who wast their deliverer.

10 For they still remembered the things that came to pass in
the time of their sojourning,
How that instead of ¹bearing ²cattle the land brought forth
³lice,
And instead of ⁴fish the river cast up a multitude of frogs.

11 But afterwards they saw also a new ⁵race of birds,
When, led on by desire, they asked for luxurious dainties;

12 For, to solace them, there came up for them quails from
the sea.

13 And upon the sinners came the punishments

¹ Or, *birth of cattle*   ² Gr. *living creatures.*   ³ Or, *sand flies*
⁴ Gr. *creatures of the waters.*   ⁵ Or, *production* Gr. *generation.*

skipped about] Cp. Ps. cxiv. 4, and Mal. iv. 2.
wast their deliverer] So אB, rather than as AC (foll. by Vulg.
liberasti) "hadst delivered them."
Praising thee, O Lord] See Ex. xv. 1—19; and Philo, *Mos.* ii. 34.
10. *still remembered*] The memories of the Israelites were very
short, cp. xvi. 11: but the miracles of land and water at the passage of
the Red Sea recalled the special plagues through land and water in Egypt.
instead of bearing cattle] The normal products of the earth were
replaced by abnormal. There is a contrast between Gen. i. 24 and
Ex. viii. 17.
brought forth lice] For the generic use of the singular, cp. "the frog,"
Ex. viii. 6.
instead of fish] So Vulg. *pro piscibus*, but marg. translates literally.
Fish are the characteristic product of water, Gen. i. 20, 21: on this
occasion the water teemed with amphibians. The Greek word (Vulg.
eructauit, belched forth) comes from Ex. viii. 3, and is a variant in R
for *swarmed with* in Ps. cv. 30 LXX.
11. *afterwards they saw*] A loose and hardly logical continuation
of the amplification of "*having beheld*" in *v.* 8.
new race of birds] Marg. *production*, cp. Vulg. *creaturam*, is better,
because there was nothing new about the quails as birds, though the
extraordinary quantity and the unfailing supply were undoubtedly new,
cp. xvi. 2; Ex. xvi. 11; Num. xi. 18.
led on by desire] Cp. Num. xi. 34.
asked for] Ps. cv. 40. The writer ignores the Scriptural account
(Num. xi. 4—23), and treats the sending of the quails as a gracious
answer to a reasonable request.
12. *to solace them*] Cp. Philo, *Mos.* i. 37.
there came up...quails from the sea] See ch. xvi. 2, 3. Cp. Ex. xvi. 13,
and Num. xi. 31. The quails came from the sea, not in the sense of

Not without the tokens that were given ¹beforehand by the
force of the thunders;
For justly did they suffer through their own wickednesses,
For ²grievous indeed was the hatred which they practised
toward guests.

¹ Some authorities omit *beforehand*.   ² Or, *yet more grievous was*

v. 10 (although perhaps the writer had some such idea in his mind as
that the coming of the quails from the sea was an analogous reversal
of nature to those in *v.* 10), but because they had crossed over the sea in
one of their annual migrations, and dropped down tired as soon as they
reached the shore.

vv. 13—17.   THE PUNISHMENT OF THE EGYPTIANS FOR THEIR VIOLATION OF HOSPITALITY TO ISRAEL.

13.   *And upon the sinners*]   i.e. the Egyptians.   This section follows
upon the previous one, (*a*) depending upon *they remembered v.* 10,
(*b*) providing a contrast with *v.* 12; to the Israelites came solace, to the
Egyptians punishment; and (*c*) being suggested by the mention of the
Red Sea *v.* 7, which was a blessing to Israel and the reverse to Egypt.

that were given beforehand]   Text reads with ℵAC Vulg.   The
destruction of the Egyptians was preceded by signs of the divine anger.

the force of the thunders]   There was a Jewish tradition that the
drowning of the Egyptians occurred after or during a great war of the
elements, cp. Ps. lxxvii. 16—19; Ex. xiv. 24 (see *Jerus. Targum*,
Etheridge, p. 489 "The Lord looked forth...from the column of fire, to
hurl upon them flakes of fire and hail"); and Jos. (*Ant.* ii. 16. 3)
"Showers of rain also came down from the sky, and dreadful thunders
and lightning with flashes of fire.   Thunderbolts also were darted upon
them: nor was there any indication of God's wrath which did not
happen at this time.   For a dark and dismal night oppressed them."

justly did they suffer]   Dramatic justice is always appreciated by
Jewish writers, cp. 2 Macc. ix. 6, xiii. 8.   The justice of the punishment
is shown by comparing it with that of Sodom.   The men of Sodom
violated the sanctities of hospitality, Gen. xix., and were punished by
the descent of fire and the irruption of the Dead Sea: a similar fate
came upon the Egyptians.

grievous indeed]   Vulg. *detestabiliorem*, as marg., probably rightly,
for the comparison is being pointed to the disadvantage of the Egyptians.   The Egyptians were even worse than the men of Sodom, or
any other people who had been false to their guests.   Philo (*Mos.* i. 7)
writes "They came to dwell in Egypt under guarantee of security, and
Pharaoh enslaved them as if they had been taken captive in war or
bought from slave-dealers, and he treated as slaves those who were not
only free but guests, suppliants, and resident foreigners, with never a
thought of his obligation to the god of freedom, of hospitality, of
sanctuary, and of the hearth."

14 [1]For whereas the *men of Sodom* received not [2]the strangers
when they came among *them* ;
[3]The Egyptians made slaves of guests who were their benefactors.

15 And not only so, *but God* shall [4]visit [5]the men of Sodom
after another sort,
Since they received as enemies them that were aliens ;

16 Whereas these *first* welcomed with feastings,
And *then* afflicted with dreadful toils,
Them that had already shared *with them* in the same rights.

[1] The Greek text of this and the following verse is perhaps corrupt.
[2] Gr. *them who knew them not.*   [3] Gr. *These.*   [4] Or, *visit them...
sort; since* the men of Sodom *received...aliens*   [5] Gr. *them.*

14. *whereas the* men of Sodom] lit. *they.* The writer as usual
expects his readers to interpret his allusions.

received not] Vulg. *recipiebant,* i.e. "were not for receiving." The
writer suggests that the men of Sodom did not wish to receive the angel
visitors.

the strangers] Text renders with Vulg. *ignotos, unknown.* Marg.
gives the lit. translation "them who knew them not."

made slaves of] Cp. Philo, *Somn.* i. 18 "thou didst seize Israel,
making a slave by compulsion of him who by nature is free."

guests who were their benefactors] The Israelites might be spoken of
as *benefactors* because both of their great ancestor Joseph, and of their
services rendered during the years of their captivity : they were
guests inasmuch as they had been invited to come into Egypt, Gen.
xlv. 17, 18. *vv.* 14—16 seem to be written in a not altogether dis-
passionate strain, and point perhaps to a lingering sense of the injustices
frequently perpetrated by the Egyptians upon the Jews resident in Egypt.

15. but God...*after another sort*] Vulg. *sed et alius quidam* suggests
the conjecture adopted by R.V. οὐ μόνον, ἀλλ' ἄλλη τις, lit. *there shall
be another visitation of them.* The writer's special pleading carries
him on to making excuses for Sodom, and asserting that extenuating
circumstances are to be found. Visitation (ἐπισκοπή) is used in a good
sense, cp. iii. 7, iv. 15. The men of Sodom are pictured as receiving
their visitants under constraint *as enemies*: there was uncompromising
hostility from the first, and consequently no change of face : they treated
their guests as they had received them. They did not add fickleness to
their crimes, cp. Philo, *Conf. l.* § 8.

16. The Egyptians began in one way, and ended in another. *with
feastings,* cp. Gen. xlv. 17—20, xlvii. 1—12. The contrast is height-
ened by this fanciful embellishment of the scriptural account.

with dreadful toils] Ex. i. and v.

shared...the same rights] Possibly civil privileges, as was the case
under the Ptolemies, cp. Jos. *Ant.* xii. 1.

And moreover they were stricken with loss of sight   17
(Even as were those *others* at the righteous man's doors),
When, being compassed about with yawning darkness,
They sought every one the passage through his own door.
For as the notes of a psaltery vary the character of the 18
   rhythm,
Even so *did* the elements, changing their order one with
   another,
Continuing always *the same, each* in its *several* sound;
As may clearly be ¹divined from the sight of the things that
   are come to pass.

> ¹ Gr. *conjectured.*

17. *stricken with loss of sight*] Cp. Dt. xxviii. 28. Another correspondence between the men of Sodom and of Egypt. Philo uses this
Greek expression of the Egyptian darkness (*Somn.* i. 18). *Even as...*
those, i.e. the men of Sodom, Gen. xix. 11, cp. Philo, *Conf. l.* § 8.
the righteous man] Lot, cp. x. 6.
   yawning darkness] Vulg. *subitaneis tenebris.* The meaning of
ἀχανής is not certain. Probably it is as in text, or perhaps *speechless,*
i.e. reducing to speechlessness.

   vv. 18—21. A REVERSION TO THE SUBJECT OF THE
            MIRACLES IN *vv.* 6—12.

18. Grammatically this verse is difficult to unravel, though in sense
it is quite simple. Farrar rightly says the obscurity arises from the
confusion of the comparison with the thing to which it is compared.
The full sentence would read : "For the elements, changing their order
one with another, [but continuing always the same, vary their combina-
tions], just as the notes of a psaltery, continuing always the same, each
in its several sound, vary the character of the rhythm." The idea is
that the relations in which a thing stands can modify completely the
effect which it produces : the notes of the instrument, in whatever key
they are played, are the same notes, but the alteration of their relations
seems (but only seems) entirely to have altered their sound.
   the elements, changing] Cp. *v.* 6, and xvi. 21, 25. See Philo, *Mos.*
i. 17; 28 "Each of the elements rendered obedience as to a master,
changing its power and submitting to his decrees"; ii. 12 "The three
elements all undergo variations and transmutations."
   Continuing...sound] *Continuing* is neuter, agreeing with *elements,*
though properly referring to *notes* as is shown by "each in its several
sound." For the musical comparison, see Philo, *Post. C.* § 32 "Just as
instruments change in accordance with the endless combinations of
sound, so does the Logos vary." For the word, cp. Ps. xxxiii. 2
LXX., where the psaltery is s⸱ ɔken of as ten stringed.
   As may clearly be divined] The incidents of the Exodus are adduced

19 For creatures of the dry land were turned into creatures of
   the waters,
   And creatures that swim trode *now* upon the earth :
20 Fire kept the mastery of its own power in *the midst of* water,
   And water forgat its quenching nature:
21 Contrariwise, flames wasted not the flesh of perishable
   creatures that walked among them;
   Neither ¹melted they the ²ice-like grains of ambrosial food,
   that were *of nature* apt to melt.

¹ The Greek authorities read *could be melted.*   The Latin seems to
have preserved the original Greek text.   ² Gr. *ice-like kind.*

as evidence that the philosophic theory of interchange between the
elements was then further illustrated: see next *v.*

19.   *creatures of the dry land*]   The Israelites and their cattle passed
through the waters, obtaining for the time the powers of water-dwellers,
Ex. xii. 38, xiv. 29; Ps. lxvi. 6.   Philo applies the same doctrine of
transmutation as in *vv.* 18, 19 to Xerxes at the Hellespont (*Somn.* ii.
17).   For the adjectives *of the dry land, of the waters* (χερσαῖα, ἔνυδρα),
cp. Philo, *Q. R. D. H.* § 27.

creatures that swim]   This can only refer to the plague of frogs, Ex.
viii. 3.   Philo writes (*Mos.* i. 18) "It seemed as though nature were
planning to send out a colony of water-dwelling creatures into an
enemy's country: for dry land and sea are opposed."

20.   *kept the mastery*]   Vulg. *ualebat supra suam uirtutem*, seems to
point to the conjecture πῦρ (ὑπερ)ίσχυεν ἐν ὕδατι, i.e. fire waxed more
fierce than ever in water.   For the ref. see xvi. 17, 19.

its quenching nature]   This *l.* is almost a repetition of the preceding.
Cp. Philo, *Mos.* i. 20 "The thunder-bolts, shooting through the hail,
neither melted it nor were put out themselves, for all the incompatibility
of their natures," and id. *Somn.* i. 3 "Springs of boiling water are
known in mid sea, which all the water around them could not overcome
(σβέσαι), nor even check in the least degree."

21.   *flames wasted not*]   Cp. xvi. 18.   This *v.* and the prec. *v.* are
merely repetitions of marvels previously dealt with.   As before he
postulates that the locusts, flies, etc. were still in existence when the
plague of hail was sent.   Cp. Dan. iii. 27.

Neither melted they]   Vulg. *nec dissoluebant*, points to the true reading
οὐδ' ἔτηκον.

icelike...food]   For the rather forced comparison of manna to snow
and ice, see xvi. 22.   *ambrosial* has reference rather to the source (bread
from heaven, angels' food, xvi. 20) than to the pleasantness of the
manna (xvi. 21).   Farrar writes "By reverting to what he has already
dwelt on, the writer is able to illustrate his thesis that the elements
changed their normal operations: and he thus ends in a blaze of futile
paradoxes."

For in all things, O Lord, thou didst magnify thy people,   22
And thou didst glorify them and not lightly regard them;
Standing by their side in every time and place.

22. *For in all things*] The book comes to an abrupt conclusion
with this *v.* It sums up what the writer has been urging through the
latter half of the book, viz. that history is conducted on behalf of the
chosen people: that Israel is always true to its destiny, and that God is
always on the side of Israel.

in every time and place] Even to the writer's own day. There was
no reason why the book should end at this place: no culminating point
has been reached, at which the argument finds a natural conclusion. A
continuation of the interpretation of the history of Israel down to the
time of Solomon might have been expected (see ch. vi. 22). But this
is not to say that the original ending has been lost. Grimm compares
v. 22 with the closing words of 3 Macc. "Blessed be the Saviour of
Israel unto all times for ever." The brief summary indicates that the
later period would be found to illustrate the same principles as the
earlier. At the same time it does not offer equal possibilities of
dramatic contrast, and therefore any prolongation of the book might
only serve to detract from the cogency of the earlier argument. "It is
obvious that the scope of the argument is fully satisfied by the investi-
gation of the providential history of the Jews up to the time of the
occupation of Canaan, and the last verse furnishes a complete epilogue
to the treatise" (Westcott, in Smith's *D. B.*).

INDEX.

CAMBRIDGE: PRINTED BY JOHN CLAY, M.A. AT THE UNIVERSITY PRESS.